DISCOVERED BUT FORGOTTEN

Discovered but Forgotten

THE MALDIVES IN CHINESE HISTORY, C. 1100–1620

Bin Yang

Columbia University Press
New York

Columbia University Press
Publishers Since 1893
New York   Chichester, West Sussex

Copyright © 2025 Bin Yang
All rights reserved

Columbia University Press gratefully acknowledges the support provided by the
Harvard-Yenching Institute Publication Grant.

Library of Congress Cataloging-in-Publication Data
Names: Yang, Bin, 1972– author.
Title: Discovered but forgotten : the Maldives in Chinese history, c. 1100–1620 / Bin Yang.
Description: New York : Columbia University Press, [2024] |
Includes bibliographical references and index.
Identifiers: LCCN 2024008901 (print) | LCCN 2024008902 (ebook) |
ISBN 9780231212328 (hardback) | ISBN 9780231212335 (trade paperback) |
ISBN 9780231559324 (ebook)
Subjects: LCSH: Sea-power—China—History. | China—Relations—Maldives. |
Maldives—Relations—China. | Indian Ocean—Discovery and exploration—Chinese. |
China—History, Naval—To 1644. | Maldives—History. | China—History—
Song dynasty, 960-1279. | China—History—Yuan dynasty, 1260-1368. |
China—History—Ming dynasty, 1368-1644.
Classification: LCC DS740.5.M415 Y36 2024 (print) | LCC DS740.5.M415 (ebook) |
DDC 359/.030951—dc23/eng/20240404

Cover design: Chang Jae Lee
Cover image: Reproduced by permission of the Bodleian Libraries,
University of Oxford. *Selden Map of China* (1620–1629), MS.Selden supra 105.

CONTENTS

LIST OF FIGURES, MAPS, AND TABLES ix

NOTE ON CHINESE WEIGHTS AND MEASURES
IN THE MING DYNASTY xi

ACKNOWLEDGMENTS xiii

Part I. The Stage

Chapter One
Small, Remote, but Significant 3

Chapter Two
From Zaitun 17

Chapter Three
Sailing to the Indian Ocean 30

Part II. A Destination

Chapter Four
Who Once Landed in the Maldives? 53

Chapter Five
The Kingdom of Atolls 72

Chapter Six
Monsoons and Currents 94

Chapter Seven
Between the Son of Heaven and the Sultan 103

Part III. The Cargo

Chapter Eight
The Trees of the Maldives 121

Chapter Nine
Ships Without Nails 129

Chapter Ten
Cowrie Shells 148

Chapter Eleven
Dried Fish, Grains, and Handkerchiefs 168

Chapter Twelve
Dragon's Spittle 180

Chapter Thirteen
Laka Wood and Frankincense 217

CONTENTS

Part IV. Reminiscences

Chapter Fourteen
A Ruined Buddhist Past   225

Chapter Fifteen
Port Marriage   235

Chapter Sixteen
A True Romance   254

Chapter Seventeen
An Echo: The "China Bird"   263

NOTES   281

BIBLIOGRAPHY   333

INDEX   353

FIGURES, MAPS, AND TABLES

FIGURES

FIGURE 3.1.   The China Pagoda at Nagapattinam, 1846   47
FIGURE 5.1.   A Chinese compass   86
FIGURE 9.1.   The bronze mirror from the Belitung shipwreck   141
FIGURE 10.1.   Bronze cowrie coin mold   160
FIGURE 10.2.   The *Hezun*   162
FIGURE 17.1.   *Louwa* (Cormorant) by Johan Nieuhof   269
FIGURE 17.2.   *The Fishing Cormorants* by William Alexander   270

MAPS

MAP 1.1.   The Maldives in maritime Asia   7
MAP 5.1.   The Maldives (*Wandao*) in the Ricci Map   79
MAP 5.2.   Physical features of the Maldives   84
MAP 5.3.   The nine *liu* and their navigation routes in the *Zheng He Hanghai Tu*   86
MAP 12.1.   *Longxian Yu* in the *Zheng He Hanghai Tu*   197
MAP 17.1.   The Maldives and Liushan in Chu-Si-Ling's map of China   275

TABLES

TABLE 3.1. The calculated size of *Quanzhou I* 34
TABLE 4.1. Indian Ocean products found in the compartments of *Quanzhou I* 56
TABLE 4.2. Travelers/scholars and their records concerning the Maldives 64
TABLE 5.1. Different estimates of the number of islands in the Maldives 78
TABLE 7.1. The itinerary of Zheng He's seventh voyage (1431–1433) 110
TABLE 7.2. The kings of the Maldives during the Zheng He voyages (1405–1433) 116
TABLE 10.1. Statistics of cowrie shells in the early Ming by the Ministry of Revenue (*Hubu* 户部) 164
TABLE 13.1. Taxation rates for the *Xiang* materials in Moon Harbor, Zhangzhou (1589 and 1615) 220

NOTE ON CHINESE WEIGHTS AND MEASURES IN THE MING DYNASTY

WEIGHT

1 *jin* 斤 = 16 *liang* 两 = 1.3 pounds (596.80 g)
1 *liang* 两 = 10 *qian* 钱 = 100 *fen* 分 = 1,000 *li* 厘

LENGTH

1 *li* 里 = 1,935 feet (c. 590 m)
1 *zhang* 丈 = 10 *chi* 尺 = 100 *cun* 寸 = 1,000 *fen* 分

SILVER

1 *liang* 两 = 1.32 ounces (37.3 g) = 10 *qian* 钱 = 100 *fen* 分 = 1,000 copper coins

ACKNOWLEDGMENTS

No academic monograph could have been completed solely by the author alone. This genuinely is the case.

I must admit that I had no background in maritime history or Sino–Indian Ocean interactions. I received BA and MA degrees from Renmin University of China (Beijing) with the unusual major of "History of the Chinese Communist Party," which was more of an ideological doctrine than anything else. I gave up my academic program there in September 1998, waved a farewell, and was fortunate enough to be admitted to the World History Center in the History Department of Northeastern University in Boston.

Studying world history in the United States greatly expanded my horizons, and I intended to study Chinese history from a global perspective. My research on Yunnan, China's southwestern ethnic and frontier region, was the result, thanks to the remarkable support and supervision of Christina Gilmartin (1949–2012), Adam McKeown (1965–2017), John Wills Jr. (1936–2017), and Patrick Manning. My paper was one of the first to advocate for a global perspective on Chinese frontiers (and imperial China), and it received the 2004 Gutenberg-E prize before being published by Columbia University Press in 2008 as a Gutenberg-E book and in 2009 in print.

But I still knew little about maritime China.

In 2003, the fifth year of my studies at Northeastern, I was no longer financially supported by any assistantship, but I required at least one more year to complete my research and writing. To survive became my top priority. I read a variety of academic announcements and advisements, and I applied for funding, scholarships, and one-year positions created by professors on sabbatical. A local university in central Connecticut offered me one-year position, but to my dismay, a foreign student was not permitted to work. The suit I'd bought for $100 or more at a Macy's basement in downtown Boston, in anticipation of the interview, became my most expensive and pointless expenditure.

And then something happened.

An email from Singapore sent a lifeboat. The Asian Research Institute (ARI), recently established by the National University of Singapore (NUS) and directed by Anthony Reid, offered me a writing fellowship grant. I hurried to complete as much of my writing as possible before boarding an aircraft in Logan Airport bound for Singapore.

It was at ARI that I was pulled into maritime Asia. Despite knowing next to nothing, I was motivated by the expertise and presentations there. During the brief period (November 2003–July 2004), in addition to my four supervisors, I became deeply indebted to numerous scholars, particularly Wang Gungwu, Anthony Reid, Barbara Andaya, Geoff Wade, John Miksic, Liu Hong, Huang Jianli, and Sun Laichen, who enlightened me on maritime history and other fields.

I rushed to the College of William & Mary a few days after officially presenting my research at Northeastern in early August, working as visiting assistant professor for one year. When invited to create a new course for the college, I instantly thought of "Maritime China," which was perhaps the first time such a subject had been offered in the United States. I hadn't studied much about China's maritime history until that point, but it had piqued my attention.

As fate would have it, I returned to Singapore on December 16, 2005, to work as a tenure-track assistant professor in the History Department at NUS. I was promoted and tenured in August 2010. At NUS, one important course I oversaw was "Past and Present: China and Southeast Asia," through which I had broadened my research from China's southwestern border into Sino–Southeast Asian–Indian interactions. This subdiscipline is inextricably linked to overseas Chinese studies and maritime history. I also created

ACKNOWLEDGMENTS

a new seminar there called "Approaches to World History," which introduced global history to graduate students. Maritime history, indeed, was naturally born as a global history.

There were, however, many more maritime specialists I had missed in Singapore, including my former colleague Michael Feener, an associate professor who joined the NUS History Department at the same time I did. He specialized in Southeast Asian history and Islamic studies, but we didn't share any academic field because I was mostly constrained by Chinese borders. Before he left for Oxford, we became "good colleagues" without troubling each other. In July 2017 I resigned from NUS because the school rarely promotes historians to the rank of full professor and relocated to the University of Macao, where I began writing a book manuscript, *Cowrie Shells and Cowrie Money: A Global History* (Routledge, 2019). I accidentally discovered that Michael directed a giant project, "the Maldives Heritage Survey (MHS, 2017–2020)." I contacted him right away and sent him a draft of my work. Michael patiently and graciously shared feedback and suggestions. In 2020, Michael relocated to the Kyoto University Center for Southeast Asian Studies (CSEAS), and MHS was renamed "the Maritime Asia Heritage Survey (MAHS)," with field teams operating in Indonesia, Thailand, and Vietnam as well as the Maldives. I sent him a manuscript of the present book, hoping for his feedback. Michael not only read and commented on the manuscript, but he also scheduled a Zoom meeting with me, bringing numerous questions, recommendations, and theoretical reflections with him. I can't thank him enough for his assistance.

Many recognized scholars in the field of maritime Asia have inspired and left me indebted throughout the two decades after 2003. Chinese scholars include Feng Chengjun, Xiang Da, Su Jiqing, Xie Fang (Yu Sili), Chen Jiarong, Lu Junling, Zhang Yi, Xia Nai, Rao Zongyi, Yang Bowen, Yang Wuquan, Zhang Xun, Yao Nan, Han Zhenhua, Wang Bangwei, Geng Sheng, He Gaoji, Chen Gaohua, Qian Jiang, Zhang Bincun, Chen Guodong, Li Bozhong, Rong Xinjiang, Cao Shuji, Jin Guoping, Wu Zhiliang, Liu Hong, and Wu Xiaoan; international scholars include William W. Rockhill, Friedrich Hirth, Gabriel Ferrand, Paul Pelliot, J. V. G. Mills, Henry Yule, Jitsuzō Kuwabara, Namio Egami, Charles Boxer, Edward H. Schafer, Kentaro Yamada, Roderich Ptak, Victor Mair, Pierre-Yves Manguin, Takeshi Hamashita, Leonard Blussé, Hans Ulrich Vogel, John Deyell, Himanshu

Prabha Ray, Tansen Sen, and Eric Tagliacozzo. Of course, they are only a portion of the lengthy list.

Many people assisted me in various ways during my book preparation, particularly in discovering and gaining access to specific sources. From Leiden, Atsushi Ota assisted in obtaining a crucial article written by Kentaro Yamada. Huang Ming, Gan Liangyong, Sun Fulei, and Zhang Chen were helpful in creating maps and locating sources. Friends such as Cheng Yinghong, Du Chunmei, Wang Yuanchong, Li Ji, Zou Kunyi, Sittithep Eaksittipong, Ji Yun, Zhang Changhong, Dong Fengyun, Li Xiaen, Chen Ye, and Lu Haiyue have all offered advice and encouragement. Susan Amy has proofread all draft versions, as she has for my previous books and articles over the last fifteen years. Finally, I would like to express my gratitude to Columbia University Press, particularly Caelyn Cobb and her team, for the tremendous efforts to publish this book.

This book is the intellectual manifestation of my research project MYRG2022–00043-FAH, which was funded by the Faculty of Arts and Humanities at the University of Macao. The Harvard-Yenching Institute offered me a special fellowship to support this effort for three months at the Institute in 2022, but because of Macao's local pandemic policy, I was compelled to give it up. Lose in the beginning but gain at the end. On the eve of publication, the Harvard-Yenching Institute generously offers its publication grant, for which I have been sincerely graceful.

Early results of this research project have been presented at the University of Macao, Southern University of Science and Technology (Shenzhen), Shantou University, Xiamen University, and Yale University (Third Middle Period China Humanities Conference, June 22–25, 2023). I appreciate the hosts' and audience's comments, questions, and suggestions. Special thanks are owed to *Journal of World History* for allowing the revision and publication of my article on ambergris.

PART I
The Stage

Chapter One

SMALL, REMOTE, BUT SIGNIFICANT

> Except for exceedingly scant glimpses afforded in the very few notices put on record by casual visitors who have alluded to the Maldives from time to time, the veil of information had been, up till 1880, temporarily lifted only thrice-in the Fourteenth Century by the Maghrabín traveler, Ibn Baṭúṭa (A.C. 1343-4); in the Seventeenth Century by the French castaway captive François Pyrard (A.C. 1602–07); and in the Nineteenth Century by Lieutenants Christopher and Powell of the Indian Navy (A.C. 1835). Even at this day, in the Twentieth Century, the world still knows little of the history of the Maldive Islands, and the manner of men who inhabit them.
>
> —H. C. P. BELL

The Maldives islands are nowadays more known for being an exotic and distant resort for romantic holidays than anything else, and few people stop to think about their history. These beach lovers, on the other hand, are not to blame. H. C. P. Bell's comprehensive studies made in the early twentieth century uncovered their history at a time when few people in the modern world, whether in the West or the East, showed any serious interest in this tiny Indian Ocean archipelago.

Born in British India, Harry Charles Purvis Bell (1851–1937) spent almost all his life (apart from his school days in Britain) in Ceylon, serving the British Empire. He started his career in the civil service in Ceylon in 1873 and was appointed archaeological commissioner from 1890 to 1912, reflecting his interest and talents in local history, language, and archaeology.[1] Concurrently, he took over the position of secretary of the Ceylon Branch of the Royal Asiatic Society, playing an eminent role in producing and spreading imperial knowledge on South Asia. After his retirement Bell was assigned to investigate the archaeology and epigraphy of the Maldives, a protectorate then attached to Ceylon. Bell had once adventitiously visited the Maldives in November 1879 when he had been shipwrecked. Forty years later, he paid two subsequent visits from January 20 to February 21, 1920, and from February 2 to September 22, 1922, respectively.[2] Bell mastered the

Maldivian language, and his pioneering works in this field and other areas made him the acknowledged father of Maldivian studies.

While he highlighted the contributions made by Western travelers such as Ibn Battuta and François Pyrard, who first made the world aware of these formerly "unknown" islands, Bell did not know that it was Wang Dayuan 汪大渊 (c. 1311—?), a Chinese merchant during the Pax Mongolica, who might have been the first Chinese person to land in the Maldives and who provided a relatively detailed and accurate albeit extraordinarily brief textual description of the Indian Ocean archipelago. Although contemporary with Ibn Battuta (1304–1377), the traveler Wang Dayuan is far less known. Wang was a member of the Chinese literati and most probably also a merchant who traveled from Quanzhou 泉州, a southeastern port city in Fujian Province, via Southeast Asia to the Indian Ocean. Indeed, Wang visited the Maldives more than a decade earlier than Ibn Battuta.

Thanks to Wang Dayuan, the Maldives began to feature on the Chinese knowledge horizon in the early fourteenth century. And it was the Zheng He 郑和 voyages (1405–1433) that brought the Sino-Maldivian interactions to their heyday. Then, rather surprisingly, the Maldives disappeared from Chinese records in the post-1600 period. From 1600 onward, no single Chinese recorder seemed to have had anything to say about the Sino-Maldivian relationship. This was not true of Ceylon, commonly known then in China as the Kingdom of the Lion (*Shiziguo* 狮子国), another island and powerful neighbor of the Maldives, which was frequently mentioned in imperial Chinese texts, given its paramount role as a center of Theravada Buddhism. Eclipsed by its more religiously significant neighbor, within a period of less than three hundred years, the spotlight on the islands of the Maldives in the Chinese world had been like a tiny meteor, seemingly confirming its place in the trading world as small, fleeting, and insignificant.

The Sino-Maldivian relationship deserves our special attention simply because it was asymmetrical: China was a huge empire in terms of territory, population, power, history, and culture, while the Maldives was just a tiny dot in the Indian Ocean. Such an unbalanced association has rarely been addressed in the traditional world and may yield some significance for our understanding of the current One-Belt-One-Road Initiative launched by the People's Republic of China, a new maritime power, especially in the Asia-Pacific region and Africa.

SMALL, REMOTE, BUT SIGNIFICANT

Before the arrival of Ibn Battuta, Western travelers contributed little if any knowledge on the Maldives, except that it was repeatedly mentioned that this archipelago consisted of more than ten thousand islands. During his almost thirty years of travel (1325–1354), the Moroccan explorer crossed Africa, the Arabian Peninsula, Europe, India, Southeast Asia, and China. Specifically, he visited the Maldives twice, spending more than eighteen months there altogether.[3] Ibn Battuta went on to marry four wives in the Maldives in addition to acquiring several concubines. No wonder he was able to provide so comprehensive a description of this island society.[4]

In 1345 Ibn Battuta docked at Quanzhou (Zaitun was the name given by Marco Polo), a port city from which Wang Dayuan had departed for the Indian Ocean fifteen years earlier. Wang Dayuan was born in Nanchang 南昌, Jiangxi Province, where porcelain (especially the blue and white style produced in Jingdezhen 景德镇) had been the best-known Chinese artifact in the maritime world from the Song (960–1279) and especially the Yuan (1279–1368) periods onward.[5] The contemporary porcelain network probably inspired Wang to travel from Nanchang to Quanzhou, perhaps the largest port in the world at that time, a port at which both Marco Polo and Ibn Battuta marveled. On this first overseas trip from Quanzhou in 1330, Wang visited the Maldives in the winter of 1330, left in the spring of 1331 for South India, and might have visited North or East Africa before his return to Quanzhou in 1334. Between 1337 and 1339 Wang Dayuan made his second maritime voyage, which was mainly confined to modern Southeast Asia. In 1349 Wang completed the *Daoyi Zhilue* 岛夷志略, in which more than 220 foreign places were recorded, mostly in maritime Asia.[6] Wang's book was used as a key travel guide by Zheng He, the Chinese eunuch of the Ming dynasty (1368–1644), during his seven voyages to the Indian Ocean nearly six decades later.[7]

Thus, during certain years of the 1330s and the 1340s, Wang Dayuan and Ibn Battuta, one from the East and the other from the West, could be said to have traveled toward each other, although as it turned out they were never once in the same place at the same time so as to meet one another. Fortunately, they separately provided priceless information on maritime Asia, including the Maldives.

6

THE STAGE

A REMOTE ARCHIPELAGO THAT SHAPED IMPERIAL CHINA

Chinese scholars, whether imperial or modern, seem never to have concerned themselves much about the Maldives.[8] Compared with other medieval polities across the Indian Ocean, including Ceylon, Chola, Kollam, Cochin, Ma'bar, and Bengal, the Maldives did not receive any Chinese attention until the era of Wang Dayuan. Decades later the Zheng He fleets followed in Wang's footsteps to visit this island kingdom and brought its tributary envoys all the way to Nanjing and Beijing. More information was obtained through Chinese agents in the Zheng He fleets, but from 1600 onward mention of the Maldives simply disappeared from Chinese writings.

In the nineteenth and twentieth centuries China was beset by both internal and external turmoil. While the slogan "Learn from the West" pushed Chinese people to pay attention to the outside world, this exhortation mainly referred to studying major Western powers and the fates of certain colonial victims such as Ethiopia and Poland. Not surprisingly, the Maldives remained in obscurity in Chinese scholarship during this period. I learned of the name of this island country myself from a middle school geography textbook only in the 1980s and hardly retained any impression of its features except for its being an archipelago. While occasionally paying some slight attention to the Maldives when studying the Maritime Silk Road, Chinese scholars have consistently failed to realize its significance in the history of maritime Asia, let alone in Chinese history.

Yet the Maldives has been widely acknowledged outside China as having commanded a strategic location and been an active participant in East-West maritime interactions from medieval to modern times.[9] What has remained almost entirely unknown is that this small and remote archipelago, even if inadvertently, made a great contribution to the formation and transformation of Chinese civilization and empire building. First, records drafted on the Maldives demonstrate China's increasing knowledge of the Indian Ocean and maritime Asia and recount the golden age of Chinese activities in the Indian Ocean. Second, the presence of Maldivian envoys at the Ming court illustrated the expansion of the Chinese tributary world into the Indian Ocean, establishing the imperial image of China as the center of maritime Asia and thus "All under Heaven (*Tianxia* 天下)," at least as conceptualized by the Ming emperors themselves and shared by their elite scholar-officials.

SMALL, REMOTE, BUT SIGNIFICANT

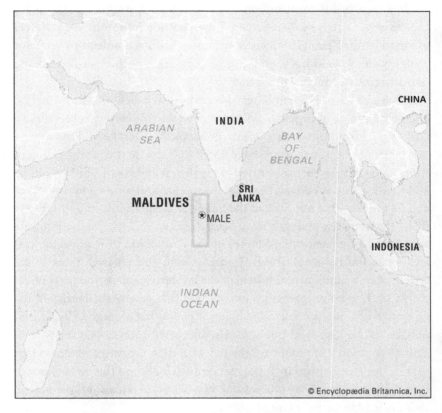

MAP 1.1 The Maldives in maritime Asia. *Source*: Based on "Maldives," *Encyclopaedia Britannica*.

Was the Maldives, a mere island kingdom among so many, so very important to China, a giant empire far away to the east? Ideologically it was, especially to Emperor Yongle 永乐 (r. 1402–1422) of the Ming dynasty. As a usurper who had seized power from his nephew, Emperor Yongle was as anxious as Kublai Khan to legitimize his throne under heaven. He followed Kublai's practice of dispatching Chinese envoys to maritime Asia, including the so-called Western Ocean (*Xiyang* 西洋), soliciting tributary missions from various kingdoms.[10] Audiences with tributary envoys from "ten thousand" kingdoms at his court were dazzling extravaganzas, and the glittering array of exotic peoples from far-flung places all coming to pay tribute to him as the Son of Heaven (*Tianzi* 天子) at the center of All Under Heaven made a significant contribution to his legitimacy. Any doubt about his throne would surely be disregarded. Tributary missions from the Maldives escorted by the Zheng He fleets were hence thrilling emblems of Emperor Yongle's glory, legitimacy, and thus confirmation of the half-factual and half-imagined Chinese world order.

What was the most central but so far overlooked factor in the formation and development of Chinese civilization was the role played by the humble cowrie shell from the Indian Ocean (presumably from the Maldives in the very early period). Few people have noted that cowrie shells originating in the Indian Ocean were transported to northwest and north China via India and Central Asia as early as the Neolithic period and went on to play a crucial role in the state building of the Shang-Zhou period (c. 1600 BCE–256 BCE), the formative and early stage of Chinese civilization. Cowrie-granting was the most frequent ritual adopted by the Zhou kings through which various lords and nobles established, maintained, and renewed their feudal relationship, a fundamental system of the Western Zhou period (1045 BCE–771 BCE). It is no exaggeration to conclude that cowrie shells shaped the formation of Chinese civilization in terms of politics, economy, rituals, and religion.[11] The long-held popular misconception that cowrie shells were China's first form of money originated with such recorders as Sima Qian 司马迁, the grand historian in the first century BCE, and this error was reiterated all the way up to present day historians, showcasing how cowrie shells helped to shape imperial China.

While cowrie shells did not in fact become a form of money in early China, the two non-Chinese kingdoms of Nanzhao 南诏 (c. 7th century–902) and Dali 大理 (937–1254) roughly based in modern Yunnan, southwestern China, flourished and adopted cowrie money from the ninth or tenth century onward. After the Mongol conquest of Dali in 1254, cowrie money continued there until the mid-seventeenth century. Therefore, the Maldives' remarkable influence continued in the Chinese incorporation of a frontier province where a variety of peoples lived. Furthermore, during the Song-Yuan-Ming period (960–1644) cowrie shells were shipped to the Yangzi Delta, in addition to Yunnan. From the Yangzi Delta, Maldivian cowries shells were transported both by the Yuan and Ming imperial states and by private merchants to Yunnan in exchange for local goods such as gold. Therefore, it is fair to conclude that the Maldivian shells to some extent also shaped imperial China's economy and society.

SMALL, REMOTE, BUT SIGNIFICANT

In addition to cowrie shells, ambergris, known by the euphemistic Chinese title of "Dragon's Spittle," was a centrally important product of the Maldives (with the Indian Ocean being the major supplier) that began to be consumed widely in Song China (960–1279). Acquired by Zheng He's treasure ships, ambergris later held significant appeal among the Chinese upper class, particularly during the reign of Ming Emperor Jiajing 嘉靖 (1507–1567, r. 1522–1567). Jiajing's attempts to create elixirs with ambergris as a crucial element afforded a brief respite for the Portuguese. As the only supplier of this Indian Ocean medicinal material, the Portuguese were granted the right by the Chinese to settle at Macao in 1557, a trading base they had failed to obtain through diplomacy, bribery, military assistance in suppressing local piracy, or political submission. Macao in 1557, like Malacca in 1519, Goa in 1511, and Fort Manuel in 1505, illustrates the severe changes brought about by the Europeans, a new force represented by the Portuguese to maritime Asia decades after the retreat of the Chinese treasure ship in 1433. Few people, however, have realized that ambergris, whether from the Maldives or not, played a key in creating the new landscape in maritime China. Small and remote as the Maldives was, no other kingdom in the Indian Ocean played such a significant longue durée role in Chinese political, economic, and cultural history.

China's involvement in Indian Ocean trade was abruptly halted when the Ming state reissued the maritime ban policy in 1433 after the last voyage of Zheng He, and thereafter, no ships were permitted to sail to the Indian Ocean. The archives and charts of the Zheng He voyages were either burned, destroyed, or went missing. As a result, Chinese scholars missed out on the opportunity to increase their knowledge of the Maldives and the Indian Ocean world, and more unfortunately for latter-day historians, their great body of ontological knowledge gradually became diluted, ambiguous, and even downright erroneous. Not surprisingly, China's knowledge of the Maldives and the Indian Ocean in the post-1600 era never again surpassed the era of Wang Dayuan, let alone that of Zheng He.

SOURCES: TEXTS, SHIPWRECKS, AND MAPS

The seven voyages of Admiral Zheng He in the Indian Ocean are well known across the world for their astonishing scope and impact. Oddly though, few people have thought the Chinese maritime achievements in the pre-Zheng He period that contributed to and provided a solid foundation for the Ming treasure fleets worthy of closer study. Nor has the drastic curbing of travel in the post-Zheng He period received serious attention, when abruptly, no Chinese ships sailed into the Indian Ocean, even when the maritime ban policy was partially lifted in 1567. These interesting and significant periods are elaborated in this book.

This book explores the cross-regional topic of Sino-Maldivian interactions to shed fresh light on both maritime China and the Indian Ocean world in the broad context of maritime Asia. By scrutinizing the waxing and waning of China's maritime activities in the Indian Ocean from the medieval period to the arrival of the Jesuits in East Asia, it crosses the boundaries of China, Southeast Asia, and South Asia and integrates Chinese, Indian Ocean, economic, and maritime histories, as well as the history of science, technology, and society.

While Albert Gray, with the help of H. C. P. Bell, compiled almost all non-Chinese texts concerning the Maldives from the *Periplus* to French notes produced at the beginning of the seventeenth century, the Chinese understanding of these islands has not been appropriately addressed, especially in the broader context of either the Sino-Indian Ocean interactions or maritime Asia.[12] Unfortunately, mention of the Maldives in early Chinese texts amounts to only a couple of pages, beginning with Wang Dayuan, and these scant notes would have been copied in the following centuries, literally speaking, word for word. Not long after the copying of these sources stopped altogether as Chinese interest in the region disappeared. "Discovered" and named by the Chinese in the 1330s, the island kingdom would be forgotten in post-1600 China.

Su Jiqing 苏继庼 (1894–1973) and Xie Fang 谢方(1932–2021) were the first Chinese scholars to make pioneering efforts to examine the imperial geographical knowledge of these islands, the former having annotated the *Daoyi Zhilue* and the latter having collected imperial sources and discussed Chinese knowledge on the Maldives.[13] John Carswell was the first scholar to seriously consider the Sino-Maldivian relationship, and Andrew D. W. Forbes provided a bibliographical review on Maldivian history up until the year 1980, together with a collection of Maldivian items sold to the British Museum in 1981, but his Chinese list remains essentially incomplete.[14] Roderich Ptak has made remarkable progress in this respect by gathering and analyzing a comprehensive list of Chinese textual sources produced in the Yuan, Ming, and Qing periods.[15] In a brief but inspiring paper, Ptak has discussed many key issues such as Chinese etymology, official contacts, and navigational routes. In addition, my recent work on cowrie shells casts a spotlight on the role of the Maldives in maritime Asia and China in particular.[16]

In addition to texts there have been some monumental discoveries in both marine archaeology (especially shipwrecks) and cartography. In 1974, a Chinese shipwreck dated to the end of the Southern Song (1127–1279) was discovered on the seabed in Quanzhou Bay. After a comprehensive analysis of the ship and its remains, Chinese scholars concluded that the ship sank on its return journey from Southeast Asia (highly likely from the port of Palembang), and this opinion has been widely accepted for nearly half a century. Recently, however, I have reexamined the remains of its cargo, especially the cowrie shells, ambergris, peppers, and marine animals, and argued that this Chinese oceangoing ship was more probably on its return journey from the Indian Ocean.[17] Due to its paramount significance in understanding China's maritime history, I would like to propose that this ship be named *Quanzhou I*.

In 1998, the so-called Belitung ship was discovered in Indonesia. This ship, a typical example of Arab-style oceangoing vessels, the earliest of which completed the journey between West Asia and China as early as the mid-ninth century, could have been produced anywhere from North Africa to Gujarat in India.[18] The Belitung ship belonged to the "stitched ship" type, which the Maldivian people also commonly constructed and used during the medieval period.[19] Thus, in addition to a few other Chinese and non-Chinese shipwrecks, the Belitung ship facilitates an understanding of maritime connections between the Indian Ocean world (including the Maldives) and China during the Tang-Song period before the advent of Wang Dayuan.

Recently, *Nanhai I*, another Southern Song shipwreck, was excavated from the coastal sea off Guangzhou.[20] Unlike *Quanzhou I*, the vessel fortuitously had most of its goods extant and thus provides fresh and rich information on maritime China. Exotic items, especially gold ones, have indicated that this Chinese oceangoing ship was bound for some Indian Ocean ports, en route about one hundred years earlier than *Quanzhou I*.

The two Song ships, *Nanhai I* sailing for the Indian Ocean around the 1170s and *Quanzhou I* returning from the Indian Ocean in the 1270s, therefore have provided firsthand marine archaeological evidence to illustrate the movements of Chinese ships, merchants, and goods between the China Sea and the Indian Ocean before the era of Wang Dayuan and Ibn Battuta. The Belitung shipwreck, *Nanhai I*, and *Quanzhou I* hence present solid evidence to support what Geoff Wade has coined "an early commerce age in Southeast Asia" and beyond, roughly the period of 900–1300 CE,[21] in which commercial activities and networks had crossed maritime Asia and engulfed China, Southeast Asia, and the Indian Ocean world.

Imperial maps made during the Ming-Qing period (1368–1911) can contribute a great deal to the study of ocean navigation, especially the favored routes. The *Selden Map of China* (Bodleian Library, University of Oxford), one of the first Chinese maps to reach Europe, completed no later than the 1620s, followed traditional Chinese navigational charts such as the *Zheng He Hanghai Tu* 郑和航海图 (the Zheng He Nautical Chart) that was presumably used and updated by Zheng He, and it showed the retreat of Chinese activities from the Indian Ocean during the post-1600 period.[22] Meanwhile, other imperial maps made from the early seventeenth century onward, especially official ones, absorbed European geographical knowledge that had been spread to China by Jesuits such as Matteo Ricci (Chinese name Li Maodou 利玛窦, 1552–1610) and Ferdinand Verbiest (Chinese name Nan Huairen 南怀仁, 1623–1688). Very interestingly, the two epistemological systems concerning the Maldives were both marked on some maps drawn by Qing scholars. Unfortunately, the Chinese elite failed to realize that the two places were in fact one and the same Indian Ocean kingdom. The presence, absence, and juxtaposition of the Maldives on imperial maps present a fresh view to understand the waxing and waning of this Indian Ocean Archipelago in the Chinese mindset.

Firmly based on the foundation built by the scholars mentioned above, I attempt in this book to conduct a relatively comprehensive scrutiny of textual and cartographical sources (both Chinese and non-Chinese) as well as archaeological findings, such as shipwrecks and porcelain sherds in the Maldives. Imperial Chinese records consist of official history, private works, miscellaneous essays, stories (which remain an underexplored treasure), and maps produced during the discussed period that have not been sufficiently addressed. Ambitious as it is, this book is expected to illustrate the dynamics of maritime Asia on the eve of the sighting of European sails in these vast waters.

PERIODIZING AND STRUCTURE

History is but a narrative that reconstructs the past. By deliberately using "in Chinese history" in the title, I adopt a paralleling, contesting, and thus broadly defining concept of history, as Paul Cohen has done in his classic *History in Three Keys*, in which the term "history" accommodates the reconstruction of the past alongside experience and myth.[23] Taking the Maldives as a case, angle, and approach, this book aims to kill three birds with one stone. First, by exploiting broadly untapped or unknown Chinese sources, this book diversifies and thus enriches the understanding of the Maldivian history and culture. Second, by examining the Sino-Maldivian interactions with a cross-regional approach, this book illustrates how this small and remote archipelago (and thus the Indian Ocean world) shaped the state-building of the giant Chinese empire, a theme that has yet to be attempted. There are few such extraordinary asymmetrical relationships between a giant empire and a miniature island kingdom seen in world history. Third, by showcasing the Sino-Maldivian interactions, this book examines imperial China's maritime activities and thus its knowledge production of the Indian Ocean world before and after the Zheng He era during the period of ca.1100 to 1620. What is behind these three themes is the historical process in which the waxing and waning of maritime China expanded into and departed from the Indian Ocean, paralleling the entrance and exit of the small and remote Indian Ocean sultanate of the Maldives in the Chinese world order.

To some degree, this book is inspired by Edward H. Schafer's *The Golden Peaches of Samarkand: A Study of T'ang Exotics*, a classic Sinological work on foreign exotics and their influence in Tang China.[24] The time period covered in this book starts from ca. 1100, based on a few crucial sources illustrating China's active participation in the Indian Ocean. After losing the Central Plain (the Yellow River region) in a crushing defeat to the non-Chinese Jin dynasty (1115–1234), the Southern Song dynasty then made the Yangzi Delta its political center and adopted an unprecedented policy shift by encouraging maritime trade, a surging industry that constituted the dynasty's key financial income. Chinese oceangoing ships, invested in and sponsored by Chinese businessmen, operated by Chinese captains and sailors, and loaded with Chinese cargo and merchants, began to sail to Southeast Asia and the Indian Ocean. As a result, Chinese knowledge of the Indian Ocean reached a new era.

In his *Pingzhou Ketan* 萍州可谈 completed in 1119, Zhu Yu 朱彧 (?–1148?) shared his firsthand witness of the maritime network based in Guangzhou when he accompanied his father, who was an official there in the last decade of the eleventh century.[25] While he explicitly mentioned Chinese merchants venturing to the Arab empire by sea, Zhu Yu was probably not aware that the maritime epicenter had shifted from Guangzhou to Quanzhou in his time, a tendency more visible in the *Lingwai Daida* 岭外代答 (Answers for Questions Concerning Out of Range) by Zhou Qufei 周去非 (1135–1189).[26] Zhou recorded navigation routes from both Guangzhou and Quanzhou to the Indian Ocean, and his work was based on his own service in Guangxi from 1172 onward. *Nanhai I*, highly likely departing from Quanzhou, was probably wrecked in 1166–1174. Considering other textual sources, I believe that the beginning of the twelfth century is a good period to pin as a starting point for this book. By the same token, 1620 makes a suitable closing date because of the completion in 1617 of the *Dongxiyang Kao* 东西洋考 (An Examination of the Eastern and Western Oceans), a maritime treatise compiled by Zhang Xie 张燮 (1574–1640) that largely ignored or forgot China's previous activities in or connections with the Indian Ocean.[27] In addition, the *Selden Map of China* which drew the whole of East and Southeast Asia but paid little attention to the Indian Ocean was completed around 1620. Thus, in this book, I draw the action to a close in 1620 when the Indian Ocean was no longer a part of the Chinese world, whether real or imagined.

This book is divided into four parts, consisting of seventeen chapters. Part I, "The Stage," consists of three chapters and establishes the setting. Chapter 2 spotlights Quanzhou, probably the largest port city in the world at that time, from which Chinese ships departed for the Indian Ocean, and chapter 3 scrutinizes Chinese navigation technology, merchant organization, and ships to highlight the background of the voyages of Wang Dayuan. In part II, "A Destination," chapter 4 recounts all the medieval travelers or scholars who either visited the Maldives or who wrote about these islands. Chapters 5 and 6 examine the different aspects of the island sultanate, such as the Chinese nomenclature of the Maldives, atolls, monsoons, and coconut trees. Chapter 7 turns to discuss the political interactions between Ming China and the island sultanate. Part III, "The Cargo," consisting of six chapters, examines the local products and commodities of the Maldives, such as coir rope, dried fish, grains, handkerchiefs, cowrie shells, ambergris, and scented woods. This diverse range of commercial goods not only distinguished the islands, but also made them a hub of maritime trade. Finally, part IV, "Reminiscences," deals with how the Maldivian past became blurred and forgotten in China. Chapter 14 attempts to reconstruct the Buddhist landscape, at least partially, in the pre-Islamic Maldives of which Chinese travelers such as Wang Dayuan and Ma Huan had no conception. Chapter 15 explores a special contracted marriage between native women and foreign sojourners that constituted a popular practice in port societies across maritime Asia. Chapter 16, examines how the *Sanbao Taijian Xiyangji Tongsu Yanyi* 三宝太监西洋记通俗演义, a Chinese novel composed by Luo Maodeng 罗懋登 in the 1590s, romanticized the Zheng He voyages and presented its fabricated knowledge on the Maldives and the Indian Ocean world.[28] Chapter 17 traces the circulation of Chinese knowledge within and beyond maritime Asia through the case of "the China Bird" discovered in the Maldives. While the episode stood as the last echo of Chinese activities in this remote island kingdom, there emerged the parallel trajectories of European and Chinese cartographic knowledge of the Maldives, both strands making their mark on imperial cartographic works produced in China.

Links, exchanges, and interactions among kingdoms and peoples over time rarely take a linear or cumulative course. They are sometimes disrupted, or they decline, and some are even deliberately dropped. Disconnection essentially constitutes the other side of various interactions. China's discovery of the Maldives primarily resulted from commercial activities backed up by the market under the Southern Song and the Yuan. China's rapid increase of its knowledge of the Maldives was an immediate consequence of the Zheng He voyages, an official campaign made by a state with a strong willingness and capability that as fate would have it could not last long without the appropriate support from the hands of the market. While the force of the market continued to move cowrie shells from the Maldives to China's southwestern and southeastern frontiers through transit trade, the people at that time hardly had an inkling of the actual origin of this marine substance. Once political zeal cooled down, connections were discontinued. Ming China's sudden withdrawal from the Indian Ocean and reissue of maritime ban policy in 1433 expunged former commercial connections with the Indian Ocean, and such a pattern went on until the late nineteenth century. As a result, discovering was replaced with discarding, with fragmentary information on the Indian Ocean being indirectly provided by Europeans. From the Ming-Qing transition onward, with Chinese attention shifting to the Nanyang 南洋 (lit. the "South Sea," referring to modern Southeast Asia), the age of the Nanyang kicked off, and Qing China embarked on its long eighteenth century of trade and exploration in this region. The Indian Ocean once again became a far-off place, a forgotten world.

Chapter Two

FROM ZAITUN

It is indeed impossible to convey an idea of the number of merchants and the accumulation of goods in this place, which is held to be one of the largest ports in the world.

—MARCO POLO

The port of Zaytun is one of the largest in the world or perhaps the very largest.

—IBN BATTUTA

Quanzhou, or Zaitun as it was known in the medieval west, thanks to Marco Polo and Ibn Battuta, was the city from which Wang Dayuan departed for the Indian Ocean world and at which Ibn Battuta landed to begin his visit to China at the beginning of the mid-fourteenth century. There have been numerous studies on the so-called foreign merchants (and their community) in Quanzhou; among these the best-known is the life of Pu Shougeng 蒲寿庚 during the Song-Yuan transition period of the thirteenth century.[1]

Pu Shougeng was a descendant of foreign merchants (Cham, Persian, Arab, Malay, or other such origins) who had settled in Guangzhou and then moved to Quanzhou, fitting well in the shift of maritime trade from Guangzhou to Quanzhou during the period. Pu took charge of the Shiboshi 市舶使 (Maritime Customs Superintendent) of Quanzhou, established himself as a rich tycoon through maritime trade, and played an eminent role in the maritime trade and dynastic politics during the Song-Yuan transition. The Pu family continued to hold enormous power and wealth throughout the Yuan period (1279–1368), and hence symbolized the prosperity of maritime trade centered on Quanzhou, where multiculturalism thrived. Indeed, Billy So has insightfully pointed out that Pu and his family were "clearly a South Fukienese family, despite its foreign origin."[2] Studies of stone inscriptions and images discovered in local temples, tombs, and other structures of the period have illustrated the localization and development of various religions such as Nestorianism, Buddhism, Hinduism, Manichaeism, Islam, Daoism, and Confucianism in this world-class port city.[3] It is not necessary to repeatedly highlight all of these foreign connections and contributions. The following section instead focuses on how Chinese merchants from Quanzhou explored maritime Asia, thus revealing how the trading network worked from the China end.

Quanzhou lies on the southeast coast of Fujian Province, about 118 miles (190 km) south of Fuzhou 福州, a maritime port that developed earlier than Quanzhou, and 75 miles (120 km) north of Zhangzhou 漳州, a port city that was to replace Quanzhou during the late Ming period. Mountainous as it is, the Quanzhou area lacks arable land and is crisscrossed by many rivers such as the Jin River (*Jinjiang* 晋江), which flows from the western mountains to the eastern coast and joins the sea. In the Tang period (618–907), southern Fujian (*Minnan* 闽南) in which Quanzhou was located had remained largely agrarian. It was chiefly during the second half of the tenth century that Quanzhou began to take off as an international port, and by the beginning of the eleventh century Quanzhou merchants had been active participants in the transit maritime trade, especially with Koryo (*Gaoli* 高丽).[4]

A breakthrough was made in 1087 when the Shibosi 市舶司 (the Maritime Customs Office) was set up in Quanzhou. While the reason for its establishment was possibly more political than economic, the Shibosi would have furthered the development of maritime trade in Quanzhou and southern Fujian.[5] The fall of the Northern Song (960–1127) and thus the founding of the Southern Song in 1127 indicated the southern shift of politics and economy, which tendered a new opportunity for Quanzhou and its overseas trade.

CHINESE MERCHANTS

It was during the Song period that Chinese merchants traveled overseas, particularly starting from Quanzhou. In 1095 Jiang Gongwang 江公望, a magistrate of Yongchun 永春 County under Quanzhou, vividly detailed the activities there. "Here sea ships communicate with foreign countries. With a tail wind, they could sail a few hundred *li* 里 in one moment.

Precious and exotic goods such as pearls, turtle shells, rhinoceros horn, ivory, cinnabar, mercury, sandalwood, frankincense, and so on, are coming ashore. Eminent merchants crowd the streets, shoulder to shoulder and heel to heel."[6] Jiang's observations mainly referred to foreign ships and foreign merchants at the end of the eleventh century, but things were to change within a few decades. Along with foreign merchants who had been Sinicized in China represented by Pu Shougeng, many native Chinese merchants were inspired and went to sea, their exploits inspiring many stories set out in the *Yijian Zhi* 夷坚志 written by Hong Mai 洪迈 (1123–1202).[7]

Hong Mai, a native of Raozhou 饶州, Jiangxi Province, and a *jinshi* 进士 (the highest degree through a series of examinations in imperial China) in 1145, once served as the prefect of Quanzhou in 1163–1166, in addition to that of Jizhou 吉州 (Jiangxi), Ganzhou 赣州 (Jiangxi), Wuzhou 婺州 (Zhejiang), and Shaoxing 绍兴 (Zhejiang), all being either coastal cities or very close to the coast. His *Yijian Zhi* provides many details about the maritime trade conducted by Chinese merchants in southern Fujian, especially in Quanzhou. One such episode was related by Bencheng 本偁, a Quanzhou monk, whose cousin was caught in a storm during the voyage to *Sanfoqi* 三佛齐 (Srivijaya). By holding on for dear life to a piece of wood that fortuitously floated within his reach, his cousin was carried to an island where a naked woman saved him. There they lived together for seven or eight years and had three boys. One day a Quanzhou ship passed by, and the man boarded it for home.[8]

Another story, said to have occurred in the seventh month of the twentieth year of the Shaoqing 绍庆 reign (1150), shares a similar narrative. A ship, formed from a single log, arrived from the southeast (*dongnan* 东南). On this ship was a native of Fuzhou, his wife, and the woman's two brothers, together with a cargo of sandal and aloe wood amounting to a few thousand *jin* 斤. The man said that some thirteen years earlier he had been lost at sea and came across a big island where he had stayed. The local chief had married him to his daughter and treated him well. Two months earlier, he had left for home on this canoe/ship. The author of the *Yijian Zhi*, Hong Mai himself, boarded the ship, examined its inner cabin, and saw these three foreigners. In another anecdote from the *Yijian Zhi*, Yang, a maritime merchant in business for more than ten years, had accumulated wealth to the tune of two hundred million *min* 缗 (one *min* is equivalent to 1,000 copper coins).⁹

While the above tales are fascinating, perhaps there was no one better than Wang Yuanmao 王元懋 to illustrate the actual contemporary maritime commercial activities of Quanzhou merchants.¹⁰ A native of Quanzhou, Wang Yuanmao served in a kind of "Buddhist temple" (*sengsi* 僧寺) when he was young, and his master taught him some of the written languages of certain southern barbarian countries (*nanfan zhuguo shu* 南蕃诸国书) in which he became fluent. He then boarded an oceangoing ship to Zhancheng 占城 (Champa) where the king of Champa so appreciated his multilingual talents that he married Wang to his daughter. Ten years later Wang returned to Quanzhou a wealthy man, worth over one million *min*. He then devoted himself to maritime trade. In the fifth year of the Chunxi 淳熙 reign (1178), he hired Wu Da 吴大 (lit. "Wu the Oldest") as the head merchant (*gangshou* 纲首) to oversee thirty-eight people on an overseas trip that would last for ten years. When Wu Da returned in 1188 with pearls, agar wood, camphor, and musk, he realized a profit over a few dozen times the price he had paid for the goods (*shushibei* 数十倍).

Wang's legendary life provides a wonderful insight into maritime activities in Quanzhou. One should bear in mind that Wang was born only a few decades earlier than Hong Mai, and thus Hong's record was highly reliable. The "Buddhist temple" he stayed in was by no means a conventional Chinese one and seems to have been strongly influenced by Hinduism, since his master was said to have taught Wang some of the languages of the southern countries, likely to have been South Indian or West Asian languages such as Tamil and Arabic. After his return to Quanzhou Wang hired local men to conduct overseas trade, and one of the voyages lasted for as long as a decade. The mentions of *gangshou* (head merchant or captain) and various foreign aromatic materials all fit well in the Song context. For example, in 1167, there were two voyages that originated in Quanzhou and sailed to Champa, one of these consisting of five ships.¹¹ When the Yuan envoy Zhou Daguan 周达观 visited Zhenla 真腊 (Cambodia) in 1296–1297, he came across a fellow countryman, Xue (*xiangren Xueshi* 乡人薛氏), who had been in that foreign land for 35 years.¹² This means that Xue, who was from Wenzhou, a coastal city in Zhejiang, must have reached Cambodia in the 1260s, the closing years of the Southern Song, in which *Quanzhou I* sailed between Quanzhou and the Indian Ocean.

FROM ZAITUN

The 1260s–1270s seem to have been very eventful decades for China's maritime activities, since quite a few testimonies refer to considerable feats undertaken during that period. In addition to Xue's exploits, *Quanzhou I*, the China pagoda built in 1267 in Nagapattinam (on the southeastern Indian coast), and cowrie shells stored in the Jiangnan warehouse in 1275 (more on these latter two in chapters 3 and 10), the tombstone of a Master Pu (*Pugong* 蒲公) dated 1274 was discovered in 1972 in Brunei.[13] Its inscription includes ten big Chinese characters: *Yong Song Quanzhou Panguan Pugong Zhimu* 有宋泉州判官蒲公之墓 (lit. "the tomb of Master Pu, Panguan of Quanzhou, the Song Dynasty") and eight small ones, *Jingding Jiazi Nan Yingjia li* 景定甲子男应 [?]甲立 (lit. "erected by Son Yingjia in the Jiazi year of the Jingding reign"). The Jiazi year refers to 1274, the last year in the Jingding reign (1260–1264) of Emperor Lizong of the Southern Song dynasty, while the title *Panguan* 判官 might refer to a low-ranking Song official position once held by Master Pu in Quanzhou. It seems curious that a Song official from Quanzhou would have been buried in a Muslim cemetery in Brunei. The Chinese character Pu 蒲 might be a transliteration of Abu, but whether Master Pu was a Muslim remains a pure speculation. What can be deduced is that he once served in Song Quanzhou, died in or around 1264, and was buried by his son in Borneo. And very interestingly, the type of stone the stele is made from does not occur naturally in Borneo.[14] Did Master Pu die in Borneo or not? Was Master Pu an imperial envoy, a retired official, a merchant, or a political refugee? Why did his son decide to bury him overseas in Borneo? And what was his son doing in Borneo in the first place? All these questions have remained unanswered. Nevertheless, the tombstone of Master Pu, certainly the oldest known Chinese epigraph in Southeast Asia, does illustrate the intensive network in maritime Asia in which Chinese people and especially those in Quanzhou played an extremely active role.

Chinese merchants such as Wang Dayuan continued their overseas trade during the Yuan period. A 1365 biographical essay that recorded the activities of a certain Sun Tianfu 孙天富 and a Chen Baosheng 陈宝生 provides a window on the world of fourteenth-century Chinese commercial maritime enterprises. Sun and Chen, sworn brothers and native traders from Quanzhou, had been overseas for a decade, doing business in Korea, Java, Lov, and various other places.[15] The two shared every penny made from trade and won the nickname among foreigners: "The Two Righteous Men from Quanzhou" (*Quanzhou liang yishi* 泉州两义士). Other evidence suggests that Chen's father was drowned overseas, indicating that international trade was a family tradition.

THE STORY OF WEN SHI

These cases reveal that Quanzhou and its merchants had been active participants in maritime trade during the Song-Yuan period. The story of Wen Shi 文实 (lit. "Wen the Honest") created in the *Paian Jingqi* 拍案惊奇 (Amazing Tales) and authored by Ling Mengchu 凌濛初 (1580–1644) shares the legendary experience of a literati merchant (just like Wang Dayuan) who made his fortune on an incidental overseas trip.[16]

Wen Shi was a native of Suzhou 苏州, a prosperous coastal port city along the Grand Canal during the Chenghua 成化 reign (1465–1487). While he was talented and well educated, a series of misfortunes in his domestic trade cost him the entire wealth he had inherited from his family. He desperately appealed to Zhang Chengyun 张乘运 (lit. "Zhang the Lucky") who headed a group of merchants comprising more than forty men specializing in overseas trade. Zhang kindly agreed, since he thought that Wen's mix of tales and yarns would amuse his fellow merchants, bringing some fun and entertainment to their long and dull sea voyage. Zhang and the other merchants also kindly provided one tael of silver for Wen to buy any Chinese goods for the maritime trade. Such a small sum could hardly buy any fine goods, so Wen bought a basket of oranges and became a minor passenger-merchant, occupying a small corner of a cabin. In their first landing at a port in the kingdom of Jiling 吉零 in Southeast Asia, Wen's oranges were sold for over 1,000 silver coins, approximately 900 taels.[17] When a storm blew the ship to a desolate island, Wen happened to find a giant turtle shell that could be made into two beds. On its return journey, the ship called at a port in Fujian, and Mabaoha 玛宝哈, a local "Persian foreigner" (*Bosi hu* 波斯胡) who had been in China so long that his dress, language, and behavior were almost entirely Chinese, combined all his assets, including cash in silver, shops, houses, and servants amounting to 50,000 taels of silver, to purchase Wen's shell. Everyone was surprised until Mabaoha, after completing the deal, explained that the shell was that of *tuolong* 鼍龙 (one of the nine sons of the legendary dragon) and that within the shell there were twenty-four large night-shining pearls (*yemingzhu* 夜明珠). The "Persian merchant" thereafter returned to his homeland, while Wen decided to settle in the Fujian port.

A few points need to be highlighted here. First, Ling Mengchu, the author of the *Paian Jingqi*, was a scholar, but his scholarly route to the imperial exams was not a straightforward or smooth one. As a native of Huzhou 湖州, Zhejiang Province, then the center of the silk industry and bronze mirror manufacturing, Ling was supposed to understand trade and business very well. While Ling underlined the themes of the Buddhist worldview by starting his novel with the legend of Wen Shi, this story gives a good idea of the daily reach of overseas trade in China. Like Ling Mengchu, the Wen Shi in the story was well educated but unlucky in his business. However, an unplanned overseas trip brought him an unexpected fortune, indicating the widely accepted belief that equated maritime trade with instant wealth.

Like his sea trade success hero Wen Shi, Ling was not a native of Fujian, but he understood the role of this region in China's overseas trade. In the story of Wen, Ling did not specify the port in Fujian, whereas circumstantial evidence suggests that the port city was none other than Quanzhou. The connection with the Indian Ocean was also hinted at in the mention of the so-called Persian merchant. Another telling detail pointing to this connection was that the treasured night-shining pearls were wrapped in a Xiyang cloth (*xiyang bu* 西洋布).[18] The *Xiyang bu* in the Ming and early Qing texts referred to cotton cloth produced in South India, especially Ma'bar. Therefore, the story of Wen Shi created by Ling Mengchu must have had its social prototype, and the protagonist Wen Shi bears a remarkable similarity to Wang Dayuan, a member of the literati who, though not native to Quanzhou, participated in the Sino-Indian Ocean trade in which Quanzhou played the key role.

Finally, Mabaoha, the so-called *Bosi hu*, has its historical base. As early as in the Yongxi 雍熙 reign (984–988), Luohuna 啰护哪, a monk who claimed to be native to Tanzhu 天竺 (India) arrived at Quanzhou, and with donations from foreign merchants was able to build the Baolinyuan 宝林院, a "Buddhist monastery (*focha* 佛刹)" in the southern part of the city.[19] Such anecdotes lead us to understand that by the end of the tenth century, a community of foreign merchants, especially from South Asia and West Asia, had been already formed in Quanzhou. Owing to the wealth that they had accumulated they were active in sponsoring religious activities, in addition to their intimate association with local Chinese officials. For example, in the tenth month of the fourth year of the Jiatai 嘉泰 reign (1204), Luoba

罗巴 and Zhiligan 智力干, two prominent heads of the scores of foreign merchants, took part in the customary funerary wailing outside the house of the recently deceased Guo Xizong 郭晞宗, the Shiboshi in Quanzhou.[20] Twenty years later when Zhao Rukuo 赵汝适 took over the position of the Shiboshi there, he might have been acquainted with these same foreign resident traders. In his *Zhufan Zhi* 诸蕃志 (A Record of Barbarians), Zhao particularly mentioned that a father Luoba 罗巴 and his son Zhiligan 智力干, "currently living in southern Quanzhou," belonged to the same people as those of the Kingdom of Nanpi 南毗.[21] Nanpi, located near today's Calicut (Khozikode), on southeastern coastal India, was regarded by Zhao as the furthermost country from Quanzhou (and thus Song China). The father, Luoba, and the son, Zhiligan, might have been the abovementioned foreign chiefs who had mourned the demise of Guo Xizong, and they represent the earliest foreign sojourners in Quanzhou, especially those from South India, who must have inspired and guided Chinese merchants and their ships to South India. "The country (of *Nanpi*) is the furthest, and foreign ships seldom call at Quanzhou"; nevertheless, owing to the father and the son, "many (Chinese) ships have sailed to the country," concluded the *Song Shi* 宋史 (History of the Song Dynasty).[22] Obviously, the advent and residence of foreign merchants in Quanzhou played a key role in encouraging, guiding, and supporting Chinese ships on their initial journeys to the Indian Ocean.

THROUGH THE LENS OF MARCO POLO AND IBN BATTUTA

Thus, by the early twelfth century, a foreign merchant community was prosperous and well established in Quanzhou. Lin Zhiqi 林之奇 (1112–1176), a *jinshi* of 1151, once served as the Shiboshi of Quanzhou. One of his essays commemorated the establishing a cemetery for foreigners who had died in Quanzhou, a task that would have fallen to the superintendent.

> Among the three prefectures dealing with the South Sea and responsible for taxing mercantile ships is Quanzhou prefecture. Among the scores of countries that have trade connections with Quanzhou is Srivijaya. Among the scores of rich merchants from Srivijaya who are living or were born in Quanzhou is a man called Shi Nawei 试舻围. Shi was famous for his generosity among his fellow foreign residents in Quanzhou. The building of a

cemetery was but one of his many generous deeds. This cemetery project was first proposed by another foreigner named Pu Xiaxin 蒲霞辛 (Abu Hasan?), but it was carried out and accomplished by Shi. The cemetery is located on the *Dongban* 东坂 (lit. "eastern hillslope") at the east of the city. After the wild weeds and rubble were cleared, many graves have been built, with the cemetery being covered with a roof, enclosed by a wall, and safely locked. All foreign merchants who die in Quanzhou are to be buried there. Construction started in the year of *Renwu* 壬午 (1162) and was finished in the year of *Guiwei* 癸未 (1163). Such a benevolent deed by Shi releases all foreigners in this land from worrying about their fates and enables the dead to be free of regrets. Such kindness will certainly promote overseas trade and encourage foreigners to come. I am very pleased with what he has done, and thus I write this essay to commemorate the event so that [news of it] will be widely circulated overseas.[23]

This bustling overseas commercial network and large foreign community made Quanzhou the prime destination for Ibn Battuta when he landed in China.

Both the Moroccan traveler and Marco Polo provided vivid descriptions of this very cosmopolitan oriental city. Marco Polo was impressed by the extent of maritime trade in Quanzhou.

> The noble and handsome city of Zai-tun, which has a port on the sea coast celebrated for the resort of shipping, loaded with merchandise, that is afterwards distributed through every part of the province of Manji. The quality of pepper imported there is so considerable, that what is carried to Alexandria, to supply the demand of the western parts of the world, is trifling in comparison, perhaps not more than the hundredth part. It is indeed impossible to convey an idea of the number of merchants and the accumulation of goods in this place, which is held to be one of the largest ports in the world. The Great Khan derives a vast revenue from this place, as every merchant is obliged to pay ten per cent, upon the amount of his investment. The ships are freighted by them at the rate of thirty per cent for fine goods, forty-four for pepper, and for sandal, and other drugs, as well as articles of trade in general, forty per cent. It is computed by the merchants, that their charges, including customs and freight, amount to half the value of the cargo; and yet upon the half that remains to them their profit is so considerable, that

they are always disposed to return to the same market with a further stock or merchandise.²⁴

Differentiation of the tax rate, a point noted by Marco Polo, had certainly been carried out from as late as the Song period. According to Zhu Yu writing in the early twelfth century, when foreign ships in arrived in Guangzhou, the Shiboshi dispatched officials and clerks on board the vessels to levy tax in kind (*choujie* 抽解), 10 percent for pearls and camphor (*longnao* 龙脑), 30 percent for turtle shells (*daimao* 玳瑁), sappanwood (*sumu* 苏木), and so on. The Song state monopolized the purchase of ivory weighing over thirty *jin* and all quantities of frankincense (*ruxiang* 乳香), with fixed official prices after being taxed.²⁵ In order to avoid the official monopoly, merchants deliberately cut large chunks of ivory into smaller pieces, each piece intentionally lighter than thirty *jin*. Negotiations between the Shiboshi and foreign merchants in Quanzhou were likely to have been carried out in a similar manner.

Urban life in Quanzhou was pleasant for foreigners. According to Marco Polo, "The country is delightful. The people are idolaters, and have all the necessaries of life in plenty. Their disposition is peaceable, and they are fond of ease and indulgence. Many persons arrive in this city from the interior parts of India for the purpose of having their persons ornamented by puncturing with needles in the manner before described, as it is celebrated for the number of its artists skilled in that practice." Clearly, the Venetian understood that merchants from Quanzhou (and Fujian) had regular trade with Japan to the east, Champa to the southwest (where Wang Yuanmao had made his fortune), and Java to the south. Ziamba (Indo-China) was "fifteen hundred miles across" the sea from Zaitun, and Java "abounds with rich commodities. Pepper, nutmegs, spikenards, galangal, cubes, cloves, and all the other valuable spices and drugs, are the produce of the island." "From thence it is that the merchants of Zai-tun and of Manji in general have imported."²⁶ Commercial connections between Quanzhou and these countries, though very briefly mentioned, were in line with those that Zhou Qufei and Zhao Rukuo had remarked on around a century earlier. It was from Quanzhou that Marco Polo made his way home.

Chinese connections with the Indian Ocean world were observed by Ibn Battuta. He found that the Chinese vessels (and merchants, of course) spent their winter in "Fandarayná [Panderani], a large and fine town with orchards and bazaars," the town certainly being one of the oldest ports in Kerala on the Malabar Coast. The city of Quilon was "the nearest of the Mulaybar towns to China and it is to it that most of the merchants [from China] come." The ship that Ibn Battuta planned to board in Calicut met with a storm and broke into pieces, as did the one in which "the ambassador from the king of China" had traveled. In Quilon, Ibn Battuta met the Chinese ambassador once again. "They had embarked on one of the junks which was wrecked like the others. The Chinese merchants provided them with cloths and they returned to China, where I met them again later."[27] This vague reference to Chinese people cannot help to identify at all whether or not Quanzhou merchants were included in their number, but on a few occasions Ibn Battuta specifically referred to the Quanzhou connections with Ceylon.

In Ceylon,

> The blessed Footprint, the Foot of our father Adam, is on a lofty black rock in a wide plateau. The blessed Foot sank into the rock far enough to leave its impression hollowed out. It is eleven spans long. In ancient days, the Chinese came here and cut out of the rock the mark of the great toe and the adjoining parts. They put this in a temple at Zaytun where it is visited by men from the farthest parts of the land. In the rock where the Foot is there are nine holes cut out, in which the infidel pilgrims place offerings of gold, precious stones, and jewels.[28]

This Buddhist link between Ceylon and Quanzhou claimed by Ibn Battuta was by no means a simple myth. A religious connection between the two had begun much earlier and had been supported by maritime trade. Both Faxian's visit to Ceylon during his return journey at the beginning of the fifth century and Wang Dayuan's stopover in the 1330s reveal these Sino-Ceylonese interactions. While discussing Buddha's footprints, Wang Dayuan mentioned a similar story about a Chinese man who came to fetch a Buddhist alms bowl (*boyu* 钵盂),[29] further confirming the Buddhist link.

Like Marco Polo, Ibn Battuta spared no ink when extolling the glories of Quanzhou:

> The first city which we reached after our sea voyage was the city of Zaytun. [Now although *zaytun* means "olives"] there are no olives in this city, nor

indeed in all the lands of the Chinese nor in India; it is simply a name which has been given to the place. Zaytun is an immense city. In it are woven the damask silk and satin fabrics which go by its name, and which are superior to the fabrics of Khansá and Khán-Báli. The port of Zaytun is one of the largest in the world or perhaps the very largest. I saw in it about a hundred large junks; as for small junks, they could not be counted for multitudes. It is formed by a large inlet of the sea which penetrates the land to the point where it unites with the great river. In this city, as in all Chinese towns, a man will have a fruit garden and a field with his house set in the middle of it, just as in the town of Sijilmása in our own country. For this reason their towns are extensive.[30]

Ibn Battuta particularly detailed the presence of porcelain and silk, the two most famous Chinese export goods.

Chinese pottery [porcelain] is manufactured only in the towns of Zaytun and Sin-kalan. It is made of the soil of some mountains in that district which takes fire like charcoal, as we shall relate subsequently. They mix this with some stones which they have, burn the whole for three days, then pour water over it. This gives a kind of clay which they cause to ferment. The best quality of [porcelain is made from] clay that has fermented for a complete month, but no more, the poorer quality [from clay] that has fermented for ten days. The price of porcelain there is the same as, or even less than, that of ordinary pottery in our country. It is exported to India and other countries, even reaching as far as our own lands in the West. And it is the finest of all makes of pottery.[31]

While Ibn Battuta claimed that porcelain was made in Canton (Sin-kalan), the place he had visited might have been Jingdezhen, the foremost porcelain center of the world for several centuries and the one with which Wang Dayuan had been acquainted. Ibn Battuta described how a river took him to Canton where porcelain was "manufactured as well as at Zaytun."[32] But there is no river connecting Quanzhou and Canton. A few rivers did most certainly link Jingdezhen and Quanzhou with a short course of land transportation in between, and porcelain from Jingdezhen was shipped to Quanzhou before its overseas trip. Perhaps Ibn Battuta confused Jingdezhen with Canton? After all, his writing was completed years after his China trip, and his memory of the place might have been less reliable.

Both Marco Polo and Ibn Battuta regarded Quanzhou as the largest port in the world, and Ibn Battuta mentioned that the Quanzhou port could accommodate one hundred large (oceangoing) junks and numerous smaller ships. What we know for sure is that a few centuries earlier, Chinese ships had begun to parallel Indian Ocean ships in Sino-Indian Ocean navigation.

Chapter Three

SAILING TO THE INDIAN OCEAN

Dashi, located northwest of Quanzhou, is the furthermost one.

—ZHOU QUFEI

Some ships of the larger class have as many as thirteen bulk-heads or divisions in the hold, formed of thick planks mortised into each other.

—MARCO POLO

Approximately from the twelfth century onward, Chinese oceangoing ships began to sail to the Indian Ocean, passing through Southeast Asia. In coastal India, Ibn Battuta observed the Chinese ships and merchants and concluded that "On the Sea of China traveling is done in Chinese ships only." In Calicut, "there were at the time thirteen Chinese vessels, and disembarked. Every one of us was lodged in a house and we stayed there three months as the guests of the infidel, awaiting the season of the voyage to China."[1] Whether the "thirteen Chinese vessels" were ships made in China and owned by Chinese merchants or were those made in the Indian Ocean world and owned by Indian or Arabic merchants but sailing to China is unfortunately not clear.

The discovery of a shipwreck will surely provide some clues. In August 1974 a Song shipwreck was discovered in Quanzhou Bay, providing crucial information about the oceangoing Chinese junks in which Marco Polo, Odorico da Pordenone, Wang Dayuan, and Ibn Battuta sailed across the China Sea. Because of its significance in the history of maritime China and especially the Sino-Indian Ocean interactions, I hence name it *Quanzhou I*.

Scholars in the 1970s–1980s carried out a thorough study of this Chinese ship and found that this wooden Chinese oceangoing junk had been built before 1271, the seventh year of the Xianchun 咸淳 reign (1265–1274), eight years before the end of the Southern Song.² A large quantity of spices, aromatic woods, incense, and aromatic medicines (*xiangyao* 香药) amounting to 5,181 pounds (2,350 kg) before hydration were found in the holds (especially in holds 3, 4, and 5), in addition to copper coins dating to the Tang and Song period, copper wares, ceramics, wooden articles (including ninety-six labels and lots, most bearing characters written in Chinese ink), bamboo strip weavings and ropes, rattan helmets, Chinese chess pieces, fruit stones (peach, plum, red bayberry, apricot, Chinese olive, and lychee), coconut shells, cowrie shells, coral, animal bones (pig, dog, goat, mouse, fish, and bird), and other items.³ The cargo categories are in accordance with the maritime trade of the Song period in which the *xiangyao* dominated commodities imported from Southeast Asia, South Asia, and West Asia to China. Scholars argued that *Quanzhou I* had completed a few voyages and after its last return journey from Southeast Asia, came across the turbulent upheaval of the Song-Yuan transition in Quanzhou and was abandoned probably in the Summer-Autumn period of 1277.⁴ All the evidence gleaned suggests that the Song ship must have passed through Southeast Asia and anchored at Palembang, which served as the key port in these waters for Chinese merchants. However, whether Southeast Asia was the destination or just the transit station to the Indian Ocean remains an unanswered question. Combined with recent textual and archaeological findings, I have critically reexamined the goods recovered from the ship (especially the *xiangyao*) and marine organisms such as cowrie shells found in or attached to the shipwreck, and pointed out that it is more likely that *Quanzhou I* had in fact just completed a return journey *from* the Indian Ocean.⁵

Aromatic articles in the shipwreck consist of laka wood (*jiangxiang* 降香), aloe wood (*chenxiang* 沉香), sandalwood (*tanxiang* 檀香), frankincense (*ruxiang* 乳香), ambergris (*longxianxiang* 龙涎香), betelnut (*binlang* 槟榔), and pepper (*hujiao* 胡椒).⁶ Most woods were in the form of broken splinters about 1.2 to 3.9 inches (3–10 cm) long, a few being as long as 66 inches (168 cm).⁷ Previous scholars pointed out that most aromatic articles were produced or purchased in Southeast Asia and thus argued that the destination of the ship had been Southeast Asia. Nevertheless, while Southeast Asia produced laka and aloe wood, these were also found in India.

Furthermore, a scientific analysis of the laka wood on board this ship showed that India was most likely to have been its origin.[8]

In terms of sandalwood and pepper, previous scholars were mistaken when they stated that these were produced in Java. India was their primary producer and earliest exporter. In addition, while ambergris was discovered in East Africa (on its coastal waters, in fact), the Indian Ocean communities were its primary and major discoverers and thus "producers" (see chapter 12). Therefore, considering the original homes of these items, it is extremely likely that the Indian Ocean was the actual destination of this Chinese vessel.

The discovery of more than two thousand cowrie shells (*Monetaria moneta* and *Monetaria annulus*) further strengthens the Indian Ocean destination hypothesis. While these two types of cowrie shell have been known to live across vast areas of tropical and subtropical oceans, historically, it was only the Maldives that has had an astronomical abundance of these shells. Tiny as the Maldives was, the massive supply of cowries and its fortuitously central geographical pivot point in maritime trading routes between Africa, Arabia, and its neighboring giant, India, a market that required hard coins, ensured its place as the only major supplier. It is true that there is evidence that the Philippines also produced cowrie shells, but its documentation occurred a few centuries later than *Quanzhou I*. Neither textual nor archaeological evidence supports the speculation that the South China Sea had once supplied cowrie shells to imperial China.[9] Finally, the size of the shells (most being .7 inches [1.8 cm] long, .55 inches [1.4 cm] wide, and 0.3 inches [0.8 cm] high) documented in the archaeological reports refers to their Maldivian origin. Therefore, it is almost certain that these cowrie shells were from the Maldives and extremely likely that they were brought by the ship owners from the Maldives or India as ballast. More cowrie shells were thought to have been stored in the holds of this Chinese vessel found in Quanzhou Bay.

In the holds there were seven other types of shell lodged between the planks or attached to the hull, including various maggots, *martesia striata*, and ostreas (lapha).[10] While early studies concluded that most of these originated in the Southeast Asian or East Asian oceans (90.8 percent from the South China Sea), I have taken a closer look and found that nine of the fifteen kinds of shells were without a doubt native to the Indian Ocean as well.[11] Therefore, marine biology further strengthens the Indian Ocean destination of *Quanzhou I*. Considering all the information, it is fair to conclude that *Quanzhou I* had just completed a return journey from the Indian Ocean for its Quanzhou home in the summer or autumn of 1277. Hence, the Quanzhou shipwreck could well be the vivid remains of the so-called *Quanbo* 泉舶 (lit. "the Quanzhou ship") recorded by Zhou Qufei in the 1160s and Zhao Rukuo in the early thirteenth century that sailed between Quanzhou and the Indian Ocean, thus providing firsthand evidence about the technology of medieval oceangoing navigation in imperial China.[12]

While Zhou Qufei's *Lingwai Daida* adopted a Guangzhou point of view, sharing information on the direction, distance, dates, and routes of Chinese ships in the twelfth century sailing from this southern port to the Indian Ocean, Zhao Rukuo's *Zhufan Zhi* was primarily based on activities originating in Quanzhou. According to Zhao, with a good wind it took a Chinese ship over twenty *cheng* 程 from Quanzhou to Zhancheng (Champa), over a month to Zhenla (Cambodia), Sanfoqi (Palembang), or Shepo 闍婆 (Java).[13] As for Indian Ocean ports, the journey took much longer. Forty days out from Quanzhou, a Chinese ship could anchor in Lanli 蓝里 (Lambri) for the winter; and when the monsoon changed in the following year, it took the ship one more month to Gulin 故临 (Quilon) and from there five more days to Nanpi (Calicut). Zhunian 注輦 (Chola) was more than 411,400 *li* from Quanzhou by sea, and Chinese merchants had to stop over at Gulin to change their ship, while Dashi, located northwest of Quanzhou, was the furthermost one. A Chinese ship from Quanzhou had to sail for more than forty days, anchoring in Lambri where in the winter for the change of monsoon, and then with a tail wind it took over sixty days to reach Dashi. Though briefly, Zhao's notes on these voyage lengths provide an accurate summary of the navigation routes used by Song ships from Quanzhou to the Indian Ocean world.

SIZE, STRUCTURE, AND TECHNOLOGY

The discovery of the *Quanzhou I* wreck has provided a wonderful opportunity to glimpse the Chinese technology of oceangoing ship construction and life on board. The wreck is 79 feet (24.20 m) long and 6.5 feet (1.98 m) deep, with a 58-foot (17.65 m)-long keel (which means that it was originally under the loaded waterline). A comparison with modern Fujian junks leads to the conclusion that the ship itself should have been about 112 feet (34 m) long and 36 feet (11 m) wide, with its waterline 82–85 feet (25–26 m) long, and with a displacement of nearly 400 tons (table 3.1).[14] Its relatively small ratio (2.55) between the length and beam facilitated its stability in ocean-going navigation. However, while certain other scholars have principally agreed on the length, they have argued that that the displacement would have been 120 or 200 tons, much smaller than 400 tons.[15]

In terms of shipbuilding, the use of local woods, the structure, and the construction features of its keel, hull, and watertight compartments follow the typical Chinese conventions during the Song period.[16] The keel of *Quanzhou I* was made of two pine logs and the peak pillar of one single camphor wood log, both kinds of trees being widely available then in Fujian. The keel and frames formed a solid tripod and thus increased the transverse strength to resist sea waves and storms. The hull was strengthened by its formation of two-ply camphor wood planks at the bottom and three-ply camphor wood planks on the sides, which was confirmed by Marco Polo who concluded that Chinese ships "are all doubled-planked."[17] The planks were connected either by overlapping or by leveling, and the interior hull planks were integrally connected vertically with tenons and troughs. Camphor wood is famous for its strength and water- and rot-resistance, and it has been widely used in the making of furniture, especially for clothing cabinets that could withstand the humid weather of south China (as I have experienced in my home in the Yangzi Delta). It became the primary and major material for the construction of ships.

TABLE 3.1
The calculated size of *Quanzhou I*

Length	34 m	Stern–mast	14.5 m
Waterline	25–26 m	Main anchor	6.6 m
Width	11m	Second anchor	4.5 m
Draught	3.5 m	Third anchor	3.6
Mold depth	3.8 m	Main sail	187 m^2
Bow height	7.5 m	Fore sail	97.5 m^2
Stern height	10 m	Stern sail	49.5 m^2
Midmast	32 m	Rudder blade	11.6 m^2
Foremast	25.6 m	Displacement	Approx. 393.4 tons

Source: *Quanzhouwan Songdai Haichuan Fajue yu Yanjiu Xiudingban* (A Report on the Excavation of the Song Boat in Quanzhou Bay), ed. Fujian Quanzhou Haiwajiaotongshi Bowuguan (Beijing: Haiyang Chubanshe, 2017), 68–75 and 128–37.

SAILING TO THE INDIAN OCEAN

Transversely and vertically connected, the planks were fixed with nails, with seams caulked with oil-lime that was mixed with flaxen threads. "These are caulked with oakum both inside and without, and are fastened with iron nails," Marco Polo detailed. These iron nails, due to their diverse uses in different parts of the ship, varied in shape being square, round, or flat, and all with a cap head. The use of iron nails and caulk differentiated the Chinese ships from the Indian Ocean ones, which had been the earliest vessels sailing between the China Sea and the Indian Ocean, and which were famous for their nail-free construction, as was illustrated by the Belitung ship of the early ninth century discovered in 1998. Marco Polo again impresses upon the reader the difference between the two. "They are not coated with pitch, as the country does not produce that substance, but the bottoms are smeared over with the following preparation. The people take quick-lime and hemp, which latter they cut small, and with these, when pounded together, they mix oil procured from a certain tree, making of the whole a kind of unguent, which retains its viscous properties more firmly, and is a better material than pitch." In addition, Marco Polo noted that a Chinese ship needed to be repaired or it would become unsafe after it had sailed for a year or more.[18] And although no compass was found on the wreck, contemporary sources show that *Quanzhou I* must have been equipped with one. At night the Chinese sailors watched the stars, and during the day the sun. When the sky was overcast, the compass would be used.[19] Of course, the sailors would have known all the very familiar landscapes of mountains, islands, or positions of reefs, the variety of currents, fish, birds, winds, and types of soil from the seabed, all of which helped them to determine their geographical location.

Last but not least, *Quanzhou I* was divided into thirteen watertight compartments in turn divided by twelve partitions, in each of which there was a small drain hole. The watertight compartment was a Chinese invention as early as the Tang period, designed such that if one compartment was broken, the others would not be affected, thus increasing the safety of the cargo and the ship. The following description by Marco Polo indicates that he had seen such a design, along with other Chinese shipbuilding technologies.

> Some ships of the larger class have as many as thirteen bulk-heads or divisions in the hold formed of thick planks mortised into each other. The object

of these is to guard against accidents which may occasion the vessel to spring a leak, such as striking on a rock or receiving a stroke from a whale, a circumstance that not unfrequently occurs; for, when sailing at night, the motion through the waves causes a white foam that attracts the notice of the hungry animal. Expecting food, it rushes violently to the spot, strikes the ship, and often staves in some part of the bottom. The water, running in at the place where the injury has been sustained, makes its way to the well, which is always kept clear. The crew, upon discovering the situation of the leak, immediately remove the goods from the division affected by the water, which, in consequence of the boards being so well fitted, cannot pass from one division to another. They then repair the damage and return the goods to their place in the hold.[20]

Here Marco Polo provides a firsthand and thus highly detailed account of the function of the watertight compartments and the drain holes in the partitions, although a further investigation of this matter is needed. Almost all major Chinese shipbuilding features discovered in the Quanzhou shipwreck were mentioned by the Venetian, who also highlighted that the Chinese sea ships organized themselves into small fleets. He observed that a large ship might be accompanied by two or three middle-sized ships and up to ten smaller boats and that each middle-sized ship also had its own small boat in tow. "Ships of the largest size require a crew of three hundred men; others, two hundred; and some, one hundred and fifty only, according to their greater or less bulk. They carry from five to six thousand baskets, or mat bags, of pepper."[21]

Those of the larger class are accompanied by two or three large barks, capable of containing about one thousand baskets of pepper, and are manned with sixty, eighty, or one hundred sailors. These small craft are often employed to tow the larger, when working their oars, or even under sail, provided the wind be on the quarter, but not when right aft, because, in that case, the sails of the larger vessel must becalm those of the smaller. The ships also carry with them as many as ten small boats, for the purpose of carrying out anchors, tor fishing, and a variety of other services. They are slung over the sides and lowered into the water when there is occasion to use them. The barks are in like manner provided with their small boats.[22]

SAILING TO THE INDIAN OCEAN

Marco Polo's detailed descriptions were backed up by Ibn Battuta, who also classified Chinese ships anchored at Calicut based on their size into three classes: "large ships called *chunks*, middle-sized ones called *zaws* [dhows], and small ones called *kakam*s." The large ship could have as many sails from three up to twelve, and the sails were "made of bamboo rods plaited like mats," as discovered in *Quanzhou I*, and these sails "are never lowered, but turned according to the direction of the wind; at anchor they are left floating in the wind."[23] Each large ship was "accompanied by three smaller ones, the 'half,' the 'third,' and the 'quarter.'"[24] The words "half," "third," and "quarter" might refer to the comparative size of these small ones to the large ship. Although his ratio between the large ship and smaller ones differed from that of Marco Polo, the three-tiered hierarchical system of the Chinese commercial fleet was also recorded in Song and later texts.

Not coincidentally, *Nanhai I*, another Song shipwreck discovered in the coastal waters of Guangdong Province in 1987 and raised from the seabed in December 2007, significantly improves our understanding of Song navigation and maritime trade. The latest coins discovered were minted in the Qiandao 乾道 reign (1165–1173) of the Southern Song dynasty, which indicates the ship might have sunk in the late 1160s or early 1170s. Unlike *Quanzhou I*, *Nanhai I* remains a relatively complete body with tidily piled commodities, among which the porcelain and iron items immediately caught the attention of its discoverers. Iron and utensils (especially cooking pots) made from it were highly welcome in Southeast Asian societies and Indian Ocean islands such as the Nicobar Islands, a trading opportunity long known to Chinese and Western traders. This ship was dated to the early Southern Song period, more than a hundred years earlier than *Quanzhou I*, while its size (98 feet [30 m] long and 33 feet [10 m] wide) was principally the same as the latter.[25] More than 160,000 pieces of cargo were discovered. Considering that most of the porcelain on board the ship was made in Fujian, Jiangxi (Jingdezhen), and Zhejiang, together with South Asian or Arab items such as gilt silver belts and cobra bones, it is highly likely that *Nanhai I* departed from Quanzhou and planned to travel through Southeast Asia into the Indian Ocean.[26] As such, *Nanhai I* and *Quanzhou I* have constituted the most vivid legacy of the Quanzhou–Indian Ocean connections, the former one dated the early Southern Song and sunk after its departure for the Indian Ocean, while the latter one dated the close of the Southern Song and abandoned after its return from the Indian Ocean.

The size of a large Chinese ship and the number of Chinese passengers including its crew are controversial points, however. Ibn Battuta claimed that a large, four-decked ship could carry a thousand men, including a crew of six hundred and four hundred "men-at-arms" (being merchants who were also armed against pirate attacks), while Marco Polo stated that a large ship might be "manned with sixty, eighty, or one hundred sailors."[27] According to its size, *Quanzhou I* is estimated to have been crewed by around forty sailors.[28] This figure, however, was much smaller than that of the smallest "large ship" mentioned by Macro Polo, or that of the two Southeast Asian junks in 1512, probably with a weight of two hundred tons apiece and each with more than eighty crew members.[29]

Were the Chinese ships really so large that they could accommodate a thousand people on a single vessel, as Ibn Battuta stated? Imperial texts of the Song-Yuan period provide a range of estimates from dozens to five hundred to six hundred people, smaller than the numbers both Marco Polo and Ibn Battuta estimated. Ibn Battuta might have been referring to the minifleet consisting of the major ship and its three small accompanying boats. The famous ship *Mayflower*, also heavily armed, measuring 100 feet (30 m) in length, about 25 feet (7.6 m) in width, and with a tonnage of 180–200 tons, was a relatively small cargo ship, not an oceangoing ship, but it successfully transported around 132 people (along with two dogs, one mastiff and the other a spaniel) in an ocean-crossing journey of sixty-six days from England to the New World in 1620.[30] *Quanzhou I* was larger in size, and its passengers would have amounted to the same number as *Mayflower* or even more, considering the fact that the latter was a kind of refugee ship.

Due to its dimensions, life on board *Mayflower* was described by some of its passengers as horrible, like a long imprisonment at sea. While storms, diseases, and other accidental challenges beset all ships, a prominent problem on *Mayflower* was the suffocatingly small space the many passengers had to share. A quick calculation based on the dimensions of the ship shows that the maximum space per person was "slightly less than the size of a standard single bed."[31] Having a few hundred people living together in a compact space on an arduous journey that crossed turbulent seas over several months and sometimes even taking more than a year to get back home must have posed a challenge for the ship's management. Now it is time to examine what life must have been like on board ship for the Chinese captains, merchants, passengers, and crew on their south and westbound voyages.

CREWS, MERCHANTS, AND SHIP LIFE

The Chinese merchants who ventured overseas were well organized and coordinated, due to the large sum of investment capital and governmental supervision (mainly for revenue and security purposes). A large oceangoing ship could accommodate as many as a few hundred people, with a chief merchant as the head (*gangshou*), vice heads (*fu gangshou* 副纲首), general manager or accountant (*zhiku* 直库), assistants (*zashi* 杂事), subheads (*buling* 部领), and helmsman (*shaogong* 艄公), who were authorized by the Maritime Customs Office to handle the ship and its people during the voyage.[32] The *gangshou* was almost certainly the captain of the ship and might also have been its owner or else been hired by some investors who did not want to venture overseas themselves, as is seen in the story of Wang Yuanmao. Many merchants were not just passengers but also acted as ship's crew, participating in the operations of the ship. Other merchants were simply passengers who stowed their goods on board, shared the navigation risk, and paid for the space in the ship for their goods and their berth. It is highly likely that Wang Dayuan was one such passenger-merchant. Being well educated, he might have helped the captain with the accounts or other paperwork. He might also have been a welcome fellow passenger among passenger-merchants and crew members, as Wang was able to tell stories from the many books that he had read, judging by the Ming story cited earlier about Wen Shi.

The descriptions given earlier of the Song Chinese merchants were confirmed by Ibn Battuta's observations.

> These vessels are built only in the towns of Zaytun and Sin-Kalán [Canton]. The vessel has four decks and contains rooms, cabins, and saloons for merchants; a cabin has chambers and a lavatory, and can be locked by its occupant, who takes along with him slave girls and wives. Often a man will live in his cabin unknown to any of the others on board until they meet on reaching some town. The sailors have their children living on board ship, and they cultivate green stuffs, vegetables and ginger in wooden tanks. The

owner's factor on board ship is like a great amír. When he goes on shore he is preceded by archers and Abyssinians with javelins, swords, drums, trumpets and bugles. On reaching the house where he stays they stand their lances on both sides of the door and continue thus during his stay. Some of the Chinese own large numbers of ships on which their factors are sent to foreign countries. There is no people in the world wealthier than the Chinese.[33]

Did Chinese ships really need to be so heavily armed when going overseas? Most assuredly. The Yuan dynasty requirements clearly stated that ocean-going vessels should declare their weapons (*bingqi* 兵器) as well as their gongs (*luo* 锣), all of which had to be kept in the official warehouse until the departure of the ship,[34] and this might have been a Song legacy. Zhu Yu mentioned that there were many pirates who attacked any ships that avoided going to their country. A ship purposing to visit Zhancheng (Champa) might be blown to Zhenla (Cambodia), and local pirates would take all the goods and sell off the northerners (*beiren* 北人, referring to the Chinese merchants and sailors), claiming that "after all you guys had no plan to visit here."[35] In 1138 twenty-six Chinese pirates were arrested in Fuzhou.[36] Another interesting question would be: Did the Chinese use 40 percent of its crew in defense, as Ibn Battuta claimed? Perhaps not. However, when attacked by pirates, all the crew and merchants would be mobilized to defend the ship.

It is very intriguing that Ibn Battuta mentioned that in Chinese ships, children were employed to cultivate vegetables to increase the food variety and supply vitamins crucial for long-distance navigation. Interestingly, there were also around thirty children on *Mayflower*, some being passengers while others were probably more likely to have been wards or servants. Due to their small size, these children were more agile in moving about the parts of the ship, and so saved precious sleeping space. They probably raised more than just vegetables, too: remains of bones of animals including pigs, goats, dogs, chicken, and geese discovered on *Nanhai I* suggest another role for these children.[37] One may wonder who these children were. Ibn Battuta confidently described them as the sailors' children, which might not have been altogether accurate. It is highly possible that these children were either adopted, hired, or bought as slaves. Wang Dayuan himself most likely took a boy (*tongzi* 童子) with him on his Indian Ocean trip. He once asked the boy to dive for a coral in the shallow seabed around Ceylon.[38] With daily experience and training on board, some of these children would grow up to become excellent sailors, merchants, and leaders of maritime life. If Wang Yuanmao had begun his overseas career as a teenager, he might have done similar things. These boys, tasked to do minor but somehow crucial tasks, continued to find a role in modern navies. Known as cabin boys, quite a few of them grew up to become excellent captains. In Charles Dickens's (1812–1870) *Oliver Twist*, for example, Oliver would have been sent away to sea by the "gentlemen" of the board as a cabin boy before he became apprentice to a coffin maker. These boys might also have had a sexual role similar to the *puer* (boy) in ancient Rome. After all, homosexual relationships were not uncommonly observed at least in imperial piracy during the Ming-Qing period.

Having said that, these boys might truly have been the children of sailors or merchants. Based on textual sources, it became very popular for a local family in Fujian to adopt or to purchase a boy with a different surname during the Ming period. Many motives accounted for such a widespread custom. First, lineage tensions among different migrants and indigenous villagers in a land-hungry environment precipitated violent clashes that required male labor and fighters. Having more boys meant a greater combined strength in the competition for land and other resources. Second, overseas trade also demanded males as agents, sailors, and laborers. Local merchants understood the difficulties and risks of life at sea, so they kept their own children at home but sent their adopted boys to do the dangerous overseas business. He Qiaoyuan, a native of Quanzhou at the end of the Ming era, explained such a practice, placing it in the maritime context. "Haicheng 海澄 is filled with foreign vessels, Chinese merchants travel overseas, and local settlers invest money. Some people adopt children of poor families or orphans the same as their own sons; when growing up, they are dispatched to communicate with barbarians, since their life and death was of no great concern."[39] As a result, it was widely observed that during the Ming-Qing period the Fujianese tended to have adopted sons even when they had sons of their own. The Chinese children that Ibn Battuta observed on board ship, whether adopted or not, would have been derived from such maritime practices.

The comparison of big merchants or ship owners in China and Amir mentioned by Ibn Battuta due to their wealth, power, and grandeur would surely not have escaped his readers. The merchants he referred to were the *gangshou*, the heads of the maritime trade. Whenever one of these *gangshou* landed, he was surrounded, protected, and served by dozens of people. The Malay Maritime Code (*Undang-undang Laut*), probably compiled in the mid-seventeenth century, provides a similar account: "The captain is, as it were, a Caliph on board his own ship" and "The captain [Nakhoda] is as a king on board his ship."[40] Wang Zhi 王直 (or 汪直?—1559), both a head merchant and a chief of the *wakou* 倭寇, had already established his own giant fleet and built a maritime empire of great splendor at the time the Portuguese were just attempting to build a direct trading relationship with China in the early sixteenth century.[41] This was also true of Zheng Zhilong 郑芝龙 and his son Zheng Chenggong 郑成功 (known as Koxinga among Western traders) during the Ming-Qing transition, a momentous time when their maritime empire dominated Chinese waters for decades and enabled China to defeat the first European colonists.

Ibn Battuta described the Chinese cabins on board their ships in detail. A Chinese ship had four decks, and contained rooms, cabins, and saloons, each cabin being equipped with chambers and a lavatory so that the occupant could have his slave girls and wives on the journey.[42] Obviously, those who occupied their own cabins would have been eminent merchants or agents, as minor merchants could only divide and occupy a few *chi* 尺 of the ship's space to store their goods over which they slept.[43] The space of a few *chi* was the so-called *kewei* 客位 (lit. "passenger space"), a name that would have been adopted into various languages in Asia and Europe, thanks to the expansion of overseas trade from Fujian to maritime Asia.

In his analysis of the Malay Maritime Code that dealt with the division of cargo space, Anthony Reid noted the Malay word *kiwi*.[44] Many scholars have participated in the discussion on this word.[45] While almost all scholars understand that the term in historical texts referred to maritime merchants or brokers, its origin has remained debatable. Scholars such as Leonard Blussé and Chen Xiyu have pointed out that the Dutch *quewij* meant adopted sons,[46] which reminds us of those children aboard the ship described by Ibn Battuta. Chen Guodong has argued that *quevees* or *kiwi* instead was a transliteration of *kehuo* 客伙 (lit. "merchants" or "fellow merchants"), a term popularly used in Ming novels, to refer to minor merchants renting ship space.[47] Obviously, the Malay *kiwi* was a loaned Chinese word, probably from the Amoy dialect term *kheh-ui* (kewei), the latter being recorded by Westerners as early as 1873.[48] The section *hukum kiwi* in the Malay Maritime Code summarized four different types of financial relationships between the *Nakhoda* (ship owner) and the *kiwi*.⁴⁹ Each merchant had its own *petak* (partition) in the ship space. While the *nakhoda* was in charge during the voyage, he had to consult with merchants and their representative (*maula kiwi* or *mulkiwi*) regularly, especially on the issue of any cargo to be jettisoned. Like their Chinese counterparts, Southeast Asian sailors were primarily traders who were rewarded by goods, which constituted their substantial allowance. It was ruled that one *petak* (partition) each was due to the leading officers and half a *petak* to the sailors not categorized as slaves.⁵⁰ It is fairly clear that the term *kiwi* originally derived from passenger space and gradually referred to merchants who owned the partition of this hold space.

Recently, this discussion has begun to include Portuguese terms such as *queve*, *queue*, or *quevees*.⁵¹ While agreeing on the origin of *kheh-ui*, Jin Guoping has pointed out that these terms in the Portuguese context developed over time to refer to a range of personnel, including brokers, agents, and even *hong* 行 merchants (Chinese merchants in Canton authorized by the Qing State to deal with Western trade and Western merchants prior to the first Opium War). Moreover, Jin has linked *queve* with *kegang* 客纲 and *keji* 客纪 in the Ming official and private documents appearing as late as the 1550s. The *gang* in *kegang* might be an abbreviation of *gangshou*, which was recorded in Song texts, referring to the head of maritime merchants acknowledged by the imperial state; and the *ji* in *keji* might be an abbreviation of *jingji* 经纪, namely, brokers. In this case, due to the increasing influence of maritime merchants, *queve* began to refer to the *hong* merchants who very seldom went overseas for trade but functioned as semiofficial agents between the Celestial Dynasty and European merchants under the Canton system.

Under the firm authority of the ship owner or captain, ship crews were crucial for oceanic navigation. They consisted of various professions that were required for sailing and operating the ship, including professionals such as security heads, accountants, managers, compass masters (*zhoushi* 舟师 or *huozhang* 火长), and sailors who were in charge of rudders, masts, anchors, and cords.⁵² Zhang Xie specified that sailors were allowed to take their own goods for sale, and this gradually became a maritime rule.⁵³ It was a well-collaborated hierarchical system, and crews needed to build a relationship of mutual trust in addition to their mastery of navigational skills. That is why both natural and social associations such as lineage, clans, fellow countrymen alliances, sworn brotherhoods, adoptive relations, and shareholders were widely employed in maritime trade to make the team work well together.

The *Quanzhou I* wreck is also invaluable in helping us understand Chinese commercial organizations and how they carried out maritime trade. A total of ninety-six wooden labels/lots (seventy-seven written with Chinese characters) discovered in the Quanzhou shipwreck help reveal the diverse nature of the ship's merchants and their cargos.[54] These wooden items, based on their characters, can be divided into a few categories, some of which overlap. First, those with the Chinese character *gan* 幹 might refer to official merchants or cargo. The term *gan* might be an abbreviation of *ganguan* 幹官 or *ganbanguan* 幹办官, a low-ranking officer, or *bogan* 舶官, a ship clerk assigned by the Maritime Customs Office, though some scholars argue that it referred to salaried agents employed by rich landlords or merchants. In either case, the *gan* labels indicate the existence of employed commercial agents for the risky long-distance maritime trade who surely accompanied their own goods. Chinese surnames such as Zeng 曾, Lin 林, and Zhang 张, all popular in Fujian, were preceded by the character of *gan* to claim the specific ownership of goods.

Second, many wooden labels were written with the Chinese character *ji* 记. The term *ji* refers to a trademark and remains the term most popularly adopted in present-day Chinese commerce. These *ji* labels consisted of names referring to officers, merchants, agents, and crew members. Wooden labels belonging to crew members are revealed by the character *gong* 工, an abbreviation of *chuangong* 船工 (lit. "ship crew").

Third, some labels were written with the character *jun* 郡. The term *jun*, meaning a commandery or prefecture, was an administrative unit in early and medieval China. No longer extant by the time of the Southern Song, *jun* was then used to refer to the geographical origin of a cargo or person, especially for large clans or major lineages. Therefore, these wooden labels illustrate the diversity of the cargos, merchants, and trading shops, and provide an invaluable glimpse into a complex and sophisticated maritime commercial community.

It is certain that decades before Wang Dayuan, Chinese ships and merchants were known to frequent the Indian Ocean. Unfortunately, very few textual or archaeological remains provide definitive evidence of these early activities. This is why the recent discussions on the China Pagoda at Nagapattinam (Tamil Nadu, India) are so crucial.

THE CHINA PAGODA AT NAGAPATTINAM

It was quite normal for Song merchants to stay in foreign countries for weeks, months, years, or even permanently, and these traders were called the *zhufan* 住蕃 (lit. "living in a foreign land") while foreigners who stayed in Guangzhou or Quanzhou were known as the *zhutang* 住唐 (lit. "living in Tang [China]").[55] Buddhist pilgrims from Tang China, for example, had remained in India for years or even for the rest of their lives. Many of them such as Yijing 义净 (635–713) naturally also spent months or years on their round trips to and from Southeast Asia. The China Pagoda at the extreme south of the Indian subcontinent indicates that by the mid-thirteenth century, Chinese merchants had sojourned in coastal India.

Wang Dayuan paid special attention to a so-called Tuta 土塔 (lit. native pagoda) in Badan 八丹, known as Nagapattinam in southeastern coastal India. The word *tu*, literally meaning indigenous, local, or native, here certainly referred to Chinese people, as Wang Dayuan used it to mean Chinese travelers like himself.[56] Under the entry of "Tuta," Wang Dayuan provided a detailed description. The pagoda was located on the plain of Badan, surrounded by logs and stones. It was made of earthen bricks, a few *zhang* 丈 high, and on it, the inscribed Chinese characters (*hanzi* 汉字) read: "Completed in the eighth month of the third year of the Xianchun reign (1265–1274)" (*Xianchun sannian bayue bigong* 咸淳三年八月毕工), which was approximately September 1267, ten years earlier than the sinking of *Quanzhou I*.[57]

Wang Dayuan's *tuta* was known as the China Pagoda or Chinese Pagoda among local people and western colonists. The Dutch traveler Wouter Schouten saw and described it in the 1660s. Sir Walter Elliot (1803–1887) and Henry Yule (1820–1889) were among some of the earliest scholars to study the pagoda.[58] Sir Walter Elliot, a British civil servant in colonial India and an eminent orientalist, visited the pagoda in 1846 and had someone draw him a sketch of the pagoda (figure 3.1), which he shared with Henry Yule. The pagoda, "a tall weather-beaten tower," had many names including "the old pagoda," "Chinese pagoda," "black pagoda," "the Puduveli-gôpuram," or "the Jeyna (Jaina) pagoda;" located "between one and two miles to the north of Negapatam," it stood as "a useful landmark to vessels passing up and down the coast."[59]

> I found it to be a somewhat four-sided tower of three stories, constructed of bricks closely fitted together without cement, the first and second stories divided by corniced mouldings, with an opening for a door or window in the middle of each side. At the top of the lowest story were marks in the wall, showing where the floor of the second had been fixed. The top was open. The base of the ground-story was worn at the angles, from collision with passers-by and cattle, but the structure was solid and firm. No trace of sculpture or inscription was visible.[60]

Sir Walter Elliott immediately realized that "this building differed essentially from any type of Hindu architecture with which he was acquainted, but being without inscription or sculpture, it was impossible to assign to it any authentic origin." "Negapatam was, however, celebrated as a seat of Buddhist worship, and this may have been a remnant of their work." He told Yule that the brickwork of the pagoda, "very fine and closely fitted but without cement, corresponds to that of the Burmese and Ceylonese medieval Buddhist buildings. The architecture has a slight resemblance to that of Pollanarua in Ceylon."[61] In 1859, thirteen years after Sir Walter Elliot's visit, the pagoda was "in too dilapidated a state for repair." In 1866 Dr. Burnell found that the China pagoda "had become merely a shapeless mass of bricks," and on August 28, 1867, "The Governor in Council is pleased to sanction the removal of the old tower at Negapatam."[62] Henry Yule explained that the pagoda "popularly bears (or bore) the name of the Chinese Pagoda. I do not mean to imply that the building was Chinese, but that the application of that name to a ruin of strange character pointed to some tradition of Chinese visitors." He used this Chinese pagoda to illustrate the Sino-Indian trade, evidence of which was partially supported by many coins, Chinese, Byzantine, and Hindu. These coins were picked up by Sir W. Elliott "in the sand, at several stations on this coast."[63] In addition there were five Buddhist statues discovered near the pagoda, four bronze, and the fifth being "a mixture of porcelain and clay, of exquisite workmanship."[64] The fifth piece raised the possibility of its Chinese origin.

The hard facts observed by these colonial scholars about the China Pagoda certainly confirmed Wang Dayuan's notes. In addition, in 1856, an

THE TOWER AS IT EXISTED IN 1846.

FIGURE 3.1 The China Pagoda at Nagapattinam, 1846. *Source*: Sketch by Sir Walter Elliot, "The Edifice."

old Mohwa tree (*Bassia latifolia L.*) near the tower was cut down, and its diameter was more than a meter, "indicating, according to the usual growth of the tree, an age of 700 to 800 years."[65] This dating was roughly in accordance with the year 1267 Wang Dayuan had mentioned.

Himanshu Prabha Ray carried out a comprehensive study of this pagoda and illustrated the China connection indicated by Wang Dayuan. The China Pagoda was essentially a part of the Cudamanivihara, a Buddhist monastic complex established in the tenth and eleventh centuries by the king of Srivijaya at Nagapattinam, which was a multireligious sacred place before and after the period under discussion. Many archaeological findings in the complex from 1856 onward have illustrated the intensive religious, commercial, and political interactions among South India, Southeast Asia (such as the Malay Peninsula and Sumatra), and China. Two leyden copper plates, one in Sanskrit and the other in Tamil, bear inscriptions indicating that the construction of the *vihara*, at the initiative of the kings of Srivijaya, was begun during the reign of the Chola King Rajaraja I (985–1016) and completed during the reign of his son and successor Rajendra I (1012–1044).[66] In addition, Burmese monks might also have visited the *vihara*. In the case, the Chinese connections could be traced as early as the eleventh century.

In 1856 the Jesuits decided to remove the remains of the pagoda to their own college. As a result, a lot of Buddhist bronze images were discovered. From then on up until the 1930s, 350 Buddhist images were recovered at Nagapattinam. The inscription on the pedestal of one Buddha image, 27.2 inches (69.2 cm) high, bore a note about who had made it: "The prefect of artisan manufactories for the merchants of the eighteen countries."[67]

In addition to Buddhist tradition, Shaivism shaped Nagapattinam too, where the Kayarohanaswami temple, for example, was dedicated to Shiva. Inscriptions on the temple walls dated to the eleventh and twelfth centuries further confirm the cross-regional network. While the king of Srivijaya made various donations, these inscriptions also record donations of gold coins from China for the worship of an image of Ardhanarishvara installed on the premises of the temple by the king of Kedah.[68]

It is interesting to note that several clusters of Tamil inscriptions have been found from the eastern coast of India, via Burma, the Malay Peninsula, north and west Sumatra, right to the Quanzhou in China, and the bilingual Tamil and Chinese inscription in Quanzhou, dated the second half of the thirteenth century, is found to be associated with a local Shiva temple.[69] The particular association between the Tamil language and Shiva worship provides a glimpse of this wide and intensive network across maritime Asia around the age of *Quanzhou I*, as well as the century when Wang Dayuan and Ibn Battuta were on their extensive travels.

Considering all these findings, circumstantial or otherwise, Nagapattinam was an important port on the southeastern Indian coast, indeed an active part of the maritime empire of Chola that had built intensive interactions with Southeast Asia and China. Unfortunately, the remains of the China Pagoda are gone, and it is impossible to ascertain the brick inscribed with the Chinese characters recorded or perhaps even seen by Wang Dayuan. Undoubtedly, Chinese merchants as well as Southeast Asians and local people jointly contributed to the construction of this tower, the Buddhist community, the port city, and other structures beyond. The discussion here about the pagoda serves to demonstrate that Wang Dayuan did indeed land in South India. Chapter 4 now moves on to examine who, in addition to Wang, visited the islands of the Maldives.

PART II
A Destination

Chapter Four

WHO ONCE LANDED IN THE MALDIVES?

When a ship sailing for the Western Ocean has passed near *Sengjiala* 僧伽剌 (Ceylon), the set of tidal currents rapidly changes. If the ship falls in with a head wind, it is driven to this country.

—WANG DAYUAN

We reached these islands, which are one of the wonders of the world.

—IBN BATTUTA

Before Kublai Khan established the Yuan Dynasty, very few Chinese had traveled to the Indian Ocean.[1] Imperial eunuchs and Buddhist monks were most certainly the earliest pioneers, followed by official envoys and private merchants.

When the Han dynasty (202 BCE–220 CE) dramatically expanded its power to the so-called Western Region (*Xiyu* 西域), a Chinese term referring to a vast region including today's Xinjiang and much of Central Asia, many Chinese envoys were sent to kingdoms in the west. In 97 CE, the Han envoy Gan Ying 甘英 was dispatched to *Daqin* 大秦 in the Mediterranean world. When he reached the eastern bank of the *Xihai* 西海 (lit. "West Ocean"), sailors of the Parthian Empire (*Anxi* 安息) warned him about the dangers of those waters. Disheartened, Gan Ying discontinued his western journey and turned back for home.[2]

The imperial yearning for exotic goods, especially pearls, *biliuli* 璧流离, precious stones, and some other exotic items drove Chinese missions to go overseas.[3] Probably around the reign of Emperor Wudi (141 BCE—87 BCE), the *Huangmen* 黄门 (lit. "Yellow Gate," referring to court eunuchs) were dispatched to the so-called *Huangzhi* 黄支, most likely referring to Conjevaram in the state of Tamil Nadu, southern India.[4] This round-trip expedition began in China's southern ports of Xuwen 徐闻 and Hepu 合浦,

followed coastal navigation routes, crossed the Malay Peninsula on foot, sailed into the Bay of Bengal, and then returned to China; it took a couple of years to complete.[5] Waves, storms, and pirates posed major issues for the expedition, including fatalities, and are likely to have been the reason it did not continue in the post-Han period.

From the first century, the expansion of Buddhism from India and Central Asia to China greatly aroused a curiosity about what the western world contained. While many monks and merchants from India, Central Asia, or Ceylon reached China, far fewer Chinese ventured westward. In 399, the Buddhist pilgrim Faxian 法显 set out at the grand age of sixty on the overland Silk Road to India. He visited various kingdoms in India, stayed there for ten years, reached Ceylon in 410, and returned home via the maritime Silk Road in 412. Faxian was the first Chinese traveler to visit India and the Indian Ocean. Like later pilgrims, Faxian's primary goal was to learn more about the teachings of the Buddha, and so he kept rather scant information on what life was like in the Indian Ocean back then.

During the Tang-Song period (607–1279) many Chinese monks followed in Faxian's footsteps. Among dozens of Buddhist pilgrims during the Tang dynasty, Xuanzang 玄奘 (600–664) and Yijing were the two most famous pilgrims who left detailed records of their journeys. Xuanzang's round journey was completed via the overland Silk Road, so he did not sail across the Indian Ocean. Yijing rather took the maritime Silk Road for his round trip and provided unprecedented navigational knowledge of the routes between China, Southeast Asia, and India. Nevertheless, due to the nature of his mission, once again little new knowledge was shared about the Indian Ocean world. Furthermore, Yijing only knew of the eastern part of the Indian Ocean, that is, the Bay of Bengal.

Tang China was a great world empire, and several official missions took place between China and the world to the west during this period. Wang Xuance 王玄策, a Tang diplomat, paid four visits to India, in 643, 647, 657, and 664 respectively, either taking the overland Silk Road or the Tibet-Nepal Road. Not surprisingly, he contributed little to the understanding of the Indian Ocean world.[6] Indeed, before the eighth century, most people used the overland Silk Road to reach India and beyond. Nonetheless, the Tang dynasty witnessed the advent of the golden age of the maritime Silk Road and a remarkable accumulation of Chinese knowledge of the Indian Ocean and the Arab world occurred at this time.[7]

While Tang China continued to receive monks and missions who arrived by sea, it began to send official envoys on ships from Guangzhou to the Indian Ocean. Daxi Hongtong 达奚弘通 (or Daxi Tong 达奚通) in the reign of Shangyuan 上元 (674–676) is said to have taken a journey from Guangzhou via Chitu 赤土 (lit. "Red Soil"), a polity in the western Malay Peninsula, to Qianna 虔那, probably Kanain on the southern Arabian Peninsula.[8] The eunuch Yang Liangyao 杨良瑶 (736–806) was dispatched to *Heiyi Dashi* 黑衣大食 (the Abbasid Caliphate) in 785, and completed his mission across the seas and oceans. Although his epitaph, discovered in 1984, was very brief, circumstantial information indicated that his trip contributed a great deal to Tang China's geographical knowledge and especially navigational particulars, from Guangzhou to the Arab world.[9]

And very interestingly, Du Huan 杜环, a Tang military officer, had a legendary experience in the West. In 751, Du Huan was captured by Arab forces in the Battle of Talas. Along with a few other Chinese captives, Du Huan was taken to the Arab world. In 762, Du Huan managed to return to Guangzhou by ship. Although Du Huan traveled through West Asia and the western parts of the Indian Ocean such as the Persian Gulf, the Arabian Sea, and probably the Mediterranean, his knowledge was not widely circulated. Sadly, only a few passages of his book the *Jingxing Ji* 经行记 (Record of Travels) are extant.[10]

The eminent sinologist Edward Schafer (1913–1991) once briefly described the maritime route from the Persian Gulf to Tang China in the following way. A Persian or Arab ship started at Muscat in Oman and sailed into the Indian Ocean. It might have stopped at the coastal port of Sind, or directly headed for Malabar, after which it passed Ceylon (known to the Chinese as the Lion Country and famous for all kinds of precious stones), then it sailed eastward to the Nicobar Islands, where iron was exchanged for coconuts or ambergris offered by local naked savages. The ship proceeded to land in Kedah on the Malay Peninsula, and then went through the Malacca Strait, visiting a few port cities in Sumatra before sailing north to Hanoi or Canton.[11] Du Huan and Yang Liangyao must have taken this or a similar route back home.

A DESTINATION

Song China's maritime activities were principally commercial rather than exploratory or religious, and private merchants began to frequent the Indian Ocean. While the Song dynasty (907–1279) received quite a few missions from kingdoms in the Indian Ocean such as Chola and Ceylon, no Chinese envoys were correspondingly dispatched in response. In contrast, private ships and merchants from China frequently visited certain Indian kingdoms such as Nanpi, Gulin, and even Dashi 大食 (the Arab world).[12] Thanks to the plethora of both Chinese and foreign traders, Zhou Qufei and Zhao Rukuo, the two Song officials in coastal China (one in Guangxi, and the other in Quanzhou), compiled the *Lingwai Daida* and the *Zhufan Zhi*, respectively, based on their surveys, and provided meticulously in-depth information on overseas kingdoms, goods, navigation, and social customs.

Relics found in *Quanzhou I* provide a convincing case, revealing the bustling commercial and cultural interactions between Song China and the Indian Ocean world. The Chinese ship carried a large quantity of rare woods and aromatic materials that had originated in Indian Ocean trading centers (table 4.1).[13] The frankincense, ambergris, and pepper in watertight compartments (2, 3, 5, 6, 9, 10, and 13) suggest that these Indian Ocean products might have been of the same origin and been owned by

TABLE 4.1
Indian Ocean products found in the compartments of *Quanzhou I*

Compartments	Pepper	Ambergris	Frankincense	Cowrie shells (unit)	Coconut fruit
1	X			11	
2	X	X	X	17	X
3	X	X	X	50	X
4	X			48	
5	X	X	X		
6	X			12	X
7	X				
8	X				
9	X	X	X	1,000	
10	X	X	X		
11	X				X
12	X			69	
13	X	X	X	1,079	1
Total				2,286	

Source: *Quanzhouwan Songdai Haichuan Fajue yu Yanjiu Xiudingban* (A Report on the Excavation of the Song Boat in Quanzhou Bay), ed. Fujian Quanzhou Haiwajiaotongshi Bowuguan (Beijing: Haiyang Chubanshe, 2017), 24–26.

the same merchant(s), especially since the two kinds of shells in and around the shipwreck, *Monetaria moneta* and *Monetaria annulus*, must in my opinion have come from the Maldives.[14]

THE MONGOL ENVOYS

Broadly speaking, the Pax Mongolica facilitated political, economic, and cultural exchanges within Eurasia. That is why this period produced some of the best-known travelers, including Marco Polo, Odorico da Pordenone, and Ibn Battuta, but there was also Wang Dayuan, who though renowned in China has remained little known to Western readers.

Unlike the Song, the Mongol Yuan dynasty under Kublai Khan was aggressive in its maritime expansion. The thirteenth century witnessed the establishing of the Mongol Empire, the largest land empire in world history. However, the disputes of succession soon divided this empire into the Golden Horde Khanate in the northwest, the Chagatai Khanate in Central Asia, the Ilkhanate in the southwest, and the Yuan dynasty in China. The Toluid Civil War (1260–1264) broke out between the brothers Ariq Böke and Kublai Khan (r. 1272–1294), and the latter was unable to obtain the unanimous support his grandfather Genghis Khan had garnered. Being anxious to establish his legitimacy across the world, Kublai Khan sent numerous envoys to solicit tributary submissions from various kingdoms in East Asia, Southeast Asia, and South Asia, and maritime exchanges of official envoys became unprecedentedly frequent. The ostensible reason for Marco Polo's return journey in 1291, for example, was to escort the Mongol princess Kököchin on her journey to marry the Ilkhanate Khan Arghun in Persia.

The Indian Ocean was of particular interest to Kublai Khan, who engineered Sino-Indian official interactions to an unprecedented degree. At least sixteen missions were dispatched to India within the twenty-four years of 1272–1296, and eighteen embassies from India, principally Kollam and Ma'bar, were received at the Yuan court.[15] Three Yuan officials among the Mongol envoys established their roles: Yiheimishi 亦黑迷失, Yang Tingbi 杨庭璧, and Yang Shu 杨枢.

Yiheimishi, of Uighur extraction and a prominent imperial bodyguard, was dispatched on four missions to southern India. In the ninth year of the Zhiyuan 至元 reign (1272), Kublai Khan sent him to Baluoboguo 八罗孛国 (Ma'bar) on the southwestern coast of India, and two years later, he returned to China bringing with him local people and exotic treasures. In 1275 he went to Ma'bar a second time and escorted its imperial master (*guoshi* 国师) along with a quantity of the region's famous medicine (*mingyao* 名药). In 1281 he went to Champa to solicit its submission. In 1284 Kublai Khan ordered him to visit the kingdom of Sengjiala (Ceylon), offering devotional worship to the Buddha's alms bowl and *sarīradhātu* (*fobo sheli* 佛钵舍利), and presenting jade belts, clothes, and saddles to local people. It seems that his trip was completed within that year, so that he was still in time to participate in the Mongol campaign against Champa in the same year. In 1287 he was dispatched to Mabaerguo 马八儿国 (Ma'bar) for the third time to obtain Buddha's alms bowl and *sarīradhātu*. This voyage met with a series of storms, and it took him a year to reach his destination. He managed to bring back famous physicians and efficacious medicines (*liangyi mingyao* 良医名药) and used his own money to buy the *zitan* 紫檀 (*Pterocarpus santalinus*) for Kublai Khan's palace construction.[16] An envoy from Ma'bar joined his return journey to pay tribute to the Mongols. In 1292 Yiheimishi became the maritime leader for the Mongol campaign against Java. Clearly Yiheimishi was a trusted official in the Kublai court who was seen as a specialist in maritime affairs. He had accumulated a remarkably rich experience through his seven overseas trips (three to Ma'bar, one to Ceylon, two to Champa, and one to Java). His four visits to the Indian Ocean indicated the special role of Ma'bar in the Mongol empire, and the mention of the Buddha's alms bowl and the *sarīradhātu* reveal the Buddhist connection that spanned maritime Asia. Very interestingly, the Mongol missions for Buddhist relics in Ceylon were to be noted by both Marco Polo a few years later and Wang Dayuan some four decades after Yiheimishi.

Marco Polo mentioned that Kublai Khan desired the "grandest ruby" possessed by the king of Zeilan (Ceylon), and thus dispatched his envoy to exchange the stone for the value of a city.[17] While the great Khan failed in his first attempt, he finally achieved it by sending his ambassadors in 1284 on a long and tedious journey to obtain the Buddha's relics. Kublai Khan and his party of officials poured out of the city of Beijing to welcome the arrival of the Buddha's relics. Marco Polo omitted to mention the alms bowl, but Wang Dayuan noted down a description of it. "There used to be an alms bowl in front of the Buddha; it was not made from jade, copper, or iron, with a color of purple and mild; when knocked, it sounds like glass (*boli* 玻

璃). And that is why in the beginning of our Dynasty three imperial envoys were dispatched to obtain it."[18]

Wang Dayuan made note of three Mongol envoy trips, which does not seem to match up with the two trips said to have been made by Yiheimishi, but Wang was adamant about the Mongol missions to Ceylon. Yang Tingbi was another Mongol envoy who visited Kollam four times in 1280, 1281 (twice), and 1283.[19] In his second mission in early 1281 Yang Tingbi departed from Quanzhou, was blocked by a storm near Ceylon, and had to land in the Kingdom of Ma'bar. Ma'bar seemed to be at odds with Kollam at that time, and later a local official called Boali 孛阿里 (Abu Ali) when being prosecuted by the king of Ma'bar sought asylum in China.[20]

Yang Shu paid two visits to the Indian Ocean in 1301 and 1304, starting his first trip at the age of nineteen, and on his return journey he was joined by the envoys sent by Ghazan, the Ilkhanate khan to the Yuan court.[21] On his second trip (1304–1307), Yang reached Ormuz, the furthest westward destination the Chinese had made at the time. These official interactions must have simultaneously stimulated commercial activities, which was very much what local officials and merchants in coastal China desired and promoted. The prosperous international port city of Quanzhou not only received foreign merchants (especially from the Indian Ocean) for centuries, but also witnessed the departure of many Chinese to trade and even to reside overseas. It is important to remember that these Chinese envoys sometimes boarded official ships, that is, ships owned or confiscated by the government, while other times they boarded commercial ships (occasionally they prepared ships themselves). These latter instances imply that these official expeditions were also involved in maritime trading.

In terms of regulating maritime commerce, the Yuan generally followed the Song model, despite intermittent (and unsuccessful) efforts to control private trade. Yang Shu, for example, in his first Western Ocean trip, took the *Guanbenchuan* 官本船 (lit. "official-invested ship").[22] The *Guanbenchuan* regulation was proposed in 1285 with the intention of monopolizing maritime trade and forbidding private maritime activities. Under this new policy, the government provided oceangoing ships and capital, and selected appropriate men to conduct maritime trade. The profits derived were split between the government (70 percent) and the agent (30 percent). The regulation was so unpragmatic that in the same year it was abolished. Private operations of maritime trade resumed. Nevertheless, the maritime profit was so tempting that the state re-issued the *Guanbenchuan* under the *Zhiyongyuan* 制用院 that was established in 1298, with an important revision that private activities were not banned.[23] Yang Shu's second maritime voyage, though dispatched as a Yuan envoy, did not involve the government, and he prepared his own ships and took care of all the other expenses. Obviously, he simultaneously made this trip into a commercial one and used his own money to purchase some white horses (*baima* 白马), black dogs (*heiquan* 黑犬), amber (*hupo* 琥珀, highly likely ambergris), grape wine (*putaojiu* 蒲萄酒), and foreign salt (*fanyan* 蕃盐), all famous Arab or Indian Ocean luxuries, which he presented at court.[24]

Probably due to the increasing interactions between China and the Indian Ocean World during the reign of Kublai Khan, Chen Dazhen 陈大震(1228–1307), a native of Canton, compiled a book in 1304 entitled the *Nanhai Zhi* 南海志, mentioning the trading of treasured items (*baowu* 宝物), clothing (*bupi* 布疋), various incenses and perfumes (*xianghuo* 香货), medicines (*yaowu* 药物), various woods (*zhumu* 诸木), skins and furs (*pihuo* 皮货), ox hooves and horns (*niutijiao* 牛蹄角), and miscellaneous exotica (*zawu* 杂物), alongside the mention of various foreign kingdoms (*zhufanguo* 诸番国).[25] Some kingdoms, though mentioned by Song sources such as the *Lingwai Daida*, were provided with new transcriptions, indicating new sources of information and thus the expansion of Chinese knowledge.[26] While many kingdoms in Southeast Asia, India, and even East Africa were named here, the Maldives was probably not listed. It is within such a historical context that Wang Dayuan distinguished himself for us to see the Chinese understanding of the Indian Ocean, especially the Maldives, whose role in the Indian Ocean, imperial China, and maritime Asia of that period cannot be overestimated. Wang was one of the first Chinese travelers to visit the Indian Ocean and left us with an account of what he experienced and observed.

THE CHINESE DISCOVERY OF THE MALDIVES

Compared with those Chinese who had been to the Indian Ocean, Wang Dayuan's position in the 1330s was different and unique, for the following simple reasons. First, he was neither an official envoy dispatched by the Chinese state nor a Buddhist pilgrim. He was a private visitor, traveler, or adventurer, and he might have been involved in maritime trade during his journey, as this was a popular practice. Second, Wang Dayuan traveled to maritime Asia twice, the first time to the Indian Ocean around 1330–1331 and the second to the region now known as Southeast Asia, probably traveling as far east as the island of Timor in 1333–1334.[27] His experience in the vast waters of maritime Asia dwarfed all other Chinese fellow adventurers and made him an iconic figure alongside Marco Polo and Ibn Battuta. Indeed, only in the colonial period did European explorers exceed Wang Dayuan in terms of the breadth of their maritime travel.

More important, Wang Dayuan was the first Chinese traveler to compose an incredibly informative work on maritime Asia by recording at least ninety-nine foreign places, all of which he claimed that he himself had personally been to. Whether or not he visited every single one of these ninety-nine places is uncertain, but he certainly landed in most of them. Before Wang's time the Indian Ocean (and maritime Asia) had never been a major focus in the works of Chinese travelers, including those pious Buddhist pilgrims, although in the Song period, the *Lingwai Daida* and the *Zhufan Zhi* did pay considerable attention to maritime Asia. As officials, neither Zhou Qufei nor Zhao Rukuo went overseas themselves. Their records were based on previous texts, official archives, and interviews with merchants (both Chinese and foreign), but not on personal experience. In contrast, Wang Dayuan's *Daoyi Zhilue*, devoted to maritime Asia, was primarily based on where he had traveled, what he had observed and experienced, and what had been related to him. Indeed, Wang was the first Chinese traveler to consider maritime Asia as a single unit, and he was also the first to introduce many foreign places to the Chinese world, such as the Maldives in the Indian Ocean and Ormuz, a major commercial center in the Persian Gulf.[28]

Unlike most merchants, Wang was well educated. Although little information on his education and postmaritime life exists, the writing style of the *Daoyi Zhilue* indicates that he was well trained in traditional Chinese education. In Ceylon, Wang was so inspired by a beautiful coral branch that he composed one hundred Chinese poems in praise of it overnight, all exquisitely written, as was his short essay on this episode.[29] On another occasion Wang Dayuan compared Mantuolang 曼陀郎, probably Mundra in the port of Mandvi along the Gujarat coast, with the so-called Zhu-Chen Village (*Zhuchen Cun* 朱陈村) in Xuzhou 徐州, located in today's northern part of Jiangsu Province, due to their shared common marriage custom of marrying within just two clans over generations—in the case of the Xuzhou village, those of the Zhu and the Chen.[30] Such a marriage custom in the Zhu-Chen Village was highly praised in a poem composed by Bai Juyi 白居易 (772–846), a famous Tang poet, and two poems by Su Dongpo 苏东坡 (1037–1101), a brilliant scholar of the Song dynasty. Both among the most productive poets in Chinese history, Bai has left us with more than 3,800 poems and Su with more than 2,700, and the fact that Wang Dayuan was able to notice their references to the Zhu-Chen Village in three of the less popular ones shows an amazing breadth of reading and a tremendous feat of memory.

It seems that Wang Dayuan had gotten along with many local official scholars. Zhang Zhu 张翥, a member of the Imperial Academy (*Hanli* 翰林), for example, provided a preface for the *Daoyi Zhilue*. Another preface and postscript by Wu Jian 吴鉴, a local scholar who was in charge of the compilation of the Quanzhou Gazetteer, also illustrated Wang's interactions with imperial official scholars.[31] Therefore, the literati background distinguished Wang Dayuan from common Chinese traders who were exclusively devoted to commerce and who were usually unable to write or reflect upon their overseas trips.

In addition, while many official envoys had presented their reports to the court, such accounts were brief, vague, and tempered with necessarily Sinocentric perspectives. Some of these might have been referenced in official histories, but most of them eventually went missing. Wang Dayuan was also wealthy or fortunate enough to secure financial resources to print his encyclopedic book and thus circulate his knowledge. Wang Dayuan and his *Daoyi Zhilue* thus represent the cream of the contemporary Chinese knowledge of maritime Asia, especially the Indian Ocean, and went on to be a crucial travel reference for the Zheng He voyages.

None of these Chinese travelers who visited India or the Arab world had ever reported on the Maldives, a seemingly unimportant island kingdom situated in the middle of the Indian Ocean and so very remote from the Middle Kingdom, until Wang Dayuan's records in the 1330s. The great distance between the Maldives and China and the extremely small size of the island kingdom assuredly constituted the reason for this neglect, yet in truth, the Maldives contributed to Chinese culture to such a degree that it could hardly be exaggerated.

WHO ONCE LANDED IN THE MALDIVES?

Thanks to Wang Dayuan, the Maldives entered the Chinese world for the first time. Previously, major ports or polities in coastal India such as Chola, Nanpi, Kollam, and Ma'bar, the Arab Caliphate, and some kingdoms in East Africa and the Mediterranean world had been recorded by the Chinese, but the Maldives, owing to its small size and geographical location and being surrounded by water, had remained unknown to the Chinese. Reputedly the first Chinese man to visit the Maldives, Wang Dayuan, invented the Chinese name and provided a brief but informative description of this island kingdom. Facts on the geography, climate, commerce, and even certain customs provided by Wang Dayuan are highly reliable, as has been confirmed by other previous and contemporary sources and the significance of his *Daoyi Zhilue* has been noticed by scholars such as William Woodville Rockhill, Fujita Toyohashi, Paul Eugène Pelliot, Roderich Ptak, Hyunhee Park, and others.[32] Undeniably, like all other Chinese works on foreign kingdoms and peoples, the *Daoyi Zhilue* remains essentially a biased ethnographical account, shaped by a Chinese worldview and displaying its cultural values.[33]

The Maldives is located in the navigation route connecting Southeast Asia and China on one end and India, the Middle East, and beyond on the other. Its rich resources, such as foodstuffs including coconut products and dried fish, coir ropes for ship construction and navigation, and cowrie shells for ballast, decoration, and as a form of money, had attracted various merchants and sailors. By the age of Wang Dayuan and Ibn Battuta, the Maldives had developed into a trading pivot in the Indian Ocean and maritime Asia.

The early history of the Maldives remains obscure. It was not until the middle of the first millennium when oceangoing navigation became widely practiced that people began to visit and write about the islands. Hence, it is necessary to present a brief introduction about those people who once visited or wrote about the Maldives before going on to discuss the Chinese conceptualization of these islands.

MEDIEVAL TRAVELERS TO THE MALDIVES

Table 4.2 lists all known travelers and scholars whose works have provided invaluable information on the Maldives before the early seventeenth

A DESTINATION

TABLE 4.2
Travelers/scholars and their records concerning the Maldives

Name	Date	Visits to the Maldives, Ceylon, or India
Faxian	400–413	India and Ceylon
Palladius	5th century?	?
Cosmas the Monk	6th century	India and Ceylon
Xuanzang	600–664	India (629–644)
Sulaiman	Mid-9th century	India
Al Mas'udi	10th century	Ceylon (916)
Alberuni	11th century	India
Edrisi	1099–1186	n/a
Marco Polo	1292	India
John of Montecorvino	1292	India
Prince Hayton	1307	n/a
Friar Jordanus	1321–1323	India
Odorico da Pordenone	1321–1322	India and Ceylon
Wang Dayuan	1330–1331	The Maldives (1330–1331) and India
Ibn Battuta	1304–1377	The Maldives (1343–1344; 1346) and India
Ma Huan	1420s–1430s	The Maldives and India
Fei Xin	1420s–1430s	The Maldives and India
Gong Zhen	1420s–1430s	The Maldives (?) and India
Abd-er-Razzak	1442–1445	India
Hieronimo di Santo Stefano	1497	The Maldives and India
Duarte Barbosa	1480–1521	India (1500–1517)
Joao de Barros	1496–1570	n/a
The Brothers Parmentier	1529	The Maldives
Francois Pyrard	1602–1607	The Maldives and India
H.C.P. Bell	Three Visits to the Maldives (1879, 1920 and 1922)	Ceylon, the Maldives, and India

Source: Non-Chinese travelers and scholars except for Odorico da Pordenone and Bell are based on Albert Gray and H. C. P. Bell, "Early Notices of the Maldives," in François Pyrard, *The Voyage of François Pyrard of Laval to the East Indies, the Maldives, the Moluccas and Brazil*, ed. Albert Gray and H. C. P. Bell (Cambridge: Cambridge University Press, 2011), which omits Chinese official texts and Portuguese sources in the transition of the sixteenth century.

century. Many of these certainly visited the Maldives or the Indian Ocean world themselves, and their descriptions concerning the Maldives are essentially consistent. In this book the focus is principally on the accumulation of Chinese knowledge from the twelfth century to the 1620s, particularly around the fourteenth and fifteenth centuries (the Yuan and early Ming period) when the Chinese frequented the Indian Ocean.

A brief introduction to each of these travelers is necessary. Faxian was the first Chinese Buddhist pilgrim to India, completing his return journey through the maritime Silk Road in 412. Palladius of Galatia remains something of a myth to us, thought to have lived a couple of centuries later than the era of Alexander, but his work *De Bragmanibus* provides a brief account of the lands around the River Ganges, and more interestingly, it also records a meeting between Alexander and a Brahmin philosopher.[34] Cosmas the Monk (Cosmas Indicopleustes) was a merchant (and later a hermit) from Egypt in the sixth century who sailed to India. Xuanzang was the best-known Chinese Buddhist pilgrim to India in the mid-seventh century. Sulaiman (Sulaiman al-Tajir) was a ninth-century Persian merchant who traveled to India and China. Al Mas'udi was an Arab historian, geographer, and traveler in the tenth century who visited India. The Italian explorer Marco Polo is probably the best-known of Western travelers, traversing the entire length of the Silk Road to visit the emperor of the Mongol Yuan dynasty in China (1271–1295). John of Montecorvino (1247–1328) was an Italian Franciscan missionary dispatched to the Mongol Yuan court who later became the founder of the earliest Roman Catholic missions in India and China and the archbishop of Beijing. Prince Hayton, a contemporary of Marco Polo and John of Montecorvino, was an Armenian nobleman who authored a historiographical work of the East. Friar Jordanus (c. 1330), a Catalan Dominican missionary in Asia, was the first bishop of the Roman Catholic Diocese of Quilon, the first Catholic diocese in India. Odorico da Pordenone (1286–1331), an Italian Franciscan friar and missionary explorer to the Mongol Yuan court, traveled via India and Southeast Asia to China (indeed passing my home county in southwestern Zhejiang Province), where he probably stayed more than five years (1322–1328).

After Wang Dayuan and Ibn Battuta, the Zheng He fleet sailed to the Indian Ocean seven times in the early fifteenth century. Ma Huan 马欢, who served as an interpreter, joined the fourth (1413–1415), sixth (1421–1422), and final (1431–1433) expeditions and completed a book entitled *Yingya Shenglan* 瀛涯胜览 (Overall Survey of the Ocean's Shores). Fei Xin 费信, a military officer, joined the third (1409–1411), fifth (1417–1419), and final expedition, compiling a book called *Xingcha Shenglan* 星槎胜览 (Overall Survey of the Star Raft).[35] Gong Zhen 巩珍, a soldier who was later promoted to the role of secretary, joined the seventh expedition (1431–1433) and compiled a book entitled *Xiyang Fanguo Zhi* 西洋番国志 (Record of the Western Ocean Barbarian Kingdoms).[36] Ma Huan's work was the most original of the three, with Fei Xin lifting fairly heavily and Gong Zhen more or less copying Ma Huan verbatim. Together their works represent the zenith of Chinese knowledge on the Indian Ocean and have been well studied.

A DESTINATION

Moving on to the succeeding visitors to the Indian Ocean world, Abder-Razzak (1413–1482) was the ambassador of Shah Rukh, the Timurid dynasty ruler of Persia to Calicut (1442–1445). The Genoese merchant Hieronimo di Santo Stefano traveled to India, Pegu, Sumatra, and the Maldives at the end of the fifteenth century. Between 1501 to 1517 the Portuguese soldier Duarte Barbosa served in various parts of the east and left his account of them. Almost around the same period as Duarte Barbosa, Huang Xingzeng 黄省曾, a scholar who never once stepped outside the borders of China, compiled a book including the edited body of Chinese knowledge of the Maldives in 1520. Another vicarious commenter, Joao de Barros (1496–1570), a treasure-seeker and trader based at India House in Lisbon, never visited Asia but accumulated a great deal of knowledge due to his role in recording navigational expertise. The French Parmentier brothers navigated numerous voyages to Brazil, North America, West Africa, India, and Sumatra, and died in 1529 in Sumatra. Finally, the French navigator François Pyrard (c. 1578–c. 1623) traveled in the Indian Ocean, was captured during a shipwreck in the Maldives in 1602, and stayed in the islands until 1607, providing a highly detailed record of the sultanate at that time.

While all these early and medieval writers contributed in their own way to our understanding of the Maldives, it was H. C. P. Bell who established the modern paradigm of its history.

H. C. P. BELL: FATHER OF MALDIVIAN STUDIES

The name of H. C. P. Bell has long been essentially associated with Ceylon and the Maldives, because he is seen as the founding father of their archaeological and archival studies. Born in British India in 1851 and educated at Cheltenham College in England, Bell became a British civil officer in Ceylon in 1873 until his retirement there. In July 1890 the governor of Ceylon, Sir Arthur Gordon, appointed Bell as the first archaeological commissioner and head of the Archaeological Survey of Ceylon, and from then until his retirement in 1912 Bell devoted himself to the island's archaeology. In 1887 the Maldives became a British protectorate, so after his retirement Bell was invited to investigate the archaeology and epigraphy of the Maldives. He was able to study and master the Maldivian language and became a good friend of its sultan, the latter providing generous support for Bell's fieldwork. These experiences and privileges hence made Bell indisputably the authority on Maldivian language, culture, and history.

Bell, the acknowledged father of Maldivian studies, visited the Maldives three times, first during November 1879, second from January 20 to February 21, 1920, and third from February 2 to September 22, 1922.[37] In that first visit, in 1879, the stranding of the SS *Sea Gull* on Gafaru Reef caused Bell to land up inadvertently in the Maldives on his way to Ceylon. He boarded a native ship and visited Male, the "Sultan's Island," for two or three days before returning to his newly repaired ship and heading for Ceylon. Some years later Bell submitted a report "The Maldive Islands: An Account of the Physical Features, Climate, History, Inhabitants, Production and Trade (*Ceylon Sessional Paper* XLIII., 1881)" to the Ceylon Government on this providential albeit unofficial trip.

Forty years later Bell paid his second visit to the island kingdom. HMS *Comus* took him from Colombo on January 20, 1920, and it docked at Male the following day. The purpose of his second visit was articulately stated by the Ceylon Government to His Highness Sultan Muhammad Shams-ud-din III: "To enable information to be gathered necessary" for Bell's 1881 report; to "peruse, and arrange for a copy to be made of, the State Historical Record, known as the '*Tárîkh*,' which is among His Highness's Archives, containing information of great historical value and interest;" and to "make careful investigation regarding the alleged existence (a) of the Buddhist Cult on the Maldives prior to the Conversion to Islam of the Islanders in the Twelfth Century, and (b) of any Archaeological Remains on the Group distinctly assignable to a Buddhist origin."[38] Certainly Bell made it his principal task to trace the Buddhist footprints in the pre-Islamic period of the islands.

Bell stayed on Male until February 18 whence he departed for Colombo and where he submitted the "Report on a Visit to Male, January 20 to February 21, 1920" (*Ceylon Sessional Paper XV.*, 1921) to the Ceylon government, including a revised edition of his 1881 report. He did little revision to the first sections of the 1881 report, but sections III–VIII were substantially updated, or even "virtually re-written."[39] While the sultan graciously promised "every possible assistance," the short-term stay certainly compromised this high expectation. Soon after Bell made a third and final visit to the Maldives.

A DESTINATION

On February 2, 1922, Bell boarded HMS *Comus*, accompanied by W. L. De Silva, a young, active, and intelligent Sinhalese, and a very capable Malay servant, bound for Male. Bell was deputed by the Ceylon Government to visit the Maldives Island in order to investigate the early existence of Buddhism in these islands and to collect notes for the compilation of the revised edition of his two Maldives Reports, published as Sessional Papers Nos. LIII. of 1881 and XV. of 1921 by the Ceylon Government, respectively.[40] His final and lengthy stay there was divided into his first archaeological expedition to the southern atolls from February 9 to 18, his second expedition to the southern atolls from March 7 to April 9, his return voyage to Male from March 23 to April 9, and his stays in Male during February 3 to 9, February 17 to March 7, and April 9 to September 17.

Bell was accompanied on his first southern expedition by H. Haji Ismail Didi, former ambassador to Ceylon, who spoke Sinhalese fluently and thus served as interpreter. They visited Addu Atoll, the southernmost region of the Maldives. In the islands of Gan and Hitadu (the largest island in the atoll), they examined two ancient sites: a ruined *dagaba* mound (*ustubu* or stupa) and a connected monastic site on Gan Island, and "the dilapidated shell of an old coral-built Fort" at Hitadu.[41]

The second southern expedition took Bell to Haddhunmathi Atoll. They spent ten days in the investigation of the two congeries of Buddhist ruins in Gan, the "larger group, lying about half a mile from the clustered habitants" and "a smaller coterie at the South end of the Island, known as Kuruhinna." After that they examined the remains of a small Buddhist monastery on the island of Mundoo, where nothing but a "very diminished mound," once a *dagaba*, was surveyed.[42]

Bell's archaeological work on the third mission provided a definitive answer to "the vexed question of the existence of the Buddhist Cult in the Maldives, prior to the Muhammadan Conversion of the Twelfth Century."[43] Buddhism prevailed in the pre-Islamic period, and Buddhist ruins though considerably dilapidated continued to be discovered in a few atolls over the following decades after Bell's trip.

On his third mission, Bell also collected and deciphered copperplate grants, and his epigraphical findings indicated the prior existence of a complex society. One set of the plates "definitely dated in the sixteenth year of the reigning Queen, Rehendi Khadijah, who ruled thrice in the middle of the Fourteenth Century, bears on its cover the Arabic Seal of her father

Sultan 'Umar Vira Jalal-ud-din, and Hijra date 758 (A.C. 1356-7)." The other three sets including a complete one, belonged to earlier dates. Two sets dated in A.H. 582 and 583 (1186–1188), belonged to a sultan in the last quarter of the twelfth century, and the third to a ruler of the thirteenth century, probably the seventh sultan.[44] These plates were roughly contemporary with the era of Marco Polo, Ibn Battuta, and Wang Dayuan.

In 1937 Bell died in Kandy, Ceylon, with his final report left uncompleted. Bell's ground-breaking contribution lies in his archaeological, epigraphical, and linguistic studies that have established a multicultural history of Maldivian society. He definitively accomplished the key purpose of his visits to prove the pre-Islamic existence of Buddhism, thus providing a solid foundation for future scholars such as Albert Gray and Clarence Maloney. This present book attempts to add a few small stones to the giant pyramid that Bell bequeathed us.

THOSE WHO NEVER VISITED THE MALDIVES

There surely exist many works written by people who never visited the Maldives but who somehow collected other travelers' accounts of the archipelago.

The *Ming Shilu* 明实录 (Veritable Records of the Ming Dynasty) were the official archives compiled by Ming official scholars and thus serve as the most reliable source for the study of Ming history. The *Ming Shi* 明史 (History of the Ming Dynasty), based on Ming archives but compiled by the Qing state, is also very useful. In addition, some Chinese sources compiled in the post–Zheng He period contain information on the Maldives, but most of these writers merely copied the aforementioned works of the Yuan and early Ming period, and thus contribute little to the understanding of the Maldives.[45] Some original information nevertheless is provided in the *Xiyang Chaogong Dianlu* 西洋朝贡典录 by Huang Xingzeng, the *Shuyu Zhouzilu* 殊域周咨录 (Comprehensive Survey and Record of Foreign Territories) by Yan Congjian 严从简, and the *Zheng He Hanghai Tu* by Mao Yuanyi 茅元仪 (1594-1640).

Huang Xingzeng was an imperial scholar born in Suzhou, a prosperous city involved in both domestic and international trade in Jiangsu Province, due to its advantageous key location along the Grand Canal. Although he did not travel overseas, Huang Xingzeng managed to gain access to many

Ming works on overseas trade and the Zheng He voyages, some of which certainly went missing and thus were not available to later readers. Therefore, his *Xiyang Chaogong Dianlu* contains some information not found in Ma Huan's *Yingya Shenglan*, for example.[46]

Like Huang Xingzeng, Yan Congjian (active in the second half of the sixteenth century), the author of the *Shuyu Zhouzilu*, did not go overseas himself, but his official position provided him with a rare opportunity to gain access to official archives, memorials, and reports.[47] In 1559 Yan obtained the highest imperial degree of *jinshi*, and thus served in the Division of *Xingren* 行人 (lit. "walking man"). This division was created by Emperor Taizu 太祖 (r. 1368–1398) in 1380 to send the *Xingren* as Chinese envoys to foreign countries to solicit tributes. Yan was never assigned a place on any tribute-seeking trip, but the nature of his position allowed him to read quantities of official documents. Therefore, his work confirms, revises, and supplements early Ming sources.

Another late Ming source of great importance was the *Zheng He Hanghai Tu* presented by Mao Yuanyi in 1628.[48] Mao Yuanyi served as a Ming general, mainly on the northeastern frontiers, but Yuanyi's grandfather, Mao Kun 茅坤 (1512–1601), was a military advisor to Hu Zongxian 胡宗宪, a high-ranking official in southeast China once in charge of the suppression of the *Wakou* (lit. "Japanese pirates"), and thus familiar with maritime frontiers. This work was in fact a set of navigation charts comprising twenty maps and four star charts. Presumably based on maps used and information collected on the Zheng He voyages, this work provides more than five hundred place names in Asia and Africa and shows the navigation routes from Ming China through Southeast Asia into the Indian Ocean and the Arab world, as well as along coastal East Africa.

Literary works such as the *Xiyangji* also help fill in the details. The *Xiyang Ji* was a novel completed by Luo Maodeng in 1597 that romanticized the Zheng He expeditions and deserves some attention here.[49] Fictitious and fantastical as it is, this novel has some historical veracity, possibly sourcing some of its facts from works by Wang Dayuan, Ma Huan, and other contemporary travelers, while other details were gleaned elsewhere from origins unknown to modern scholars.[50] Its citations are sometimes identical word-for-word with the original sources. Many details and clues must have been gained not only from the Chinese but also the western conceptualization of the Indian Ocean world.

WHO ONCE LANDED IN THE MALDIVES?

The *Dongxiyang Kao* (Survey of the Eastern and Western Oceans) printed in 1617 by Zhang Xie seems to include the Indian Ocean by mentioning the "Western Ocean," but it clearly indicates the shift of Chinese interest from the Indian Ocean to Southeast Asia. Zhang Xie barely mentioned areas, kingdoms, or people further west than the Malay Peninsula, while he took a keen interest in European colonial activities in Southeast Asia.[51]

In the West there are some early works that are not directly linked to the Maldives but are nevertheless useful for reference, including the *Periplus* (90 CE?), passages by Ptolemy, Ammianus Marcellinus (320–390 CE), and Moses Chorenensis.[52]

Finally, archaeological findings in China, Southeast Asia, and the Maldives are utilized to test, supplement, or revise textual analysis. Recent archaeological discoveries of Chinese porcelain in the Maldives, the well-known Belitung shipwreck found in Indonesia, and in China, findings since the beginning of the twentieth century of hoards of cowrie shells and several bronze inscriptions that mention cowrie shells will be referred to in subsequent chapters to highlight the extensive significance of the Maldives in maritime Asia.

Chapter Five

THE KINGDOM OF ATOLLS

The land is low, with a thousand islands and ten thousand islets (*qianyuwandao* 千屿万岛).

—WANG DAYUAN

A hundred or less of these islands lie together in a circle in the form of a ring: the group has an entrance as to a harbor, and ships get through by that alone.

—IBN BATTUTA

Known as the pearls of the Indian Ocean, the islands of the Maldives lie across the equator more than 620 miles (1,000 km) southwest of Sri Lanka, and between the Lakshadweep Islands to the north and the Chagos Islands to the south. According to government statistics, the Maldives consists of 1,190 coral reef islands (199 of which are inhabited) that form an archipelago of twenty-six major atolls (groups of neighboring coral islands) and stretches 510 miles (820 km) from north to south and 75 miles (120 km) from east to west. It is no wonder that the Chinese named it the Kingdom of Atolls (*Liushanguo* 溜山国). The actual word "atoll" in French and English was borrowed from the Devehi word *atoḷu*,[1] which reveals how this prominent geographical feature of the Maldives impressed European visitors. Indeed, the islands as a whole look like a double row of atolls, elongated in the shape of a garland.[2]

The term Maldives has its Sanskrit origin *maladvipa*, which means "garland of islands," a vivid description of these islets and atolls forming themselves into a kind of lei. However, from early times onward the Maldives was also well known for its other characteristic landscape feature: coconut trees. While to its neighbors the Maldives was named after its typographical features of islands or the cowrie shell, its most distinctive product, the first impression that its Chinese travelers had, though indirectly, was its coconut trees.

THE KINGDOM OF ATOLLS

During his stay in India (629–643), Xuanzang, the Tang Buddhist pilgrim, traveled extensively in the South Asian subcontinent, but he never crossed the sea to the kingdom of *Sengjialuo* 僧伽罗, a transcription of Simghala, referring to Ceylon, let alone the Maldives. His records of Ceylon were based on what he had heard. "A few thousand *li* south of the kingdom, (it) reaches Naluojiluo Island (*Naluojiluo zhou* 那罗稽罗洲). Local people are short and small, less than three *chi* high, with a human body but a bird head. (They) do not have any grain, and only rely on coconuts," noted Xuanzang.[3] The Chinese term *Naluojiluo* was derived from the Sanskrit *nārikela*, referring to coconut trees, and the so-called Naluojiluo Island, based on its geographical location and local customs, seems to refer to the Maldives. If so, this was the first Chinese record of the Maldives. Although Xuanzang himself did not land there, he understood that the islands were filled with trees on which the local people depended. This was doubtless why the islands were so named. Clearly the Maldives was also known to its neighbors as the islands of coconut palm trees.

Coconut palms were crucial not only to the people of the Maldives, but also to many other societies in South Asia. Xuanzang made mention of them on two other occasions. When listing local products, Xuanzang included "the fruit of naliluo (*naliluo guo* 那利罗果)," with *naliluo* being a word derived from *nārikela*. In Kamarupa (*Jiamolübo* 迦摩屡波), also known as Assam, he recorded that it produced "fruits of naluojiluo (*naluojiluo guo* 那罗鸡罗果); although there grew a lot of these trees, they were still highly valuable."[4] "*Naluojiluo* was simply a variation of the word *nārikela*. Xuanzang's accounts illustrate that coconut trees were intensively associated with people's daily life in South Asia.

While many Chinese monks after Xuanzang went to India, none of them seemed to pay any attention to the Maldives. After all, the islands were on the periphery of the Buddhist world. That silence continued for the following seven hundred years. It was for Wang Dayuan to leave us with a brief but informative passage on these islands.

TEN THOUSAND ISLANDS

While Xuanzang thought the Maldives a big island or continent (*zhou* 洲), Wang Dayuan had a categorical idea that the Maldives, together with parts of the Laccadives, were simply groups of islands. Naming it *Beiliu* 北溜, Wang Dayuan used some 110 Chinese characters to introduce the islands.

> The land is low, with a thousand islands and ten thousand islets. When a ship sails to the Western Ocean and passes near *Sengjiala* [Ceylon], the tidal currents are fast and rapid; and if facing a head wind, it would be driven to this country. Waiting for the southeastern wind in the following summer, the ship could proceed to the north of the islands (*liu* 溜). In the waters there are rocky ledges like teeth, as sharp as the points and edges (of a knife), (if a ship crashes into them), it would become an incomplete one.
> The land produces coir ropes, cowrie shells, dried fishes, and big handkerchiefs. Every sea-trader who takes one shipload of cowrie shells to *Wudie* 乌爹 [Pegu] and *Pengjiala* 朋家剌 [Bengal], could exchange for more than a shipload of rice. In these areas people use cowrie shells as money, a long-time method to make a living.[5]

The 110-Chinese-character passage, brief as it is, mentions almost all the essential features of the Maldives. It not only presents comprehensive information about the Maldives in terms of location, the difficulty and danger of access, local products including coir ropes, cowrie shells, dried fish, big handkerchiefs, and the cowrie–rice trade, but it also sets up the pattern of definition for future Chinese travelers to follow. This first introduction of the Maldives by Wang Dayuan hence represents China's increasing understanding of the Indian Ocean, a result of China's intensive activities in what they called the Western Ocean. While Ma Huan and his fellow visitors in the fifteenth century provided more information, nothing fundamental was added to Wang's description. Put simply, it was Wang Dayuan who "discovered" the Maldives for the Chinese world.

The first thing that Wang Dayuan observed was that the Maldive islands were "low," and many were small, which is an accurate description. H. C. P. Bell concluded that in general these islands were not higher than six feet above sea level, and therefore they "appear to be coconut groves growing out of the water." Only a few, such as Gan and Fua Mulaku, are as large as four miles in length and breadth, while most of them are small, "not many exceeding a mile," many being mere sandbanks. Many islands are still in the process of changing, being reshaped and shifted by the tides and winds.

When an islet washes away, all that remains is a group of coconut palms standing in the sea or in the submerged black soil of the land at low water outside the beach. "Contrariwise, barren reef-borne sand-banks are known to have risen and become habitable wooded islands," Bell noted.[6]

What most impressed Wang Dayuan was the great number of islands, and this feature was highlighted by every other subsequent visitor. The four-Chinese-character term *qianyuwangao* 千屿万岛 (A Thousand Islets and Ten Thousand Islands), while describing the geographical components of the Maldives, seems to exaggerate this island number greatly. Having said this, the number of ten thousand was a common convention regarding the Maldives among medieval travelers, since such a scene hardly existed in the Mediterranean, in the Gulf, or in the western Pacific.

Initially, people understood that there were a great number of islands in the Indian Ocean, sometimes roughly referring to the Maldives. Faxian commented that "On every side are small islands, perhaps amounting to one hundred in number," but the islands he in fact referred to were those lying to the north and northwest of Ceylon, where Faxian resided for months, and this is shown by his descriptions of the local products such as precious stones and pearls.[7] These precious stones and pearls (the larger in size the higher in value) were the exotic foreign goods that had been highly sought after by the Chinese since the Han dynasty, and it was no wonder that both of these were mentioned by this Chinese Buddhist pilgrim. While these two were famous products from Ceylon, early travelers were often unable to distinguish the Maldives from Ceylon and thus wrongly attributed these prized goods to the Maldives.

In the mid-sixth century, Cosmos the monk landed in Ceylon and noted: "Round about it are a number of small islands, in all of which you find fresh water and coco-nuts."[8] Although he got the geographical location wrong, since the Maldives is not close to Ceylon, his mention of fresh water and coconuts indicates that this is the country he might have been referring to. He knew that there were quite a number of islets, but he did not state a specific number.

Palladius was the first person to provide the closest number to the actual island count for the Maldives. "Round about it (unless the report be false) lie a thousand other islands, through which the Red Sea flows."[9] Here the number one thousand appeared, although the origin of this estimate remains unknown.

Al Mas'udi (895–957) visited Ceylon in 916 and provides some specific numbers, too. "There are, as had been said a great number of islands, forming, as it were, separate groups. There are counted of them 2,000, or more exactly, 1,900."[10] The range of 1,900 to 2,000 seems to be a number known to the Ceylonese, and it is not far from the actual number.

The conventional island count for the Maldives at around the time of Al Mas'udi appeared to be ten thousand. Exaggerated as this number was, it reveals the first impression of the island kingdom in the maritime world. This geographical feature, so widely spread and believed in, might have been the result of the increasing role of the archipelago in maritime Asia.

Although he did not visit the Maldives or speak directly about the islands, Marco Polo stated: "It is a fact that in this Sea of India there are 12,700 Islands, inhabited and uninhabited, according to the charts and documents of experienced mariners who navigate the Indian Sea."[11] Not specifying the location of these islands in the Indian Ocean, the legendary Venetian traveler must have meant the Maldives by this number. His numbering the islands as 12,700 was clearly a variation of the traditional number associated with the islands of the Maldives.

Both Prince Hayton in 1307 and Friar Jordanus in the early fourteenth century vaguely mentioned "a quantity of islands" or "many islands, and more than 10,000" that were inhabited. The two seemed to be more interested in Ceylon where "the best precious stones" were found. Writing just a few years earlier than Wang Dayuan, Friar Jordanus, the first bishop of the Roman Catholic Diocese of Quilon (and thus the first Catholic diocese in India), repeated that "In this India be many islands, and more than 10,000 of them inhabited, as I have heard."[12] Odorico da Pordenone visited India in 1321 and was told that "it included in its limits a good twenty-four thousand islands."[13] Therefore, by the era of Wang Dayuan, the phrase "10,000 islands" seemed to have been well established and widely taken for granted. His word *qianyuwandao* was not a figure pulled out of thin air, nor simply a conventional Chinese estimate.

Probably because of his long stay in the Maldives, Ibn Battuta returned to a realistic number: "These islands are among the wonders of the world: they number about 2,000."[14] Ibn Battuta's number deserves some attention. It seems that while the ten-thousand count stood as a fuzzy impression describing the numerous islands, people began to realize the actual size of the island kingdom. This might have had something to do with a centralized sultanate having been well established before the arrival of the Moroccan Muslim traveler.

While on his return voyage from Pegu and Sumatra in 1497, Hieronimo di Santo Stefano, a Genoese merchant, took refuge in the Maldives for six months, but he wrote only a brief passage, mentioning that the islands were "from seven to eight thousand in number."[15] But with the arrival of the Portuguese at the end of the fifteenth century, the number 12,000 continued to be repeated. Traditionally, a twelve-based counting system dominated in the Maldives, a practice not found either in Ceylon or India.[16] Probably that is why the number of the islands was given as 12,000 (1,000 × 12). Duarte Barbosa, a Portuguese soldier in the early sixteenth century, stated that there "lies an archipelago of islands, said by the Moors to number 12,000."[17] However, after being subjected to a European navigation survey, the 10,000–12,000 range gradually disappeared.

Clearly, in the time before Wang Dayuan, there had existed across the Indian Ocean world a conventional narrative about the number of islands, which points to 10,000 or upward, and more specifically, 12,000 or 12,700 (table 5.1). Therefore, while Wang Dayuan's descriptive word was a multiplication of the actual number of islands in the Maldives, it was historically true to his contemporary travelers. Wang Dayuan's knowledge indeed might have been shared by the Maldivian or the Indian Ocean world natives. In the decades to come, Ma Huan and Gong Zhen did not mention *qianyuwandao* or any specific number of islands. Fei Xin was the only person in the treasure fleet to mention that "it is said there are over 38,000 *liu* mountains."[18] Interestingly, 38,000 is approximately equal to 12,700 thrice multiplied.

When the Jesuits led by Matteo Ricci brought with them updated geographical knowledge to China, the idea of "ten thousand islands" (*wandao* 万岛) reappeared. On the groundbreaking Ricci Map made by the Jesuits in 1602, the Americas were for the first time revealed to the Chinese, and *wandao*, referring to the Maldives, was located west of Ceylon (*Xilangdao* 锡狼岛) below India (*Yingdiya* 应帝亚) (map 5.1).[19] It is highly likely that this *wandao* was a legacy of Indian Ocean knowledge, transmitted to China through the Jesuits, and translated and written into the two traditional Chinese characters 萬島, rather than being extracted from prior Chinese knowledge from Wang Dayuan onward. While imperial scholars were amazed by this brand-new knowledge and the value system behind this

A DESTINATION

TABLE 5.1
Different estimates of the number of islands in the Maldives

Source	Century	Number of Islands
Commentary on Bharu Jātaka		1,000
Khuddakapaṭha		2,000
Ptolemy	2nd A.D.	1,387
Papps of Alexandria	4th	1,370
Sholasticus the Theban	5th	1,000
Palladius	5th	1,000
Mose Chorence	5th	1,372
Narasimha Varman II Inscription	7–8th	100,000
Sulaiman	9th	1,900 (13,700)
Al Mas'udi	10th	1,900–2,000
Rajaraja Cola Inscription	11th	12,000
Mugaddasī		1,700
Marco Polo	13th	12,700
John of Montecorvino	13th	12,000
Prince Hayton	14th	10,000
Friar Jordanus	14th	10,000 inhabited ones
Ibn Battuta	14th	2,000
Wang Dayuan	14th	10,000
Fei Xin	15th	38,000
Hieronimo	15th	7,000–8,000
Duarte Barbosa	16th	12,000
D'Alboquerque	16th	11,000
Matteo Ricci	Early 17th	10,000
Giulio Aleni	Early 17th	A few thousand

Source: Based on Clarence Maloney, *People of the Maldive Islands* (Bombay: Oriental Longman, 1980), 5–6. I have deleted Faxian and added Prince Hayton, Fei Xin, and Giulio Aleni.

map, no one seems to have paid any attention to this tiny group of islands in the Indian Ocean.

Compared with this number, the Chinese seemed to be more interested in the formation of these islands that represented such a formidable barrier for the entry of foreign ships.

THE KINGDOM OF ATOLLS

In his *Daoyi Zhilue*, Wang Dayuan called the Maldives (along with some islets from the Laccadives) *Beiliu*. The name is worth some attention. Wang Dayuan was the first Chinese traveler to use the character *liu* to refer to the Maldives, and other Chinese visitors such as Ma Huan followed this convention. In other words, it is highly possible that Wang invented the name himself.

THE KINGDOM OF ATOLLS

MAP 5.1 The Maldives (*Wandao*) in the Ricci Map. Note the rectangle referring to "Wandao (The Maldives)," the hexagon "Xilangdao (Ceylon)," and the three circles "Yingdiya (India)" of the three vertical characters, respectively. *Source*: Courtesy of the University of Minnesota Libraries.

What does the Chinese phrase *Beiliu* mean? And why did Wang Dayuan choose it to refer to the Maldives? Some scholars argue that the term *Beiliu* was a transcription of Male, the capital of the kingdom. Fujita Toyohachi (1869–1929) argues that *Beiliu* was a transliteration of Mal (Bal) where the Zheng He Fleet established an official islet (*guanyu* 官嶼) as a base, which also appears on the *Zheng He Hanghai Tu*. Su Jiqing agrees with Fujita Toyohachi, and further explains that *ma* could be pronounced as *ba*, from which the Chinese *bei* 北 (lit. "north") was derived. Meanwhile, Su suspects that *liu* might have had something to do with the local names for currents,[20] but he could not find any supporting evidence to substantiate this theory.

In fact, Rockhill was the first scholar to point out that *Beiliu* literally means "northern islands," which most scholars including Xie Fang, an eminent scholar and editor in the field of Sino-foreign interactions, agree with.[21] Xie Fang disagrees that *bei* could be a transliteration of *ma* via *ba*. He explains that there has never been another case in which *ma* was translated into *bei*, at least not in Cantonese or Hokkien. Instead, he points out that *bei*, meaning north or northern, simply refers to a geographical location.[22]

One of the puzzling issues is the meaning of the character *liu*. The basic meaning of the character *liu* in Chinese refers to "turbulent current." Xie Fang refuses to believe that *liu* was an accurate transcription, stressing that *liu* literally means "rapid currents" and thus could extend itself to refer to islands surrounded by the currents that occur around the Maldives.[23] Roderich Ptak, however, argues that *liu* is a transliteration of *diu* (island), "derived from Sanskrit *dvipa* (other forms: *diva, dive, diba* etc.)," and that "most likely it has nothing to do with the meaning of 'current.'"[24] A good case for foreign terms having been translated into Chinese usually combines translation and transliteration. The character *liu* hence might have been a deliberate decision made by the well-educated Wang Dayuan. Therefore, the character *bei* means "north" or "northern," *liu* refers to "islands surrounded by currents," and *beiliu* means "northern islands," which accords with "garland of islands," the Sanskrit meaning of the Maldives.

The discussion on *liu* made by Clarence Maloney is very interesting.[25] The *Dīpavamsa* and the *Mahāvamsa*, two Ceylon chronicles, both mention that a previous Buddha made both the island of Ceylon and the island of Giri (Giridīpa) inhabitable as desired. Giridīpa was of "low land." "In the great and deep ocean, in the midst of the water of the sea, waves always break, surrounded by the inaccessible chain of mountains, it is difficult to go inside against the wish," so "Gotama drew the island by means of miraculous power like a bullock bound with a strong rope and dragged. The sage placed the island close to the island, like a pair of ships feeling the firm hold." Giridīpa literally means "mountain island," but no mountain exists in the Maldives. However, the word *giri* means a "reef" and reefs in the sea are like mountains. Therefore, the geographical features of Giridīpa lead us to the conclusion that the islands in this context must be the Maldives. This was probably why Ma Huan called the Maldives "the Kingdom of Liu Mountains" (*Liushanguo*), although he must have known that the country had no mountains. Clarence Maloney argues that Ma Huan's *liu* "is a Chinese transliteration of *tīvu, dīv, dipa, dupa,* or *dū*, all meaning 'mountain,' and his term 'mountain' is a translation of the word *giri*, as at least thirty-six reefs of the Maldives are named *giri* or have the suffix *giri*."[26] Although Ma Huan lived much later than the age of the Dīpavamsa, the Maldives as "the inaccessible chain of mountains" and "difficult to go inside" had remained the main impressions for Chinese visitors.

The existence of a northern *liu* seems to imply there should also have been a southern one. If so, where was that southern one? Xie Fang points out that the southern *liu* (*nanliu* 南溜) would have been the southern atolls of the Maldives, including Suvadiva Atoll and Addu Atoll. He goes on to explain that the southern atolls were not necessarily part of the trading route, and that Wang Dayuan only paid a visit to the northern part of the Maldives.[27] When introducing the islands of Dabadan 大八丹 (lit. "Big Badan"), Wang Dayuan mentioned that the local people wore *nanliu bu* 南溜布 (lit. "southern atolls clothing").[28] The term *nanliu bu* suggests the existence of *nanliu*, or southern islands, in Chinese knowledge. In addition, Dabadan was also known to have a southern silk (*nansi* 南丝), which might refer to the silk produced in the southern atolls.[29]

Xie Fang's speculation about the southern atolls fits perfectly with the physical features of the Maldives, as considerable differences exist between the northern and the southern atolls.[30] Comparatively speaking, the northern atolls are more subject to monsoons and the occurrence of hurricanes, which was unfortunate, since they were strategic to maritime trade. By contrast, in the southern atolls rainfall was greater, the humidity more equable, and there were fewer violent winds.[31] R. Michael Feener comments that Xie's north-south division might in fact be the One-and-a-half Degree Channel, which was also an important route for trans-Indian Ocean crossings, and that the southern atolls were different, in terms of dialect and political relations with Male during the Islamic period. Nevertheless, they were obviously involved in transregional exchanges. On the Fuamulah Atoll, a southernmost island of the Maldives, there exist the remains of an extensive Buddhist ritual complex. In early 2018 Feener's team "unearthed a large statue base, underneath which a coral stone casket contained a devotional deposit of cowrie shells."[32] European latecomers noticed the difference between the north and the south, too. To them, the difference was more than geographical. The north remained a center of politics, economy, and culture, as "the nobles" "are all in the north, where too, the soldiers are obtained."[33]

While Bell surely observed the natural difference between the south and north, he highlighted more foreign contacts and thus influence in the north, including the mixed blood.[34] The south, from Pyrard's point of view, was culturally underdeveloped, and he credited this to the more frequent marriages between the Maldivian people in the north and their foreign visitors.

> Add to this, that a large number of foreigners from all parts meet there and make it their home; besides many Indians who from time to time are wrecked there, as we were, and remain at the islands. This is why the people living at Male and the neighbouring parts toward the north are more polished, genteel, and civilised, while those toward the south are ruder in language and habits, and also are less well-formed in body, and darker, and you see many women, chiefly the poor, go about naked, without any shame, with nothing on but a little cloth to cover their private parts. The northern parts, therefore, are more frequented by foreigners, who usually marry there. There, too, pass all the ships, which enrich the country and tend to civilise it, and so people of quality and means go there more willingly than to the south, whither, as I have said, the king sends those who he would punish with banishment.[35]

Pyrard's view clearly imposed his own cultural and racial judgment on what he saw. Having said this, he did acknowledge that "the people of the south are no less well-informed and clever than the rest, perhaps more so in some ways."[36] The popular *nanliu bu* indicated the high skills of the southern people.

Borrowing the concept of *liu* from Wang Dayuan, Ma Huan called the Maldives *Liushanguo* (Kingdom of Atolls), and this referred to both the northern and southern islands of the Maldives. Obviously he had obtained more information than Wang Dayuan. "There is no city or town (and people) living up against mountains. (Each island) is surrounded by the sea on all four sides; it is like an islet, without much large territory," related Ma Huan. Ma Huan stated that the indigenous name (*fanming* 番名) was *diegan* 牒幹.[37] Some scholars agree that the second character *gan* 幹 could have been a hand-copying error for the character of *wo* 斡, and that *diegan* was meant to be *diewo* 牒斡, the latter being a transliteration of *dewa* or *dwa* that in turn were derived from the Sanskrit *dvipa*.[38] Su Jiqing noticed that the *Nanhai Zhi* 南海志 (Record of South Sea), another Yuan source compiled a few decades earlier than the *Daoyi Zhilue*, listed a foreign kingdom known as "Tiaoji" 条垍, and he suspected that "Tiaoji" was a copying error and was meant to be "Tiaopei" 条培, which was a transcription of the

THE KINGDOM OF ATOLLS

Arabic Diba or Dvia.[39] If so, "Tiaopei" instead of "Beiliu" or "Liushanguo" was indeed the first Chinese name for the Maldives.

THE NINE *LIU*

The word "atoll" essentially defines the Maldives. An atoll is a ring-shaped coral island, or series of islets that surrounds a lagoon. Sometimes, atolls and lagoons protect a central island. Channels between islets connect a lagoon to an ocean or a sea. With the earliest French word *atollon* at the beginning of the seventeenth century, "atoll" appears to have been a word specifically invented in early descriptions for the Maldives Islands. When Ibn Battuta landed on the islands, he immediately realized this fundamental feature. "These islands are among the wonders of the world: they number about 2,000. A hundred or less of these islands lie together in a circle in the form of a ring: the group has an entrance as to a harbor, and ships get through by that alone. When a ship arrives near one of these islands it must of necessity have a pilot from among its natives so that it may reach the other islands under his guidance."[40]

The thousand-odd islands in the Maldives (map 5.2) are formed into clusters or atolls, which the Chinese called the *liu*. It must be pointed out that while the Chinese divided the Laccadive and the Maldive islands into eight or nine *liu* (major atolls), the 1,192 islands that form the Maldives are naturally divided into 26 major atolls. Obviously, the Chinese did not know many of these. Due to its paramount role, the atoll impressed the Chinese so much that they followed Wang Dayuan and used the term to name the Maldives.

Although Ma Huan did not adopt the name *Beiliu* invented by Wang Dayuan, he did stick to Wang's principal conceptualization of the local landscape. To the Chinese, islands in the sea were just like mountains on land, so Ma Huan instead called the Maldives "Liushanguo," literally meaning "Atoll Mountain Kingdom." Fei Xin made his own contribution by calling it "Liuyangguo 溜洋国," meaning "Atoll Ocean Kingdom," quite an accurate geographical description of islands in the sea, although he also used the name *Liushan*.[41] In general, all these names derived from Wang Dayuan's *Beiliu*, and the name "Liushanguo" became the most popular one in Ming China. Very interestingly, products from the Maldives were named by the same token. Cloth processed in the Maldives was called the *liu* cloth

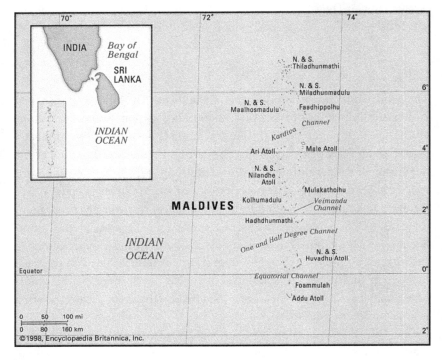

MAP 5.2 Physical features of the Maldives. *Source*: "Physical Features of Maldives," *Encyclopaedia Britannica*.

(*liubu* 溜布), dried fish the *liu* fish (*liuyu* 溜鱼), and reefs the *liu* reefs (*liujiao* 溜礁).

Ma Huan further described the atolls as being like stone gates for a city, with the atolls (*liu*) forming eight groups. "There is no city or town (and people) living up against mountains. (Each island) is surrounded by the sea on all four sides; it is like an islet, without much big space," Ma Huan observed. Each name for the eight groups contained the character *liu*, such as Sha Liu 沙溜 (lit. "Sand Atoll"), Renbuzhi Liu 人不知溜 (lit. "People-Know-Nothing Atoll"), Qilai Liu 起来溜 (*Qilai*, probably the transliteration of Kalai Island), Maliqi Liu 麻里奇溜 (perhaps Maamigili Island?), Jiabannian Liu 加半年溜 (lit. "Add-Half-Year Liu"), Jiajia Liu 加加溜, Anduli Liu 安都里溜, and Guanyu Liu 官屿溜 (lit. "Official Island Atoll," referring to Male).[42] Late Ming texts added Silong Liu 巳龙溜 to the list, so the number increased to nine. Quite a few scholars have made efforts to identify the eight *liu*.[43]

THE KINGDOM OF ATOLLS

Guanyu Liu refers to Male Island, which was connected to India and Ceylon by four navigation routes and to Mugudushu (East Africa) by one route.[44] The frequency of these trading routes established the atoll at the center of the Maldives. Sha Liu, also called Shala Liu 沙喇溜, refers to Mulaku Atoll. Renbuzhi Liu, according to Xie Fang, refers to Miladu Madulu Atoll, while Mills and Ptak believe that this was in fact Fodiffolu Atoll.[45] Qilai Liu, with "Qilai" probably being the transliteration of "Kelai," refers to Kelai Island in Tiladummati Atoll.[46] Maliqi Liu, probably also derived from a transliteration, refers to Minicoy Island in the Laccadives. Jiabannian Liu, most likely an erroneous version of Jiapingnian Liu, is thought to be a transliteration of Kalpeni Island in the Laccadives. Anduli Liu was a transliteration of Androth Island in the Laccadives.[47] The location of Jiajia Liu has not been agreed upon. Phillips referred to the group of islands called Coronelli Isole di Divandurou, Mills deduces that it might be the island of Kaka-diwa of the Muhit, Xie Fang estimates it to have been some islet or rock east of Androth Island (Anduli Liu), while Ptak believes that it might be Sacrifice Rock.

As a matter of fact, at least half of the eight *liu* lie in the Laccadives, which may suggest that Ma Huan (and the Zheng He fleet) was more familiar with the north than the south, since the former must be visited if traveling to the west coast of India, the Arabic world, and East Africa. That is why Ma Huan claimed that trading ships called at all these places, as they served as important stopovers for Chinese ships.[48]

All these eight atolls are marked on the *Zheng He Hanghai Tu*, which highly likely originated from the nautical charts used by Zheng He. Indeed, Silong Liu, the ninth atoll, south of all other atolls, was only found on this chart. Its large size together with its relative geographical location as drawn on this chart indicates that Silong Liu was the largest island and refers to Haddhunmathi Atoll.[49] Here arises the question, how did Ma Huan, Fei Xin, and Gong Zhen all miss mentioning this atoll? Perhaps the expeditions they joined failed to land there or they had simply omitted to mention this southern island among their other information? As mentioned, the Chinese were more familiar with the northern rather than the southern part of the Maldives for trade reasons.

There might be another possibility for Silong Liu. George Phillips referred to the Chagos Archipelago, and Roderich Ptak has intensively discussed this issue.[50] He has pointed out that Chinese sailors might have known of an ocean-crossing route from the Sunda Strait, along the west side of Sumatra,

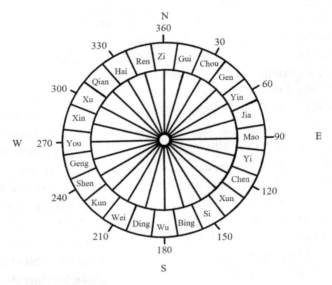

FIGURE 5.1 A Chinese compass. Author's drawing.

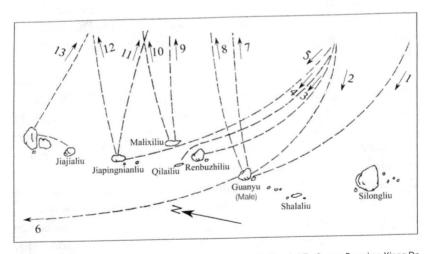

MAP 5.3 The nine *liu* and their navigation routes in the *Zheng He Hanghai Tu*. Source: Based on Xiang Da, "Fulu" (appendix), in the *Zheng He Hanghai Tu*, 3–45; Xie Fang, "Zhongguo Shiji zhong zhi Maerdaifu Kao" (A Study of the Maldives in Chinese Historical Texts), *Nanya Yanjiu* (South Asia Studies) 2 (1982): 4; Roderich Ptak, "The Maldives and Laccadive Islands (*liu-shan* 溜山) in Ming Records," *Journal of the American Oriental Society* 107, no. 4 (1987): 690, figure 2, redrawn by Huang Ming. Xie's map was made for contemporary readers.

THE KINGDOM OF ATOLLS

directly to the Chagos Islands (if this was indeed the Chinese Silong Liu). That route then led to the Seychelles, Madagascar, and the Comoros Islands, or due north to the Maldives. This navigation route through the southern section of the Indian Ocean might have been obtained from Arab sailors, whereas Zheng He and his fellows did not understand it very well, let alone have experience sailing on it.

Figure 5.1 provides a simplified version of the traditional Chinese compass used in navigation. The compass circle is divided into the forty-eight sections, each equal to 7.5 degrees, thus helping to explain the navigation routes textually described in the *Zheng He Hanghai Tu*.

On the *Zheng He Hanghai Tu* there are at least thirteen navigation routes (map 5.3), all marked with Chinese characters, referring to navigation routes in the Indian Ocean taken by the Zheng He voyages.

1. From Qianfootang 千佛堂 (Dondra Head), using the *Dangeng* 丹庚 needle (to Male);
2. (From Bieluoli 别罗里 [Beruwala]), using the *Gengyou* 庚酉 needle, after 45 *geng* 更 to Guanyu (Male);[51]
3. (From Bieluoli [Beruwala]), using the *Xinyou* 辛酉 needle, after 45 *geng* to Renbuzhi Liu (Fadiffolu);
4. (From Bieluoli [Beruwala]), using the *Xinxu* 辛戌 needle, after 50 *geng* to Qilai Liu (Kelai);
5. (From Bieluoli [Beruwala]), using the *Danxu* 丹戌 needle, after 55 geng to Jiapingnian Liu (Kalpeni);
6. From Guanyu Liu (Male Island), using the *Gengyou* 庚酉 needle, after 150 *geng*, the ship reaching Mugudu[shu] 木骨都 [朮] (Mogadishu);
7. (From Male), using the *Jiamao* 甲卯 needle, after 29 *geng*, the ship reaching Ganbali[tou] 甘八里 [头] (Cape Comorin);
8. (From Male), using the *Danshen* 丹申 needle , after 45 *geng*, the ship reaching *Xiao Gelan* 小葛兰 (Quilon);
9. (From Malixi Liu [Minicoy]), using the *Yin* 寅 needle , after 25 *geng*, the ship reaching Kezhi 柯枝 (Cochin);
10. (From Malixi Liu [Minicoy], using the *Yin* needle, after 50 *geng*, the ship reaching Guliguo 古里国 (Calicut);
11. (From Jiapingnian Liu [Kalpeni]), using the *Yimao* 乙卯 needle, after 25 *geng*, to Kezhiguo 柯枝国 (Cochin);

12. (From Jiapingnian Liu [Kalpeni]), using the *Jiamao* needle, after 28 *geng*, the ship reaching Guliguo (Calicut); and
13. (From Anduli Liu [Androth]), using the *Mao* 卯 needle, after 15 *geng*, the ship reaching Guliguo (Calicut).

There was also Route 14, which starts from Androth to Jiajia Liu (Sacrifice Rock?) using the *Mao* 卯 needle and navigating for 16 *geng*. In this case, the location of Jiajialiu would be further inland than Calicut. Obviously these Chinese texts had been wrongly copied.[52]

In sum, thirteen or fourteen navigation routes around the Maldives were marked by the Chinese in the early Ming period. Routes 1–5 linked the Maldives to Ceylon, routes 7–13 linked the Maldives to coastal India, and route 6 linked the Maldives to East Africa.

THE RUOSHUI

The treasure fleet explorers also noticed other smaller and narrower atolls (*xiaozhai zhi liu* 小窄之溜), more than three thousand in number, according to Ma Huan, but Fei Xin and Huang Xingzeng claimed that these atolls amounted to more than 38,000.[53] The so-called *xiaozhai zhi liu*, located in the western part of the Maldives, from the Chinese point of view, was primitive. "The inhabitants all dwell in caves; they know nothing about rice and grain, (and) they only catch fish and shrimps to eat; they do not understand wearing cloths, (and) they use the leaves of trees to cover the privates in front and behind," said Ma Huan. Fei Xin highlighted that these people "nest in trees and dwell in caves," being "naked and unclothed" with only tree-leaves to cover themselves.[54] Their words corroborated Prince Hayton's account around a century earlier in 1307, where he noted that local "inhabitants are black. They go naked by reasons of the heat, and in their folly worship idols. In these islands are found precious stones, pearls, gold, and many kinds of simples useful in medicine to the human race. In this region also is situated an island called *Celan*."[55]

"Dark skinned" and "naked" were the two points of description also recorded by these Chinese travelers, but Prince Hayton's mention of their folly in worshiping idols is interesting. He might thus have referred to the Buddhist faith. If so, by the early fourteenth century, Buddhism might still have been practicing in the southern atolls, after the general conversion of the Maldivians to Islam in the twelfth century. Meanwhile, Hayton's statement on Buddhism might have been outdated, as his ignorance of the religious change resulted from the fact that he never himself visited either India or the Maldives. He also confused local products produced in this kingdom with those in Ceylon, a persistent error, but he was correct in saying that in the Maldives there were "many kinds of simples useful in medicine," a fact that certainly made the islands attractive to the Chinese.

The discovery of the *xiaozhai zhi liu* indicates the east–west perspective adopted by the Chinese. Xie Fang points out that from east to west the Maldives consisted of two parallel lines of atolls, and the so-called *xiaozhai zhi liu* referred to western atolls that were smaller in terms of size but more numerous.[56] Bell observed that while northern and southern atolls were more fertile than central ones, the eastern atolls were better than the western.[57]

What made *Xiaozhai zhi liu* noticeable was its extreme danger for navigation, causing Ming travelers to compare it with the Ruoshui 弱水 (lit. "Weak River/Water"), a notorious and legendary river in Chinese history that was a metaphor for any unnavigable body of water. The Ruoshui had its own earliest records in the *Shanghai Jing* 山海经 (The Classic Compendium of Mountains and Seas) compiled in the final centuries of the first millennium BCE.[58] One entry states that the Ruoshui was located north of Mount Kunlun 昆仑, a legendary mountain in northwest China, and that the river was too weak to float even mustard seeds (*qili buneng shengjie* 其力不能胜芥). Generally speaking, a few instances of a river called Ruoshui have been recorded in the north, west, and northwest of China, referring to different rivers, both factual and fictional. The key feature of the Ruoshui, wherever it might have been, was that it was hostile to navigation. It was so named because even tiny and light things were unable to float on its surface, let alone human beings and ships. Indeed, in the Ming novel the *Xiyou Ji* 西游记 (Journey to the West) based on Xuanzang's story, even the Monkey King (*Sun Wukong* 孙悟空) who possessed magic superpowers, was unable to help his Master Xuanzang to cross it. Although completed in the sixteenth century, the origins of the *Xiyou Ji* can be traced back to as early as the Southern Song. The story goes that Friar Sandy (*Shaseng* 沙僧), later converted to become the third disciple of Master Xuanzang, occupied the Floating-Sand-River (*Liushahe* 流沙河), and posed a fatal barrier for Xuanzang and his two disciples, Monkey and Pigsy (*Zhu Bajie* 猪八戒), who were on their westward journey to seek Buddhist sutras in India. It mentions the four-line poem carved on a stone tablet that was erected on the bank of the river:

Eight hundred *li* of the Floating-Sand-Territory,
Three thousand *chi* deep of the Weak Water (Ruoshui);
On which even a goose feather is unable to float,
and the flower of the reed surely sinks into the bottom of the river.[59]

Therefore, by the Ming period, the stereotype of the Ruoshui had taken root as a concept in the Chinese mind. Considering its grave risks for navigation and its location west of China, it made a lot of sense for Ma Huan to claim that the rapid and strong currents near the Maldives were like the waters of the so-called Ruoshui. Following this assumption, the Chinese Ruoshui was thereafter placed in the foreign land of the Maldives in the remote Indian Ocean, so incorporating this archipelago into the Chinese conceptualization of its maritime world.

In the sixteenth century Huang Xingzeng was further amazed by the phenomenon that created so many "weak waters." The *Shanghai Jing* and other ancient books mentioned several Ruoshui, but even these knowledgeable men were unable to tell for certain one from the other, let alone identify the one in the Maldives (Liushan). "We may broaden our views, but the vastness of Heaven and Earth (*tiandi* 天地), could not be exhausted," concluded Huang.[60]

THE *SHIMEN*

Early visitors noticed how the sharp reefs posed a deadly risk for any foreign ship calling at the Maldives. First, these islets were clustered into groups, so that the water channel between any two islets was very narrow. "Each island is separated from its neighbor by a distance of a mile, or one, two, or three parasangs," claimed Al Mas'udi.[61] Ibn Battuta confirmed that these islands "are so close to each other that the tops of the palms which grow on one seem to belong to its neighbor." These islets are "small and low, through which the sea for the most part enters, the space from one to another being about a mile and a half," continued the Genoese merchant Hieronimo di Santo Stefano in 1497.

THE KINGDOM OF ATOLLS

J. de Barros probably made the best description of all how closely clustered these islands were.

> As regards their situation, though some of the larger islands are distant apart some five, ten, fifteen, or twenty leagues, the great majority are so close-set that they look like an orchard half inundated by a flood, equal parts of which are visible and concealed; and you can leap from one to another without wetting the feet, or else swing across by means of the branches of the trees.
>
> And while many of these channels are so deep as to carry very large vessels, yet are they so narrow in some places that the yards will strike the palm trees.[62]

In addition to the narrowness of openings between islands, the reefs themselves, especially the parts under the sea surface, constituted another great danger, since they were solid and sharp enough to damage a ship that crashed into them. "In the waters, there are rocky ledges with teeth as sharp as the points and edges of (weapons), which no vessel can withstand," so observed Wang Dayuan.[63]

Like many others before him, the British civil servant H. C. P. Bell was shipwrecked in the Maldives and stayed there for two or three days in 1879, probably making him one of the best-known victims in Maldivian history. Indeed, shipwrecks happened so often that Clarence Maloney once argued that it was "one of the factors contributing to the cultural complexity and civilisational growth of the country." In 1885, a Lieutenant Christopher found that the local people believed themselves to be of Sinhalese descent, their forefathers having ended up staying there after a wreck five hundred or six hundred years before them.[64]

Having said that, these natural formations simultaneously made the Maldives accessible. The channels, sandwiched on either side by rocks or islets, functioned as highways for ships. Ma Huan was greatly amazed by such a natural wonder. "In the middle of the sea there are natural stone gates (*tian sheng shimen* 天生石門), resembling gateways in a city-wall."[65] "There is in the sea a natural marvel: three stone gates resembling city gates, when looked from afar; through them ships can pass," added Fei Xin.[66]

At that time, Chinese cities were usually encircled by wall made by earthen bricks and wherever possible, gates were constructed at the four cardinal directions for transportation. The channels between two reef rocks or islets in the Maldives thus seemed a very familiar feature to these Chinese visitors, who were immediately reminded of their own city gate system. They called the entrances to these reefs/islets *shimen* 石門, "stone gate channel." To them, a waterway passing though stone gates before landing in a country looked just like a gateway that connected the inside of a Chinese city with the wild and arable land outside its walls.

Ibn Battuta had no concept of a Chinese city gate, so he simply saw the gateway functionally as an entrance to a port.[67] "A hundred or less of these islands lie together in a circle in the form of a ring: the group has an entrance as to a harbor, and ships get through by that alone." Hence, "When a ship arrives near one of these islands it must of necessity have a pilot from among its natives so that it may reach the other islands under his guidance."[68]

During his stay, Pyrard sailed among the islands often and described these channels.

> During my sojourn I was in all the *atollons*, and sailed about them with the natives. Each of these *atollons* is separated from its neighbour by a sea channel and these vary, some being narrow and some wide; but whichever they be, you cannot pass them in large ships without disaster. Albeit there are four much wider than the others, which the largest ships can pass; but even these are very dangerous, and it is hazardous to go by them, especially by night; for then you are infallibly lost, as we were, for you must meet with some shallows and reefs, which ought to be avoided.[69]

Pyrard followed Ibn Battuta's use of the word "entrance."

> For the rest, these entrances to the *atollons* vary in size. Some are broad, some narrow; the broadest is not more than two hundred paces or thereabouts; while some are hardly thirty, and even less. At each side of these entrances to each *atollon* are two islands, and you might say that they were for the very purpose of guarding the entrance; for, in fact, it would be easy with cannon to prevent ships from entering, seeing that the broadest is no more than two hundred paces.[70]

The phrase "guarding the entrance" fits well into "stone gate" and "gateway" in the Chinese context. In this sense, both the Chinese and the westerners appreciated the natural defenses the Maldives were endowed with to protect them from foreign invasions.

Although the Chinese used the term "city gate" to describe the rocks on either side of the entrance, one must bear in mind that the Maldives did not have cities or towns in this traditional period. Unlike villages that consist of the basic and fundamental communal unit for identity in most traditional societies, in the Maldives, it was the "Ra," meaning "island," that constituted the key feature for local people. There is no word for city, town, or village in the Maldivian language. Clarence Maloney pointed out that people from Male, the only urban area in the country, for example, called all the other Maldivians "islanders."[71]

Further details about these island entrances or channels are provided by Pyrard. "As for the channels, called by them *Candou*, which separate the *atollons*, four of them are navigable for large ships passing the Maldives; all sorts of foreign craft use them, but not without danger, and many are lost every year."[72] Then, one by one, he introduced the four channels that ships had no choice but to sail through.

> The first (channel) to take from the north is that at the entering in whereof we were wrecked on the reef of Malosmadou *atollon*. The second, nearer to Male, is called *Caridou*, in the midst of which is the largest of all the islands, surrounded by reefs, as I have described. The third is beyond Male, to the south, and is called *Addou*. The fourth is called *Souadou*, which is directly under the equinoctial line, and is the widest of all, being more than twenty leagues broad.[73]

Three of the four channels detailed by Pyrard were located in the northern part of the Maldives, and it is highly likely that these were the three stone gates mentioned only by Fei Xin. Wang Dayuan did not say anything about a channel or an entrance, and Ma Huan and Gong Zhen did not specify the number of stone gates; nevertheless, over time, the Chinese accumulated highly accurate information on Maldivian geography. Apart from these natural defenses, all of them were much impressed by the local winds and currents, the subject of the next chapter.

Chapter Six

MONSOONS AND CURRENTS

The following year in the spring with the southeastern wind, may the ship again proceed to the north of the island.

—WANG DAYUAN

We were obliged to stay here for six months to wait for favorable weather for our departure.

—HIERONIMO DI SANTO STEFANO

The monsoon winds have played another key natural factor that have shaped the history of the Maldives. Wang Dayuan and his fellow Chinese sailors understood their critical role in navigation, especially since he was inadvertently brought to the shores of the Maldives by a sudden change of the monsoon winds in the closing months of 1330. Back in Quanzhou, local officials had established a twice-yearly ritual tradition (usually in April and November) to pray for the punctual arrival of the seasonal winds, and evidence of this practice can be found in many stone inscriptions dating from as early as the twelfth century.

Wang Dayuan had to remain in the islands for a few months to catch the southeastern monsoon in the spring to blow him toward South India. Ma Huan and his fellows in the treasure fleet also understood the change of monsoon seasons very well. Ma Huan made a particular mention of how a good wind (*haofeng* 好风) could take a ship from Weh Island, northwest of Sumatra, to the Maldives in ten days. On the other hand, if it met with a head wind, a ship might miss the Maldives or even sink.[1]

The change of monsoon or the surprising arrival of a storm could harm the local Maldivians as much as it could the foreigners. Many locals sailing to Sri Lanka, South India, or Bengal were blown away as far eastward as Burma, the Andaman Islands, or the Nicobar Islands, known as "Minikā

Rājje" (lit. "Country of the Cannibals") in Maldives folklore. Their return journeys were even more fraught with danger, since they might be swept off course westward to the western part of the Indian Ocean or somewhere along coastal East Africa.[2] In December 1951 a Maldivian ship left Colombo, but a few squalls blew it to Providence Atoll in the Seychelles. The crew had to wait to be shipped to Aden, whence they were transferred to Cochin, from which they boarded yet another ship and finally reached home safely. This return journey from Colombo to the Maldives usually took less than a week, but instead it had taken them more than six months. Local folklore also tells the tale of how a gale took a ship with sixteen people southward to the Chagos Islands.[3] Badly damaged, the ship lost its ability to steer or sail, and they were stuck on the island. A brilliant idea struck them when they noticed some frigatebirds, and they taped an SOS message to the legs of some of them, since the birds were known to migrate annually northward to the Maldives. The people in Fua Mulaku caught frigatebirds for food, and they found the message and went to the rescue of the castaways.

The monsoons constituted a primary determining factor on activity for premodern ships whose oceangoing navigation fundamentally relied on the winds. There are two monsoon seasons in the Maldives: the northeast monsoon (*iruvai* in Dhivehi) from December to March, blowing from the east-northeast and bringing dry weather, and the southwestern monsoon (*hulhangu* in Dhivehi) from May to November, blowing from the west-northwest and bringing with it torrential rain. The two months of April and December are the transitional periods in which the wind makes its annual change. The local people invented the festival Havaru-bassavá Duvahu, an annual gathering to celebrate the advent of the southwest monsoon. H. C. P. Bell joined in the celebrations on May 6, 1922.[4] The appropriate day for this festival sometimes fell in April, depending on the arrival of the monsoon. During the festival, muffins and mats produced in five islands of Huvadhu Atoll were presented and distributed to soldiers and sailors.

In his report Bell provided a detailed introduction to the monsoons and their uneven influence on different regions of the islands. During the "winter" season, the northeast monsoon affects islands as far south as Huvadhu Atoll in January, and it is also present in Addu, forty miles south of the equator until March, while the further southern atolls are "almost beyond its influence," where winds and weather "are very irregular here, with intermittent squalls." In terms of rainfall, it is greater in the southern atolls, "with less violent winds and more equable humidity than further North." From June to August, Bell added, the southwest monsoon follows, accompanied by heavy rain storms blowing up with frequent recurrence. In the transitional period between the two monsoons, light winds prevail.[5] Light or no winds, just like violent or surprising winds, may cause problems for sailing, too.

With the two monsoon seasons determining the arrival and departure of the trading ships that visited the islands, these seasonal winds always imposed enormous pressure on sailors, especially when they were not familiar with local conditions and weather patterns. Furthermore, the change of monsoon might come earlier or later than usual, which unpredictably would pose an immediate and sometimes fatal threat. "When a ship sailing for the Western Ocean has passed near Ceylon, the set of tidal currents rapidly changes. If the ship falls in with a head wind, it is driven at once to this country," warned Wang Dayuan.[6] Unexpected squalls often caused trouble, including shipwrecks and deaths. No wonder Fonadhoo Island, less than a mile north of Male, was reserved for the ceremony of burying foreigners who had perished while in the Maldives, and this is where Bell discovered two English graves, one being that of a Captain Overend, whose demise was due to the wreck of the *Tranquebar* in 1797, and the other of the captain of HMS *Proserpine*, who drowned in 1909.[7]

When Wang Dayuan described the monsoons, he was certainly drawing from his own experience. "On the second day of the tenth month in the winter of the Gengwu 庚午, the Zhishun 至順 reign (1330–1333)," or November 22, 1330, the ship Wang Dayuan had boarded anchored at the foot of Dafoshan 大佛山 (Lit. "Big Buddha Mount," probably referring to Adam's Peak) on the west coast of Ceylon. He might well have boarded a ship that had intended to head up north to Ma'bar along the Coromandel Coast. However, the headwind (the northeast monsoon in winter) unintentionally pushed the ship toward the Maldives. Like many other foreign sailors, Wang Dayuan surely understood the changes of the monsoon. "The following year in the spring with the southeastern wind," added Wang Dayuan, "may the ship again proceed to the north of the island."[8] After a few months in the Maldives up until the spring of 1331, the southwest monsoon carried him to South India.

MONSOONS AND CURRENTS

According to the *Zheng He Hanghai Tu*, the Chinese were able to approach the Maldives either from the south and southwestern coasts of India or from Ceylon. Four routes linked Male with India and Ceylon, one route linked Fadiffolu Atoll with Ceylon, while another linked Tiladummati Atoll with Ceylon.[9] The Chinese might have reached Cochin or Kollam and then departed in the winter for the Maldives, or, like Wang Dayuan, they might have reached Ceylon before visiting the Maldives. Huang Xingzeng provided a seventh route from Bengal to the Maldives, and this route might have included a stopover in Ceylon.[10] Indeed, Yijing, writing in the seventh century, sketchily alluded to this route.[11] In 685 the Chinese Buddhist pilgrim arrived at the kingdom of Danmolidi 耽摩立底 (Tamralipta or Tamralipti), a port city along the Bay of Bengal where people sailed southeastward for the Malay Peninsula, Sri Vijaya, and Tang China, or southwestward for the Shizizhou 师子洲 (Sri Lanka). Ibn Battuta certainly took the seventh route when departing from the Maldives, and his journey took him forty-three days to reach Bengal. He must have had a few stops during that journey.[12]

THE DEATH OF SULTAN IBRAHIM II

Sailors in medieval times were often forced to stay in a place as dictated by the monsoon season. During his return voyage from Sumatra and Pegu in 1497, Hieronimo di Santo Stefano took refuge in the Maldives for half a year, complaining, "We were obliged to stay here for six months to wait for favorable weather for our departure."[13] Very interestingly, his experience was exactly what had occurred to Wang Dayuan some 167 years earlier.

The power of wind in containing or facilitating navigation is again illustrated by Bell's experience. On his second expedition to the southern atolls in 1922, it took the schooner only four days from Male to reach the lagoon of Haddhunmathi Atoll. However, the return journey took eighteen days from March 23 to April 9 and proved to be far more troublesome. The lack of wind made sailing extremely slow, and elusive currents pulled the ship backward a few miles south at night. Sometimes the schooner had to be aided by rowboats, log rafts, and various forms of guidance from the local people. On this visit, Bell had meant to travel back to Sri Lanka on the Maldivian government schooner *Mary*, which planned to reach Male from India in April or May. However, the *Mary* was pushed off course by adverse winds when sailing between Rangoon and the Maldives. The schooner was forced to "take shelter in Madras Roads, and later at Paumban," causing a delay of three months. Bell had to wait for its arrival on August 20, which in turn extended his six-month mission by two additional months. In his diary on that day, Bell wrote, "The Schooner *Mary*, much overdue, entered Male Atol, after a very protracted, and often storm-beaten, voyage from Rangoon to Madras, Paumban, &c. The vessel needs much overhauling, and cannot sail for Ceylon for about a month." At 5:00 p.m. on September 17 the *Mary* finally departed Male, but it took her four and a half days to reach Colombo. Unfortunately, on its last voyage on October 31, the *Mary* went missing, having probably foundered at sea, as had six other vessels owned by the Maldivian government in previous years.[14]

A sudden calm in the wind could cause more than just a traveler's delay. It could even be as fatal as an overwhelming storm. On February 2, 1607 (or 1609, depending on different records), a Malabar pirate fleet consisting of fourteen (or sixteen) galleys launched a raid on the Maldives. Sultan Ibrahim II (1547–1607 or 1609), the only son of Sultan Mohamed Thakurufan the Great Uteemu, the legendary hero who defeated the Portuguese and restored independence to the islands, was speared to death by a pirate's lance on February 4.[15] One may wonder why Sultan Ibrahim II did not simply escape with his royal ship, since the Maldivians were known to be good at sailing and had an unmatched familiarity with the local topography. He certainly had been warned and was planning to sail away, together with his wives and his nephew. Fatefully, however, the needed wind did not arrive. The French traveler François Pyrard might have witnessed this surprising attack and recorded the fate of the Sultan. "The cause of the taking and death of the king was that there was no wind, but the greatest calm possible, and that the enemy's galleys were better for rowing than those of the king, which were only good for sailing, and of no use for oars. Had there been but a little wind they could not have caught him; but his ill-fortune cast him into this fate."[16] As a result, the lull in wind brought about the death of Sultan Ibrahim II and the capture of his four wives, while his nephew drowned, perhaps attempting to escape from the piratical attack.

CURRENTS

Internal communication from atoll to atoll in the Maldives was dependent on the channels that lay between them. Bell highlighted the importance of

MONSOONS AND CURRENTS

these channels for internal communication. "Every enclosing atoll reef contains openings (*kandu*), which constitutes convenient 'passage' used by Maldivian boats in sailing from one atoll to another; some will admit the largest ships. Within the atolls the sea from storms, and secure lagoon anchorages is found in 20 to 40 fathoms smooth water which bottom of coral sand or mud."[17] The channels between the islands, along with the seasonal monsoons, created turbulent currents, which when combined with the sharp reefs posed another natural threat to shipping. Some channels were deep and broad, while others were shallow, narrow, and risky. As an aid to navigation and to reduce and avoid risk when entering a channel, stakes attached with palm fronds were set up in the coral reefs, functioning as a kind of lighthouse for wary ships.

Wang Dayuan only briefly mentioned the rapid change of "the set of tidal currents," and this was later corroborated by Pyrard who pointed out that "the currents, more than anything else, carry the ships out of their course during calms and contrary winds, when sails are of no avail to escape the currents."[18] "When a ship loses its bearing and the rudder is destroyed, the ship passing these *liu* drifts into ebbing waters, gradually loses its control, and sinks; (and), as a general rule, when you travel by ship it is always right to avoid these," emphasized Ma Huan.[19] Thus these foreign visitors, whether Chinese or European, were all aware of how a ship could be confounded by the combination of an unfavorable wind and rapid currents. And here we are reminded that the original meaning of the Chinese character *liu* was "rapid current(s)." The Maldivian people had their own name, *oyuarou*, for these local currents. Pyrard clearly explained the formation and danger of these currents created by the combination of channels and monsoon winds:

> They are most troubled by the currents *oyuarou*, which run now to the east, now to the west, through the island channels, and in other parts of the sea, six months one way and six months the other; and not six months for certain either way, but sometimes more and sometimes less, and this is what deceives them, and usually causes the loss of their vessels. The winds are often steady, like the currents from the east or the west; but they vary even more, and are not so regular, sometimes veering to the north or south; while the current always keeps its accustomed course until the season changes. This, as I have said, is variable and is the cause of disasters to the shipping. I shall note some instances hereafter.[20]

While there existed a seasonal pattern that would "run six months to the east and six months to the west," it sometimes became unpredictable due to the local landscape and thus posed a great challenge even for inter-atoll communication.

Simultaneously, channels and thus entrances provided natural communication portals among the atolls, so "you can go from one *atollon* to another, notwithstanding the current, at all seasons, and traffic and communicate freely, as in fact they do." However, if the two entrances "were not opposite each other, but one on towards the east and the other towards the west, you could easily get across and enter, but you could not return until after the six months were past and the current changed," warned Pyrard.[21]

Ibn Battuta shared the same concern. "When a ship arrives near one of these islands it must of necessity have a pilot from among its natives so that it may reach the other islands under his guidance. They are so close to each other that the tops of the palms which grow on one seem to belong to its neighbour. If the vessel misses its way it cannot reach the islands, and is driven by the wind to *Ma'bar* or towards Ceylon."[22] Being remarkably familiar with local life, Pyrard explained how important it was to understand the way that the currents travel from one atoll to the other.

> For each *atollon* has an opening at four places, corresponding to its two neighbours; for example, there is an opening toward the east, which is almost directly opposite the entrance to the other *atollon*: and on the western side there is another, which is likewise over against that of the neighbour on that side; so that if the current is running from east to west, you cannot cross direct from opening to opening; but in this case you set out from the eastern opening, which is the higher up the current, and over-thwarting it, enter the other *atollon* by the western opening. And so you can speedily return at all times without awaiting the change of season; but then you must set out from the eastern opening, which is opposite the one you started from, and, over-thwarting the current, make the western opening of the other *atollon*. When the current changes, and runs from west to east, you must do the opposite to what I have said: that is, set out from up the current and enter by the opening of the other *atollon*, which is down the stream, that will be towards the east.[23]

Even so, "barques and boats are very often lost, being carried out of their course by the currents, and chiefly when they are caught by calms or contrary winds on their passage; but if these openings were not where I have described them, it would be much worse, and you could not navigate from *atollon* to *atollon*."[24]

Bell's fieldwork expeditions also suffered setbacks from these currents. He observed a general rule that the currents ran eastward from June to September, and when the northeast monsoon came and struck along the west side of the islands, the currents ran westward, "strongly through the Channels as far South as the Equator; and so run till April, being thereafter variable until the S.W. Monsoon succeeds." The currents are largely dependent on winds and tides, and when going through channels between atolls, they could accumulate great strength. A three-to-four-knot current is not uncommon, Bell added, and sometimes, it could reach six and a half knots.[25] Typically, a traditional sailboat such as a Chinese junk could reach a speed of five to eight knots, although the famous clippers could sail as fast as twenty knots. Therefore, an adverse current of three to six knots would pose an almost insurmountable challenge to a ship that had no other resources or optional routes. Bell's return journey from the southern atolls to Male in 1922 faced such an awkward situation, causing the delay of his trip.

Living in the islands and communicating by boat, the Maldivian people were naturally great swimmers. "As for the men, they can swim so well that in these sea passages they always save themselves; and in truth, they are half fish, so accustomed are they to the sea, in which they pass their days, either swimming or wading or in boats," witnessed Pyrard. They were incredible navigators and geographers, too. They had "many marine charts, in which all this was very precisely laid down." Mastering local landscapes, the Maldivian people knew how and when to avoid reefs, shoals, rocks, currents, or winds, even when the channels were so narrow to pass only one boat. Pyrard manifested his great fear while in a boat "of not more than four arm-lengths, in a sea towering above me two pikes high, more stormy and swollen than ever was," which caused his host to laugh heartily.[26]

There were numerous boats in the Maldives, both large and small. Even the poorest person had his own boat, while a rich one might be the owner of a whole fleet. Expert as these sailors were, Pyrard noted their native caution: "They never navigate by night, wherefore they fetch land every evening; they steer only by eyesight and without compass, except when they go beyond their own islands on a long voyage. . . . If they made the least mistake in the world, their barque would be upset and their merchandise lost."[27]

Chapter Seven

BETWEEN THE SON OF HEAVEN AND THE SULTAN

> In the tenth year of the Yongle reign, Zheng He was dispatched to this kingdom. In the fourteenth year, its king, *Yisufu* 亦速福 sent his tributary envoys. After that, three tributary missions arrived together with those from *Hulumosi* 忽鲁谟斯 (Ormuz) and other kingdoms. In the fifth year of the Xuande 宣德 reign, Zheng He was dispatched to it again, but thereafter no more tributary mission arrived from it.
>
> —THE *MING SHI*

Wang Dayuan was the first recorded Chinese traveler to land in the Maldives, but the official relationship between the island sultanate and the Chinese empire was not established until the early fourteenth century, when the Zheng He treasure fleet made seven great voyages to the Indian Ocean. It was Zheng He who established the direct interactions between the Son of Heaven and the sultan of the Maldives for the first time, or the so-called tributary relationship between Ming China and the Maldives in the Chinese context.

Did the Zheng He voyages ever visit the Maldives? If so, which voyage, and how many times? For the first question the answer is positive. Ma Huan clearly stated that "One or two treasure ships of *Zhongguo* 中国 (the Middle Kingdom) went there, too, where they purchased ambergris, coconuts, and other goods."[1] According to the *Ming Shi*, Liushan was on the list of the thirty-eight places that the Zheng He fleet visited.[2]

The second question proves to be a difficult one to answer. Owing to the lack of firsthand documents produced on the Zheng He voyages and the vagueness of other Ming sources, it is difficult to conjecture on which voyage(s) the Maldives was included. In 1967, Su Chung-jen stated that four of the seven voyages (1405–1407, 1413–1415, 1417–1419, and 1431–1433) visited the Maldives, while Mills referred to three: 1413–1415, 1417–1419, and

1421–1422.³ Roderich Ptak has scrutinized all the Ming sources and provided a comprehensive analysis. As for the first voyage (1405–1407), only one late source claims that the Maldives was visited on that trip. No historical account has ever mentioned any visit on the second voyage (1407–1409). As for the third (1409–1411), Fei Xin joined this mission and his *Xingcha Shenglan* described the Maldives, but the itinerary of the voyage did not mention the Maldives, so there is "no sufficient proof for a Chinese visit." As for the fourth voyage (1413–1415), Ma Huan joined that one and mentioned that one or two treasure ships went to the Maldives, so the treasure fleet assuredly visited the Maldives, and this is supported by other Ming sources. As for the fifth voyage (1417–1419), Zheng He was ordered to escort foreign envoys including one from Liushan (the Maldives) to their home countries, so the treasure fleet might have taken the Maldivian ambassador back to Male, or at least to Ceylon or southern India. A similar situation occurred for the sixth one (1421–1422), when Zheng He was again ordered to ship home envoys from Southeast Asia and the Indian Ocean including the Maldivians. Ma Huan was on that voyage, and the Maldivian ambassador might then have plied the same journey as on the fifth one. As for the final voyage (1431–1433), Ma Huan and Gong Zhen joined this trip, and official Chinese archives all stated that the treasure fleet was sent to the Maldives on a "side mission," with a couple of the ships from the main fleet possibly visiting the islands.⁴

While the analysis above only manages to confirm that the Chinese fleet unquestionably visited the Maldives on its fourth voyage, given the fact that the Maldives sent three tributary missions to China, in 1416, 1421, and 1423, respectively (namely, after the fourth, fifth, and sixth voyages), Ptak has reckoned that "some Chinese diplomats must have been in touch with the Male government during these expeditions, either on the spot or, say, in Southern India or Sri Lanka, places reasonably close to the islands." "Chances that Chinese ships called at the Maldives during the first three of Cheng Ho's journeys are small; they were more likely visited in the course of the fifth, sixth, and seventh voyages, and definitely during the fourth," Ptak concluded.⁵

Meanwhile, while both the fifth and the sixth voyages brought the Maldivian tributary missions to the Ming court, the seventh did not. It is unimaginable that any sultan of the Maldives would turn down a Ming invitation had one or two ships of the treasure fleet anchored in his kingdom. After all, the Ming envoys were eager to be the ones to introduce foreign ambassadors during an audience with Emperor Xuande (r. 1426–1435), who had recently ascended the throne. Therefore, it is reasonable to suppose that Zheng He's last voyage did not land in the Maldives. Nonetheless, the *Ming Shilu* does record that the Maldives was among the foreign countries and that Zheng He was ordered to visit and present gifts to their king on the seventh voyage.[6] The *Ming Shi* also states that Zheng He was again dispatched to this country (*fushi qiguo* 复使其国).[7] Might it be remotely possible that Zheng He requested that a king of Ceylon or the head of some other southern Indian kingdom, or even some merchants, pass the Ming gifts on to the Maldivian sultan?

SHERDS OF CHINESE PORCELAINS

Hundreds of sherds, broken pieces of Chinese porcelain, that were still widely available in the 1970s are probably the only footprint left of the Sino-Maldivian interactions from the Song period onward, both directly and indirectly. In the collection of items from the Maldives sold by Andrew Forbes in conjunction with Fawzia Ali to the British Museum in 1981, there are four pieces of Chinese porcelain, two of which are obviously the so-called blue and white porcelain. Based on its floral pattern but particularly from the type of blue glaze, the first one, as observed and judged by Chen Ye, a porcelain expert and friend of mine, is dated to the end of the Yuan to the early Ming.[8] This piece, labeled as a potsherd, was certainly the bottom part of a blue and white bowl, and is likely a legacy of the Zheng He treasure fleet. Another blue and white sherd also dates from the early Ming period. Whether these porcelain sherds were once the porcelainware carried by the Zheng He treasure fleet forever remains a puzzle.[9]

Recently archaeological fieldwork on the island of Kinolhas (Raa Atoll) has unearthed 237 Chinese sherds. Among these is one blue and white sherd dated to the fourteenth century, belonging to the recently coined Yuan Qinghua 元青花 (Blue-White Porcelain of the Yuan Period), exclusively made for the court and elites in the Yuan dynasty.[10] This piece of Yuan Qinghua corroborates the records of Wang Dayuan and Yuan official envoys and is a tiny piece of evidence that points to the intensive exchange between the Mongols and the Indian Ocean through maritime Asia.

Another single sherd produced in the official kiln for the court and elites was unearthed from Kinolhas and it is highly likely to have been part of a porcelain item carried by the Zheng He fleet. This sherd, "hard, smooth, white, and pure" and thus of a very fine quality, is covered with an evenly applied transparent glaze with a very slight grayish-white shade. On the outer glaze, it is incised with a very thin and fine pattern called *anhua* 暗花 (secret decoration) that is "only visible when held up to the light." Scholars have coined this type of white porcelain *tianbai* 甜白 (lit. "sweet-white") because the glaze reminds people of a thin layer of icing sugar, a type most famously made in the reign of Yongle (1402–1424). A stem cup of *tianbai* can be seen in the British Museum, marked with a four-character-seal-script *Yongle nian zhi* 永乐年制 (lit. "made in the Yongle years").[11] This *tianbai* sherd was produced in the same period and most likely belonged to a set of imperial drinking vessels. Imperial porcelain was a privileged luxury during the Ming-Qing period, and commoners were forbidden to use it. Considering all these factors, this sherd might have been part of a container gifted by Emperor Yongle, the Chinese Son of Heaven, to a certain Maldivian envoy or probably meant for the sultan himself. As such, this piece remains the only palpable evidence of the forgotten history of royal interactions between the Maldives and Ming China.

Discoveries of Chinese porcelain sherds indeed throw fresh light on the framework of Sino-Maldivian interactions. More than six hundred Chinese potsherds discovered by Carswell in his 1974 visit of Male that date from the late Song period (960–1279) to the Ming period (1368–1644) or later, fit well overall in the exchange framework, but the recent Kinolhas project has provided a contesting trajectory with what I have attempted to reconstruct.[12] Apart from the Longquan celadon dated to the Yuan period of the fourteenth century (bearing in mind that the Yuan merchant Wang Dayuan once stayed in the Maldives), the fifteenth-century Chinese ceramics discovered in Kinolhas remain minimal, in sharp contrast with the frequency of findings of ceramics from the Zheng He voyages.[13] Even more surprisingly, there were "unusually common" discoveries of blue-white porcelain on Kinolhas that date to the sixteenth-seventeenth centuries, the post–Zheng He period when the official relationship between China and Indian Ocean kingdoms had ended. It is highly likely that these Ming ceramics reached the Maldives through transit trade via Southeast Asian, South Asian, and European agents. Of course, it is no surprise that Chinese ceramics disappeared after the seventeenth century, when direct connections between China and the Indian Ocean had ceased.

Whatever the case, the textual evidence here supports the conclusion that the Zheng He fleet visited the Maldives on the fourth and seventh voyages and indicates that the Chinese fleet might also have visited the islands during the fifth and sixth voyages, while archaeological findings supply evidence of the arrival of imperial gifts from Ming court. But another tough question raises its head here: Who from the Chinese Fleet actually landed in the Maldives?

THE MING ENVOYS WHO LANDED IN THE MALDIVES

Did Zheng He himself, admiral of the Chinese treasure fleet, land in the Maldives? It is highly possible, since it looks as if the fleet possibly visited the island sultanate on four occasions. Meanwhile, it is hard to confirm if the Chinese eunuch did so, since no direct evidence exists.

However, based on the works by Ma Huan and his fellow travelers, it is fairly evident that Ma Huan himself visited the Maldives. Ma Huan was present on three voyages altogether, the fourth one, during which the Chinese landed in the Maldives, and the last two (the sixth and seventh), on which it is highly probable that the Chinese visited the Maldives. As an interpreter, Ma Huan might have been asked to accompany the Chinese envoys on their first visit, and that is why Ma Huan was able to provide a very detailed account of this island sultanate. His mention of the treasure fleet's calling at the Maldives is the only direct extant evidence of the Chinese visit, and the account suggests that he had visited the islands himself as it shows that he was very familiar with the Chinese agenda there.

Did Fei Xin ever set foot in the Maldives? It seems that his description largely copied Ma Huan's details, but he did make his own contribution. First, he stated that three stone gates were erected there. Ma Huan had noticed a stone gate but failed to mention how many there were. Therefore, it is reasonable to deduce that Fei Xin had in fact landed and remained in the Maldives for some days. Furthermore, Fei Xin noticed one local product that Ma Huan had missed, and that was frankincense. In addition, while Fei Xin emphasized that local people did not plant rice or any other grain, he stated that rice and grains (*migu* 米谷) together with porcelain (*ciqi* 磁器), colorful satins (*seduan* 色段), colorful silks (*sejuan* 色绢), gold, and silver were used in transactions, none of these mentioned by Ma Huan.[14] In one edition of his *Xingcha Shenglan* Fei Xin stated that the chiefs in the Maldives often presented local goods to Ming China.[15] Finally, in his own preface, Fei Xin wrote that from the reign of Yongle to that of Xuande he himself had participated in four voyages.[16] Therefore, in addition to his first voyage (1409–1411), Fei Xin must have joined the last voyage (1431–1433) and two other voyages: the fourth, fifth, or sixth. As Ptak concluded, all Fei Xin's last three voyages most likely took him to the Maldives.[17] All these clues, whether circumstantial or not, seem to lead to the conclusion that Fei Xin must have set foot in the Maldives.

But it is surprising that Fei Xin omitted the mention of other such obvious local products as cowrie shells, dried fish, and coconuts. Was he trying to relate some fresh detail to distinguish himself from Ma Huan? Possibly. Nonetheless, it is impossible for anyone who visited the Maldives at that time to overlook the presence of quantities of cowrie shells or dried fish, all mentioned by all other medieval travelers. Fei Xin did in fact answer the question of whether he had visited the Maldives. His *Xingcha Shenglan* was divided into two parts, the first part listing the places he had witnessed (*mushi zhi suozhi* 目识之所至), while the second was based on his interpretations of what he had been told (*chuanyi* 传译).[18] Liuyangguo, or the Maldives, was placed in the second part. Therefore, Fei Xin himself acknowledged that he had not visited the Maldives, although part of the fleet most likely called at the Maldives on the voyages that Fei Xin joined.

Gong Zhen joined the final voyage. Originally a soldier, Gong Zhen was promoted to secretary, which shows that he must have been relatively well educated.[19] His work was long missing from historical records and was rediscovered and publicized only in the 1950s. To our disappointment, his *Xiyang Fanguo Zhi* remains a literal, word-for-word copy of the *Yingya Shenglan*, possibly because of his limited participation in the Chinese expedition. So that is the case of Gong Zhen's entry on *Liushan guo*: it is no different from that of Ma Huan.[20] While it remains unknown whether or not Gong Zhen himself landed on this island kingdom, I tend to believe that he did not. No direct evidence supports or indicates any visit.

Apart than the Chinese texts, no Maldivian records ever mention the visits of the Chinese fleets, and even the maritime archaeology of the Maldives only provides a brief glimpse of the Chinese commercial involvement in these islands. Michael Feener has shared his concerns about maritime archaeological findings and goes some way to explaining the lack of evidence. If a ship were wrecked on the outside of a reef, it could sink to a very great depth, but if it sank inside the reef then it would typically be picked clean by order of the king, and this was a well-established custom for most of the recorded historical period.[21]

Certainly we have Chinese ceramics of almost all kinds, such as Longquan celadon and the blue-white porcelain, dated to the first and second millennium CE, which has been discovered in the Maldives. In the Kuruhinna Tharaagadu Ceramic Assemblage, the Chinese ceramics ware "were all serving vessels," and "formed the largest portion of the sample," dating from the twelfth to the seventeenth centuries. In addition to chinaware, a Chinese bronze coin was also discovered, dating to the beginning of the Northern Song period (the closing years of the tenth century).[22] It is highly likely that this coin was brought there by a Southeast Asian merchant, but we cannot exclude a Chinese or an Indian one.

THE ITINERARY OF THE SEVENTH VOYAGE (1431–1433)

Chinese sources are generally silent about the itinerary of the treasure fleet, except for the seventh voyage. Zhu Yunming 祝允明 (1460–1526), a native of Suzhou and an extraordinarily talented painter and calligrapher, retained one piece of detailed information in his *Qianwenji* 前闻记 (A Record of What Has Been Heard) that relates to the last voyage about the number of people involved, the names of the ships, and particularly the itinerary.[23]

The treasure fleet involved 27,550 people, including officers, soldiers, pilots, sailors, chefs, secretaries, interpreters, dealers, accountants, physicians, all kinds of smiths, and others.[24] Although the fleet left Nanjing on the sixth day of the twelfth month of the fifth year of the Xuande reign (January 19, 1431) and arrived at Changle 长乐 Port, Fujian, on the twenty-sixth day of the second month in the sixth year of the Xuande reign (April 8, 1431), it remained in the latter port to await the northeastern monsoon. On the twelfth day of the eleventh month (December 16, 1431) the fleet departed, passing Mount Fudou (*Fudoushan* 福斗山) near Fuzhou, and on the ninth day of the twelfth month (January 12, 1432) it sailed through the Five-Tiger Gate (*Wuhumen* 五虎门) located at the entrance of the Min River, and embarked on its ocean-going journey.[25] Table 7.1 briefly summarizes the itinerary of Zheng He's seventh voyage.

A DESTINATION

TABLE 7.1
The itinerary of Zheng He's seventh voyage (1431-1433)

Port/kingdom	Arrival date (d/m/y)	Departure date (d/m/y)	Days spent
Fudou Mount		16/12/1431	
Wuhumen		12/01/1432	
Qui Nhon, Champa	27/01/1432	12/02/1432	16 days
Java	07/03/1432	13/07/1432	25 days
Palembang	24/07/1432	27/07/1432	11 days
Malacca	03/08/1432	02/09/1432	7 days
Samudra	12/09/1432	02/11/1432	10 days
Ceylon	28/11/1432	02/12/1432	36 days
Calicut	10/12/1432	14/12/1432	9 days
Ormuz	17/01/1433	09/03/1433	35 days
Calicut	31/03/1433	09/04/1433	23 days
Semudera	25/04/1433	01/05/1433	17 days
Malacca	09/05/1433		9 days
Kunlun Ocean (Condore Island)	28/05/1433		
Chikan (Ke Ga Point)	10/06/1433		
Qui Nhon, Champa	13/06/1433	17/06/1433	
Wailuo Mount (Culao Re)	19/06/1433		
Nanao Island (near Shantou, Guangdong)	25/06/1433		

Source: Zhu Yungming, "Qianwenji Xiaxiyang" (Down to the West Ocean in Record of What Has Been Heard), in Gong Zhen, *Xiyang Fanguo Zhi* (A Record of Foreign Kingdoms in the Western Ocean), ed. Xiang Da (Beijing: Zhonghua Shuju, 2000), 55–57; Ma Huan, *Ying-yai sheng-lan: "The Overall Survey of the Ocean's Shores,"* [1433]; translated from the Chinese text edited by Feng Ch'eng-chün with introduction, notes, and appendices by J. V. G. Mills (London: Hakluyt Society, 1970), 14–19.

Soon afterward the treasure fleet passed by Champa, directly crossed the South China Sea to Java, moved westward through the Malacca Strait, sailed across the Bay of Bengal to Ceylon, reached Calicut in South India on December 10, 1432, and then Ormuz in the Persian Gulf on January 17, 1433.[26] So as to catch the winter monsoon from the north, the fleet did not linger long in Ormuz. Departing from the Persian Gulf on March 9, 1433, its return journey was simply the reverse of the outgoing voyage.

A few more places along the Vietnam and South China coasts appeared in the return journey in Zhu Yunming's note. Nan'ao 南澳 Island was located along the Guangdong-Fujian border, and the treasure fleet continued to sail north through the Taiwan Strait.[27] On July 7, 1433, it reached Taicang 太倉, a port base at the entrance of the Yangzi River. From Taicang, one could take a ship through the Yangzi River to Nanjing, the southern capital of Ming China. Indeed, imperial envoys arrived in Beijing on July 22, 1433 (which must have been an extremely tight journey from Nanjing to Beijing), officially ending China's last voyage to the Indian Ocean.

Obviously Zhu Yunming copied this entry from some official archive or document, and he even confessed that he had omitted some lengthy details from the original text. Other sources, such as those by Ma Huan, Fei Xin, and Gong Zhen, as well as the biography of Zheng He in the *Ming Shi*, provide supplementary and sometimes key information.[28]

First, the seventh voyage visited many more polities/ports than the eight mentioned by Zhu Yunming. For example, Fei Xin recorded that due to a storm on November 15, 1432 (the twenty-third day of the tenth month), the fleet was forced to anchor in the Nicobar Islands (*Cuilanyu* 翠蓝屿) for three days and nights (November 15–17, 1432).[29] He witnessed the welcoming party of the barely clad local people, in their canoes, who came to sell coconuts. Liushan was on the list of over twenty kingdoms that were visited in the *Ming Shilu*, together with Dhofar, Lasa, Mogadishu, and Brava.[30] It seems that Zheng He had dispatched a few smaller fleets to visit various other ports while the main fleet followed the route described by Zhu Yunming. One of the subfleets, speculated Paul Eugène Pelliot, was led by eunuch Hong Bao 洪保 and was joined by Ma Huan, sailing from Sumatra directly to Bengal.[31]

Second, the treasure fleet stayed in Java, Malacca, and Semudera for at least a few weeks each time. The fleet was in Java for more than four months while waiting to catch a favorable wind to sail through the Malacca Strait, and meanwhile, branch ships were dispatched to various ports along the coasts of Java and other islands. The one-month stay in Malacca was due to a Ming depot being established at the strategic port that controlled the strait, with another depot set up in Semudera. These official depots served as bases for the Ming expeditions to the Indian Ocean.

Here is another question: If the seventh voyage did visit the Maldives, when exactly during the outward and homeward voyages did it do that? According to Zhu Yunming, the fleet called at Ceylon on November 28, 1432, and departed for Calicut on December 2, 1432. If the imperial envoys had gone to the island kingdom and granted gifts from the Son of Heaven to the sultan, it must have taken place after the visit to Ceylon. A few treasure ships might have sailed from Ceylon to the Maldives on or soon after December 2, 1432. Indeed, 102 years earlier, Wang Dayuan had taken the same route from Ceylon to the Maldives in almost the same month.

It seems highly unlikely that the seventh voyage visited the Maldives on its return journey. Its return journey was a hurried one, since Zheng He's body had to be conveyed back home for the necessary funeral rites. The fleet had to rush to catch the monsoon winds, sailing straight across the Indian Ocean to Sumatra. It took less than four months from Ormuz for the fleet to reach Taicang at the entrance of the Yangzi River, and it does not seem likely that there would have been time or inclination for a subfleet to have been dispatched to the Maldives during that voyage.

THE MALDIVIAN TRIBUTES TO THE MING COURT

The *Ming Shi*, which was compiled by the Qing official scholars, stated that in 1416 King Yisufu of the Maldives sent his envoys to China, and that after 1416 three more tributary missions arrived, together with those from Ormuz (*Hulumosi* 忽鲁谟斯) and other kingdoms.[32] Therefore, according to the *Ming Shi*, at least four tributary missions were sent by the Maldivian kings to Ming China. However, the king of the Maldives from 1411–1412 to 1419–1420 was Ibrahim, and this name hardly accords with that in the Chinese records, while King Yusub (r. 1420/21–1442/43) seems to fit better, at least in terms of pronunciation.[33] Could there have been a bureaucratic error in that Yusub had sent the 1421 and 1423 missions to Ming China so that Ming sources wrongly assumed that the 1416 mission had been sent by the same king?

In addition, another tributary mission from the Maldives was recorded either in the Hongwu reign (1368–1399) or in 1407 during the Yongle reign. At the end of the sixteenth century, Luo Yuejiong 罗日褧 in his *Xianbin Lu* 咸宾录 (A Record of All Guests) claimed that the Maldives (Liushan) had sent a mission to China during the Hongwu reign,[34] which was too early to have been correct. Huang Xingzeng recorded a Maldivian envoy in the fifth year of the Yongle reign (1407).[35] This again, as the only source, seems doubtful. Indeed, the exact number of Maldivian missions to Ming China is worth discussing. The *Ming Shilu*, the firsthand Ming archives, mentioned the Maldives six times, and all these were related to the Zheng He voyages, thus helping to clarify and determine the mission issue.

In 1412 Zheng He was commanded to visit the Maldives, along with Malacca, Java, Champa, Semudera, Aru, Cochin, Calicut, Lambri, Ormuz, and other places, offering silk and other gracious gifts to the rulers of these lands.³⁶ In 1416 Emperor Yongle had an audience with the ambassadors from the Maldives, Malacca, Calicut, Java, Champa, Ceylon, Mogadishu, Lambri, Brava, Ormuz, Cochin, Pahang, and the Palembang Pacification Commission, among others, with a banquet promptly prepared for them.³⁷ Most of these ambassadors, if not all, must have been conveyed to China on the fourth voyage (1413–1415) and were later escorted back home on the fifth voyage (1417–1419). They arrived in China before September 1415 at the end of the southeastern monsoon and had stayed in China for over a year before this farewell party. During their long stay, much must have been done to please the Son of Heaven. While the guests were well treated, they would have been trained to perform all kinds of rituals appropriate to appearing before the emperor, while their Chinese hosts busied themselves drafting and translating official documents into a tributary language, which must have proved a long and exhausting process. This was the first Maldivian mission to the Ming court.

One month after the farewell banquet, on the tenth day of the twelfth month, the fourteenth year of the Yongle reign (1416), Emperor Yongle ordered Zheng He to escort these ambassadors back to their own countries.³⁸ The fifth voyage proved a major initiative of Ming China in the Indian Ocean. In addition to the routine gifts to all the kings of these countries, Cochin was singled out because the Ming conferred a seal upon its king and honored a mountain in Cochin with the title of "Protecting-Country-Mountain" (*zhenguo zhi shan* 镇国之山). A stone tablet was provided on which a proclamation, composed by Emperor Yongle himself, was inscribed. It seems that the Ming state might have intended to develop Cochin into its alliance or base on the southwestern coast of India.³⁹

On the twenty-fifth day of the first month in the nineteenth year of the Yongle reign (1421), the envoys from sixteen kingdoms including the Maldives, Ormuz, Aden, Dhofar, Mogadishu, Calicut, Ceylon, Lambri, Semudera, Aru, and Malacca presented themselves before the emperor, offering prized local artifacts such as excellent horses. Emperor Yongle ordered the Ministry of Ritual to treat them to a banquet.⁴⁰ These envoys are known to have arrived between the fifth voyage (1417–1419) and the sixth (1421–1422), and it is highly likely that they were invited to travel to China on the fifth voyage. If they had been in Zheng He's fleet, they must have reached China in 1419. This was the second Maldivian mission to the Ming court.

On the twentieth day of the ninth month in the twenty-first year of the Yongle reign (1423), the Maldives and fifteen other kingdoms again sent some 1,200 people as members of tributary to Beijing.[41] The Ministry of Ritual provided a banquet and routine gifts, the envoys brought with them exotic and prized local products from their home countries, and in turn they were recompensed with Chinese paper money (chao 钞).[42] As on previous voyages, the envoy parties were collectively invited and conveyed to China on the sixth voyage (1421–1422). This was the third Maldivian mission to the Ming court.

On the ninth day of the sixth month in the fifth year of the Xuande reign (1430), Emperor Xuande announced that he would send Zheng He and Wang Jinghong 王景弘 on another expedition. All kinds of gifts would be presented to the kings of more than twenty countries, including the Maldives, Ormuz, Cochin, Calicut, Ceylon, and Malacca.[43] In 1431 Zheng He began his seventh and last visit to the Indian Ocean. However, while the last voyage might have included the Maldives, it did not bring the Maldivian mission back to Beijing.

In 1433, Semudera, Calicut, Cochin, Ceylon, Dhofar, Aden, Ormuz, Mecca, and other kingdoms all duly sent their tributary missions, but the Maldives was noticeably not on the list. Perhaps the court historian omitted the Maldives by mistake? This is highly unlikely, since the *Ming Shilu* explicitly provided the names of all the other kings and their ambassadors. Nineteen days later all these envoys were granted with gifts, and again the Maldives was not mentioned here either.[44] It is safe to conclude that the Maldives did not send its envoy to the Ming court on that occasion.

The *Gujin Tushu Jicheng* 古今图书集成 (Complete Collection of Illustrations and Writings from the Earliest to Current Times), a massive imperial encyclopedic work begun in 1700 and completed in 1725, cited the *Guangdong Tongzhi* 广东通志 (Provincial Gazetteer of Guangdong), whence it gleaned that in 1445 the king of Liushan had dispatched his envoy Yebala Modeliya 耶巴剌谟的里哑 (?Abd al Muttīʻ) to the Chinese court to present the emperor with local Maldivian products, and that in 1459, Gelishengxialaxilibajiaola 葛力生夏剌昔利把交剌 (?Ghaisullah Inayatullah), the king of Liushan once again dispatched his envoys to China.[45] His name is not found in the list of Maldivian kings, nor was mention of the two envoys seen in any other Chinese source.[46] It is highly likely that the two self-claimed envoys might have been merchants from the Indian Ocean wishing to obtain official Chinese endorsement for their commercial activities, a popular (mal)practice in the Chinese tributary context.

In sum, the *Ming Shilu* provides an insightful and a more informative glimpse into the official exchanges between Ming China and the Maldives Kingdom. Three tributary missions (instead of the four claimed by the *Ming Shi*) dispatched by the Maldives safely arrived in Beijing or Nanjing, and all three visits were certainly sought for and arranged by Zheng He. The first mission was brought to China in 1415 on the return trip of Zheng He's fourth expedition and the envoys were in Nanjing in 1416. The second came to China in 1419 on Zheng He's fifth return voyage, and the envoys were in Nanjing in 1421. The third arrived in China in 1422 with Zheng He's sixth voyage, and the envoys were in Beijing in 1423. Roderich Ptak has confirmed these three missions.[47] While authors of the *Ming Shi* must have erred in claiming three subsequent tributary missions from the Maldives after 1416, they correctly pointed out that the Maldives did not participate or were not invited to participate in Zheng He's last voyage.[48]

Internal power struggles in the Maldives might account for their reluctance to send tributes to Ming China on that last voyage. During the Zheng He period, the Maldives witnessed a frequent change of kings, which might have been one reason why the island kingdom, flooded with internal political strife, had no time or energy left to focus on furthering the Sino-Maldivian relationship.

Located in the Persian Gulf, Ormuz was further from China than the Maldives. According to the *Ming Shi*, the three post-1416 missions from the Maldives came to China together with the envoys from Ormuz.[49] It is also true that emissaries from both Ormuz and the Maldives joined the fifth and sixth voyages to Ming China. However, while the Maldives did not send its envoys to Beijing in 1433, Ormuz did. In addition, even after the end of the Zheng He expeditions, Ormuz continued to send its missions to Ming China.

In 1436 Emperor Yingzong 英宗 (1436–1449 and 1457–1464) returned to their kingdoms the eleven envoys from Calicut, Semudera, Ceylon, Cochin, Mecca, Aden, Ormuz, Dhofar, Zhenla, and other states.[50] The edict stated that their arrival occurred in the Xuande reign (1426–1435), meaning that these visitors were certainly escorted to China on the return leg of the seventh voyage. This is further proof that the Maldives did not dispatch its tributary mission in 1433.

TABLE 7.2
The kings of the Maldives during the Zheng He voyages (1405–1433)

Reign	King	Duration of reign
1397–1409	-S. Husain I	10 years
1408–1411	-S. Nsr-ud-din	3 years
1410–1412	-S. Hasan II	9 months
1411–1412	-S. Isa	3 months
1411–1420	-.S. Ibrahim I	8 years and 9 months
1419–1421	-S.'Usman II	3 months
1420–1421	-S. Danna Muhammad	11 months
1420–1443	-S.Yusud II	23 years

Source: H. C. P. Bell, *The Maldive Islands: Monograph on the History, Archaeology and Epigraph* (Colombo: Ceylon Government Press, 1940), 22–23. This table, however, is not conclusive. The list of kings in "Timelines of Maldives History" is slightly different, while its frequent changes of reigns also indicate the intensive power struggle during the period discussed. "Timelines of Maldives History," https://maritimeasiaheritage.cseas.kyoto-u.ac.jp/wp-content/uploads/2021/03/Maldives-Timeline-MHS.pdf, 4–5.

In 1442, Sultan Tūrānshāh (*Sulutan Tulansha* 速魯檀土兰沙) of Ormuz sent his ambassador Hājj ʿAli (*Hazhi Ali* 哈只阿里) to the Ming court, where he presented such prized local commodities as horses and asked for permission to resume the routine tribute as had been proffered in the past, but Emperor Yingzong politely declined this appeal.[51] This was the last mention of the sultanate of Ormuz in the *Ming Shilu*.

From this note we can conclude that Ormuz was more zealous than the Maldives in wanting to establish a formal relationship with the Ming Dynasty. Compared with the Maldives, Ormuz sent more missions to China during and even after the Zheng He voyages. This was probably because the Ming court was a profitable market for Ormuz in the horse trade.[52] As Ma Huan noted, Ormuz was famous for its horses, and the Ming court always listed horses as one of its most desired tributary goods, often paying a handsome price to acquire them, indeed, with a much higher profit than Ormuz traders would have gained in the horse trading markets closer to home. By contrast, the Maldives seemed less interested, both politically and commercially, to develop its relationship with Ming China. After all, China was not special, since there existed a seemingly insatiable demand from the rest of the international world for its goods such as cowrie shells, dried fish, and coir rope.

With the closing of the Zheng He voyages, the Chinese no longer visited the Maldives, the Chinese connections withered, and the Chinese influence died out. China again became a far-off place. Today, one notable legacy of the Chinese cultural influence on the Maldives seems to be the term for "China," which is "Sīnu Kara" from the Devehi language, included on the list of foreign places known to the inhabitants of the Maldives of yesteryear.[53] This, interestingly, reflects the asymmetrical relationship between the Maldives and China. While Chinese influence was voluminous, abrupt, and aggressive, its legacy in the Maldives proved to be fleeting and evaporating, unable to last long after the retreat of the Chinese emissaries, yet the Maldivian influence in China was slow and less perceptible, but longer lasting, and helped to shape the formation and development of imperial China over the course of more than three thousand years. In chapter 10 we will examine the basis for this grand claim.

PART III
The Cargo

Chapter Eight

THE TREES OF THE MALDIVES

> Coconuts are very abundant; people come from every place to purchase them, and go to other countries to sell them as merchandise.
>
> —MA HUAN

> From the fruit are obtained milk, oil, and honey.
>
> —IBN BATTUTA

From his Indian informants, Xuanzang heard that there was a kingdom called Naluojiluo, literally meaning "the kingdom of coconut trees" where people were short, "do not have any grain, and only rely on coconuts."[1] This piece of hearsay would be confirmed and detailed by later Chinese visitors such as Ma Huan. Wang Dayuan noted the production and export of coir rope in the Maldives, but for some reason, he had no words to spare for coconut trees, though all other visitors mentioned these prominent features of the Maldives.

Ma Huan observed that coconut trees were a key part of the local landscape and an important resource for living. While also depending on fishing, the local people "plant coconut-trees for a living," and even Chinese treasure ships visiting the Maldives purchased coconuts. "Coconuts are very abundant; people come from every place to purchase them, and go to other countries to sell them as merchandise. They have a kind of coconut with a small-shaped shell, which the people there convert into wine-cups; they make the feet of rose-wood, and varnish the mouth and feet with foreign vanish; they are most uncommon." Ma Huan also mentioned that the fiber from coconut shells was made into rope, which was another much sought-after product exported from the Maldives.[2] (This rope production will be discussed in chapter 9.)

The fruit of the coconut trees was attractive to maritime people because it proved to be a convenient supplier of fresh water for sailors. Compared with fresh water, which required containers to carry it, coconuts enjoyed a lot of advantages. They could be tucked into any small corner of the ship, a most treasured feature considering the precious space of shipload, could be stored much longer and more hygienically than fresh water, and tasted pleasant when served as a kind of food. In addition, the shells served many other functions on a long voyage. That is why foreign ships including Chinese ones purchased a load of coconuts before their departure from the Maldives. No wonder coconut shells and even whole coconuts were found on *Quanzhou I* in the Bay of Quanzhou.[3]

While the plantation of coconut trees, the harvest of the coconuts, wine cups made from coconut shells, and coir rope were observed in the Maldives, their significance was only later elaborated upon by Ma Huan in his introduction to *Guli* (Calicut). In Calicut:

> Wealthy families mostly cultivate coconut trees—sometimes a thousand trees, sometimes two thousand or three thousand—; this constitutes their property. The coconut has ten different uses. The young tree has a syrup, very sweet, and good to drink; it can be made into wine by fermentation. The old coconut has flesh, from which they express oil, and make sugar, and make a foodstuff for eating. From the fibre which envelops the outside (of the nut) they make ropes for ship building. The shells of the coconut make bowls and cups; they are also good for burning to ash for the delicate operation of inlaying gold or silver. The trees are good for building houses, and the leaves are good for roofing houses.[4]

In Ceylon, Ma Huan noted, "the coconut is very abundant. Oil, sugar, and wine are all manufactured from this article for human consumption."[5] Hence, in addition to serving as the fundamental source of food, coconut trees were widely utilized in local societies, especially for the making of ships and houses. Thus, coconut trees provided three of the four basic necessities required by the Chinese travelers: clothing, eating, living, and transportation (*yishizhuxing* 衣食住行).

As Ma Huan described, almost all parts of the coconut tree were skillfully utilized in Calicut and Ceylon, and this surely must have been true of the

Maldives and elsewhere. Wang Dayuan noted abundant coconut plantations in Southeast Asia and South Asia, and many societies such as those in Pahang, Palembang, and Ma'bar made coconut wine. In *Hualuo* 华罗, probably Verawal in Gujarat, coconut trees were planted as borders to mark one's territory apart from others' land.[6] Not surprisingly, these trees constituted an integral part of property, and in the Maldives no bequest was worthier for a father to leave to his children than a plantation of coconut trees.

The Chinese had certainly long been familiar with coconut trees, which also grew in the south of China. Though he had never been there, the Tang monk Huilin 慧琳 (737–820) mentioned that this tree grew in Guangzhou, with its leaves being made into mats, its shell fibers being processed into coir rope to secure ship planking, its inner shell being fashioned into wine cups, its fruit being tasty, and the pulp of the fruit being as sweet as honey.[7] Liu Xun 刘恂, an official in Guangzhou at the end of the ninth century, described the fruit in detail, noting that it was round, shaggy on the outside, with a solid shell under the hair.[8] This shell was made into fine containers and its milk tasted fresh, making people feel cool and causing them to belch.

During the Song period, the Chinese came to learn about the wide use of coconuts in the Indian Ocean world. In his *Lingwai Daida*, Zhou Qufei introduced the region's geography, countries, customs, goods, and flora and fauna, including coconut trees in southern China and beyond.[9] This tree had its fruits hidden among leaves, he noted, and the fruit could be as large as a five-peck (*dou* 斗) container, of a size that only a jackfruit (*boluobi* 波罗蜜) could surpass. When picked up its color was initially green, but it gradually turned yellow and eventually dried out. The shell inside the fruit was made into containers. Its flesh, white as jade, tasted like cow's milk, and its water, while fresh and fragrant at first, turned cloudy and undrinkable when kept for too long. Zhao Rukuo repeated this same description but added one more sentence, noting that in the countries around Nanpi people mixed its flower juice with honey to make wine.[10] The *Song Shi* recorded coconuts as local products in Zhancheng (Champa), Sanfoqi (Srivijaya), and Zhunian (Chola), adding Boni 勃泥 (Borneo) and Shepo (Java) to the list of places where coconut wine was made.[11] Obviously, by the Song period, the Chinese had already understood the importance of this tree and its fruits in the broad context of maritime Asia.

At the end of the Ming period coconuts were listed as one of the import goods, and the tax rate was two *fen* in silver per one hundred coconuts in 1589 and one *fen* and seven *li* in silver per one hundred in 1615.[12] The fruits in this period, however, were most likely not from the Maldives, the Island of Coconut Trees, but from Southeast Asia.

THE TREES OF THE MALDIVES

The coconut tree has shaped the culture of the Maldivian people and local life since the very beginning. Its significance to local people was self-evident. In Waqf endowments, whenever trees were mentioned, coconut trees always led the list.[13]

Generally speaking, while Maldives coconuts were smaller than those in India, they were thought to be sweeter and to yield more oil. Each and every part of the coconut tree had its important function in the Maldives: leaf fronds were for thatching, matting, and baskets, matted fiber was for strainers and matting, stems were for making brushes or as firewood, trunks were for making into boats and houses, and shells were for making into containers, kindling, charcoal, and not the least important of uses, for making coir rope.[14]

Western travelers supplied similar if not further information on coconut trees and their role in the Maldives. Coconut trees were deliberately planted and were visible everywhere in the islands. "These islands, which are governed by a woman, are planted with coco-tree," and "They are all inhabited, and all produce coco-trees," pronounced Sulaiman. "Coco-nuts flourish there," continued Al Mas'udi. Edrisi went on to mention that local people "cultivate there the coco-tree and the sugar-cane."[15] However, none of these could beat the descriptions penned by Ibn Battuta, who regarded coconut trees as "the Trees of the Maldives." "Most of the trees on these islands are coconuts: they furnish the food of the inhabitants along with the fish."[16] He was amazed by the magical functions of the coconut.

> The nature of the coconut is marvelous. Each of these palms produces annually twelve crops, one a month. Some are small, others large: many are yellow; the rest are green, and remain always so. From the fruit are obtained milk, oil, and honey, as we have said in the first part of this book. With the honey is made pastry, which they eat with the dried coconut. All the food

made from the coconut, and the fish eaten at the same time, effect an extraordinary and unequalled vigour in manhood.[17]

While Ibn Battuta provided more details, his description of coconuts being used for food stuff was mostly the same as Ma Huan would later share. Ibn Battuta believed that it was coconuts that made "the inhabitants of the islands accomplish astonishing feats," and he himself was one of the beneficiaries too when he boasted. "I had in that country four legitimate wives, besides concubines. I visited them all every day, and spent the night with each in turn. I continued this course of life during the year and a half that I spent at the Maldives."[18] Obviously, Ibn Battuta believed that coconuts provided him with the vigor he needed for that busy schedule. Indeed, a local folk tale highlights how the first coconut trees grew up out from the magic mixture made by a great sorcerer and put into the mouth of every dead person.[19] The first settlers in the islands hence were saved from famine, and this tree, known by the Maldivians as *Divehi ruh* (Maldivian palm), had its place as the national emblem.

Maldivian coconuts continued to amaze visitors. More than two centuries later, J. de Barros, a clerk writing from his Lisbon office, had been so impressed by the flavor of the juice that he expended a great deal of ink on this exotic item. "These palm trees do not yield dates, as do those of Barbary and all Africa, but a fruit of the size of a man's head. Before reaching the kernel, it has two husks, after the manner of nuts. The first, although on the outside, is quite smooth; beneath this is another all of fibre, which excels the *esparto*."[20] He went on to describe the inside of the fruit, probably with a view to helping European people who had never seen let alone tasted this tropical fruit.

> The kernel within this second shell is about the size of a large quince, but of a different appearance, resembling the filbert in its outer surface and inner substance; it has, however, a hollow space within. It is of the same taste, but of greater bulk, and is more oily in its consistency than the filbert. Within the cavity is distilled some water, which is very sweet and cordial, principally when the nut is young. When the nut is planted, all this cavity in which the water was becomes a thick mass like cream, called *lanka*. It is very sweet and tasty, and better than almonds, when it thickens on the tree; and as this fruit in its substance and edibility is very like

the almond or filbert, so, too, its outer surface is fawn-coloured, and its interior white.[21]

Barros then turned to introduce the wonderful dishes made from the fruit that had been praised by Ibn Battuta. "This nut and the palm which yields it have other profitable uses, ordained of God for the support and necessities of man, for besides those mentioned it supplies him with honey, vinegar, oil, and wine, and is itself a substantial food, either eaten alone or with rice, or served in other modes employed by the Indians in their cookery." He went on to introduce the use of coconut trees in the construction of houses. "The palm trees also are used for timber, logs, and tiles, for the natives cover their houses with the leaves, which prevent any water getting in." In addition, "these also serve them for paper, and their *palmitos* put them in no need of the *palmitos* of Barbary."[22]

"AN ARTICLE OF MEDICINE"

Through local adaptation, one variety of the coconut tree that grew in seawater was famous for its medical uses.

> Besides these trees, which in those islands grow above ground, it seems their seed is endowed by nature with such virtue that it has produced in some places beneath the salt water another species, which yields a larger nut than the coco. The second shell of this nut is found by experience to be more efficacious against poison than the Bezoar stone, which also comes from the East, growing in the stomach of an animal called by the Persians *Pazon*.[23]

Barros's description was later to be confirmed by François Pyrard and the Italian Jesuit Giulio Aleni in the early seventeenth century. Giulio Aleni mentioned that around the Maldives, "In the sea grows a kind of coco-tree, with fairly small fruits, which can cure many diseases."[24] Pyrard elaborated with further details. "It is the same with a certain nut, cast up by the sea from time to time, and as big as a man's head, which one might liken to a couple of large melons joined together: this they call *Tauarcarré*, believing that it comes of certain trees under the sea: the Portuguese call it 'coco des Maldives,' it is an article of medicine, and fetches a high price."[25]

Because of its extensive and essential use in local life, the Maldivian people conflated this coconut (and ambergris) with wealth or treasure. "In short, when a man of those parts has a pair of these palm trees he has everything necessary for existence; and when they wish to praise one for his benefactions, they are wont to say, 'He is more fruitful and profitable than a palm tree.' "[26] Pyrard made a statement similar to Barros's: "when one becomes suddenly rich, it is commonly said that he had found *Tauarcarré*, or amber, as though it were treasures." The term *tauarcarré* means "hard (shelled) nut," while amber refers to ambergris.[27]

Living in the Maldives for years, Pyrard developed a personal attachment to coconuts.

> None, however, is more useful than the coco or Indian nut, which they call *Roul*, and the fruit *Caré* which is more plentiful at the Maldives than elsewhere. The islands supply many neighbouring countries, and the natives there know better than others how to extract its substance and the commodities it yields. It is, indeed, the most wondrous manna imaginable: for this single tree can supply everything necessary to man, furnishing him in plenty with wine, honey, sugar, milk, and butter. Besides, the kernel or almond is good to eat with all kinds of viands. Instead of bread: there, they neither make bread nor ever see it; indeed, I was five years or more without tasting it, or even seeing it, and I got so accustomed to that style of living that it seemed not strange to me. Moreover, the wood, bark, leaves, and nuts provide the greater part of their furniture and utensils.[28]

Pyrard surely could not have known that the Spaniards had similarly reported these same details two decades earlier in Manila, a few thousand miles away from the Maldives. When the Spaniards departing from Mexico had arrived in the Philippines, they were told by merchants from the Maldives that:

> in all the Iland of Maldiuia from whence they came, they haue no other sustainment, but onely that which this tree yeeldeth: they do make houses hereof, and tyles for to couer the same, the fruit doth yeeld a meollio or curnell, which is very sauory and healthfull, the sauor thereof is much like to greene hasell nuts, and if you do cut the branch there whereas the coco

commeth forth is the principal fruite, and euery one of them hath ordinarily a pinte of Water, the which is very sweet and delicate: al the said substance doth returne into the trunke of the tree, whereas they doo bore a hole, and thereat they do draw out all that water, which is much: and mingling it with other thinges they make thereof good wine, the which is drunk in al those ilands and in the kingdome of China. Of the same water they make vineger, and of the meollio kernel aforesaide, oile verie medicinall, milke like vnto almon milke: hony and suger very sauorie.[29]

All these uses were only some of its limitless functions, according to the Spaniards.

It must be highlighted that due to the diminutive size and thus the limited resources in the Maldives, all the available materials were fully made use of in daily life. In addition to coconut trees, coral stones mined from neighboring reefs were another primary material for construction from the second century up until 1992, establishing the Maldives as one of the best examples in exploiting this unusual sea material.[30] Once made into small tools for carving Buddhist statues of a relatively large size, these coral stones were then shaped or chipped and sometimes engraved with beautiful decorations or scripts, and assembled by way of a locally invented carpentry technique to construct buildings from simple block sets all the way to sophisticated mosques such as the Male Old Friday Mosque. Built in 1658 with a size of 240 square meters, this mosque can accommodate three hundred people and is regarded as one of the finest coral stone projects in the world.[31]

Both coconut trees and coral stones illustrate the impressive adaptability of the Maldivian people to their environment. It is no exaggeration to conclude that coconut trees, along with other local resources of a limited variety, provided all necessities the people of the Maldives needed, not just for sustenance but also for trade. The greatest importance of this tree, indeed, was not confined to the islands but spread across the broader Indian Ocean world. The Maldivian coir rope processed from coconut fiber was "in common and universal use for the ships of the whole East," concluded Barros, writing comfortably from his desk in Lisbon.[32]

Chapter Nine

SHIPS WITHOUT NAILS

The land produces coir ropes, cowrie shells, dried fish, and big handkerchiefs.

—WANG DAYUAN

The Indian and Yemenite ships are sewn together with them, for the Indian Ocean is full of reefs, and if a ship is nailed with iron nails it breaks up on striking the rocks, whereas if it is sewn together with cords, it is given a certain resilience and does not fall into pieces.

—IBN BATTUTA

The significance of the coconut tree in Maldivian society resulted not only from its being a key source for food, but also for the basic materials derived from its parts that were used for house and shipbuilding. Of the four local products listed by Wang Dayuan, coir rope was placed in order of importance ahead of cowrie shells, dried fish, and large handkerchief cloths.[1] During medieval times, western Indian Ocean ships used coconut tree trunks as beams and planks, and more interestingly and importantly here, these planks were tied together with coir rope. Popularly known as "stitched ships," these vessels were constructed without using a single iron nail. Coir rope that was made from the fiber of coconut shells was thus crucial for navigation and maritime trade.

Wang Dayuan was the first Chinese person to specifically mention this kind of ship in Ganmaili 甘埋里, a place located somewhere in the Persian Gulf.

In this place the ships are called horse ships (*machuan* 马船), larger than commercial vessels (*shangbo* 商舶). (They) do not use iron nails (*ding* 钉) or caulking (*hui* 灰), but instead use coir rope (*yesuo* 椰索) to (sew) planks together. Each ship has two or three decks, with planks used to (construct) the cross sheds; seawater seeps in continuously, so sailors take turns to bail water out day and night, to prevent its submersion. In the lower hold frankincense (*ruxiang*) is loaded as ballast, and on the upper part a few hundred horses are carried.[2]

The horse ship was also used to transport goods such as pepper, cloves, nutmeg, porcelain, glass beads, and so on, so it sailed frequently between the Persian Gulf and coastal India. Wang Dayuan noted that horses were carried on the horse ships from the Arab world to Calicut (*Gulifo* 古里佛), and trade between Kollam (*Xiaoju'nan* 小唄喃) and Calicut, for example, relied on horse ships, too.[3]

Wang's record was brief but informative. Clearly this kind of ship was made from coconut tree planks that were fastened together with coir ropes. The ship did not use any iron nail or caulking so that seawater tended to come into the ship, which is why sailors had to bail out water constantly. Marco Polo certainly had a negative view of these horse ships, probably because he had had firsthand experience of what he thought were the superior large oceangoing ships that sailed across the Mediterranean world or between the Indian Ocean and China.

> The vessels built at Ormus are of the worst kind, and dangerous for navigation, exposing the merchants and others who make use of them to great hazards. Their defects proceed from the circumstance of nails not being employed in the construction; the wood being of too hard a quality, and liable to split to crack like earthenware. When an attempt is made to drive a nail, it rebounds, and is frequently broken. The planks are bored, as carefully as possibly, with an iron auger, near the extremities; and wooden pins or trenails being driven into them, they are in this manner fastened. After this they are bound, or rather sewed together, with a kind of rope-yarn stripped from the husk of the Indian nuts, which are of a large size, and covered with a fibrous stuff like horse-hair. This being steeped in water until the softer parts putrefy, the threads or strings remain clean, and of these they make twine for sewing the planks, which lasts long under water. Pitch is not used for preserving the bottoms of vessels, but they are smeared with an oil made from the fat of fish, and then caulked with oakum. The vessel had no more than one mast, one helm, and one deck. When she has taken in her lading it is covered over with hides, and upon these hides, they place the

horses which they carry to India. They have no iron anchors, but in their stead employ another kind of ground-tackle; the consequence of which is that in bad weather—and these seas are very tempestuous—they are frequently driven on shore and lost.[4]

Marco Polo's description largely concurs with Wang Dayuan's account. The horse ship had no iron fittings at all, because no iron nails or anchors were employed when making it. For the planks, these were lashed together with coir rope, the manufacture of which Marco Polo detailed from coconut shells to rope. While Marco Polo seemed to disparage the poor quality of the horse ship, he was generous enough to state how adroitly the indigenous people made full use of their local resources. Iron nails were not used because the local wood was too hard to knock nails into, for example. Marco Polo also noted that the ships were used to carry horses, a popular commodity in the Persian Gulf.

While Wang Dayuan claimed there were two to three decks, Marco Polo stated that the horse ship had just one deck. Nor did he mention the men employed to bail out water, but he did note the use of hides to waterproof the ship. Wang Dayuan claimed that a horse ship could provide sufficient space to load a few hundred horses, but this number might have been an exaggeration, especially considering that sailors had to bail out water without stopping.[5] More than 150 years earlier, Zhou Qufei had claimed that the Mulan ships (*Mulanzhou* 木兰舟) in the foreign ocean could accommodate a few hundred men. "South to the South Sea (*nanhai er nan* 南海而南), there are ships large as giant houses (*jushi* 巨室), their sails like hanging clouds from sky (*chuitian zhi yun* 垂天之云), rudders (*duo* 柂) as long as a few *zhang*; one ship could hold a few hundred people, with a storage of grain that could support them for a year; pigs are raised and wines are made in the ship; these people have put their life and death out of account."[6]

"South to the South Sea" refers to the Indian Ocean (especially the Arabian Sea) or possibly even the Mediterranean. The people on board the Mulan ship were excellent navigators. They could tell the location of various countries by the shape of mountains. If they planned to go to a given country, they could calculate the days it would take with a tail wind before they would see a certain mountain and then turn to the destination. If the wind was too strong, they would reach the mountain ahead of schedule and adjust the direction accordingly. If the ship sailed too fast, it could rush into shallow water and be smashed to pieces on the rocks. Although the ship was large enough to withstand waves and storms, it was fragile in shallow water. On the other side of the kingdom of the Dashi in the Western Sea (the Mediterranean), the ships were even bigger in size and could accommodate a few thousand people.[7] What Zhou Qufei described might have been based on information including stories he may have heard from Chinese and foreign merchants. Partly true and partly fictitious, he certainly did realistically recount the advances in navigation mastered by the Arab people and paint the scene of the Roman fleets sailing across the Mediterranean.

The ships without nails also attracted Wang Dayuan's Western contemporaries, such as Odorico da Pordenone and Ibn Battuta. At the beginning of the eleventh century, Alberuni observed this especially in the Maldives. "Diva-Kanbar, the island of the cords twisted from coco-nut fibre, and used for fastening together the planks of their ship."[8] In the late thirteenth century, John of Montecorvino saw how these boats plied their way between the Maldives and India.

> Their ships in these parts are mighty frail and uncouth with no iron in them and no caulking. They are sewn like clothes with twine. And so if the twine breaks anywhere, there is a break indeed! Once every year therefore there is a mending of this, more or less, if they propose to go to sea. And they have a frail and flimsy rudder, like the top of a table, a cubit in width, in the middle of the stern; and when they have to tack, it is done with a vast deal of trouble; and if it is blowing in any way hard, they cannot tack at all. They have but one sail and one mast, and the sails are either of matting or some miserable cloth. The ropes are of husk.[9]

Fascinated by the "ships that have no iron in their frame," Odorico da Pordenone boarded such a ship himself during his ocean-crossing trip to India. "In this country men make use of a kind of vessel which they call *Jase*, which is fastened only with stitching of twine. On one of these vessels I embarked, and I could find no iron at all therein. And having thus embarked, I passed over in twenty-eight days to Tana."[10] Tana was on the western coast of India. Obviously, this ship without nails had been regularly used for long-distance ocean trips.

CONSTRUCTING "SHIPS WITHOUT NAILS"

Marco Polo's disparaging view of horse ships is in sharp contrast to the views of other visitors who thought highly of these vessels. Perhaps Marco Polo and Wang Dayuan were describing an early stage of the horse ship that was intended for short-distance journeys, while Ma Huan was looking at a more sophisticated stage or a different type of horse ship. In Calicut, according to Ma Huan, people used coir rope in the construction of ships, and in the Maldives, coir rope "filled one house after another; foreign ships from various places came here to purchase, and sell to other countries, for the uses of ship-buildings and so on. Here the ships do not use nails; the lock holes (*suokong* 锁孔) are fastened with ropes, inserted with wooden wedges (*muxie* 木楔), and smeared with foreign bitumen (*fan liqing* 番沥青)."[11]

While Wang Dayuan commented that no caulking was used, Marco Polo mentioned that wood pins, fish oil, and oakum (but not pitch) were employed to solidify the joints and make the ship watertight. Ma Huan also mentioned that wooden pins as well as pitch were used in ship construction. It seems that the horse ship was continuously improved upon over time.

Huang Xingzeng noted a similar use of coir rope to fasten planks together, but he stated that it was ambergris (*longxian* 龙涎) rather than bitumen that was used to make the ship watertight. It could well be suspected that Huang might have made a mistake here, since he never actually traveled overseas.[12] However, a contemporary Portuguese traveler from Cochin found that local fishermen along the Malabar Coast regarded ambergris as a kind of bitumen and used it for the caulking of ships; in addition, he also noted that local people sometimes mistook ambergris for bitumen.[13] Therefore, Huang might have been correct, and it is highly possible that ambergris had been used for caulking by indigenous fishermen before its great value was fully realized.

The marine archaeologist Michael Flecker provides a detailed description of ships constructed without the use of nails.

> A canted stem-post connects to the keel at a horizontal mortise and tenon joint. Hull plank edges are faired to the correct angle and butted directly against the flat surface of the keel and stem-post, where they were stitched in place. The stern post is either vertical or has a slight cant. A strong

keelson supplements the light keel in providing longitudinal stiffness to the vessel. Sawn hull planks are stitched edge-to-edge with coconut fibre twine, or coir, passing right through the planks in a criss-cross manner. Wadding material is placed under the stitching both inside and outside the hull. Frames are notched where they pass over plank edge-joints to allow for the stitching and wadding, and two holes are provided between each notch for fastening light frames to the hull planks. Teak thwart beams protrude through the hull just below the gunnel, just as they do on still extant Omani fishing boats. So-called ceiling timbers, or cargo trays, may be placed longitudinally across the keelson, stringers, and frames as a supporting bed for ballast and cargo.[14]

While this description is much more detailed and technical than anything provided by Wang Dayuan or Ma Huan, the basic structure is clearly the same. The hulls were made of teak or coconut wood, as these types of timber were easily available, durable, elastic, and strong. Coconut trees were native to India, Ceylon, the Maldives, and the Laccadive Islands and gradually spread to Arabia. The shipbuilders in the Maldives and the Laccadive Islands made full use of "the diverse products of the coconut trees: hulls, masts, stitches, ropes, and even sails." While a simple way to build a ship was as Wang Dayuan described, oceangoing ships must have had reinforcing ribs to resist the buffeting of waves and winds. The sides of the hull were made of carved planks laid side by side, coir ropes were used to stitch through "holes bored at intervals near the edges of the adjacent planks," and to prevent the seawater from coming in, caulking was necessary. Bitumen (noted by Ma Huan) or resin, mixed with whale oil (mentioned by Marco Polo), was often made into caulking.[15]

Scholars have long realized that medieval Arab (or western Indian Ocean) ships were distinctive, with the planks of their hulls being sewn together, not nailed.[16] The earliest European mention of such a ship was *The Periplus of the Erythraean Sea*, an anonymous geographical work completed around the first century, while archaeological findings have confirmed the use of such a ship as early as the mid-third millennium BCE in Oman.[17] A popular misconception was that stitched ships were only an Arab practice, confined to the Indian Ocean, but in fact they were constructed and employed widely in Arabia, East Africa, India, Southeast Asia, the Mediterranean, the Americas, and even northern Europe.[18] In the Indian Ocean there emerged two types of sewn ship: one being the Arab-Indian type found in the western Indian Ocean, and the other the Southeast Asian variety used in South China Sea and the Bay of Bengal.[19] Through influences from the Indian Ocean world as well as from the Chinese empire, traditional Southeast Asian ships were divided into two stages of development: the early one using the "stitched-plank and lashed-lug" technique and the later one only the "lashed-lug method."[20] The early type belonged to the "ships without nails" category, while the later one used iron nails, thanks to Chinese influence. Probably in the late thirteenth century or even earlier, Southeast Asian shipbuilders adopted the Chinese feature of transverse bulkheads to create a tradition of shipbuilding techniques in the South China Sea. These hybrid vessels, built from tropical hardwood joined by wooden dowels and thus retaining the essential feature of sewn boats, began the supplementary use of iron nails to fasten the transverse bulkheads to the frames at the hull, a newly added Chinese element.[21]

While the Maldivians had learnt their shipbuilding from some of their neighbors, its basic no-nail technique for stitched boats remained. Meanwhile, their craftsmen knew how to make good use of local resources. The coconut trunks in the Maldives were denser than those in India, providing a better option for local preferences, and these same trees provided the quality fiber for famous coconut coir ropes.

THE TALE OF THE MAGNETIC ROCK

Ibn Battuta noticed that the Maldivians used coir rope "instead of nails to bind their ships together and also as cables." He pointed out the advantages of these ships. "The Indian and Yemenite ships are sewn together with them, for the Indian Ocean is full of reefs, and if a ship is nailed with iron nails it breaks up on striking the rocks, whereas if it is sewn together with cords, it is given a certain resilience and does not fall into pieces."[22] Probably a thousand years earlier than Battuta's voyage, the resilience of sewn ships against sharp rocks had been thought of as a magical power in sea lore.

There existed a popular tale in maritime Asia, dating from the beginning of the first millennium, that told of some special magnetic rock on the seabed that could wreck a ship. The invention of the magnetic rock on the seabed indeed has something essentially to do with the Maldives. The earliest mention of this story seems to be by Claudius Ptolemy, who in his *Geography* (c. 150 CE) claimed that these magnetic rocks were located near the Maldives:

> There are said to be other islands here adjoining, ten in number, called Maniolae, from which they say that boats, in which there are nails, are kept away, lest at any time the magnetic stone which is found near these islands should draw them to destruction. For this reason they say that these boats are drawn up on the shore and that they are strengthened with beams of wood. They also say that these islands are occupied by cannibals called *Manioli*. There are means of approach from these islands to the mainland.[23]

From this tale, we glean the following points: There were ten islands that were connected and that were called the Maniolae Islands, and these were hazardous for any ship built with iron nails, as while passing by, the ship would be attracted to and dashed to pieces by the magnetic rock. To avert a tragedy, ships were strengthened with logs, and primitive people living in these islands could sail as far as the mainland.[24] All these circumstantial details suggest that the Maniolae Islands might in fact be based on the Maldives.

Why were the Maldives Islands chosen as the setting for this tale of the magnetic rock? It may have something to do with the strategic location of this archipelago in maritime Asia. Southwest of Sri Lanka, the islands of the Maldives stretched more than 500 miles (800 km) from north to south, constituted a natural land barrier for ships that traveled west–east between the Arabian Sea and the Bay of Bengal, and lay in the path of the two strong monsoons that could blow early ships from coastal India or Sri Lanka to these islands. With the nickname "ten thousand islands," the Maldives soon became notorious among sailors for its perilous atolls, strong winds, and treacherous currents that caused numerous shipwrecks, so it is highly likely that such events in turn grew into the myth that there was a magnetic rock in the Maldives that and attracted those ships built with iron nails.

A passage by the so-called Palladius, included in *De Bragmanibus*, a work of uncertain date and origin, highlighted the disadvantages of the ship with iron nails in the tale of the magnetic rock.

> Round about it (unless the report be false) lie a thousand other islands, through which the Red Sea flows. In these islands, which are called *Maniolae*,

the magnet-stone which attracts iron is produced; so that if any ship built with iron nails should approach these islands, it will by the virtue of this stone be drawn thither and stayed in its course. Wherefore those who sailed to Taprobane employ ships built with wooden bolts, especially for this voyage.[25]

This tale of the magnetic rock on the seabed, popularly repeated in many medieval folktales such as those included in *The Thousand and One Nights*, soon found its way to early China, too. The *Taiping Yulan* 太平御览 (Readings of the Taiping Era), a massive Chinese encyclopedia compiled in the reign of Taipingxingguo 太平兴国 (977–983), cited from the *Nanzhou Yiwuzhi* 南州异物志 (Record of Exotic Things in Southern Prefectures), a work produced in the third century, and shared the Chinese version of the magnetic rock tale. It related that at the end of the *zhanghai* 涨海 (lit. "the swollen sea") and near the farthest point (*qitou* 崎头) of land, the water was shallow and filled with magnetic rocks (*cishi* 磁石). When foreigners approached in a ship built with iron nails, the ship stopped moving, because the iron parts were attracted to the magnetic rocks.[26] The *zhanghai* is usually understood as referring to the South China Sea, and this Chinese legend reverses the Western one by emphasizing the navigational difficulty for Chinese vessels in maritime Asia. According to Rao Zongyi 饶宗颐 (1917–2018), an extremely knowledgeable scholar, the Chinese magnetic rocks were located at the southern end of the Malay Peninsula.[27] Rao's interpretation is reasonable, since the Malay Peninsula seemed to be a natural barrier between China and the India in the early times.

This tale of the magnetic rock told and retold all over maritime Asia appears to attest to the navigational advantages of ships constructed without iron nails. This stitched ship must have been very popular in the Indian Ocean by the first centuries of the first millennium and were still so at the time the Portuguese arrived. These new arrivals straightaway saw that local "*Gundras* are built of palm-timber, joined and fastened with pegs of wood without any bolts. The sails also are made of mats of the dry leaves of the palm."[28] Duarte Barbosa sketched the various types of local ships.

> In these islands of Maldio they build many large ships of palm-wood, held together with matting, because they have no other timber there. In these they voyage to the mainland. These ships have keels and are of very considerable

capacity. The islanders build also small rowing crafts, like brigantines or fustas; these are of great strength, admirably built, and extremely light; they serve chiefly for going from one island to another, though they are also used for crossing over to Malabar.[29]

THE MAKING OF COIR ROPE

There are physical justifications for using coir rope instead of iron nails for the binding of ship planks. Marco Polo, for example, stated that they lasted longer in the water. J. de Barros also shared his insightful analysis on the advantages of coir rope.

> The rope made from this fibre supplies the whole of India, and chiefly for cables, because it is more secure and stands the sea better than any made from hemp. The reason is that it agrees with the salt water, and becomes so tough that it seems like hide, contracting and expanding with the strength of the sea; so that a good thick cable of this rope, when the ship is standing at her anchor in a heavy gale and straining upon it, draws out so thin that you would think it could not hold a boat; when the vessel is pitching in a mere swell, it keeps its usual thickness. This coir is also used instead of bolts, for such virtue hath it of swelling and shrinking in the sea that they join the timbers of their ships' ribs with it and consider it quite secure.[30]

This Portuguese interpretation provided a modern and scientific refutation of the fable of the magnetic rocks retold for over a thousand years.

While the Chinese observed the importance of coir rope, they failed to mention how it was made. Just like Marco Polo, Ibn Battuta briefly explained how these ropes were made from the outer husk of coconut shells. "The natives make it undergo a preparation in pits dug near the shore; then they beat it with picks, after which the women work it into rope."[31] But it was François Pyrard who shared the detailed, step-by-step method of making coir rope.

> The nut is covered with a husk or shell; some are of the size of a man's head, and some less. The husk has a yellowish hue over the green when it is ripe and is three or four inches thick. This husk is composed of fibre, whereof they make their rope. They remove the husk when green, as we should that

of a nut, and lay it to steep in the sea, covering it with sand. After it has been there for the space of three weeks they take it out and beat it with wooden mallets, such as we here use for flax or hemp. Thus, having separated the fibres, they expose it to the sun. Next, the women twist and spin it into rope with the hand on the naked thigh, for the men take no part in the labour of rope-making. The rope thus made serves for all uses, and none other is employed throughout all the Indies. The same husk, when dry, serves to caulk the ships withal.[32]

He also meticulously described the capacity of the ship without iron, hence clearing any confusion or doubt left by Marco Polo's and Wang Dayuan's accounts.

I have oftentimes seen at the Maldives an infinite number of ships of 100 or 120 tons, built entirely of this timber, without any iron or other wood or material except what this tree produces. The anchors even are made of it, and are very excellent and handy. They have a cross-piece of wood of the same tree, hollowed out and packed with flints and little stones, and then firmly closed. This is to render the anchor heavier, so that it shall catch and keep a better hold. The planks are fastened with pins, and lashed and seamed within with cordage made of the fruit. Moreover, these ships, entirely built, fitted, and equipped with the timber or fruit of this tree, are loaded with merchandise proceeding from the same tree, to wit, cordage, mats, sails of cocos, comfits, oil, wine, sugar, and other goods, all the produce of this tree. And this is true also of the provisions of the ship, whether of meat or drink; and whether the voyage be to Arabia, 800 or 900 leagues distance, or to the coast of Malabar, Cambaye, Sumatra, or elsewhere. These vessels last four or five years, and with repairs and proper treatment will make many long voyages.[33]

CALLING AT CHINA: THE BELITUNG SHIP

The ships without iron nails were local inventions, commonly built and used among islanders or coastal people who had not yet mastered metallurgy, probably because they would have to depend on imported materials for making metal. Such ships constituted a feature across the Arabian Sea and the Indian Ocean in the medieval period, as confirmed by recent maritime archaeological discoveries. The discovery of the Belitung shipwreck in Indonesia has proved that the stitched ships not only sailed across the Indian Ocean but also visited Southeast Asia and China as early as the beginning of the ninth century, more than 450 years before Marco Polo.

In 1998 a sea-cucumber diver found a shipwreck near Belitung Island, Indonesia. More than sixty thousand pieces of gold, silver, and ceramics from northern, central, and southern China were discovered in this shipwreck. Among the more than fifty thousand Changsha kiln pieces of porcelain produced in Changsha, a city on the mid–Yangzi River, one bowl was marked with the message "the 16th day of the seventh month in the second year of the Baoli 宝历 reign," or 826 CE, which meant that the ship would have sailed not long after that date.

Another interesting find was a Chinese bronze mirror that bore a lengthy Chinese inscription telling its entire story, how it was forged a hundred times in the middle of the Yangzi River, Yangzhou, on the twenty-ninth day of the eleventh month, in the first year of the Qianyuan Reign (759 CE) of the Tang dynasty (*Tang Qianyuan yuannian wuxu shiyiyue nianjiuri yu Yangzhou Yangzijiangxin bailian zaocheng* 唐乾元元年戊戌十一月廿九日于杨州扬子江心百炼造成) (figure 9.1). The *Jiangxinjing* 江心镜 (lit. "mirror [forged] in the middle of the [Yangzi] River") was a highly valued tributary item made to be presented at the Tang court and said to have been completed on the fifth day of the fifth month. No other extant Tang bronze mirror is known to match the imperial textual descriptions so precisely. Supplemented with evidence from Chinese coins and radiocarbon analysis, it has been established that the Belitung ship probably is the oldest shipwreck ever found in the South China Sea.

Astonishingly, archaeological findings and scientific analyses have gradually indicated and confirmed that the Belitung ship style was indeed as Wang Dayuan, Ibn Battuta, and Ma Huan had described. The surviving keel is 50 feet (15.3 m) long, the hull from the ship's centerline 17 feet (5.1 m) at the widest point, and many timbers used in the ship "originated in Africa, which along with ethnographic and iconographic evidence confirms a ship of Middle-Eastern origin, an Arab dhow."[34] An archaeological analysis found that "every timber was fastened with stitching, with no sign of wooden dowels or iron fastenings. This was the first suggestion that the vessel was from the western Indian Ocean. The later discovery of through-beams

SHIPS WITHOUT NAILS

FIGURE 9.1 The bronze mirror from the Belitung shipwreck. *Source*: Asian Civilization Museum, Singapore. Courtesy of Lu Haiyue.

reinforced the supposition, and identification of timber samples removed all doubt."[35] Scientific analyses of the timber further confirm that "the Belitung ship was definitely not built in India. It was most probably constructed in the Middle East (perhaps in the region of Oman or Yemen)."[36] The identification of bitumen in a sample of hard material adhering to the athwart beam also points to its Middle East origin. The use of bitumen for the caulking was something that Ma Huan had observed.

While the Belitung ship sank near Indonesia, probably overcome by a sudden storm, it is evident that this ship was on its return journey home to the Indian Ocean world. Whether or not this ship was on its way back from China or elsewhere remains a question. However, the fact that the overwhelming majority of the goods carried on the Belitung ship were Chinese porcelain, alongside some other circumstantial evidence, is convincing enough to assume that the ship most likely called at Guangzhou, one of the most prosperous ports in the medieval world, was loaded up with Chinese goods there, and then departed.

The Belitung ship is not the only wreck found in the South China Sea. In 2013 the Phanom Surin shipwreck was discovered in a swamp west of Bangkok. With the surviving keel about 59 feet (18 m) long, the ship was clearly larger than the Belitung one, probably as long as 115 feet (35 m).[37] Its stitched hull techniques are identical to that of the Belitung ship, indicating that it was also a stitched ship. Both early and recent researches have concluded that this ship was dated to the eighth or ninth century.[38] Therefore, these two ships, although discovered in Southeast Asia and once extensively repaired in this region, were of the same period and shared the same western Indian Ocean tradition.[39]

Not surprisingly, in al-Balīd, a settlement site with an Islamic citadel in Dhofar, Oman, various parts of ship timber have been found since 2004, with some "planks sewn together, some with the stitching still preserved," and this sheds some new light on the ships without nails during the period from the tenth to the fifteenth centuries. It is observed that all the techniques used in these ship timbers including carpentry, joinery, and stitching were "very similar to those in use today in traditional sewn-boat construction. Even the repairs adopted are exactly the same as those used in the present day," and the cordage and wadding used in all the observed sewn timbers "seems to be the same material used today," namely, coir.[40] Therefore, the Dhofar findings fill in the piece that the Belitung shipwreck could not provide because of its having rested at the bottom of the sea for centuries, with all traces of coir long since rotted away.

In sum, the construction materials of the Belitung ship such as timber and bitumen, its technology such as fastening beams with stitches, and the absence of any iron are all in accordance with the historical texts mentioned above, be they Chinese or western. Coir rope and wooden wedges, two crucial materials for the stitched ships, were not found in the remains of the Belitung ship, as they obviously decomposed being in seawater for over

1,100 years. Amazingly, it was this type of ironless ship that established the first direct trade between the Arabian Sea and China as early as the ninth century.

SEEN IN EARLY CHINA

When the Belitung ship might have called at Guangzhou at the beginning or middle of the ninth century, it was probably not an unusual sight for the Chinese, who were used to seeing this type of vessel arriving into port. Some early Chinese records support this fact.

Huilin was born in Kashgar in the Western Region, went to Chang'an 长安, the capital of the Tang dynasty, mastered both Sanskrit and Chinese, and trained to become an encyclopedic monk-scholar. In 810 (or 807), he completed the *Yiqie Jingyinyi* 一切经音义, the earliest Chinese lexicographical work on Buddhist sutras in which a so-called *Kunlun bo* 昆仑舶 (lit. "Kunlun ship") was mentioned. According to Huilin, the Kunlun ships belonged to the ship type without nails. They used rope made from coconut shell husks as fastening (*yezipi wei suo* 椰子皮为索) and olive sugar (*gelantang* 葛览糖) as caulking to prevent water seepage. When the coconut tree was mentioned, Huilin again emphasized that its fibers could be made into rope, which in turn was used to bind the ship's planks together, and the advantage of coir ropes was that they were corrosion-resistant.[41] Huilin's description of the use of coir rope instead of iron nails to fasten planking suggests that the so-called Kunlun ship might have been of Indian Ocean origin. In that case, the Belitung ship might have been one of those that the Tang Chinese called Kunlun ships, being unable to tell apart the ships from Southeast Asia, South Asia, or Arabia. It is amazing that Huilin, a northern monk who had never been to the south or maritime Asia, understood this oceangoing ship so well. He must have learned about it from other Chinese works when working on his great Buddhist compendium project.

The Kunlun ship was usually interpreted as being a Southeast Asian ship, sometimes called a *Bosi bo* 波斯舶 (lit. "Persian ship") or *Nanhai bo* 南海舶 (lit. "South Sea ship").[42] As non-Chinese vessels, the Kunlun ship even then had been very active in the South China Sea and the Indian Ocean. Many Buddhist pilgrims, for example, took a Kunlun ship from China to India.

Jianzhen 鉴真, another Tang monk, mentioned that in 749 there were numerous foreign ships in Guangzhou, including Poluomen 婆罗门 (Brahman), Bosi 波斯, and Kunlun 昆仑 ships, and a diversity of merchants including those from Ceylon (Shiziguo) and Dashi 大石 living there.[43]

Indeed, as early as the third century, the Chinese had noticed the use of various materials including ropes made from coconut fiber and olive tree bark for sewing ship planking together. Ji Han 嵇含 (263–306) pointed out that foreigners utilized rope made from the bark of olive trees to fasten planks, as this material became softer, more resilient, and stronger (*rouren* 柔韧) in water. This advantage was also pointed out by Ibn Battuta when he described coir. The use of olive tree bark was noted by Liu Xun, a commandant (*Sima* 司马) in Guangzhou during the reign of Emperor Zhaozong (r. 888–904). When describing the sugar palm (*guanglan* 桄榔), a southern tree, Liu Xun specifically mentioned that under its leaves there was a kind of whisker (*xu* 须) as thick as a horse's tail (and it is interesting that Marco Polo also compared coconut fiber to a horse's tail). When placed in salty water, these whiskers became swollen and tight, and people used them to bind ships together, so that these ships were made without the use of iron or thread (*buyong dingxian* 不用钉线). The advantages that Liu Xun highlighted about these fiber ropes were no different from descriptions of the coir rope known in the Indian Ocean world.[44] Although the ship described by Liu Xun was not lashed together with coir rope like the Belitung one, they both belonged to the type of ship that used no iron in their construction.

In addition, Liu Xun recorded the use of olive sugar for caulking. Southern people collected the resin from olive trees, mixed it with olive bark and leaves, and boiled all together with water into a black decoction they called the *Ganlantang* 橄榄糖 (the *ganlan* sugar). When dried and used as caulking, *ganlan* sugar became more solid than lacquer (*lao yu jiaoqi* 牢于胶漆), and even harder when it met with water (*zhuoshui yijian* 著水益坚).[45] The use of different materials such as coconut and olive trees, sugar palm, olive sugar, and *ganlan* sugar reveals the indigenous wisdom that variously exploited the available local natural resources to build a ship without the use of a single iron nail.

It must be pointed out that ships without iron nails were the earliest type of ship and universal among early peoples. Canoes, for example, were adopted across the world by all kinds of peoples. As late as the twelfth century, the Chinese still employed such kinds of ships. In Guangdong and

SHIPS WITHOUT NAILS

Guangxi, ships were constructed without the use of iron nails or Tung oil (*tongyou* 桐油, "China wood oil"), planks were lashed together with rattan (*teng* 藤), and dried madder (*qiancao* 茜草) was used for stitching. During a voyage, dried madder became wet and helped to make the ship watertight, just like the hides in the horse ships observed by Marco Polo. Zhou Qufei called these rattan ships (*tengzhou* 藤舟) and noted that they could be large enough to be used for cross-ocean commerce.[46]

Interestingly, by the twelfth century, the legend of the magnetic rocks at the bottom of the sea told by Ptolemy and Palladius had moved its location from the ocean to a Chinese river. According to Zhou Qufei, it was said that the rattan ship was so designated to pass the so-called *Cishishan* 磁石山 (lit. "Mount Magnetic Rock"). Like the horse ship, the rattan ship did not have any iron fittings on board, so that Mount Magnetic Rock posed no danger. Rattan ships were also used in Sichuan, an inland province along the upper Yangzi River, where people used *Cudrania tricuspidata* wood for nails (*zhemu weiding* 柘木为钉). Iron nails were avoided there because the rivers in Sichuan were notorious for the rocks in their riverbeds, although Zhou Qufei did speculate whether the so-called Mount Magnetic Rock was to be found in Sichuan.[47]

Wang Dayuan observed that a similar rattan ship was constructed in Puben 蒲奔, probably a local kingdom along the Pembuang River in southern Kalimantan.[48] Planks were bound with rattan or thin bamboo strips (*mie* 篾), and cotton was used to fill in the gaps. Whatever and wherever the case, ships without iron fittings were invented and exploited earlier than those made with nails, and in areas where metallurgy was introduced late or where iron remained rare and expensive, these nailless ships continued to be built.

MANILA AND MACAO

During European colonial expansion in Asia, ships without nails continued to sail in the Indian Ocean, and even to China, though in declining numbers. It is assumed that with the arrival of the Portuguese in East Asia, particularly after their stay at Macao in the later 1550s, stitched ships from Indian bases such as Goa continued to call at ports in the South China Sea.

The Spanish of the 1580s, for example, regarded the stitched ship as a most remarkable phenomenon. What surprised them even more were the ships made wholly from one kind of tree and were similarly amazed that all the goods loaded in the ship were all made from that same tree.

> But amongst all other notable thinges that these Spaniards haue seene in those ilands, and in the kingdome of China, and other places whereas they passed, there is one thing which hath caused them most to maruel at, and to haue it most in memory; which is a tree, ordinarily called palma de cocos, but doth differ from that which beareth the dates, and with great reason, for that it is a plant so full of mysterie and profite, that there hath come a ship vnto these ilands, and the said ship, and all that was in her to be sold, with ropes, cords, masts, sailes and nailes, were made of this tree, and the merchandice that she brought was mantels made of the rind of the saide tree, with great subtiltie and fine works. Likewise all the victuals that was in the said ship for the sustentation of thirtie men that came in her, yea their water was of the same tree.[49]

The Spanish understood that these commercial ships were from the Maldives.[50] Combining this testimony with the shipwrecks discovered so far, suffice to say that stitched ships had played an active role sailing between ports in the Indian Ocean and those in Southeast Asia. They must have called at Burma, the Malay Peninsula, Sumatra, Java, Borneo, Siam, Champa, the Philippines, and other Southeast Asian ports.

Qu Dajun 屈大均 (1630–1696), a scholar native of Canton during the Ming-Qing once visited Portuguese Macao where he found two kinds of foreign ships. One was the Portuguese galleon, and the other the stitched one. His account of the latter was similar to those recorded by Liu Xun, Zhou Qufei, and Ma Huan, and so was his explanation why nails were not used.[51] Obviously, these Indian Ocean ships had established their own tradition, and with Portuguese encouragement, they began to call at some new ports in the South China Sea such as Macao.

As late as the mid-eighteenth century, stitched ships were still present in the Canton Bay. In 1744 Yin Guangren 印光任, the first subprefect (*Tongzhi* 同知) assigned by Emperor Qianlong 乾隆 to maintain imperial control of Macao (which had been leased to the Portuguese in 1557), and later followed by his successor Zhang Rulin 张汝霖, began to impose strict imperial regulations over foreign trade and communities in this prosperous port city. As such, the two Chinese officials became acquainted with

SHIPS WITHOUT NAILS

foreign ships calling at Macao including the *waiyang yibo* 外洋夷舶 (lit. "outer ocean foreign ships"), namely, the Portuguese carracks, and the *fanbo* 蕃舶 (lit. "foreign ships"), namely, those stitched ships.

The two celestial officials compared these two types of oceangoing ships. Smaller than the Portuguese carrack, the *fanbo* was made with planks of ironwood (*tielimu* 铁力木, lit. "iron power tree," referring to *Mesua ferrea*) as thick as two to three *cun* 寸. These planks were fastened with rattan (*teng*), sewn together with coir rope (*yesuo*), and caulked with bitumen (*liqing* 沥青) and petroleum (*shinaoyou* 石脑油). The ship had two or three masts (*qiang* 樯) and was able to accommodate a few hundred people. More interestingly, it is said that these ships were under the registration of the local maritime customs, which had issued twenty-five permits in total, but, by the time of Yin Guangren's term of command (1744–1746), only sixteen ships were extant, and this number was reduced to thirteen during Zhang Rulin's administration (1746–1749).[52]

Clearly, both Yin and Zhang were describing the so-called stitched ships documented by Marco Polo and Wang Dayuan more than four centuries earlier. Therefore, even after the dominance of European ships in maritime Asia, traditional Asian vessels such as stitched ships still participated in and were used by European traders and colonists in maritime trade, even between the Indian Ocean and the South China Sea. Macao and Manila might have been the primary and furthermost destination for these Indian Ocean vessels. Also, the role of coir rope in navigation did not decline when the Europeans arrived. Indeed, as late as the beginning of the nineteenth century, coir rope was still widely used, even in Siam, as one Chinese sailor observed.[53] However, the mid–eighteenth century witnessed the drastic decline and probably the disappearance of this kind of ship. Within a period of less than three decades, nearly half of these ships registered in Macao were no longer seaworthy as their condition had deteriorated.[54] The Chinese mention of stitched ships might be the last textual source for these traditional Asian vessels. Today stitched ships probably reside only in certain museums, especially because the 2004 tsunami destroyed the very few still used in coastal fishing.

Effective as they were, "ships without nails" had their limits. They were unable to withstand the fierce storms and waves around South Africa, for example. "True it is, these ships are not sailed through the furious gales of the Cape of Good Hope," declared J. de Barros.[55]

Chapter Ten

COWRIE SHELLS

> Every sea-trader who takes one shipload of cowrie shells to Wudie 乌爹 (Pegu) and Pengjiala (Bengal), could exchange these for more than a shipload of rice. In these areas, people use cowrie shells as money, and a very old style of currency it is.
>
> —WANG DAYUAN

Alongside coconut trees, the cowrie shells often impressed visitors to the Maldives. Even the name of the Maldives is connected with cowrie shells, illustrating their significance for these islands. In Bengali, the term *māla* means load or ballast, and it also denotes money.[1] No wonder the Maldives is known as the islands of the cowrie shells. Scholars have long noticed how important a role these Maldivian shells played in economic and social history across vast areas of Afro-Eurasia. It has however been an oversight that few scholars have noted how significant cowrie shells were in shaping early and imperial China. This chapter therefore introduces not only the Chinese understanding of the cowrie trade centered on the Maldives but also how these marine creatures from the Indian Ocean (principally the Maldives) shaped the Middle Kingdom from its early period onward.

While Wang Dayuan's description of the Maldives is extraordinarily brief, a major issue he highlighted was the production and export of cowrie shells to Pegu in Lower Burma and Bengal. Indeed, Wang was the first person to record the cowrie-rice trade across the Bay of Bengal. He mentioned that one shipload of cowrie shells from the Maldives could exchange more than a shipload of rice from Pegu or Bengal, and emphasized that "in these areas, people use cowrie shells as money, and a very old style of currency it is."[2]

COWRIE SHELLS

From approximately the fourth century to the beginning of the twentieth century, various societies in Africa and Eurasia used cowrie shells as money, and most of these marine creatures would have been exported from the Maldives.[3] More than two hundred species of cowrie shells are found across the world, but when cowrie money is mentioned, there were only two main types: *Monetaria moneta* and *Monetaria annulus*. The first type, native to the Maldives, is the most important one and is also called the money cowrie, as its scientific name indicates. The other, commonly known as the ring cowrie, while also native to the Maldives, is found in much smaller numbers.

Both money cowries and ring cowries are widely found in the subtropical and tropical areas of the Indian and Pacific oceans. To our surprise, the Maldives was the primary and principal supplier of cowries for various Afro-Eurasian societies that adopted cowrie shells as a form of money. Two key factors account for the distinctive success of the Maldivian cowrie shells: one was their extremely small size, and the other was the geographical location of the Maldives.

What made cowrie shells an obvious choice as one of the earliest forms of money essentially were their physical features, being small, solid, light, and reliably even in size. Indeed, one pound of cowrie shells amounted to approximately four hundred pieces. Therefore they were easy to count and transport, difficult to break, and hard to forge.[4] Compared with other shells in other parts of the world, the size of the money cowrie from the Maldives was distinguishably smaller, less than three-quarters of an inch (2 cm) in length and half that or less in width and height. Furthermore, the Maldives, a maritime nexus for East–West interactions, was not far from the Indian subcontinent, which cultivated thriving economies that in turn brought a demand for a form of money. All these factors contributed to the Maldivian cowries evolving into an early form of money in India and beyond.

Cowrie shells were collected in the Maldives and shipped to Bengal in exchange for rice. Around the fourth century, somewhere in Bengal or north India, cowrie shells were used as money for the first time, and this practice soon spread to the whole Bengal region, reaching Assam by the seventh century. From India cowrie money spread to mainland Southeast Asia, including Arakan, Lower Burma, the Tai world such as the Chiang Mai Kingdom, and Yunnan (southwestern China). Cowrie shells moved westward to Africa, too. Ibn Battuta witnessed the use of cowrie money in the Mali kingdom, which shows that by the fourteenth century cowrie money had reached the upper and middle Niger River region. From the sixteenth century onward European arrivals began to ship cowries from the Indian Ocean to West Africa in such quantities that these shells eventually ruined the existing West African monetary systems and economies on the one hand and brought about the European domination of the world on the other. From Africa, some cowries were carried onward by European merchant ships to the New World for use in the fur trade or during the Middle Passage, passing into North America or the Caribbean. This is the incredible journey of the Maldivian cowrie that made its presence felt around the world at the very same time as the evil nature of colonialism was witnessed.[5]

Wang Dayuan, as I have said, was the first Chinese traveler to notice the cowrie trade and the wide uses of cowrie money across the Indian Ocean world. He recorded that one ship of Maldivian cowries was exchanged for more than one ship of rice from Bengal. He added that such a trade between cowries and rice had long been in existence, and that in Pegu and Bengal, cowrie shells were used as money. In Bengal, a silver coin called a *tanka* (*tangjia* 唐加) was minted, each of which could be exchanged for more than 11,520 cowrie shells, the latter being a form of low-value money, hence convenient for the common people. In addition, cowrie shells were used as money, along with gold and silver, in Da Wudie 大乌爹 (Orissa). Wang Dayuan also noticed the use of cowrie money in Fangbai 放拜 (Bombay), although he made a mistake there, since cowrie shells did not in fact function as money along the western coast of India.[6]

COWRIE MONEY IN INDIA AND BEYOND

Clearly Wang Dayuan was not the first person to observe the use of cowrie money in India, but interestingly, several Chinese travelers were the first to record this Indian practice. At the beginning of the fifth century, Faxian mentioned that in Mathurā (Motouluo 摩头罗) transactions involved cowries (*huoyi ze yong beichi* 货易则用贝齿).[7] Xuanzang noted the use of gold and silver coins, cowrie shells, and pearls as local money in India.[8] A few decades later, Yijing remarked on the donation of cowries (*beichi* 贝齿), gold, and silver in India, and on another occasion he specifically mentioned cowrie shells and other forms of money (*chibei zhuqian* 齿贝诸钱).[9] This is probably the first explicit reference to cowrie shells being used as money, and it confirms the use of cowrie money continuing until as late as the end of the seventh century. Huilin provided detailed mentions of cowrie money in India, confirming the wide use of cowrie money in the subcontinent.[10] Chinese Buddhist pilgrims of the Tang dynasty continued to confirm the use of cowrie money in India, and this Indian practice was well known to the Chinese by the late Tang period.

By the era of Wang Dayuan, the use of cowrie money had spread to mainland Southeast Asia, especially the Tai world. In Luohu 罗斛 (Lvo, Lavo, or Lohot), Wang Dayuan stated that cowries were used as money and that the exchange rate with the *Zhongtong chao* 中统钞, a paper money of the Yuan dynasty, was 10,000 cowries for 24 taels of the *Zhongtong chao*.[11] Scholars agree that *Luohu* was located in modern Lophuri on the lower Menam River. Moving westward, Wang observed that in Siam people "still use cowries as money" (*reng yi bazi quan qian shiyong* 仍以𧵅子权钱使用). The inclusion of the word "still" leads to the conclusion that Wang Dayuan knew that cowries had been used as money in Siam long before his arrival. In Zhenlu 针路 (Mergui, in the northern region of the Malay Peninsula located in present-day Myanmar), cowries were used as money in trade deals with Siam. In Pegu each silver coin weighed two mace and eight candreens, equivalent to 10 taels of the *Zhongtong chao* and each could be exchanged for about 11,520 cowries. Because 250 cowries could buy one pointed-cone-shape basket of rice that was equivalent to 1.6 *dou*, each silver coin could buy 46 baskets of rice, that is, 73.2 pecks, more than enough to feed two men for a year.[12] Wang Dayuan's account of cowrie money in Pegu bears a remarkable similarity to other travelers' descriptions of its use in Bengal, which reveals the regulation and consistency of such a monetary system across all these regions.

Not surprisingly, Wang Dayuan's observations accord with the notes made by Marco Polo. Once dispatched by Kublai Khan to Burma, Marco Polo traveled across the cowrie money zone from Yunnan to mainland Southeast Asia. In Dali, the center of western Yunnan, he noted that "for money they employ the white porcelain shell, found in the sea, and these they also wear as ornaments about their necks. Eighty of the shells are equal in value to a *saggio* of silver, or two Venetian groats, and eight *saggi* of good silver, to one of pure gold."[13] The Venetian adventurer followed a medieval

Mediterranean tradition by calling cowrie shells porcelain, which originally meant "little pig." A Portuguese writer in the mid-sixteenth century mentioned that "shells which in Italia are called porcellette—little white ones which we call *buzios*" were "used for money in Ethiopia."[14] Cowrie shells were so called probably because of their hog-backed shape, the resemblance of the underside of the shell to the vulva of a sow, or perhaps to their whitish-yellowish flesh color. The name "porcelain" and its nickname "little pig" were frequently recorded when the cowrie trade was mentioned from medieval to modern times.

After traveling ten days westward, Marco Polo arrived at another chief city of Yunnan. "They likewise use porcelain shells in currency," and Marco Polo understood the home of these shells, "which, however, are not found in this part of the world, but are brought from India." After another five days' journey Marco Polo reached Yongchang 永昌, a border city famous for its international trade as early as the first century. "The currency of this country is gold by weight, and also porcelain shells," Marco Polo noted. Marco Polo also visited Lohu, which not only adopted cowries as money but also served as a transit center of the cowrie trade. "From hence are exported all those porcelain shells, which, being carried to other countries, are there circulated for money, as had been already noticed," he concluded.[15]

Ma Huan further confirmed the use of cowrie money in these areas. In Siam (Xianluo guo 暹罗国), "sea shells (*haiba* 海𧵅) are used as money and they do not use gold, silver, or copper coins." So it was in Bengal (Banggelaguo 榜葛剌国). "In streets and markets, cowrie shells were used in small transactions (*lingyong* 零用), with a foreign name of *kaoli* 考黎." Both cowries in Siam and in Bengal were from the Maldives, and Ma Huan indeed provided the procurement information. "As to their cowries, people there collect them and pile them into heaps like mountains; they let the flesh rot and transport them for sale in Xianluo and Bengal where they are used as money."[16] This process would be detailed briefly but accurately by many Westerners.

Gong Zhen left a similar account, noting that trade transactions involved cowries as money. He pointed out that *kaoli* was the foreign name of *haiba* (seashells), and that they were counted one by one in the trade.[17] Huang Xingzeng recorded that in Siam trade was carried out through gold and silver, (copper) cash, and cowries. In Bengal, trading involved silver known as *tangjia* and cowries called *kaoli*, the latter which were counted by *jin*. His notes could very well have been a copy of Ma Huan's work, whereas his observations about trading in Liushan are of great significance. He pointed out that local traders used silver coins and that the country benefited from its abundant supply of fish and cowries.[18] Unlike some scholars, who mistakenly thought that cowries were used as money in the Maldives, Huang categorically confirmed that silver did not serve as money there, while cowries were exported to bring wealth into the country. Yan Congjian mentioned the use of cowrie money in Siam and Bengal, and in Siam 10,000 cowries were equivalent to 20 *guan* 贯 of the *zhongtong chao*, indicating the decreasing value of cowrie shells in the Tai world.[19] In the early seventeenth century Zhang Xie provided more information about the use of cowrie money in Siam. The use of cowrie money also had a mystical significance, being part of a local superstition: if in certain year cowrie shells (*ba*) were not used, a plague would take place in the country.[20]

This discussion leads us to a tentative conclusion concerning the source and route of cowrie money in Southeast Asia. These shells originated in the Maldives, were shipped to Bengal, traveled along coastal Burma to Siam, and were taken from Siam to Chiang Mai (and to Yunnan). This route constituted a major source in the following centuries for the cowrie monetary system in Nanzhao, Dali, and Yunnan in the Yuan-Ming period. Questions remain about Burma, which was supposed to be another important source of cowrie shells in Yunnan.

In summary, cowrie money spread from Bengal and Assam to Lower Burma, the Chao Phraya River basin, up to Chiang Mai, and reached the Nanzhao Kingdom by the ninth to tenth centuries. In these Southeast Asian societies, cowries were used along with silver and gold to form a binary currency system that lasted until as late as the middle of the nineteenth century in some places, for example, Thailand.

KNOWN TO THE WEST

As latecomers to the Indian Ocean, the Chinese were certainly not the first to notice cowrie shells and cowrie money. In the ninth century, Sulaiman was the first person to mention cowrie shells, but not without some errors in understanding. "Their money consists of cowries. The queen stores these cowries in her treasuries," he claimed. Sulaiman was also the first to record how cowries were collected. "The cowries come up to the surface of the water and contain a living creature. A coco tree branch is thrown into the water, and the cowries attach themselves to it. The cowry is called *Al Kabtadj*."[21] Suleiman was correct in almost everything except for his assertion that cowries were used as an actual form of money in the Maldives. His misinterpretation was repeated over many ages of travelers and was accepted as correct even by H. C. P. Bell in the early twentieth century; Bell, however, indicated that in some areas such as Bengal that he may have heard about or visited, cowrie shells were employed as a form of money.[22]

Sulaiman's information seems to have been copied by Al Mas'udi, who repeated Sulaiman's misconception of cowries being used as money. He claimed that the queen had no other money than cowries and described the local procurement of shells. "The queen sees her treasure diminishing, she orders her islanders to cut coco branches with their leaves, and to throw them upon the surface of the water. To these the creatures attach themselves and are then collected and spread upon the sandy beach, where the sun rots them, and leaves only empty shells, which are then carried to the treasury." Later writers could hardly add any further detail to an account of this process. Around 1030 CE the Arab traveler Alberuni called the Maldives "the islands of cowries" and the Laccadives "the island of cords," based on their chief exports. In the twelfth century, the North African–Sicilian traveler Edrisi (Muhammad al-Idrisi) claimed that "commerce is carried on by means of shells" and described the use of coconut branches to catch shells.[23] Obviously, cowrie shells constituted a major local product for export, although neither traveler detailed the export of cowries.

It must be emphasized that cowrie shells were not a form of local money, but as significant exported goods, they had certain values so that they could serve as religious donations. Therefore, cowrie shells were found both in Buddhist ruins and in Waqf endowments. Two deposit boxes containing cowrie shells dated to 690–785 CE (one even containing a piece of gold) found in Buddhist ruins, for example, indicate that cowrie shells were used as part of a sacrificial offering by Buddhist priests. An excavation at the island of Kaashidhoo in Kaafu Atoll conducted in 1996–1998 unearthed four deposits of cowrie shells, with 62,000, 106, 109, and 218 shells, with the earliest dated to 156–345 CE while the latest find was from 1170–1340 CE, suggesting the close relationship between Buddhism and the cowrie shell.[24] During the Islamic period, in one case 96,000 (88 *kottey*) cowrie shells were donated to the Funadhoo Mosque. In another case, a deal of a piece of land was made in exchange for 8 *kottey* cowries (96000) and 4 *mulhi* of rice.[25] Being economically valued, the religious role of cowrie shells in the Maldives should not be ignored.

The misconception that cowrie shells were used as money in the Maldives was repeated even by Ibn Battuta. Ibn Battuta certainly conflated money with other concepts such as wealth and value, and he listed the prices of various amounts of shells.

> The money of the islanders consists of *wada'*. This is the name of a mollusc, collected in the sea and placed in pits dug out on the beach. Its flesh decays and only the white shell remains. A hundred of them is called *siya*, and 700 *fál*; 12,000 are called *kotta*, and 100,000 *bostú*. Bargains are struck through the medium of these shells, at the rate of four *bostú* to a dínár of gold. Often they are of less value, such as twelve *bostú* to a dínár. The islanders sell them for rice to the people of Bengal, where also they are used for money.[26]

He also noticed the westbound trade of cowries. "They are sold in the same way to the people of Yemen, who use them for ballast in their ships in place of sand. These shells serve also as a medium of exchange with the negroes in their native countries. I have seen them sold at Máli and Júúj, at the rate of 1,150 to a dínár." Ibn Battuta was presented by the vizier with 100,000 cowries to cover his travel expenses to Male. Ibn Battuta's observations are crucial, since by his time in the 1340s cowrie shells were being used as money in West Africa, a fact so far not mentioned by anyone else. Interestingly, Ibn Battuta once dispatched one of his servants to ship cowries and sell them in Bengal. Unfortunately, a storm at sea had prevented this venture.[27]

In 1503, when the Portuguese Chief Captain Vicente Sodré cruised off Calicut, he caught four Maldivian *gundras* (stitched ships indeed). "These vessels were laden with cairo and *caury* which are small white shells found among the islands in such quantity that ships make their cargoes of them. In these a great trade is carried on with Bengal where they are current as money."[28] From his Lisbon office, the armchair traveler Barros described the catch of cowrie shells in the Maldives.

> Now the manner in which the islanders gather these shells is this: they make large bushes of palm leaves tied together so as not to break, which they cast

into the sea. To these the shell-fish attach themselves in quest of food; and when the bushes are all covered with them, they are hauled ashore and the creatures collected. All are then buried in the earth till the fish within have rotted away. The shells (*buzios* as we, and *Igovos* as the negroes call them) are then washed in the sea, becoming quite white, and so dirtying the hands less than copper money. In this kingdom (Portugal) a quintal of them is worth from three to ten cruzados, according as the supply from India is large or small.[29]

No sooner had the Portuguese landed in India than they grasped how the cowrie trade worked, being quick to link the cowrie trade in the Indian Ocean with the cowrie money zone in West Africa. Hundreds of tons of cowrie shells were shipped by the Portuguese, Dutch, French, and British to Europe (Lisbon, London, Amsterdam, Hamburg, and so on), where these shells were auctioned and then reshipped to West Africa in exchange for slaves and palm oil in the following centuries.

THE STRONGEST MONEY CANDIDATE IN EARLY CHINA

While the role of cowrie shells in the slave trade is well known, few scholars including Chinese historians have noted the arrival of Maldivian cowrie shells in early China from the Neolithic to the Shang-Zhou period (16th century BCE–3rd century BCE), where they played a key role in politics, economy, and rituals. Most cowries found in the Shang and Zhou period (roughly the Bronze Age in China) were *Monetaria moneta* and to a lesser extent *Monetaria annulus*, as well as the even less used *erronea errones*. These three shells appear similar in terms of size and physical form and are thus not usually differentiated in Chinese archaeological reports. The first two species are found widely in warm sea waters and shallow lagoons in the basins of the Indian and Pacific oceans.

The case of China in the story of cowrie shells is certainly one of its most fascinating episodes. First and foremost, cowries have been excavated in Neolithic sites widely over northwestern and northern China, followed by numerous archaeological discoveries in the Shang and Zhou tombs, with sometimes a single tomb holding up to a few thousand cowrie shells. Such funerary hoards of cowrie shells did not disappear until the age of the first Chinese empire, around the third century BCE. These cowries were surely imported from outside the Chinese cultural sphere and were regarded as precious items that symbolized power, prestige, and wealth. Indeed, the use of the cowrie shell in China illustrates its monetary functions, such as the unit of value, which indicates that cowrie shells were a strong—in fact, the strongest—money candidate in early China.

Second, early China produced the greatest number of textual sources that record the use of cowries in its societies. Many inscriptions on oracle bones and in bronze vessels that contain messages concerning cowries have illustrated the political, economic, cultural, and religious roles of cowrie shells among the elite in early China, and this phenomenon is eye-catching in terms of cowrie cultures across the world.

Finally, cowrie shells did not in fact become an early form of money in China, although they did take on *certain* monetary functions, and thus have been envisaged by both Chinese (imperial and contemporary) and Western scholars as having taken on a full monetary role at least two thousand years ago. More interestingly, while genuine cowries failed to be adopted as money, the imitation bronze cowries became one of the earliest forms of metal money in the second half of the first millennium BCE, which has complicated the story and at the same time been an intriguing point of contention when discussing the role of cowries in early China.

In China there have been two long-held misconceptions concerning the source and nature of cowrie shells used in early China. Since the era of Sima Qian, the grand historian of the first century BCE, the Chinese have claimed that these cowrie shells unearthed in northern China originated in the South China Sea and that they functioned as money in the Shang-Zhou period. In terms of their source, a persistently dominant view has advocated the South China Sea route, while a more extreme view has referred to their coming from all coastal waters. Considering sea surface temperatures and salt concentrations, naturally and geographically, China's coastal waters were not an ideal habitat for the cowrie shell, and while the existence of cowrie shells in the South China Sea during the age in question is possible, there has been no single archaeological finding concerning the procurement, transport, or consumption of these shells from the south coast all the way to the Central Plain in the north. In sum, all archaeological, scientific, and textual analyses refute the southern origin hypothesis.

In contrast, the geographical expansion of cowrie shells in early China clearly leads us to conclude that the Indian Ocean was their origin. First, the use of cowrie shells in early China was confined to northern China, and such shells have only very rarely been discovered south of the Yangzi River. Second, archaeological findings have confirmed that the use of cowries spread from the northwest to the north and predominantly stayed in northern China. And finally, there seems to be a cowrie–bronze nexus, since wherever there were cowrie shells, bronze items were also present. The bronze culture spread from the west to China. Therefore, geographical distribution not only refutes the South China Sea hypothesis but also leads to the Indian–Central Asian connection. Since cowrie shells from the Indian Ocean had reached northern India and Central Asia before and during the period in question, they were consequently brought to northwestern and northern China, where they were appreciated by the Chinese elite.[30]

The *Quanzhou I* shipwreck provides invaluable information on the cowrie shells that had been only occasionally brought to China before the age of Wang Dayuan. In its thirteen compartments, 2,286 cowrie shells (*Monetaria moneta* and *Monetaria annulus*) were discovered, and more than a hundred were found either on the bottom of or along the sides of the ship.[31] With a size of no more than .7 inch (1.8 cm) long, .55 inch (1.4 cm) wide, and 0.3 inch (0.8 cm) tall, these shells were surely of Maldivian origin, especially considering the fact that the compartments in which they were discovered most often happened to be those where ambergris and frankincense, the two other Indian Ocean products, were placed alongside the shells. Their quantity of less than 2,400, comparatively, is no great number. Perhaps these might have been taken by the sailors or merchants for gambling or other games or simply brought on board as exotic souvenirs. Whatever their use, the discovery of these cowrie shells in a Chinese oceangoing ship dating from the thirteenth century and together with the other Indian Ocean products serves as strong evidence against the conventional opinion that cowrie shells in China originated in the South China Sea.

Meanwhile, at least two contemporary textual sources supplemented these archaeological findings. In 1276, almost the same time when *Quanzhou I* sank to the seabed, the Central Secretariat of the Yuan dynasty noted the large flow of private cowrie shells from Jiangnan (the Yangzi Delta) to Yunnan and thus proposed to follow this private practice so as to profit from the trade.[32] This purpose was rejected as possibly causing inflation in Yunnan, a recently conquered frontier. Cowrie shells stored in the official warehouses in Jiangnan obviously must have been shipped from the Bay of

COWRIE SHELLS

Bengal area via Southeast Asia, and this route was hinted at in the *Dade Nanhaizhi*. Printed in 1304, a few decades later than *Quanzhou I* sank, the *Dade Nanhaizhi* mentioned various *bohuo* 舶货 (lit. "ship goods") from the Indian Ocean, including *bazi* 贝八子 (cowrie shells).[33] This seems to be the first Chinese mention of cowrie shells harvested in the Indian Ocean. These pieces of archaeological and textual evidence work together to reveal something about how the Maldivian cowrie shells arrived along the southeast coast of China during the Song-Yuan period.

As for the functions of these cowrie shells, scholars almost unanimously agree that they were the earliest form of money in China, and this erroneous conclusion results from their conflation of money with wealth or value. Their key evidence is cowrie-granting inscriptions on the bronze items cast in the Shang-Zhou period. Gift-granting constituted a crucial ritual to help regulate, maintain, and enhance the king-vassal relationship that was fundamental for the Shang-Zhou political system. Among the long list of typical gifts including bronze, horses, bows, slaves, land, carriages, furs, jade, cloth, cattle and so on, cowrie shells distinguished themselves as the gift most frequently mentioned.

Numerous inscriptions record the bestowal of cowrie shells by the king or noble upon his subjects. A frequently found phrase with some variations was *"yong zuo baozunyi"* 用作宝尊彝, often translated as "[cowrie shells] were used to make this precious vessel." By this understanding, cowrie shells were used as either a means of payment for the casting of or as the medium of exchange to purchase bronze as a material for casting. However, this dominant interpretation endorsed by most Chinese scholars is essentially problematic. The phrase *yong zuo baozunyi* should be understood as "for this reason, a vessel is cast," or "on this occasion I made this treasured vessel." As such, the cowrie-granting inscriptions record "the casting of a vessel to commemorate an event, the king's gift," and so the inscription was not intended to be an account book to record the cost of the bronze vessel.[34] Therefore, the role of cowrie shells in the critical ritual should not be conflated with a form of money, so evidently cowrie shells did not serve as actual money during the Shang-Zhou period.

One may wonder why cowrie shells did *not* develop into actual money in early China, as would happen in early India. Geography constitutes the answer to this question. China felt a need for a kind of money as early as the mid–first millennium BCE, but because of the long distance between

THE CARGO

the Yellow River region and the Indian Ocean and unstable and precarious transportation routes over sea, land, mountain, steppe, and grassland, the insufficient supply of cowrie shells made them unfit as a form of money, which to be effective required a stable and regular supply.[35] As a result, cowrie shells in early China had remained a rare and thus precious and religious item for more than a millennium.

Interestingly, the monetary functions attributed to actual cowrie shells in early China were taken on by their metal imitations. Certain bronze coins, oval in shape, known as the ant-nose coin (*yibi qian* 蚁鼻钱), the ghost-face coin (*guilian qian* 鬼脸钱), or the money-shell coin (*huobei qian* 货贝钱) among numismatists, imitated cowrie shells and served as one of the earliest monies in China. Most bronze cowries were cast by the Chu, a giant kingdom based in the mid–Yangzi River region, which probably

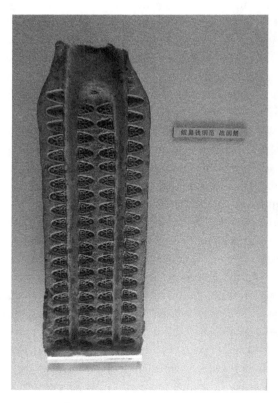

FIGURE 10.1 Bronze cowrie coin mold. *Source*: Shanghai Museum. Photo by Bin Yang.

began to produce bronze cowries with inscriptions during the Warring States period (475–222 BCE), and by the mid–Warring States period bronze cowries had become very popular. Bronze cowries were widely discovered in Hubei, Hunan, Anhui, Jiangsu, and Shandong, where the Chu Kingdom had its main influence. Overall, more than 150,000 bronze cowries have been unearthed.[36] In terms of size, they surprisingly matched the size of the actual cowrie shells, especially the Maldivian ones. One extraordinary finding was a mold (figure 10.1) used for casting bronze cowries that provides a glimpse into the process of bronze cowrie minting. The large quantity and the casting mold indicate that bronze cowries functioned in the Chu area as money.

The combination of bronze metal and cowrie shell designs in the bronze cowrie, in addition to the frequent appearance of cowrie shells in the bronze inscriptions and the noble tombs, illustrate the paramount role of these Indian Ocean shells in the economy, politics, and religion in early China. Cowrie shells probably preceded jade items, for example, in burials. The cowries were placed near or on the bodies of nobles when they were buried, suggesting their importance in the Chinese world.

Possibly, nothing is more illustrative of this practice than the inscription of the *Hezun* 何尊 (figure 10.2),[37] a bronze item in which the two-character phrase *Zhongguo* (lit. "the Middle Kingdom," referring to China itself) appeared for the first time. In an admonition to a clan member named He, King Cheng (the third king of the Western Zhou, 11th century BCE—770 BCE) mentioned that after the defeat of King Zhou 纣 (the last king of the Shang dynasty), his father, King Wu, had claimed that "I hence make *Zhongguo* my home (*yu qi zhai zi Zhongguo* 余其宅兹中国). Following this declaration, King Cheng granted thirty strings of cowrie shells to He, and He then cast a bronze vessel (*Hezun*, as it was named after its discovery in 1975) to commemorate this event.

The significance of this *Hezun* is self-evident, both substantially and symbolically. First, it was the earliest text that recorded the replacement of the Shang with the Zhou, an extremely important event in early Chinese history that has been seen as one of the first manifestations of the Heavenly Mandate (*tianming* 天命), a fundamental indigenous concept that has shaped China. Second, it was the first time that scholars learned about the origin of the *Zhongguo*, a name by which China had called itself from nearly three thousand years ago. The self-conceptualization of the Middle

THE CARGO

FIGURE 10.2 The *Hezun*. *Source*: Baoji Bronze Ware Museum, China

Kingdom hence found its earliest expression. These two pieces of evidence are invaluable and establish the role of the *Hezun* in Chinese history. However, the grant of thirty strings of cowrie shells that illustrates the king-vassal interactions from which the *Hezun* and the birth of *Zhongguo* derived have been seldom mentioned. In my view, cowrie shells from the Maldives become a metaphor for the role of foreign elements in contributing to the formation of Chinese civilization, a role that has often been underestimated and often even ignored.

COWRIE SHELLS IN THE MING TREASURY

The use of cowrie money in Yunnan, China's southwestern frontier province that borders Southeast Asia and India, illustrates how the Maldivian creature shaped late imperial China. In the first millennium BCE, cowrie shells from the Maldives came to the Dian Kingdom in Yunnan, and it symbolized political power, economic wealth, and social status. No sooner had the Tai world in mainland Southeast Asia begun the use of cowrie money than the Nanzhao Kingdom in Yunnan adopted this practice around the ninth to tenth century transition. From Nanzhao through the Dali Kingdom to Yunnan Province during the Yuan-Ming period, local people and states continued to use cowrie money for all kinds of economic activities.[38] One must bear in mind that this cowrie money practice was not a Chinese tradition, and its existence in Yunnan over nearly eight hundred years was a result of the close relationship between southwest China and the Indian Ocean world.

From Marco Polo right up to contemporary scholars, it is nearly unanimously agreed that the cowrie shells in Yunnan came from India (and originally the Maldives) through mainland Southeast Asian regions such as Thailand and Burma. Even so, as early as the Yuan period (1279–1368) officials found a large quantity of cowrie shells stored in the government treasuries in the Yangzi Delta. In 1276 the Central Secretariat of the Yuan noticed the large inflow of cowrie shells from Jiangnan.[39] A Muslim (*Huihuiren* 回回人) official in Yunnan with the personal name Qielai 怯来 reminded the officials that due to the governmental prohibition that forbade the export of cowries from the Yangzi Delta to Yunnan, great hoards of cowries had been stored up in the Shibosi, where they were of no use at all. Hence, he suggested these cowries be shipped to Yunnan in exchange for horses and gold. After careful consideration it was finally decided that the prohibition should continue to avoid the inflation of cowrie money in Yunnan. One might wonder where these cowrie shells stored in the Yangzi Delta had come from.

Although no source exists, owing to the regular trading with South Asia and the Middle East that the Yuan court favored it is fair to assume that the cowries stored in Jiangnan had been shipped from Southeast Asia or the Bay of Bengal, probably as ballast. Then, in the early fifteenth century, it is highly possible that cowrie shells were presented by the Maldivian missions to the Ming court. Unfortunately, no official records concerning such tributary gifts are extant. However, a great number of cowrie shells were held in the Ming warehouses, as table 10.1 shows.

Table 10.1 indicates that on average, the Ming court warehouses possessed around 26,000,000 cowrie shells at the end of each year listed above, equivalent to 65,000 pounds in weight, which is by no means a small store. More interestingly, before the arrival of the first Maldivian mission to the Ming court in 1416, there already existed a stock of cowrie shells in the Ming depots. For example, 63,000 pounds of shells were recorded for the year 1393. Equally interestingly, in 1402 the Ming warehouses only held about one sixth of the 1393 storage. Obviously, Emperor Taizu, the founder

THE CARGO

TABLE 10.1
Statistics of cowrie shells in the early Ming by the Ministry of Revenue (*Hubu* 户部)

Year	Cowrie shells	Year	Cowrie shells
1393	More than 25,280,000	1412	27,291,580
1402	3,911,520	1413	27,095,120
1404	25,737,680	1415	27,466,240
1406	27,385,760	1416	26,671,120
1407	2,697,600	1420	26,480,480
1408	27,237,200	1424	26,560,480
1411	26,790,640		

Source: The figures are the result of a search of "haiba 海𧵱" (cowrie shells) from "Veritable Records of the Ming & Veritable Records of the Qing," National Institute of Korean History, http://sillok.history.go.kr/mc/main.do.

of the Ming dynasty, had together with his courtiers made use of the larger part of the store of cowries. Emperor Taizu is known to have presented cowrie shells to his son who was assigned to serve in Yunnan. Another large deduction occurred in the year 1407, when over 60,000 pounds of cowrie shells were withdrawn from the reserve. A reasonable explanation for this is that they were taken on the second voyage of Zheng He to the Western Ocean as ballast in the navigation and as gifts to be presented to the Indian Ocean kingdoms. From 1408 to 1424 the storage of cowrie shells remained remarkably stable. It seems that the arrival of the Maldivian missions in 1416, 1421, and 1424 contributed little to fluctuations in the reserve.

From the occupation of Yunnan in 1384 by Emperor Taizu onward, the Ming court established a tradition of presenting cowrie shells to princes, officials, and soldiers in Yunnan, especially during the campaign against the rebellion of Luchuan 麓川 along the Ming-Burmese borderland in the 1430s and 1440s. In 1440, Emperor Yingzong ordered the transportation of half a million *jin* of cowrie shells from Nanjing to Yunnan to pay local officials.[40] This startling figure of half a million *jin* is almost tenfold the earlier yearly statistics. One may wonder how the Ming could have accumulated so many cowries.

THE RYUKYU KINGDOM

It is reasonable to conclude that cowrie shells in the early Ming came to China in the form of tributary gifts from various Indian Ocean kingdoms including the Maldives, but this still hardly explains the continuous arrival of cowrie shells as illustrated in the 1440 archive after the suspension of the Zheng He voyages. While some Southeast Asian kingdoms and merchants might have brought cowries to Ming China in the post–Zheng He era, current evidence clearly shows that the Kingdom of Ryukyu (*Liuqiu* 琉球) was the primary supplier.

The Ryukyu kingdom, located in today's Okinawa islands, did not establish its formal tributary relationship until this was solicited by Emperor Taizu in the early Ming, and from then onward it quickly became the most active tributary vassal to Ming and then Qing China, entering the nucleus of China's tributary world with the same status as Vietnam and Korea. Although the kingdom was located in the ocean world in which living cowrie shells inhabited, no evidence indicates the local procurement in and export of cowrie shells from the Ryukyu. Indeed, cowries exported by the Ryukyu to Ming China were obtained by its ships that called at Southeast Asian ports and polities such as Malacca, Sumatra, and others, where in turn these cowrie shells were obtained from Indian Ocean ships. During the period between 1373 and 1570 the Ryukyu kingdom developed an intensive trading relationship with East Asia and Southeast Asia, and a few hundred ships were sent to various kingdoms in Southeast Asia, including Annam, Siam, Patani, Malacca, Sumatra, Luzon, and Java, in addition to more voyages to China, Japan, and Korea.[41] Furthermore, the end of the Zheng He voyages provided a commercial vacuum for the Ryukyu kingdom, which soon became a pivot linking Northeast Asia and Southeast Asia. During 1430–1442 at least thirty-one Ryukyu trade missions were sent to Ayutthaya, Palembang, and Java.[42] These ships usually carried Chinese goods such as porcelain in exchange for goods produced in or imported to Southeast Asia. Understanding the use of cowrie shells in China, the Ryukyu kingdom thence purchased cowrie shells as ballast in Southeast Asia and presented these as its own tributary gift to the Ming court, a fact confirmed by a few solid archival records from both the Ming Empire and the Ryukyu kingdom.

Few historical works of the Ming recorded the export of cowrie shells from Ryukyu to China, which explains why almost no scholar has paid attention to this matter. In their entries for Liuqiu, both Huang Xingzeng and Yan Congjian listed more than a dozen tributary goods, but their contemporary annotators mistakenly combined cowrie shells (*haiba* 海巴) from the Maldives with a knife (*dao* 刀) from Japan into an odd term, *haiba dao*

海巴刀 (lit. "cowrie shell knife").[43] Both recorders listed *haiba* 海巴 from Ryukyu and *haiba* 海肥 from Bengal and Siam, which shows that modern scholars did not know that the two objects were actually were one and the same item, namely cowrie shells, let alone their both originating in the Indian Ocean.

The Ryukyu kingdom compiled its own royal archives covering the period from 1424–1867 called the *Lidai Baoan* 历代宝案 (Precious Documents of Successive Generations).[44] In 1434, its king presented gifts to the Ming including "40,000 *jin* of sulfur (*liuhuang* 硫磺), 4,000 fish skins, 6,330 *jin* of whetstone, 8,500 spiral shells (*luoke* 螺壳), and 5,500,000 cowrie shells (*haiba* 海巴)," in addition to various kinds of knives, fans, screens (*pingfeng* 屏风), and lacquer boxes.[45] Ming officials checked the inventory and found that cowrie shells numbered a staggering 5,888,465 (about 14,700 pounds).[46] Other famous tributary gifts from the Ryukyu included horses, gold, silver, various types of incense, and fragrant woods. Quite probably, apart from the whetstones and spiral shells, most of these "local products" presented by the Ryukyu were purchased either from Japan or from Southeast Asia.

Cowrie shells were markedly missing on the post-1434 tributary lists, even though circumstantial evidence indicates the continuous flow of cowrie shells from Ryukyu to Ming China. After all, the 14,700 pounds of cowries presented in 1434 compared to the half a million *jin* moved to Yunnan in 1440 was a small amount. In its negotiations to gain a tributary relationship with the Ryukyu kingdom in 1665, the Qing state referred to a Ming tradition in which cowrie shells were listed along with the other items mentioned before.[47] In addition, on the 1589 and 1615 lists of commodity taxation imposed in Zhangzhou, a commodity called *luoba* 螺蚆 was taxed at a rate of two *fen* 分 of silver per one *shi* 石 in 1589 and one *fen* and seven *li* 厘 per one *shi* in 1615. The Chinese character *ba* 蚆 seems to be identical with other *ba* characters such as 巴 or 肥, the two latter referring to cowrie shells. Its tax rate calculated by the weight unit of *shi* further indicates the *luoba* as being small and light, and thus suggesting cowrie shells. By contrast, because of their large size other *luo* were taxed based on their quantity. For example, in 1589 the tax rate of the *Yingwuluo* 鹦鹉螺 (Parrot Spiral Shell) was one *fen* and four *li* per one hundred, and the *Jianweiluo* 尖尾螺 (Pointed-Tail Spiral Shell) one *fen* and six *li* per one hundred.[48] Considering this circumstantial evidence, cowrie shells seem to have continued to reach

China through Zhangzhou after the lifting of the Maritime Ban in 1567. The volume of cowries, however, must have been small, and they must have been brought by ships from ports along the Malacca Strait.

The Ming archives also confirm that cowrie shells were presented by the Ryukyu kingdom. In 1436, a report from the Ryukyu envoy complained that personal goods including 90 spiral shells and 58,000 cowrie shells (*haiba* 海巴) were confiscated by Ming officials, and he pleaded with Emperor Yingzong to compensate him for the seized goods. The emperor graciously conceded. In the following year, a local official in Zhejiang where the Ryukyu tributary mission had landed proposed that all spiral and cowrie shells brought by the Ryukyu envoys should be confiscated. Emperor Yingzong insightfully pointed out that these items brought about a profit for these Ryukyu officials and so rejected the proposal.[49] Therefore, unknown quantities of cowrie shells must have been sold by the Ryukyu missions to Ming China at least by the mid–fifteenth century.

To sum up these pieces of evidence, from the Neolithic period to the Ming period, cowrie shells originating in the Maldives continued to reach China by transit trade in great numbers during a period of more than three thousand years. They possessed political, economic, and religious significance on the eve of the emergence of imperial China. The frequent references to the cowrie-granting ritual between the Shang-Zhou kings and their lords indicate that cowrie shells played a key role in establishing and enhancing the feudal system in early China. While cowrie shells did not become one of the earliest forms of money, their bronze imitations made up for it by becoming one of the earliest monies in the mid–first millennium BCE. Even more interestingly, cowrie shells were used as money in the southwest Chinese frontier for more than eight hundred years, and they contributed a great deal to the creation, reproduction, and expansion of the China-centered tributary world across maritime Asia. It is a shame that so few people have realized the great role of this little seashell from a small island kingdom far away in the waters of the Indian Ocean in shaping the state-building of imperial China.

Chapter Eleven

DRIED FISH, GRAINS, AND HANDKERCHIEFS

> It is eaten when perfectly dry. From this country it is exported to India, China, and Yemen. It is called *kulb almás*.
>
> —IBN BATTUTA

> The women wear a short garment on the upper (part of the body); (and) on the lower (part), they too wear a broad cotton kerchief around them; they also carry a broad, large, cotton kerchief which passes across the head and covers the face.
>
> —MA HUAN

Wang Dayuan listed dried fish as a major export of the Maldives, and Ma Huan noted that most of the indigenous population made a living by fishing, especially those in the Xiaozhailiu.[1] Brief as their accounts of this item were, the Chinese were correct in understanding that fishing was crucial to the Maldivians for both food and trade, and that is why, whether rich or poor, no one could manage without his boat. "So it would be impossible to tell the number of barques and boats upon all the islands. For the poorest will have a boat of his own, and a rich man will have many," François Pyrard concluded.[2]

Fresh fish could not last long, so most of it was processed for local consumption and international export to Sri Lanka and other neighboring countries. The ideal and prime fish was bonito that could be dried by different degrees. When fairly dry, it could be preserved for several weeks, and when extremely dry and thus very hard, it looked like a piece of black wood, about 5.9 inches (15 cm) long each, and this type could be stored for long periods.[3] Ibn Battuta elaborated on the process of drying the fish. "The food of the natives consists of fish like the *lyroûn*, which they call *kulb almás*. Its flesh is red, it had no grease, but its smell resembles that of mutton. When caught at the fishing, each fish is cut up into four pieces, and then slightly cooked: it is then placed in baskets of coco leaves and suspended in smoke.

DRIED FISH, GRAINS, AND HANDKERCHIEFS

It is eaten when perfectly dry. From this country it is exported to India, China, and Yemen."[4] While Battuta did not specify this, it is very important to note that unlike many societies that salted their fish, the Maldives did not employ this method. Sunshine was the primary way to dry fish there because the Maldives did not produce salt, and salting it would mean they would have to depend on importing salt from India, for example. Another reason for not salting the fish might have been that the Maldives did not have any spacious flat land necessary for the processing of salt from seawater.

Decades later Ma Huan provided an accurate passage on the production of dried fish. He did not say whether it was cooked as claimed by Ibn Battuta before it was sun-dried. Ma Huan described the process. "As to their *majiao* fish (*majiaoyu* 马鲛鱼), it is cut into large pieces, dried in the sun, and stored in the warehouses. Other countries also came to buy and then sell to other places too, under the name of *liu* fish (*liuyu*)."[5] Gong Zhen confirmed that after being cut into pieces as large as a human's arm, the fish was dried in the sun without being salted (*danshai zhigan* 淡晒至干) before being collected and stored in a warehouse.[6] In one version of the *Xingcha Shenglan*, Fei Xin stated that all the eight *liu* used nets to catch "big fish from the *Liu* Ocean" (*liuyang dayu* 溜洋大鱼), and this fish was "sun dried to be used as food" (*shaigan yi dai liangshi* 晒干以代粮食).[7] The so-called *majiaoyu* refers to bonito fish, and its local name was *kalu-bili-mass*. One version of the *Yingya Shenglan* identified the fish as the "sea atoll fish" (*hailiuyu* 海溜鱼) and some Chinese scholars interpreted *hailiu* 海溜 as the transcription of *kalu*, trying to link it to the indigenous word *kulb almás*.[8] Pelliot suspected that the character *hai* was a redundancy due to misprinting or miscopying.[9] If *liu* is the transcription of atoll, *hailiu* could hardly be a transcription of *kalu*.

The nearly ideal warm and shallow waters of the islands cultivated a rich variety of fish that provided ample protein for the Maldivians. From early times onward dried fish became an important trading product to sell to foreign ships. J. de Barros mentioned the prosperity of the dried fish export trade. "These islands produce abundance of fish, of which great quantities of *moxama* are made. It is exported as merchandise to many quarters and gives a good profit." He knew dried fish very well, noting that it "consists of pieces of bonito fish dried in the sun, because there is no salt at these islands: yet are they made so dry that they never go bad. Such quantities of this, too, are made at the islands, that ships are laden with it; there is no better victuals for sailors, and all seamen are provisioned upon it during their voyages."[10]

The types of fish in the Maldives impressed Pyrard, too. "The Maldives have also an infinite abundance of fish of all kinds... And so rich is the fishery, that not only have they always enough to fill their own bellies withal, but they also sell a large quantity, both cooked and dried, to foreigners. This commodity is in great demand in all parts of India, notably in Sumatra, whither whole shiploads are carried."[11]

FISHING

Fishing served as the foundational means of livelihood for the Maldivians, who were among the best fishermen in the world. Pyrard shared how fish were caught in several ways. The chief method was used in the deep sea where large fish lived. A line of one fathom and a half of thick cotton cord was fixed on a big cane, with a hook without a barb or tongue but whitened and tinned on the end. No bait was attached. However, some preparation work must have been done the day before. An abundance of little fish was caught from the reefs and shallows and kept live in the coconut cord meshes. When people went to fish, they cast these little fish into the deep sea, and as this was a rare and irresistible sight for the big fish, they rushed in, mistaking the white hooks for little fish. According to Pyrard, "They have then only to draw the line into the boat, where the fish drops at once, being hardly hooked; the line is speedily put back into the sea, and thus a marvelous quantity are taken, in such wise that in less than three or four hours their boats are nearly full."[12] It is reasonable to suspect that the French traveler somewhat exaggerated this story, but scholars have mentioned that in the Maldives during modern times two hundred or six hundred or even a thousand fish, each weighing 4–5 pounds (1.8–2.3 kg), can be fished by a team of eight to ten men in a boat within just a few hours.[13]

The fish commonly caught there was called the black fish or "*Cobolly masse*" in the local language, "because of its black colour." Indeed, the Maldivian name *kalu-bili-mass* means "black bonito fish," but this was corrupted by Europeans into the term "cobily mash." After that, the fish was cooked in seawater and dried in the sun on trays. Pyrard repeated that "there is great traffic in them, not only in the country, but throughout the rest of India, where they are in great request."[14]

Another way of fishing introduced by Pyrard was done at night on the reefs, and only twice a month when the moon was full, and these days were called the fishing festival days. Thick and strong cotton lines, as long as fifty to sixty fathoms, were used. These lines were blackened with charcoal or pitch to prevent them from rotting. Hooks with baits were cast. "With these lines they catch a quantity of fish, of a kind I have not seen elsewhere; it is three or four feet long, and broad in proportion, and all red; but within quite white and firm when cooked. It is most excellent and delicious eating, by reason whereof these people—who, in the name they give to things, full nearly express their nature—call this fish 'the king of the sea.'"[15] Obviously Pyrard loved this fish, which was eaten only when fresh.

Going fishing, one could not be too careful. Because of the dangers of navigation, even in the daytime, local fishermen did not venture more than 10–12.5 miles (16–20 km) from shore so that they could make sure that they were able to return home safely.[16] Incredibly strong currents and winds might occasionally push a boat as far as Sri Lanka or India.

Abundant as the supply of fish was, the taste buds of the Maldivian people became very picky, which impressed Pyrard a great deal.

> The Maldives abound in fish more than any place in the world. The natives are exceedingly dainty, and eat only the best and most delicate, despising the rest. There is a little fish about a foot or thereabouts in length, square at the four corners, and covered with a shell of one piece, so hard that it requires a hatchet to break it, with only the point of its tail turned back to serve it for a helm; the shell is of a yellowish colour, and marked with dark stars. On this score some call it the star-fish. It is the most delicate eating imaginable; the flesh is white, firm, and without any bones. You would say it was chicken, so good is it. You see there, too, many rays of vast size, some from six to seven feet broad; the natives, however, take no count of them, and never eat them, considering this fish not to be good. I have, however, eaten it, and found it as good as it is here. But, as I have said, they are so dainty and nice, and have so abundant a supply, that they disdain to eat most of the fish that are like ours, finding them not good enough for their tastes.[17]

Pyrard could not hide his astonishment at the wealth of sea life, saying: "one can only wonder and confess that the marvels of our Creator are more apparent in the sea than in any other portion of His handiwork."[18]

GRAINS, FRUITS, AND ANIMALS

While coconuts and fish served as primary foods for the Maldivians, the islanders were provided with many other fruits, meats, and cereals, either locally produced or exported. "The soil is very poor; rice is scarce; and there is no wheat, nor many varieties of vegetables. They have oxen, goats, fowls, and ducks, and nothing else," Ma Huan reported.[19] Fei Xin further claimed that the Maldivian people did not know rice or other grains (*bushi mimu* 不识米谷).[20]

Ma Huan was right in saying that the Maldives was short of rice. Rice was exported from Bengal and Pegu in exchange for cowrie shells. And there was no wheat. "Wheat, which is called *Godam* and rice, called *Andoue*, do not grow at all," confirmed Pyrard.[21] However, the general impression, as Ma Huan implied, that the Maldives lacked grains or food varieties was not in fact correct. In the Maldives, soil and freshwater were available, but the territory was too small to develop a large and complicated crop system. Bell noted that because of the tides "the submerged black soil of the land is discernible at low-water outside the beach," and the substructure "consists of surface-sand mixed with vegetable matter, forming a dark coloured soil, light in texture, covering two or three feet of pure sand." Below this is soft sandstone about two feet thick, "which softens again to sand, in which fresh water is found."[22] In terms of freshwater that was so crucial for islanders and for foreign ships, it was also easily accessible. Several islands contained freshwater lakes, but most people had drinking water at a little depth, easily obtainable by sinking shallow wells.

When Ibn Battuta landed on the island of Male, he was deeply impressed by the variety and abundance of food. Betel and rosewater were presented to him, and "a repast consisting of a large bowl full of rice and surrounded with dishes of salted meats dried in the sun, chickens, melted with butter, and fish" was sent to him. The following morning, another meal comprising "rice, melted butter, salt, sun-dried meat, coconuts, and honey extracted from the same fruit" was served for his breakfast. His dinner with the vizier, a prime minister and Ibn Battuta's father-in-law-to-be, "consists of rice, chickens, melted butter, fish, salt, sun-dried meat, and cooked bananas. After eating, they drink some coco-honey mingled with aromatics, which facilitates digestion." On another occasion, the vizier presented Ibn Battuta with "rice, chickens, melted butter and spices."[23] It seems that rice constituted a major role in local dishes, at least for the elite and distinguished guests such as Ibn Battuta. Therefore, Ma Huan's impression of local food might be somehow misleading and inaccurate.

First, the Maldives was rich in trees and fruits. Because of its distinctive contribution to the island society, trees (particularly coconut and palm trees), together with land, constituted the most frequent Waqf endowment. In addition to their importance for local architecture and ships, these trees also grow various fruits that served as food or food ingredients, and even leaves from trees that did not grow fruits could be eaten, supplying fiber and vitamins for local people who did not have access to many varieties of vegetables. "Among the remarkable trees of these islands are the *jumún*, the lemon, the lime, and the colocasia. From the root of the last named, the natives prepare a flour with which they make a kind of vermicelli, and this they cook in coco-milk; it is one of the most agreeable dishes in the world. I had a great taste for it and ate it often," declared Ibn Battuta, clearly with delight.[24] Pyrard provided the best testimony for local fruits: "Herbs and trees abound everywhere in the islands; a large number bear fruit, others not at all; yet of these latter the leaves are eaten, being sweet and delicate; others are applied to every sort of use."[25] He continued, providing more details about the local fruits:

> As for fruits, there are limes, pomegranates, and oranges, in the greatest possible abundance; bananas, which the Portuguese call Indian figs, but the Maldivian *Quella*. It is a large fruit, which multiplies fast, is tasty and very nourishing, so much so, that they feed their babes upon it in place of pap. There are ever so many more with which I cannot name, some of which resemble our plums, pears, figs, cucumbers, and melons, though they grow on trees.[26]

Second, while Ma Huan complained of the local scarcity of rice, which constituted the primary food staple for southern China whence he came, the situation in the Maldives seemed to have improved remarkably in the succeeding centuries, probably due to the prosperity of the cowrie-rice trade.

Rice was abundant and cheap, and many ways were invented to cook it. According to Pyrard,

> It is served and eaten in diverse ways: it is cooked by itself in water and eaten with other viands in place of bread, or else mixed with spiceries; sometimes with milk and coco-sugar, sometimes cooked with chickens or fish, which dishes they serve with great neatness and propriety. They also cook it and then dry and pound it; and with this flour, along with eggs, honey, milk, and coco-butter, they make tartlets and other very excellent cakes. Herbs and trees abound everywhere.[27]

Furthermore, although rice or wheat did not grow locally, the Maldives did grow local grains that served the people fairly well with carbohydrates. Five or six kinds of millet, originally introduced from mainland South Asia and planted by shifting cultivation, were principal crops in the northern and central Maldives. The commonest type of millet was called *bimbi*, meaning "speckled," since the small round grains are various shades of brown and red. Rich with iron and calcium, its powder is often made into a dark brown flat bread or into a fish bread for daily consumption in many islands.[28] To cite from Pyrard: "There is millet in abundance, which they call *Oura*, as well as another small grain called *Bimby*, which is like millet, except that it is black like turnip-seed. These grains are sown and reaped twice a year. They make of them a kind of flour, whereof they concoct a gruel with milk and coco-milk, and also cakes and fritters, and many other comfits."[29]

In addition, quite a few roots were abundant in the Maldives. Several kinds of tubers were also cultivated, including several types of taro, and four types of sweet potatoes were introduced in the post-1500 period from the New World.[30] Pyrard became the foreigner with the most familiar knowledge of local dishes and described them in detail:

> There grow there also roots of divers kinds, on which they live; among others, one called *Itelpoul*, which is plentiful without being sown; it is round and as large as the two fists, or thereabouts. They crush it upon a very rough stone, then they put it on a cloth in the sun to dry; it then becomes very white, like starch or flour, and keeps as long as is desired. They make it into thick soup, cakes, and biscuits, which are very good eating, except that they are

too filling for the stomach, and must be eaten fresh, to be wholesome. There are also kinds of roots called *Alas*, good to eat and plentiful, which are sown and cultivated; one kind red, like beetroot, others white, like turnips; they are in general larger than a man's thigh. They are cooked and served in several ways; and to preserve them the year round (for they are ripe only at the end of winter, in the month of September), they mix them with honey and coco-sugar, and that compound forms a great part of the food of the people.[31]

As to animals, both Barros and Pyrard provided far more detailed descriptions than Ma Huan, who only listed oxen, goats, fowl, and ducks. Goat meat was not appreciated, and cows were raised by the king on a couple of islands for festive occasions.[32] "They rear herds of sheep and cows, but not sufficient for the supply of butter, which is brought from Ceylon and other parts, and yields the carriers a good profit," said Barros.[33] More details were provided by Pyrard:

> One sees numbers of cats, polecats, and ferrets. That is all I have to say of the animals native to the island. I have seen others of all kinds, but they came from abroad. There are no beasts of burden, nor other large animals, either wild or tame. It is true there are about four or five hundred cows and bulls, but they belong to the king, who keeps them at his island of Malé. They had been brought from the continent as a curiosity and had multiplied to this number as they are never eaten, except four or five times a year at the great feasts, when the king has one killed, and sometimes to give to foreign ships which the king desires to gratify. I have also seen some sheep, which also belong to the king. He has no dogs: the people have a horror of them.[34]

Pyrard's conclusion that oxen and sheep were imported was confirmed by Ibn Battuta's experience. When Ibn Battuta planned his trip to visit the Foot of Adam in Ceylon, the vizier "sent him five sheep, a rare animal with the islanders, having to be brought from Ma'bar." In addition, horses and mares also existed at least during the age of Ibn Battuta. Horses were exported, and only reserved for the elite; but Ibn Battuta was lucky enough to get one from his father-in-law.[35]

It was a fact that the small land territory of the Maldives did not allow it to support large animals. Although there were ox and sheep, their number did not amount to many. As for chickens and ducks, Pyrard did not mention either, but Ibn Battuta witnessed that local people "buy with chickens any pottery which may be brought; a pot fetches five or six chickens."[36] Chickens were raised on a few islands, primarily for eggs.[37] So eggs frequently appeared in local dishes, which indicates that Ma Huan was correct.

Therefore, the shortage of grains or foods in the Maldives is a misleading impression created by the Chinese observers. This island kingdom was not only rich in maritime trade, but also abundant in local life. "The Maldives are very fertile in fruit and other commodities necessary for human life," Pyrard resolutely concluded.[38]

HANDKERCHIEFS

Because the Maldives lies in the tropical belt, "its seasons are hot, all like summer," but being mere islands, the Maldives did not grow any major crop, nor cultivate cotton or mulberry trees. However, Wang Dayuan listed "large handkerchiefs" (*da shoujin bu* 大手巾布) as a major export that were found as far as South India and Southeast Asia. The so-called handkerchief was a kind of sarong that could also be used for creating headdresses. Chinese visitors such as Wang Dayuan had never seen such a manner of attire and so he thought this cloth was a kind of "enlarged" Chinese handkerchief. In contrast, Ibn Battuta did not mistake them as handkerchiefs when he mentioned the local use of cotton turbans and kerchiefs as garments.[39]

An intriguing note made by Wang Dayuan was that in Xiali 下里 and Jinta 金塔 (lit. "Golden Stupa"), both located in coastal India, local people tied the *liu* cloth into clothing (*ji liubu* 系溜布).[40] Rockhill explained that it "is a cotton fabric made in the Liu (Maldives) islands."[41] The term "Liu" as a name indicating the Maldives can be confirmed by the so-called *liuyu* (lit. "*liu* fish"), the dried fish produced in the Maldives, as mentioned by Ma Huan.[42]

Although Wang Dayuan did not call the large handkerchiefs *liubu* (*liu* cloth) under the entry *Beiliu*, he understood their origin. That is why he mentioned the *liubu* a few times when the Maldivian cloth or silk was consumed by people in other places outside the Maldives. When introducing Dharmapatanam (*Dabadan*) in northwestern India, Wang Dayuan mentioned that local people wore "southern-atoll clothing" (*nanliubu* 南溜布),

DRIED FISH, GRAINS, AND HANDKERCHIEFS

namely, cloth made in the southern atolls.[43] In addition, Dabadan also had "southern silk" (*nansi* 南丝), which, by the same token, might refer to the silk cloth produced in the southern atolls. The *liu* cloth was exported not only to India, but also probably to Southeast Asia. Wang Dayuan noted the same form of clothing custom in Luowei 罗卫, where local people used purple cloth as turbans (*yi ziman chantou* 以紫缦缠头) and tied the *liu* cloth into clothing (*ji liubu*). Luowei was probably Rājaburī (Ratburi), in the Gulf of Siam, located in the previous Dvarapati Kingdom.[44]

Ma Huan thought highly of the quality of the *liu* cloth. "They also weave the first class embroidered silk kerchief, very closely woven, substantial; its length and breadth are superior to those produced elsewhere. They also have a variety of golden-woven square kerchief, with which the men bind their heads; its sale price could reach two *liang* 两 of silver."[45] Gong Zhen and Luo Yuejiong mentioned the price of up to five *liang* for this cloth,[46] an almost princely sum.

The *liu* cloth even reached China, too. First, it is reasonable to suppose that both Chinese merchants such as Wang Dayuan and the official missions of the Ming might have taken the *liu* cloth back home. In addition, the four Maldivian missions to the Ming court surely presented their indigenous products including fine cloth to the Ming emperor. Second, both Calicut and Siam presented handkerchiefs and cloths to Ming China, such as red-flower silk handkerchiefs (*honghua sishoujin* 红花丝手巾).[47] These places, as Wang Dayuan explained, were two of the destinations of the *liu* cloth made in the Maldives. In addition, the so-called red-flower silk handkerchief together with the blue-flower silk handkerchief were mentioned by Ma Huan in Ormuz.[48] Were these also brought from the Maldives? It is highly possible.

While the theory above remains speculative, another anecdote provides further background. A South Asian refugee called Bohali 孛哈里 or Buhali 不哈里 ran away from a political conflict in Ma'bar (*Mabaer* 马八儿) to take refuge in Quanzhou. To reward his submission and loyalty, Kublai Khan married him to Lady Cai, a Korean noblewoman. Sometime after, Bohali sent gifts to a Korean prince, and the list of gifts included "silk-thread hats (*yinsimao* 银丝帽), gold-embroidered handkerchiefs (*jinxiu shoupa* 金绣手帕), five *jin* and thirteen *liang* of agar wood (*chenxiang* 沉香, lit. "sinking aromatic"), and two bolts of indigenous cloth" (*tubu* 土布).[49] Perhaps gold-embroidered handkerchiefs were the same golden woven square kerchiefs mentioned by Ma Huan, and indigenous cloth referred to the cotton cloth made in India. Obviously, on his trip to China Buhali brought along with him a lot of products famously made in various parts of the Indian Ocean and sold all over that world.

To make such fine pieces of cloth from raw cotton and silk required high skills, industrious work, and remarkable patience for the processes involved. Thanks to the skill of the Maldivian artisans, the *liu* cloth was much admired. In the early tenth century, Mas'udi was amazed by the local manufacturers when he stated that "there are none whose natives are more skillful artisans, in the manufacture of stuffs, instruments, etc." In the twelfth century, Edrisi also praised the cloth makers for their refined skill and diligence. "The inhabitants are industrious, adroit, and intelligent. They manufacture wide tunics, open at the neck and supplied with pockets."[50]

The fine handkerchiefs made in the Maldives were immediately noticed by the Portuguese upon their arrival. They found that, in addition to dried fish, Maldivian vessels "also carried good stores of silks, both colored and white, of diverse fabrics and qualities, and many brilliant tissues of gold, made by the islanders themselves." They understood that the Maldivians obtained "the silk, gold, and cotton-thread from numerous ships that pass among the islands on their way from the coast of Bengal to the Straits of Meca." Therefore, the Maldive islands were "a great emporium for all parts, and the Moors of India frequent them, bartering their salt and earthenware, which are not made at the islands, and also rice and silver."[51]

In sum, it was India that supplied silk and cotton to the Maldives who in turn made these materials into fine kerchiefs. The Maldives was not only a supplier of raw material such as cowrie shells and primarily processed goods such as dried fish, but also an intensive manufacturer of goods such as the *liu* cloth. No wonder European visitors unanimously praised Maldivian artisans. "They make there also very rich cloths of cotton, silk, and gold, which fetch a high price among the Moors for their apparel," and they "wear very fine kerchiefs on their heads, so close-woven and beautiful that our workmen could not produce the like except with a wrong and a right side," commented Duarte Barbosa. His approving words echoed those of Ma Huan. Back in Lisbon, J. de Barros stated that the "fabrics made by these islanders are silk and cotton, and no finer stuffs are made in all those parts." He also knew that the "principal manufactory is at the islands Ceudú and Cudú, where there are said to be better weavers than in Bengal or Coromandel," and he highlighted the fact that "Yet all the silk and cotton, of which those stuffs are made, come to them from abroad, the islands lacking both these commodities, and also rice whereof their whole supply is imported."[52]

Truly, the Maldivian people were masters of handicrafts and manufacturing. With limited resources produced in this island country, the islanders were still able to make almost all necessities for their daily consumption such as food, houses, and ships. Local materials were also processed or manufactured for export in exchange for goods and especially grains that the local population needed. Imported materials such as cotton and silk were woven into fine kerchiefs by "the industrious, adroit, and intelligent" Maldivian people. It is by no means an exaggeration to claim that the Maldives was at that time a textile manufacturing center in the Indian Ocean world.

Chapter Twelve

DRAGON'S SPITTLE

> This islet is square and flat, with a large wide land. It looks like cloudy villages there, but there are no paddies good for crops. On a sunny day, when winds are strong and waves surge, crowds of dragons are playing around the seashore; they frequently spit spittle on the islet; and that is why the islet is so named.
>
> —WANG DAYUAN

> As for the *longxianxiang* 龙涎香 (ambergris), fishermen regularly collect it in the *liu* reefs (*liujiao* 溜礁); it is like the color of pitch (*liqing* 沥青) which has been immersed in water; when you smell it, it has no fragrance; when you burn it in the fire, there is only a fishy odour; the price is really high and expensive, (and) paid with silver.
>
> —MA HUAN

The Maldivian people lived in a culture redolent with aromatic materials of various kinds, and this deeply impressed the well-traveled Ibn Battuta, who had visited many an exotic land.

> They use a large quantity of scented oils, such as sandal-wood oil, etc., and they anoint themselves with musk from *Makdashau*. It is one of their customs, when they have said the morning prayer, for every woman to go to meet her husband or son with the collyrium box, rose-water, and musk oil. He smears his eye-lashes with collyrium, and rubs himself with rose-water and oil, and so polishes the skin and removes from his face all traces of fatigue.[1]

The sandalwood oil, rosewater, and musk oil Ibn Battuta mentions here were popular commodities being imported from the Indian Ocean world to China by that time. The Maldives did not produce either rosewater or musk oil, both being exported from India or the Arabian world. However, the Maldives did have something that Ming emperors greatly desired, and that was ambergris. According to Ma Huan, the Chinese treasure ships purchased ambergris from the Maldives.[2] Gong Zhen noted that the Maldives "produced ambergris; frequently fishermen collected it from atolls; it looks like bitumen, smells without any aroma; if burned, it exhales a fishy odor; being expensive, it is exchanged with silver."[3] It was a shared dream for Maldivians to get rich overnight with a find of ambergris.[4]

This substance was pushed onto the Maldivian atolls by winds and waves where it was discovered by local fishermen. A few centuries earlier than Wang Dayuan, the traveler Sulaiman noted that the Maldives was a supplier of ambergris. "The sea throws up on the shore of these islands big lumps of amber: some of these pieces have the form of the plant, or nearly so. Amber grows at the bottom of the sea like the plant; when the sea is much disturbed, it throws up the amber in pieces like pumpkins or truffles."[5] By "amber" he surely meant ambergris, which people then believed grew at the bottom of the sea. Around the tenth century, Ibrāhīm bin Šāṣh shared a similar story, explaining how ambergris was thrown up to the surface and was similar to bitumen.[6] At the beginning of the sixteenth century, Duarte Barbosa saw this precious substance in the islands. "Here too ambergris is found in large lumps, some white, some grey, and some black." Without knowing its real source, this Portuguese soldier was told that ambergris was the dung of birds.[7] He was kind enough to share his informative knowledge about Maldivian ambergris.

> I have ofttimes asked these moors what thing this ambergris was, and whence it sprang. Among themselves they hold it to be the dung of birds, and they say that in this Archipelago among the uninhabited islands there are certain great fowls which alight on the cliffs and rocks of the sea, and there drop this ambergris, where it is tanned and softened by the wind, the sun, and the rain, and pieces both great and small are torn by storms and tempests and fall into the sea until they are found or washed up on the strands or swallowed by whales. And those which they find white, called *Ponambar*, they say have been in the sea but a short time, and these they value the most; the grey has been long in the sea and obtains that hue; this too they hold to be good, but not so good as the white. The other which is found black and crushed they say was swallowed by whales and thus turned black, and it has such strength that the whale cannot bear it but vomits it up altogether. This they call *minambar*; it is worth less than the others. (It is heavier and lacks scent.)[8]

Francois Pyrard also thought it important to describe this rare and extremely expensive substance found in the Maldives. "Ambergris is produced from the sea, and chiefly under the Torrid Zone; I have seen great quantities of it at the Maldives, where it is found on the sea-beach. None of the natives of the countries visited by me know for certain whence it comes or how it grows. It is only known that it comes from the sea." According to the local laws, anything found on the seashore belonged to the king, no matter "it be wreckage, timber, chests, or other casualties; or ambergris, called by them *gomen*, and when prepared, *meccuare*."[9] So is it told in the local folklore.[10] This shows that the Maldivian people knew how to purify or process ambergris. During his stay, Pyrard must have witnessed the abundant collection of ambergris along the shores, as he claimed that "more is found there than in any of the East Indies," and that "it, too, belongs to the king, and he that would dare appropriate it would have his hand cut off."[11] This harsh punishment indicates the high value of ambergris.

PRODUCED IN THE INDIAN OCEAN

The Maldives was only one of many archipelagos in the Indian Ocean, a principal source for many exotic goods including ambergris. Indeed, before modern times, ambergris was almost exclusively procured in the Indian Ocean. However, the myths about the origin of ambergris had been pondered over by men from ancient up until more modern times. By some, ambergris was believed to be the dung of birds or other animals, by others a wax or gum from certain trees on the seashore, and by still others a fungus or a kind of bitumen from the sea.[12] As late as the mid–sixteenth century, the physician Garcia da Orta (1501?—1568), a Portuguese Renaissance Sephardi Jew and one of the most knowledgeable men of his era, believed that the most likely explanation was that ambergris grew at the bottom of the sea, and thus stood closer to the truth. He pointed out that the direction of the wind determined the location of ambergris: the east wind blowing it to East African coasts, and the west winds to the Maldives.[13] Giulio Aleni (1582–1649), an Italian Jesuit with the Chinese name Ai Rulue 艾儒略 who spent nearly thirty years in China (1610–1649) and introduced cutting-edge modern knowledge there, was also unable to identify the origin of ambergris. He listed several conflicting tales. One tale was that ambergris was the spittle from the mouth of a giant and a strange animal in Africa whose body could reach fifty *zhang* long. Another was that ambergris was produced in the soil, at this stage looking like liquid fat, which then flowed into the sea and formed a large lump, sometimes weighing even more than 1,000 *jin*. If sea fish chanced to eat it, ambergris might be found inside the fish's stomach.[14] According to Giulio Aleni, Africa (*Heiren guo* 黑人国, lit. "black people country") and Brazil (*Boxier* 伯西尔) were rich in ambergris, as winds and waves pushed it ashore.[15] Though deemed masters of modern knowledge in their era, the Jesuits seem to have contributed little to the debate around the origins of ambergris.

Diverse as these narratives are, they all start with the premise that ambergris somehow came from the sea. It was not until the end of the eighteenth century that scientists realized that ambergris was a digestive secretion of sperm whales, released in response to the sharp beaks of squid or cuttlefish, a principal food for this species of whale. Largely consisting of ambrein (a cholesterin), fatty oil, and benzoic, ambergris when fresh was black and mixed with blood and fecal matter but gradually became light gray and hard, with a sweet and musky odor.[16] While the formation of ambergris within the body of a sperm whale is designed to protect the whale's digestive tract, this substance could have caused sickness or even the death of an animal if it was too large for the animal to excrete. That is why fishermen traditionally found ambergris either floating on the sea or when they cut open the belly of a dead sperm whale.

Before the modern age almost all ambergris had been discovered in the Indian Ocean, and that is why this substance had long been known in India and the west. Yaqubi, an Arab geographer in the late ninth century, recorded that ambergris was exported from coastal areas to Basara in the Persian Gulf. Sulaiman referred to the sea of Harkland (the Bay of Bengal), and stated that a small quality was from the Nicobar Islands, where it was exchanged for iron.[17] While presenting a most detailed physical description, Mas'udi tended to focus on the western part of the Indian Ocean, particularly the East African coast.

> The best ambergris is found on the islands and coast of the seas of Zinj (Eastern Africa); it is round, of a pale blue, and sometimes as big as an ostrich egg. These morsels which have been swallowed by the fish called *Awal*. When

the sea is agitated it casts up fragments of *anbar* almost like lumps of rock, and the fish swallowing these is choked thereby, and floats on the surface. The men of Zinj, or wherever it be, then come in their canoes, and fall on the creature with harpoons and cables, draw it ashore, cut it up, and extract the ambergris.[18]

Mas'udi's observation stands out not only because of its rich information on the procurement process, but also because of its remarkable similarity to the accounts later written by Marco Polo and the Chinese scholars. Words and phrases such as "lump," "rock," "white," "black," "dark," "fish swallowing," "float," "canoe," "harpoon," and so on were also mentioned by such Chinese travelers or scholars as Wang Dayuan, Fei Xin, Huang Xingzeng, and Yan Congjian a few centuries later. Obviously, knowledge about this Indian Ocean tradition was observed or circulated among the Arabs, Indians, Southeast Asians, Chinese, Europeans, and many others, too.

In the twelfth century the traveler Edrisi mentioned that in some islands "is found a substance reselling liquid pitch-resin, which burns the fish at the bottom of the sea and is extinguished at the surfaces."[19] Considering the appearance, color, and smell of the "liquid pitch-resin," as well as its tendency to float on the sea surface, he must have been alluding to ambergris, although the phrase "which burns the fish at the bottom of the sea" seems to be a mythical misconception.

Marco Polo noticed ambergris in the Indian Ocean during his return journey in 1291. On the island of Socotra, located in between the Guardafui Channel and the Arabian Sea, the "inhabitants find much ambergris upon their coasts, which come from the entrails of whales," he explained, in a much more scientific way than his Chinese peers.[20] understanding that ambergris was widely desired and thus highly profitable, Marco Polo went on to explain how people came to obtain it from the sea.

> Being an article of merchandise in great demand, they make it a business to take these fish; and this they do by means of a barbed iron, which they strike into the whale so firmly that it cannot be drawn out. To the iron harpoon a long line is fastened, with a buoy at the end, for the purpose of discovering the place where the fish, when dead, is to be found. They then drag it to the shore, proceed to extract the ambergris from its belly, whilst from its head they procure several casks of oil.[21]

Some 320 years later Duarte Barbosa recorded "much fine ambergris" found in these islets, too.[22]

What Marco Polo described was a traditional method of catching whales, then widely practiced in maritime Asia. This method required highly coordinated teamwork, compared with the practice of the local collectors near Lambri as observed by the Chinese. Marco Polo noticed this practice along the East African coast, including Zanzibar. "Many trading ships visit the place, which barter the goods they bring for elephants' teeth and ambergris, of which much is found on the coasts of island, in consequence of the sea abounding with whales."[23]

The French gem merchant and traveler Jean-Baptiste Tavernier (1605–1689) made six voyages to Persia and India and showed a great interest in ambergris. His rich experience in Asia, however, did not help him to solve the mystery of its origin. He frankly acknowledged: "We do not very well know either how it is formed or where it is found; but it would appear as though it can only be in the seas of the East, although it has sometimes been found on the English and other European coasts;" and he knew that the East African coast was a major source, too, stating that "The largest quantity of it is found on the coast of Melinda, principally towards the mouths of the rivers, and especially at the mouth of that which is called Rio Di Sena." He particularly noticed that the Portuguese governor in Mozambique had made a great profit from the ambergris trade. When the Governor of Mozambique completed his term of three years and returned to Goa, "he generally brings with him about 300,000 *pardos* worth of ambergris."[24]

All these textual testimonies lead us to conclude that the Indian Ocean was the principal producer and thus supplier of ambergris.[25] A Japanese scholar deduced that those places that were famed for their ambergris must possess two conditions: the existence of many sperm whales and "Mohammedan activities."[26] The discovery and thus "production" of ambergris had something to do with the living environment of the sperm whale, in terms of its food, for example. Meanwhile, the distribution of islands and the culture of the local population constituted other key factors. Ambergris needed to be discovered, and its discoveries needed to be recorded for us to know its being discovered. That is why both the islands along the eastern coast of Africa and those in the Bay of Bengal such as the Nicobar Islands were the major producers of this substance, thanks to the literate peoples in the region, especially the Arabs. Indeed, of all the various aromatic components, ambergris was comparatively new to people, as no word in the legends or records of the Greeks and Romans referred to this substance, nor did the Egyptians, Persians, Indians, or Chinese, until the Arabs spread their knowledge.[27]

NAMING BY THE CHINESE

It was the Arabs who first exploited the substance and spread their knowledge about it to the world. The Arabs called ambergris *anbar* and were the prime and major consumers and agents who introduced this substance to India as late as some time before 1000 CE. European languages borrowed their versions of this word from the Arabic one: *ambar* in Latin, *ambra* in Italian, *ambar* in Spanish, *amber* in Portuguese, *ambre* in French, amber in English and *anbra* in German. In the medieval period, the French called it ambergris (gray amber) to distinguish it from yellow amber, the petrified resin. By the same token, most Asian languages were also derived from the Arabic *ambar*, including *ambar* and *ambāru* in various parts of the Indian continent, and *ambar* in Javanese, Sundanese, and Acehnese in Sumatra, *ambar* or *amber* in the Malayalam language along the Malabar Coast and in the Malay language, and *ámbarā* in Macassar and Bukit. Ma Huan called it *anbaer* 俺八儿, obviously a transliteration of its Arabic name.[28]

The Arabs were certainly not the first to discover ambergris, nor were they the first to exploit its uses. Islanders or coastal peoples along the Indian Ocean might have been the earliest groups who started to collect and use this marine product. Such a speculation is supported by the extant words such as *trnamani* and *tranagrāhi* in India, these words bearing no origin in common with the Arabic *ambar*.[29] Other native names of this substance did not survive.

The Chinese had long been acquainted with many kinds of aromatic materials, such as musk (*shexiang* 麝香), gum guggul, benzoin (*Anxixiang* 安息香, lit. "Arsacid/Parthian aromatic"), liquid storax (*suhexiang* 苏合香), frankincense (*ruxiang* 乳香, lit. "teat aromatic"), aloe wood (*chenxiang* 沉香), laka wood (*jiangzhenxiang* 降真香, or *jiangxiang* 降香, lit. "aromatic that brings down the True Ones"), camphor (*longnaoxiang* 龙脑香, lit. "dragon brain aromatic"), clove (*dingxiang* 丁香), and sandalwood (*tanxiang* 檀香). Ambergris came to the attention of the Chinese only in the Tang period, and indeed they first learned about it from Arab traders. Initially, the Chinese called ambergris *amoxiang* 阿末香, with *amo* derived from *ambar*. It is also argued that *amo* might be an abbreviation of the Chinese *anmole* 庵摩勒, which was found in Buddhist texts and referred to amalaka (emblic myrobalan).[30] Considering the historical context, the Arabic connection is justified.

In addition to *amoxiang* and *anbaer*, there was another Chinese term illustrating the Persian influence. Liu Yu 刘郁, a Mongol ambassador in 1263, called ambergris *sabaer* 撒八儿.[31] E. Bretschneider pointed out the Chinese word *sabaer* derived from the Arabic *sahabiri*, while Friedrich Hirth and W. W. Rockhill argued that it was originally the Persian word *shahbūy*, meaning "royal perfume," erroneously pronounced as *shahbari* by the Chinese.[32] Yamada pointed out that the Arabic *sahabiri* was derived from the Persian *shahbūy*, supporting the hypothesis raised by Hirth and Rockhill. In this case, the Persians also made contributions to the eastern spread of ambergris to China. When introducing Ormuz, Fei Xin mentioned *sahala* 撒哈剌 along with ambergris (*longxianxiang*). Yamada erroneously spelled *sahala* as *sa-pa-ir* and argued that both the Chinese words *sa-pa-er* and *sa-pa-ir* derived from the Persian *shahbūy*.[33] However, the so-called *sahala* or *sahaila* 洒海剌, derived from the Persian *saqalat* or *saqallat*, was a kind of red cloth produced in the Middle East. Obviously, Fei Xin's *sahala* had nothing to do with ambergris.

The Arabic influence in China was soon replaced with a Chinese term. *Longxian*, literally meaning "dragon's spittle," was borrowed to refer to ambergris as late as the Northern Song period and this clearly had nothing to do with the Arab culture at all. Ambergris was so named in China because it was thought to be the solidified spittle of a dragon, due to its shape, color, and smell.[34]

The Chinese term *longxian* suggests the marine origin and a fantasy the Chinese created. It is named after the *long* 龙, a Chinese mythical creature that was said to take charge of the rain and the sea, indicating its mixed nature and origin between reality and fantasy. This dragon was a seaborne creature, usually seen as very powerful and regarded as a highly popular guardian deity in Chinese mythology. The "spittle" was thought to be produced by this creature, and hence, it might have possessed some magic powers. Finally, the emperor himself was regarded as *zhenlong tianzi* 真龙天子 (lit. "Authentic Dragon and Son of Heaven"). Making this connection between the emperor and the dragon left a lot of space and potential for building links between the "Real Dragon" and "Dragon Spittle."

Many places in the Chinese maritime world were named after dragons. The Longya Men 龙牙门 (lit. "Dragon Teeth Gate") was located near Singapore, a strategic site for the control of the Malacca Strait. Together with the Longya Shan 龙牙山 (lit. "Dragon Tooth Mountain"), the Longya Men was listed in the *Dade Nanhaizhi*. Three other ports or sites also named Dragon Tooth were located somewhere in Sumatra, the Malay Peninsula, and the east coast of India, so named probably because there were high peaks or rocks that looked like a dragon's teeth. Not far from the western tip of Sumatra, there was a place called the Longxian Yu 龙涎屿 (lit. "Dragon Spittle Islet"). All these places might have been mentioned earlier, but their names associated with the Chinese dragon did not appear in any sources until the Yuan-Ming period. It indicates that the Chinese discoveries and naming of these maritime places occurred toward the end of the Song dynasty and then in the Yuan period when they extensively explored the Indian Ocean. These names were Chinese legacies in maritime Asia.

Ambergris as "dragon's spittle" in the Chinese context is culturally justified by some natural features of this substance. Ambergris is an enigmatic waxy substance, formed from a secretion of the bile duct in the digestive system of the sperm whale. It is rare because ambergris only occurs in about one in a hundred whales, and only sperm (and possibly pygmy and dwarf sperm) whales are the known natural sources.[35] Ambergris takes years to form, and once expelled from the whale it is often found floating on the sea. Therefore, the discovery of ambergris was usually connected with sea areas where sperm whales, seen by the Chinese as dragons, were active, and sometimes, it was found near a dead whale. "Whales were akin to dragons, since both were great sea spirits," and this is especially a good description of sperm whales since they are the largest of the toothed whales, with the length of a male measuring up to sixteen meters. Being light, lumpy, and floating on the water, ambergris could be mistaken for saliva that had been spat out by a "dragon" from the sea. Very soon, these exotic goods were categorized into the dragon-related group, including "dragon brain" (camphor), "dragon scale" (a kind of agalloch), "dragon eyes" (lychee, a southern fruit desired by the Tang elite in the north), and "dragon beard" grass.[36] This naming of foreign treasures along with the foreign places named after dragons enlarged and enriched the Chinese conceptualization of the world.

The word *longxian* had an earlier origin. Originally referring to the spume on dragon-infested waters, this term was used in romantic Tang poetry, as illustrated in a poem composed by Bai Juyi in 814 CE that described the gush of white foam on a pond caused by a waterfall pouring into it (*hongcheng zuishenchu, fuchu jiaolongxian* 泓澄最深处, 浮出蛟龙涎).[37] In the Tang-Song transition, especially when the import and consumption of ambergris became fashionable among the Chinese elite in the early Song, *longxian* came to refer to this exotic aromatic substance, and as a result, the original meaning of *longxian* was barely remembered.[38] One of the earliest users of *longxian* meaning ambergris might be Princess Tongchang 同昌 (849–870), a daughter of Emperor Yizong in the Tang dynasty. It is said that she suspended a large piece of wet cloth (*chengshui bo* 澄水帛) in her chamber, measuring eight to nine *chi* long, and containing *longxian*, which had the property to cool the air on a hot day.[39] In this context, considering the word *longxian* and, more important according to the Chinese belief, its alleged power to cool, Yamada concluded that here the word *longxian* referred to ambergris.[40] In this case, this might be the first mention of the use of ambergris in China. Another early mention was made by Su Dongpo, a gifted scholar and poet who, while he was in exiled in Hainan, compared local taro soup with *longxian* in terms of its aroma.[41] And Zhu Zicai 朱子才 on his journey to Canton wrote that "at night, the golden lamps are fed with ambergris and their light shines as so many pearls."[42] Hence, from Su Shi's comparison of foods with ambergris to Zhu Zicai's lamp fed with ambergris, it is clear that by the Song period the uses of ambergris were well established among the Chinese elite.

"ITS LUSTER CAN STIMULATE VARIOUS INCENSES"

To the Chinese, the Maldives was neither the largest place nor the earliest source from which ambergris was exported. It was in fact the East African coast that seemed to be the first ambergris supplier, as noted by the Chinese as early as the Tang dynasty.

According to Duan Chengshi 段成式 (803–863), in the southwestern sea, there was a kingdom called Bobali 拨拔力国, where the local people did not eat the "Five Grains" but lived on meat instead. They often drank fresh cow's blood and milk, they did not wear any clothing except sheepskin below the waist, and their women were white and pretty. They had no communication with other countries except for some trading with Persian merchants, but the Arab Caliphate of Dashi often invaded the territory. Its trading goods were scarce except for elephants' teeth and *amoxiang*.[43] The *Xin Tangshu* 新唐书 (New History of the Tang Dynasty), an official history of the Tang dynasty, copied verbatim the passage made by Duan Chengshi.[44] The Chinese term *amo* is a transliteration of *anbar*, and the so-called kingdom of Bobali, a transliteration of Berbera, was a commercial port along the Somali coast. As we know, the East African coast was a major supplier of ambergris. Nevertheless, Duan Chengshi's indirect knowledge might have been obtained from Arab traders whom he may or may not have encountered. After all, ambergris was just an unknown, exotic rumor for the Tang Chinese.[45]

By the Song period, the Chinese had obtained more information on the Indian Ocean and a localized concept of ambergris had been established. Ye Tinggui 叶庭珪, a *jinshi* in 1115 and once the Shiboshi of Quanzhou, presented a relatively comprehensive description of ambergris in terms of its origin, smell, color, and procurement.

> Ambergris originates from the Kingdom of Dashi; most of its dragons are coiled-up ones, bending over big rocks in the ocean; they lie down and spit saliva that floats over the surface; when people see flocks of exotic birds over black forests (*wulin* 乌林) and schools of fish swimming for it, so they use lances to fetch (*shuqu* 殳取) it in. Ambergris itself does not have fragrance, and its smell is close to fishy. The white one is like Chinese gall leaven (*Baiyaojian* 百药煎) with a fine texture; the black one is of secondary quality, like *excrementum pteropi* (*Wulingzhi* 五灵脂); however, its luster (*guangze* 光泽) can stimulate various incenses (*fa zhongxiang* 发众香) and it is often used to mix with other incenses.[46]

Ye's description clearly reveals the concept of ambergris in imperial China: the dragons, the rocks, the saliva, the birds, the fish, and the two Chinese medicines constituted all the key elements of future descriptions of ambergris. In addition, Ye stressed that the crucial and probably unique feature of ambergris was thought to be its ability to stimulate other incenses, and therefore ambergris was utilized in imperial China as a key ingredient for the making of mixed incenses (*hexiang* 合香 or 和香). Given that Ye had once served in Quanzhou, this information was surely obtained through his contact with the world of maritime Asia. And it is certain that ambergris from the Indian Ocean had reached China through the maritime Silk Road by the Song period, if not the Tang. Evidence from the *Quanzhou I* shipwreck supports the speculation that Ye must have witnessed ambergris.

The use of ambergris for blending various incenses, as mentioned by Ye, was certainly not a Chinese invention. The Chinese might have learnt this from the Arab world, especially considering their use of the combination of rose water and ambergris. Ma Huan noted the ambergris-rosewater combination in Mecca (*Tianfang* 天方), as the "land produces rose-water, *anbaerxiang* 俺八儿香, giraffes (*qilin* 麒麟), lions, and ostriches (*tuoji* 驼鸡)," among others. Giraffes, ostriches, and ambergris were obviously not native to Mecca and had been imported there. In a local mosque, Ma Huan discovered that "throughout the interior of the Hall, the walls are all formed of clay mixed with rosewater and ambergris, exhaling a perpetual aroma." It is told elsewhere that the 1398 ceremonial cleansing ritual involved rubbing civet, musk, and ambergris into the walls, and thus what Ma Huan related concurs with this.[47]

A few decades later Zhou Qufei largely repeated Ye's words while adding his own observations of the substance:

> In the Western Sea (*Xihai* 西海) of the Dashi Kingdom, there are many dragons; they sleep by resting heads on rocks, and their saliva floats over water; when accumulated, the saliva becomes solid; fishermen (*jiaoren* 鲛人) collect it and regard it as the finest treasure. The fresh one is of white color, and it becomes purple over time and finally dark. I once saw it in Panyu 番禺, and it is neither smoky nor smelly, and looks like but is lighter than pumice (*fushi* 浮石); some people say that ambergris has a special fragrance, others say that the fishy odor of ambergris can stimulate other incenses, (but) they are not correct. Ambergris cannot increase nor can it decrease aromas, but it can gather vapors together (*juyan* 聚烟). If mixed incenses (*hexiang*) using authentic ambergris as an ingredient, even a little being burnt, a green vapor rises up, remaining together without dispersing; guests can use scissors to cut and divide this vapor.[48]

Zhou thus determined that the key feature of ambergris was its ability to gather vapor together, seemingly magically, as vapor or smoke from other incenses usually disperses quickly. Furthermore, Zhou highlighted its change of color when stored over time and emphasized its magical power of creating a long-lasting smoke. His new explanation was fascinating if not quite scientific. A few decades after this, Zhao Rukuo copied the previous passage word for word while adding to the list the country of Zhongli (*Zhongli guo* 中理国) that was separated from the country of Bipaluo 弼琶啰 by mountains. "Bipaluo" referred to the land of Berbera and had been mentioned by Duan Chengshi a few centuries earlier. Zhao described how local people found a large dead fish that had been washed ashore, sometimes over ten *zhang* long and over two *zhang* tall. From this fish, they obtained oil out of the fish's brain and eyes, and this oil was used in ship-caulking and lamps. What this passage also provides is a description of the traditional use of the sperm whale that happened to be the producer of ambergris. It seems, however, that Zhao did not make this connection, as he claimed that nobody there knew where ambergris came from. "It suddenly appears in lumps of from three to five *jin*, sometimes ten *jin*, driven to the shores by winds. When local people find it, they divide it; sometimes they sail a ship to sea and come across and fetch it."[49]

Traveling widely during the thirteenth century in Sichuan, Zhejiang, and Fujian, Zhang Shinan 张世南 had the chance to talk with the *xiang* makers in Quanzhou and Guangzhou. Of all the *xiang* materials, ambergris was the most expensive, with premium quality sold in Guangzhou at a price of more than one hundred thousand copper coins per *liang*. The second quality could be worth fifty to sixty thousand per *liang*, and this he learned came from the Dashi but had originally been brought in from overseas. Following conventional legendary narratives, he was told by the *xiang* makers that ambergris had the ability to gather and maintain the aroma of camphor and musk for decades. Finally, based on quality, he classified ambergris into three kinds: the best floated on the water (*fanshui* 泛水), the second was mixed with sand (*cansha* 渗沙), and the third was swallowed by fish (*yushi* 鱼食).[50] This classification matched the common belief about ambergris in maritime Asia. The first kind was fresh, the second floated and was mixed with sand or soil when washed ashore by wind and waves, and the last was found inside fish that had eaten it. According to

Zhang, the Chinese thought the second and the third kinds were not good enough for making incense.

THE TALE OF THE AMBERGRIS ISLET

Wang Dayuan did not mention ambergris in the Maldives, but he was the first to notice an island in the southeastern part of the Indian Ocean that was rich in ambergris. It was the first time that the so-called Dragon Spittle Islet (*Longxian Yu*) or the Ambergris Islet, along with the mention of the Maldives, had appeared in a Chinese record. It is also highly probable that the Longxian Yu was the first name invented by the Chinese for this islet previously unknown to the outside world.

According to Wang Dayuan:

> This islet is square and flat, with a large wide land. It looks like cloudy villages there, but there are no paddies good for crops. On a sunny day, when winds are strong and waves surge, crowds of dragons are playing around the seashore; they frequently spit spittle on the islet; and that is why the islet is so named. The color of the spittle is sometimes darker than black aloes (*wuxiang* 乌香), looks like pumice (*fushi*), and has a slightly fishy smell. When used to mix various incenses together, the smell becomes extraordinarily fresh and lasting (*qingyuan* 清远); even the *qielan* agar wood (*qielanmu* 茄蓝木), plum blossom brain (*meihua nao* 梅花脑), sandalwood (*tan* 檀), musk (*she* 麝), gardenia (*zhizihua* 栀子花), *chensu* wood (*chenshumu* 沉速木), and rosewater (*qiangwei shui* 蔷薇水) and so on, must have it added to them for them to be stimulated into efficacy.
>
> Previously, nobody lived on this islet. From time to time, people from other places come; they dig a whole wood into a boat, sail it to fetch ambergris, and sell it to other countries. In transaction gold and silver are used.[51]

While he had learned that the origin of ambergris was dragon' spittle, the same as in the traditional Chinese narrative, Wang's description of this specific islet was original, indicating that he must have landed there. Furthermore, Wang must have been very familiar with various *xiang* materials, as he listed so many of them. More important, it is evident that Wang himself had seen ambergris. He not only noticed the color and smell of ambergris, but also singled out a major functional feature of ambergris: its potential for stimulating and blending various aromas together (*hexiang*). This feature, together with its capacity to hold vapor together (*juyan*), were believed by the Chinese to be the unique and somehow magical power of ambergris, making this substance distinctive, fantastical, and invaluable.

However, a tale about an ambergris islet might have spread across maritime Asia, and indeed was a very popular tale among the Arabs. *The Seven Voyages of Sinbad the Sailor* contains one of the most vivid versions of the ambergris story in the Arab world (and thus the whole medieval world). Not included in the early fourteenth manuscript of *The Thousand and One Nights*, the most famous Arab folktale produced in the Islamic Golden Age, the Sinbad story had an independent existence before being added to that collection. And thus, it is reasonable to assume that the author(s) of Sinbad might have been contemporary to Wang Dayuan, or probably a bit earlier.

Stories of Sinbad, a fictional sailor and adventurer, were set in the age of the early Abbasid Caliphate in the eighth and ninth centuries. During his seven voyages around the Indian Ocean, Sinbad experienced many wonders and thus underwent numerous fantastical adventures. On his sixth voyage, Sinbad and his fellow travelers were thrown by the waves onto a large island, where they encountered a stream made of ambergris. The beaches of the island "were covered with the remains of wrecked ships and every kind of jetsam."[52] On the island, a river fell from a cleft in the mountains, running inland and disappearing into a vase that stood at the foot of a mountain. Over the banks and beds of the river were found rubies, colored precious stones, diamonds, gold and silver, and Chinese and Comarin aloes of the first quality grew above the water. More astonishingly:

> In this island there was a stream of raw liquid amber, of the colour of tar, which flowed down to the sea shore, being melted to the consistency of boiling wax by the rays of the sun. Great fish would come out of the sea and drink greedily of this substance, which heated their bellies, so that after a certain time they would vomit it upon the face of the water. There it became hard and changed both its nature and colour: at last, it was carried back to the beach in the form of ambergris, which scented the whole island. The liquid amber, which the fish did not swallow, also spread a perfume of musk about the shore.[53]

What Sinbad described here matches the medieval tales of ambergris well. Ambergris melted under the sun and thus flowed into the sea, resembling the color of tar and smelling like musk, and large fish ate it and then vomited it out. Finally, ambergris became hardened and was washed onto the beach by the waves. This half-true and half-false narrative hence makes ambergris out to be an incredibly mythical substance. Eventually, Sinbad "collected the larger branches of the Chinese and Comarin aloes and bound them together with cords" into a raft on which he reached an island called Sarandib. "I learned that the island of Sarandib was twenty-four parasangs long by twenty-four wide, that it held the highest mountain in the whole world, on which our father Adam had lived for certain of his days, and that it was rich in pearls and precious stones (though not so fine as mine) and many cocoa-nut palms."[54] The name Sarandib came from the Sanskrit Svarna-Dipa, which means "Golden Island," and this was an Arab name for Ceylon. Furthermore, the Mount Adam Sinbad mentions, in addition to the local products of precious stones and pearls, indicates that the island of Sarandib referred to Ceylon. Sinbad's mention of coconut trees probably reminds readers of not only Ceylon, but also the Maldives. Indeed, the violent storms and waves that Sinbad encountered, the shipwrecks near the island, the discovery of ambergris, the construction of a raft made with cords and planks, in addition to coconut trees, are all familiar by now to the readers here, and echo what Wang Dayuan and Ma Huan reported about the features of the Maldives.

In the early sixteenth century, the Portuguese also mentioned the Ambergris Islet as being in the Indian Ocean. Garcia de Orta claimed that people knew of and marked the position on maps of an island of ambergris but were yet never able to find it.[55] Jan Huygen van Linschoten (1563–1611), a Dutch merchant, arrived at Goa in 1583 and shared the same tale. "They say that in India, there hath bin found whole islandes of Amber which being well marked by those that found and discovered them, whereby to come thether againe and lade thereof, when they came to the same place they could not finde them."[56]

LOCATION OF THE AMBERGRIS ISLET

It is a puzzle that Ma Huan failed to mention the Longxian Yu, because he listed Lambri, Weh Island, the Nicobar Islands, and the Andaman Islands on his voyage from Sumatra to Ceylon. Perhaps Ma Huan did not pass by this islet or he could not identify it? Meanwhile, the Longxian Yu was mentioned by Fei Xin and was clearly marked on the *Zheng He Hanghai Tu*,[57] which shows the treasure fleets must have known about and passed by this ambergris islet (map 12.1).

According to Fei Xin, the Longxian Yu

> stands alone in the Ocean of Lambri. This islet floats beautifully on the surface of the sea; waves beat it and clouds dance upon it. During every spring, crowds of dragons gather and couple there, leaving behind their spittle. The foreigners then put out canoes (*dumuzhou* 独木舟) and land on this island, collect (the spittle), and then go back. If they meet with wind and waves, all the men get into the water and while holding onto the side of the boat with one hand, they paddle the water with the other and reach shore. This dragon-spittle is at first like fat or glue: it has a blackish-yellow colour and an intensely fishy smell. After some time, it forms into large lumps of mud. Sometimes, this substance is cut out from the belly of a huge fish. It is like a pearl as big as a *dou* (peck), but still has a fishy smell. When burnt, it gives out a pure incense, most delectable. It is a trade article in the markets of Samudra. The price is not cheap: one *liang* of our official scales costs twelve gold coins of that country, and one chin costs one hundred and ninety-two of the said gold coins, this is equal to forty thousand and ninety copper cash of the Middle Kingdom. It is extraordinarily expensive.[58]

Largely copying from Wang Dayuan, Fei Xin claimed that he had visited the Longxian Yu, and thus his description of its position was highly reliable. One version of the *Xingcha Shenglan* mentioned that the Longxian Yu was west of Samudra (*Sumendala* 苏门答剌) with a distance of a day and a night by ship, and southeast of the Nicobar Islands (Cuilanyu) with a distance of five days and nights' sailing. However, there are many islets scattered in these waters, and many of these fit Wang Dayuan's and Fei Xin's descriptions pretty well. The four islands of Rondo, Nasi, Wai (We), and Bras were all listed by sinologists such as Rockhill and Pelliot as the most likely candidates. The key issue lies in the mismatch between one of the Zheng He nautical charts and its textual annotation.[59]

DRAGON'S SPITTLE

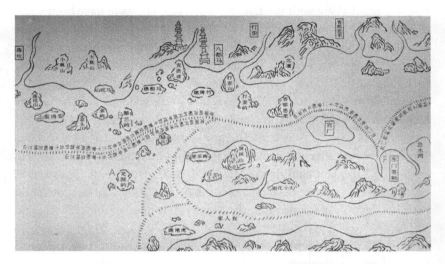

MAP 12.1 *Longxian Yu* in the *Zheng He Hanghai Tu*. (A) Longxian Yu (Ambergris Islet); (B) Nicobar Island (*Cuilanyu* 翠兰屿); (C) Andaman Islands (*Andemanshan* 安得蛮山); (D) Hat Island (*Maoshan* 帽山); (E) Lambri (*Nanwuli* 南巫里), (F) Samudra (*Sumendala* 苏门答剌). *Source*: Haijun Haiyangcehuiyanjiusuo and Dalian Haiyunxueyuan Hanghaishi Yanjiushi, eds., *Xinbian Zheng He Hanghai Tuji* (An Edited Volume of the Zheng He Nautical Chart) (Beijing: Renmin Jiaotongchubanshe, 1988), 65.

On the *Zheng He Hanghai Tu* on which the Longxian Yu was marked, the island was located southwest of Hat Island (*Maoshan*), while the compass direction in the textual annotation indicates that the Longxian Yu should be northwest of Hat Island. Su Jiqing in his review of these speculations argued that the textual annotation was authentic, so the Longxian Yu is in fact the island of Rondo.[60] However, Kentaro Yamada, with whom Su failed to consult, shared another very interesting and also plausible argument. He compared the three navigation routes listed by Ma Huan, Fei Xin, and the one on the *Zheng He Hanghai Tu* from Samudra via the Nicobar to Ceylon along which the Longxian Yu was located, and found that they did not match. Unlike other scholars who endeavored to identity the island, Yamada argued that either the Chinese imagined some island or rock in the sea was the Ambergris Island or they simply made up an imaginary island.[61]

Whether or not the so-called Longxian Yu referred to Rondo or Bras, in my point of view, does not matter so much. In fact, the lower part of the

Bay of Bengal along with the East African coast seems to have been a traditional supplier of ambergris. The Nicobar Islands, for example, were famous for ambergris. Duarte Barbosa observed that "the dwellers therein get much ambergris which is taken to Malacca and other places," probably including China.[62] That is why I tend to accept what Wang Dayuan stated as true: there was an actual ambergris islet or quite a few ambergris islets located west of Samudra and south of the Nicobar Islands, but the exact location(s) is hard to ascertain. The tale of an ambergris island circulated across maritime Asia and its description might match many candidates in the Indian Ocean, including the Maldives. Huang Xingzeng, for example, positioned the passage on the *panlong* 蟠龙 (lit. "coiled-up dragon") and their production of *longxian* on the Maldives, instead of on the Longxian Yu.[63]

Huang Xingzeng probably incorporated all imperial texts available to him and made a comprehensive description of ambergris.[64]

> As for the collection of the *longxian*, most (comes) from the *liu* islets. There are many coiled-up dragons (*panlong*) in the *liu* islets; in spring they vomit spittle (*tuxian* 吐涎), flocks of birds collect them and place them together; schools of fish sip them (*zan* 噆); the yellow kind is like glue (*jiao* 胶); the black one like *excrementum pteropi* (*wulingzhi*); the white one like Chinese gall leaven (*baiyaojian*); it smells fishy; it can also be obtained from the bellies of fish, with the size of a peck (*dou*), as round as a pearl; and its price is measured by the unit of *liang*; one *liang* can exchange twelve gold coins (*jinqian* 金钱); and one *jin* 192 gold coins.[65]

In the second half of the sixteenth century, Yan Congjian meticulously expanded Wang Dayuan's passage on the Longxian Yu.[66] In addition, he helped to reveal the value of ambergris by pointing out that 192 gold coins were equal to 9,000 Chinese copper coins. Huang Xingzeng and Yan Congjian must have accessed some sources not known to us to obtain these details.

Compared with many other *xiang* materials ambergris was a latecomer to China. It became well known in China, strangely long before a steady supply of it arrived in China during the Song period when oceangoing voyages between China, Southeast Asia, and the Indian Ocean were regular and frequent. Imperial sources indicate that the import and thus consumption of ambergris in the inner court thrived in the two periods of the Song and the early Ming.

CONSUMING AMBERGRIS IN SONG CHINA

The *xiang* was consumed and used in imperial China in many ways, as a perfume, an incense, a medicine, and as a decoration made into bracelets and necklaces. It was used to freshen and enhance both the body and spirit, and to attract both lovers and deities.[67] Very often it constituted an inseparable component in the worship of gods and ancestors. Over time its medicinal functions were gradually exploited and highlighted, especially from the Ming period onward in the Daoist tradition of processing an elixir in which ambergris was a key ingredient. Finally, when burnt or heated, the *xiang* was fragrant and gave off a light smoke, creating a magical atmosphere that brought mortals closer in their imagination to heaven or the immortal world. *Jiangzhen xiang*, for example, literally means "descending true (deities) *xiang*," probably because it was believed to be able to attract deities descending from heaven to earth, thus implying its key function in Daoist rituals.

The Chinese consumption of ambergris reached its first heyday in the Song period, and the earliest works on the production, import, processing, consumption, and appreciation of this *xiang* were completed in this period. Hong Chu 洪芻, a *jinshi* in 1094, compiled the *Xiangpu* 香谱 (Guide of the *Xiang*), the first encyclopedia on the *xiang*.[68] Its first *juan* lists the 83 *xiang*, and its second includes various matters including the making, consumption, and heresies, as well as essays, and poems dedicated to it. Hong Chu's pioneering initiative shaped future works on this subject.

At the beginning of the twelfth century, Ye Tinggui compiled the *Nanfan Xianglu* 南蕃香录 (Record of the Xiang in the South), but this work is no longer extant. Fortunately, some of its entries were cited in another *Xiangpu* compiled by Chen Jing in the thirteenth century. With a preface dated 1262, Chen Jing's *Xiangpu*, consisting of four *juan*, was another influential encyclopedia. The first *juan* lists all the names of incenses, the second provides prescriptions for the making of various *xiang*, many of which were named after members of the elite (scholars, officials, or monks) and incense shops, or directly referred to as being used in court, illustrating the active involvement of the social elite in enjoying and promoting this social fashion. The third and fourth include the making of incense beads, medications, teas, sachets, and pillows, in addition to composing essays and poems devoted to incenses.[69] An incense shop in Guangzhou managed by the Wu family, for example, was famous for its *longxianxiang*, and was mentioned in many Song records.[70]

Ambergris was not listed in the eighty-three *xiang* recorded by Hong Chu, but the term *longxianxiang* was frequently mentioned by Chen Jing. Twenty-six kinds of the *longxianxiang*, for example, are listed in the second *juan*. It seems that within less than two hundred years ambergris had become increasingly popular in China. Whatever the function of ambergris, its being a key ingredient for the making of mixed incenses was widely appreciated. And probably because it was rare and exotic, many mixed incenses, though called the *longxianxiang*, did not in fact contain any ambergris. Among the recipes of the twenty-three so-called *longxianxiang*, only three list ambergris as an ingredient. This was no careless omission, as otherwise, the processing procedure, in addition to mentioning various ingredients including the *xiang*, tea, honey, wine, and special utensils such as silver ones, was strictly detailed. It seems that the name *longxianxiang* became the synonym of *hexiang* (mixed incense), as incense producers and shops used its name to attract customers who might be unable to afford the authentic ambergris. Therefore, in the Chinese context, the name *longxianxiang* frequently refers to various mixed incenses that had been processed from base ingredients such as frankincense and aloe wood (but not necessarily and indeed seldom ambergris), while *longxian* or *lonxianxiang* as an ingredient refers to the actual ambergris.[71]

Ambergris reached Song China either as a tributary gift or as commercial goods. In 1071, a kingdom of Cengtan (*Cengtan guo* 层檀國) presented gifts including ambergris, pearls, frankincense, and coral, among other treasures. The Cengtan might refer to Zanzibar or some polity in West Asia, and thus would not have been far from the Bobali kingdom mentioned by Duan Chengshi. In 1072, a kingdom called Wuxun (*Wuxun guo* 勿巡国) under the sovereignty in some way of Dashi also presented pearls, frankincense, white dragon's and black dragon's spittle (*bailong heilongxianxiang* 白龙黑龙涎香), coral, white parrots, and other items.[72] Since the kingdom of Wuxun was either under the influence or within the territory of the Dashi, it was located somewhere in or near West Asia. In 1137, *Sanfoqi* (Palembang) in Sumatra presented its envoys at the Southern Song court.

Ambergris, together with corals, pearls, elephant trunks, and incense medicines (*xiangyao* 香药) were among its tributary gifts.[73] Zhao Yanwei 赵彦卫, a *jinshi* in 1163, explicitly listed ambergris along with rosewater, as tributary goods obtained from the Indian Ocean world kingdoms such as Dashi 大食 and Sanfoqi by the Fujian Shibosi in Quanzhou.[74] The remains of ambergris (and frankincense) discovered in the *Quanzhou I* wreck constitute solid archaeological evidence of the import of ambergris into Song China.[75]

Most of the ambergris, however, might have been presented by the Shibosi. The Song state continued and expanded this office in many key commercial port cities such as Quanzhou, Mingzhou (Ningbo, Zhejiang), Wenzhou (Zhejiang), and Mizhou (Shandong), in addition to Guangzhou, all along the southern and eastern coasts. While taxation constituted one of its major duties, the maritime customs office had the privilege of purchasing certain goods primarily intended for the imperial court. Ambergris, for example, was frequently demanded in imperial edicts issued to all maritime custom offices. No sooner had Gaozong (r. 1127–1162), the first emperor of the Southern Song dynasty, stabilized his rule in south China after the Jin Kingdom had occupied the Yellow River region than in 1133 did he order the maritime customs offices to provide ambergris for his court at Lin'an 临安 (lit. "Temporary Stay"), the new capital in the Yangzi Delta. In 1141, the edict was repeated.[76]

Gaozong's demand for ambergris might have been influenced by the court tradition of the Northern Song (960–1127). Circumstantial evidence indicates the use of the *longxianxiang* in the Northern Song's inner court, and this tradition was essentially linked with Daoism followed and practiced by a few emperors. Cai Tao 蔡绦, an official in the reign of Huizong 徽宗 (1082–1135), recorded quite a few stories about court life. Ambergris, for example, was gifted by Emperor Zhezong 哲宗 (1077–1100, Huizong's elder brother) to Cai Jing 蔡京 (1047–1126), Cai Tao's father.[77]

However, ambergris must have been very rare and was probably only presented in the inner court, which may account for why Huizong did not initially know about this substance. Huizong happened to come across two lumps of ambergris but had no idea what it was, so he distributed these to his ministers and guards. The ambergris lumps had been kept for a long time and did not look very appealing, yet even a bean-size piece when heated gave off an exotic aroma that lasted for a whole day. Extremely surprised,

Huizong ordered the ambergris he had given away to be returned. He then named it *Gu longxian* 古龙涎 (lit. "Ancient Dragon's Spittle"). Chips of ambergris, aloe wood, and camphor were inserted into candles before the wax became dry.[78] Powerful eunuchs managed to get themselves one apiece, each lump being worth one hundred *min* 缗.[79] Inserted into small gold or jade containers, ambergris was the most valuable part of the pendant. Eunuchs often showed off these pendants to one another by "wearing incense" (*peixiang* 佩香), a tradition of "hanging sachets and scent bags of all kinds in the clothing, especially on the girdle" that had been very popular as early as the Tang period.[80] Due to its aroma, ambergris was also made into beads for decoration. In the summer of 1184, 50 necklaces made of ambergris beads were presented to the empress dowager.[81] Contemporary sources also highlighted the price of ambergris. On one occasion, an empress offered 200,000 *min* (*ershiwan min* 二十万缗) for one fifth *liang* of ambergris, but her offer was turned down as the maritime merchant expected a price of up to 300,000 *min*.[82]

The *Yuan Shi* 元史 (History of the Yuan Dynasty) mentions nothing about ambergris, expect for one account that states that incenses used in a sacrificial ritual had to be aloe wood and (or) ambergris (*xiang yong chen longxian* 香用沉龙涎).[83] More ambergris than is recorded might have reached China, considering the frequent official and commercial interactions between China and the Indian Ocean.

FROM AROMATIC TO MEDICINAL

Early Ming China witnessed the arrival of ambergris from overseas, a result of the Chinese expeditions to Southeast Asia and the Indian Ocean. First, Chinese treasure fleets must have carried ambergris home to China, and second, some tributary missions presented this exotic gift at the imperial court. It is recorded that ambergris was presented in their tributes from Sumatra, Bengal, Calicut (*Guli*), Brava (*Bulawa*), Juba (*Zhubu*) and La'sa (*Lasa*) during the era of Zheng He.[84] While only a few official archives or records listed this tributary gift, Luo Maodeng's novel *Xiyang Ji* details lists of local gifts presented by foreign kingdoms as solicited by Zheng He. Among the 39 kingdoms listed in the *Xiyang Ji*, eight kingdoms presented ambergris, including an unspecified amount from Samudra, fifty *jin* from the kingdom of Jicini 吉慈尼, ten chests (*xiang* 箱) from the three kingdoms of Mogadishu (*Mugudushu*), Juba, and Brava, 500 *jin* from Cochin (*Kezhi*), four chests from La'sa, and ten chests from Dhofar (*Zufaer*).[85] All these kingdoms were located in the Indian Ocean, and the details tally with the *Ming Shi*.

But then, ambergris no longer reached China from the mid-fifteenth century onward. Emperor Jiajing, for example, was extremely disappointed, frustrated, and angry when his repeated orders for the purchase of ambergris proved to be futile. Emperor Jiajing was an intriguing and controversial ruler. In the first half of his reign, he was active, hardworking, and effective while in his post-1542 reign, he isolated himself and refused any audience with his ministers for more than two decades. What primarily occupied him was his obsession with Daoism.

Daoism attracted Emperor Jiajing because of its emphasis on being the pathway to achieve longevity or even immortality. Alchemy, the processing of Chinese *materia medica* including toxic metals such as mercury, lead, and arsenic, was an essential part of Daoist theory and practice, and with its knowledge, it was believed possible to make elixirs dreamed of by emperors who wished to stay in the secular world as long as possible or even forever. While Daoist rituals required many kinds of the *xiang*, the making of the Daoist elixir, the so-called golden cinnabar (*jindan* 金丹), required only certain key ingredients including ambergris. It was in such an imperial frenzy that Emperor Jiajing became anxious to mobilize his entire empire to obtain this Indian Ocean commodity.

Nobody was more devout in Daoist practices than Emperor Jiajing. Daoism was adopted in the early Ming court, and this might have influenced Emperor Jiajing, providing him with formal and informal channels for the teachings of this religious sect. For example, scholar-officials had presented "Prescriptions of the Inner Chamber" (*fangzhong mifang* 房中秘方, Taoist sexual practice) and aphrodisiacs (*chunyao* 春药 or *meiyao* 媚药) to the Inner Court as early as the reign of Xianzong (r. 1464–1487).[86] Daoism provided Emperor Jiajing with the pathway he needed for the two topmost goals in his forty-five-year long reign: to sire a male heir in the first half of his reign and to attain longevity in the second. He was convinced that the Daoist practices had been efficacious in helping him produce a son, who was born in 1533. And then what primarily occupied him was the making of golden cinnabars of aphrodisiac and elixir. Daoist physicians and alchemists were recruited, and key ingredients consisting of exotic and strange substances such as various *xiang* including ambergris, silver, ganoderma (*zhicao* 芝草 or *lingzhi* 灵芝), and the urine and menstrual blood of virgins were collected. Imperial officials and eunuchs were dispatched to southern China for the first three materials, the virgins were presented to the Inner Court. Menstrual blood was collected from these court girls, some of whom were so tortured by this procedure that in 1542, they got together and almost strangled the emperor to death, an unprecedented scandal in imperial China. After this incident, Jiajing became wholly devoted to Daoist practices that promised immortality.[87]

Indeed, all the Ming sources indicate that ambergris was used as a key ingredient for the making of gold cinnabar, whether it be for elixirs or aphrodisiacs. To be true, the use of ambergris for medicinal purposes had rarely been a practice before the Ming period, and it was the Daoists during the Ming period that began to exploit the medicinal properties of this substance, especially under the pressure of making golden cinnabar for the emperor.[88]

Li Shizhen 李时珍 (1518–1593), for example, could find few formulated prescriptions using this substance and his own *Compendium of Materia Medica* did not have much to say about its medicinal function. When discussing the energy of the *long* (dragon), he commented that ambergris was seldom mentioned in prescriptions, but when introducing *diao* 吊, one of the two types of eggs supposedly laid by dragons, Li Shizhen noted that the *diao* had recently been employed in the "arts of the bedchamber" (*fangzhongshu* 房中术).[89] Daoist practitioners believed that the arts of the bedchamber could promote health, longevity, and/or spiritual advancement. Li Shizhen's comments certainly reveal the rise of a trend that began to exploit the medicinal and sexual functions of ambergris, uses that Emperor Jiajing had so energetically pursued.

By the Qing period, the standard medicinal analysis of ambergris had been well established. Zhao Xuemin 赵学敏 (?1719–1805), a Qing medical practitioner, provided a further analysis of the medicinal function of ambergris that was believed to activate the blood (*huoxue* 活血), benefit the marrow and essence (*yijingsui* 益精髓), and facilitate the yang way (*zhu yangdao* 助阳道).[90] Zhao pointed out that the dragon, an eastern deity, was of a pure yang (*chunyang* 纯阳) nature, and its spittle was "yang within yang" (*yanghzongzhiyang* 阳中之阳), so that its fragrance was extremely pleasing (*qiqi juexiang* 其气绝香). Because of its yang nature, it was able to overcome the utmost yin, or female nature, especially during sexual intercourse.[91] Zhao's explanation shows ambergris evolved from an aromatic to a medicinal substance.

THE SEARCH FOR AMBERGRIS

It was Jiajing's obsession with gold cinnabar that an empire-wide mobilization was made for the search for ambergris. In 1524, Shao Yuanjie 邵元节, a Daoist priest from Dragon–Tiger Mountain (*Longhushan* 龙虎山), Jiangxi Province, the headquarters of the Daoist sect, was called to Beijing. He later recommended Tao Zhongwen 陶仲文, another Daoist priest, who was said to be able to get rid of any evil in the Inner Court, heal the smallpox of the heir apparent, and predict a fire. Probably of greatest interest to the emperor was Tao's presentation about the "Secret Prescriptions of the Inner Chamber," and many officials, though selected through the imperial exemption system, followed this method to draw Jiajing's attention.[92] Shao and Tao utilized the so-called *hongqian* 红铅, the first menstrual blood of virgin girls collected from court ladies to make an aphrodisiac, while Gu Kexue 顾可学 used the so-called *qiushi* 秋石, processed from the urine of virgins as this was thought to help achieve immortality.[93] With its medicinal potential explored for the first time in these Daoist experiments, ambergris joined other conventional materials such as ganoderma and silver in the preparation of the elixir. In 1551, Emperor Jiajing ordered the Ministry of Revenue to hand over 50,000 *liang* of silver to the Inner Court, and for the following years, 100,000 *liang* had to be presented every five years. He also ordered imperial agents to be dispatched along different routes in search of ambergris.[94]

In 1554 Emperor Jiajing warned his trusted minister Yan Song 严嵩 that the purchase of ambergris by the Ministry of Revenue had proven futile. "Amongst all incenses used in the court, this is the best," the emperor declared, emphasizing the efficacy of ambergris. He pointed out that there was a limited store of it in the Inner Court and what was there would not last long. Yan Song passed this message on to the Ministry of Revenue, which in turn justified its failure to obtain ambergris. This ambergris was obtained from remote areas of Yunnan and Guangdong, and because private stores had run out officials were unable to get their hands on any more consignments. In addition, it was difficult to tell the authentic from the forged ambergris, and people dared not present fake goods to the emperor. Emperor Jiajing read their report but still thought that the ministry had not taken his edict seriously and ordered the adoption of every single means to procure this substance.[95] Jiajing's disappointment and anger in 1554 were justified. It had been more than ten years since his first edict requesting the purchase of ambergris, but little if any had been presented to him. In 1555, the Ministry of Revenue had no choice but to send officers to coastal locations to look for ambergris one more time.[96]

However, the new efforts proved futile once again. In 1556 Emperor Jiajing was furious with the ministry and issued a warning: "over ten years, no ambergris has been presented, and your subordinates cheat and ignore to a ridiculous degree" (*shenyi* 甚矣). He ordered the production sites to be investigated. The Ministry of Revenue then "sent officials to Fujian and Guangdong, together with previously assigned ones, surveying and searching all the places where foreign ships are accessible; and high expense would not be a concern." Emperor Jiajing was patient enough to defer the punishment of those officials who failed on the ambergris mission until he saw some results. He ordered another official to Yunnan to see whether any ambergris could be obtained from any collector to whom the state would pay a high price.

Soon there appeared a campaign and competition with parties of officials and common subjects across the empire who jostled to acquire and present ganoderma to the emperor, and Wang Jian 王健 and Wang Huai 王槐 were dispatched to seek ambergris and silver ores, respectively.[97] This national mobilization did produce something. About three months later, seventeen *liang* of ambergris were presented to the court from Guangdong. In 1557 another sixteen *liang* from Fujian and nineteen *liang* from Guangdong were presented, respectively.[98]

In 1557 a new measure proposed by Wang Jiang was adopted. Because he failed to obtain any ambergris from Fujian and Guangdong, so Wang proposed that any seagoing ship (*haibo* 海舶) visiting China must surrender any ambergris before it would be allowed to enter the port. He argued that this measure would cause the arriving consignments of ambergris to be determined at a cheaper price and save on the dispatching of officials for this mission. Supported by the Ministry of Revenue and approved by Emperor Jiajing, the new measure was put into practice in Guangdong.[99]

In 1560 Emperor Jiajing issued another decree to the Ministry of Revenue that of all the ambergris presented so far, only one or two consignments had been authentic. "Concerted efforts (*yongxin* 用心) must be made to collect and present the real substance," warned Emperor Jiajing.[100]

With little authentic ambergris coming to light, it was unfortunate that a fire broke out and burned whatever stocks there had been in 1562. Three months later, Minister of Revenue Gao Yao 高燿 purchased and presented eight *liang* worth of ambergris to Emperor Jiajing, who was delighted and willingly paid the price of 760 *liang* of silver. In addition, he decided to reward Gao for his devotion with an honorary title, which Gao humbly declined but Emperor Jiajing insisted he take.[101] Eight *liang* of ambergris for 760 *liang* of silver was a shockingly bad deal, since the price of one *liang* of ambergris reached 95 *liang* of silver. According to Yan Congjian, in Lambri one *jin* (sixteen *liang*) of ambergris was worth 9,000 Chinese copper coins, which ideally speaking, was equivalent to nine *liang* of silver.[102] Therefore, Emperor Jiajing paid to Gao Yao nearly 170 times the usual price. The fact that Emperor Jiajing was willing to pay so much higher than the market price highlights his anxiety and desperation more than anything else.

Three days later eighteen *liang* of ambergris arrived from Fujian, a quantity that it was hoped might satisfy the Son of Heaven for a while. In 1563, sixty-two *liang* arrived from Guangdong and thirteen *liang* (eight *liang* the first time and five the second) was presented by Fujian. In 1565 Emperor Jiajing lost his patience once again. He accused the Ministry of Revenue of being ineffectual, saying that ambergris was an easily obtainable commodity (*changyou zhiwu* 常有之物). He refuted one official who argued that ambergris was rare all over the world, because it was so listed in *Yongle Dadian* 永乐大典, an encyclopedia compiled in the reign of Emperor Yongle. He pointed out that the ambergris presented to him was lighter in weight than had been reported, and thus had been a waste of money, and roundly scolded Gao Yao for his inability to provide ambergris.[103]

Gao Yao was in a state of fear and trepidation and asked for more officials to be sent to Guangdong and Fujian. Emperor Jiajing changed his tone and explained that his use of incense was not for Daoist cultivation and rituals (*zhaixiu* 斋修) but for the making of a "ten-thousand-year incense pie (*wansui xiangbin* 万岁香饼), a routine in the Inner Court, and he urged officials not to repeat the previous neglect shown by Liang Cai 梁材 but to seek out and obtain a steady and regular supply of a quantity of authentic ambergris. "Three to five *jin* presented each time," Emperor Jiajing detailed. Soon after, Gao Yao presented him with one *jin* and eight *liang* of ambergris which he claimed had been purchased from private markets.[104]

The name of Liang Cai was mentioned as a warning to ministers. Liang, a senior scholar-official, had once been simultaneously in charge of both the Ministry of Revenue and the Ministry of Justice, which reveals the trust and confidence the emperor had in him. However, Liang failed to provide ambergris in a timely manner and the emperor removed him on the excuse of some other offenses. In addition, Wang Gao 王杲, another minister of revenue, was removed and put into prison for the same reason. With these lessons, envoys were dispatched to obtain silver and ambergris. About a month later one official presented ambergris and was rewarded with silver and silk by the emperor.[105]

In January 1567 Emperor Jiajing died, and this put an end to the relentless pursuit of ambergris for a time. A few days after his ascent to the throne, the new Emperor Longqing 隆庆 (r. 1567–1572) announced the end of ambergris procurement.[106] However, he was obsessed with sexual pleasure and continued to take aphrodisiacs (*chunyao*), which eventually caused his death in 1572. While the lift of the Maritime Ban in 1567 witnessed a thriving oceanic trade between China and Southeast Asia, ambergris was not found in either of the two commodity-taxation lists of 1589 and 1615.[107] This exotic substance that primarily originated in the Indian Ocean almost stopped entering China for the whole of the sixteenth century and thereafter.

In the following reign of Emperor Shenzong 神宗 (r. 1573–1620), ambergris reappeared in the official archives. In 1596, a local official in Guangzhou presented forty-six *liang* of ambergris. In 1599, one decree ordered the purchase of ambergris, and about six months later, the Ministry of Revenue presented ambergris and pearls to the emperor. In 1612 a report from Guangdong shows evidence that ambergris continued to be purchased.[108] The appearance of ambergris might have something to do with Shenzong. Like grandfather, like grandson: from the time that he ascended the throne as a boy of nine and all during his youth, Shenzong worked diligently for the restoration of the Ming rule, while after 1588 he seemed to tire of administration, and followed Jiajing's retreat into the Inner Court for the next three decades. He was said to have overindulged in wine and sex. A key reason why he canceled his daily audiences with his ministers probably had to do with his poor health, most likely brought about by the excessive imbibing of aphrodisiacs and elixirs.

In August 1620, Shenzong died. Just one month after taking his place on the throne, Emperor Guangzong 光宗 (1582–1620), Shenzong's son, died of red cinnabar (*hongwan* 红丸, a nickname for aphrodisiacs) poisoning too. It seems that the Daoist faith and practices (and thus ambergris) continued in the Inner Court of Ming China until the end of the dynasty.

WHY IS AMBERGRIS NO LONGER AVAILABLE?

The detailed records above indicate that ambergris, a maritime product from the Indian Ocean, had played a critical role in imperial power struggles, court politics, religious activities, and both the secular pleasure-seeking and spiritual pursuits of emperors. Its absence caused a great sense of desperation and anxiety to the whole imperial bureaucratic apparatus including emperors, court ministers, eunuchs, and officials at all levels. While the giant empire was mobilized, its failure to procure ambergris appears to be a conundrum, especially given the emperor's determination, let alone Ming China's might and wealth.

The maritime ban carried out by the Ming state certainly accounted for the difficulty of obtaining ambergris, as this state policy cut off overseas connections, isolated China from the outside world, and prevented the arrival of exotic goods. Ming Taizu was the first emperor to issue the maritime ban policy. The launch of the Zheng He voyages with the imperial approval of Emperor Yongle, while encouraging official interactions across maritime Asia, did not allow private trade. With the end of the treasure fleets came the reissue of the maritime ban policy in 1433. In the following years, the *wakou* posed a threat to coastal China, and in 1523, a brawl between trade representatives of two Japanese *daimyo* clans in Ningbo broke out, causing massive local unrest. As a result, Emperor Jiajing ordered all other Shibosi to be closed except for the one in Guangzhou. The direct consequence of this was the end of maritime trade. No matter how the state machine was mobilized, it could not produce ambergris from thin air.

In 1567 Emperor Longqing partially lifted the maritime ban, but Zhangzhou was the only port allowing maritime trade, and all the ships approved by the state were only allowed to sail to the area now known as Southeast

Asia, not to the Indian Ocean. Meanwhile, the Indian Ocean maritime trading world faced the encroachment of European colonists and appeared to show little interest in seeking continued trade with China. After all, its tributes to China in the early Ming were essentially solicited and sponsored by the Chinese state. Once China gave up its sponsorship, the Indian Ocean lost its enthusiasm for connections with China. Direct comminutions between China and the Indian Ocean ceased, and indirect communications became rare and were often not mentioned by any source, as far as my research has shown. The presence and absence of ambergris in China thus proved to be an immediate consequence of the rise and decline of China's activities in the Indian Ocean.

With its primary attention on its northern frontiers, the Qing dynasty had no interest in the Indian Ocean at all. However, tributary relations with Southeast Asia did bring ambergris to the Qing court. Siam was a major and active player intent on developing its relationship with Qing China. In 1664, Siam presented ambergris alongside aloe wood, pepper, elephant tusks, and other local products to Emperor Kangxi 康熙 (r. 1661–1722), who was pleased with the supply of these and approved the receiving of Siamese tribute every three years to China. It is reasonable to deduce that ambergris remained on the list of tributary gifts from Siam, since in 1782 and 1797, for example, ambergris was presented by Siam to Beijing.[109] This might account for the ambergris that is still in the collection of the Forbidden City Museum.

On the wrapping that encloses six pieces of ambergris found in the Forbidden City Museum are characters that read: "Donated by Chang Ning on the eighth of the first month of the forty-fifth year" (*sishiwu nian zhengyue chubari Chang Ning jiao* 四十五年正月初八日常宁交) and "twelve *liang* weight of ambergris" (*longxianxiang zhong shier liang* 龙涎香重十二两).[110] Chang Ning was a eunuch during the Qianlong reign (1736–1796), so this package would have been presented to the Inner Court in early 1780. Whether or not it was a tributary gift, presented by Siam, is not documented.

THE PORTUGUESE SETTLEMENT OF MACAO

The *Ming Shi*, in its it chapter on Emperor Jiajing, criticizes his search for longevity. At the beginning of his reign, the supply for the Inner Court was reduced to one-tenth that of the previous emperor's reign, but, from middle age onward Jiajing began to construct Daoist altars, perform Daoist rituals, and order the purchase of special woods, incenses, pearls, and precious stones. The use of the agar wood, laka wood, and other incenses alone amounted to a few hundred thousand *jin*, and as for the ambergris they had been unable to obtain for over a decade, imperial envoys invited overseas ships to Macao for this purpose.[111] It was precisely during the 1550s that the Portuguese managed to get approval to remain in Macao.

Chinese scholars have long been aware of the connection between ambergris and the Portuguese occupation of Macao. Official archives acknowledged that during the middle of the Jiajing reign and after, very few consignments of ambergris had been obtained for over ten years, and thus oceangoing foreign ships were invited to Macao (*yin qing haibo ru ao* 因请海舶入澳) partly for this purpose, while the recorders noted that it took a long time to obtain it.[112] Many other official records imply that the Portuguese occupation of Macao, the first colonial port in China, had a lot to do with their availability of ambergris.[113]

The invitation of foreign ships to Macao occurred immediately after the 1555 edict on the procurement of ambergris issued by Emperor Jiajing. Soon, Guangdong presented seventeen *liang*.[114] This was a relatively small amount, but obtaining even these had by no means been an easy project. In 1555 the search for ambergris in Beijing had proven futile, so the Ministry of Revenue asked Guangdong to obtain some. Guangdong officials had no choice but to offer an outrageous price: 1,200 *liang* of silver for one *jin* of ambergris, but they were able to purchase only eleven *liang*, and this was immediately presented to the emperor. The Inner Court tested it and found that it was not authentic. Even so, they held onto eleven *liang* of it, and the order to local officials in Guangzhou was reissued to obtain more ambergris, but the authentic one this time.

The records show that the procurement of this seventeen *liang* of ambergris was complicated. Manabiedi 马舺别的, a foreign chief in Guangzhou, presented 1.3 *liang*, and a foreign merchant from *Mididu* 密地都 of *Midishan* 密地山 presented six *liang*, while yet another merchant from *Midishan* managed to buy some.[115] The ambergris from these three amounted to 17.25 *liang*, and it is highly likely that this was the same consignment of seventeen *liang* mentioned as being presented to the Inner Court in 1556. Jiajing was pleased to find it authentic and kept this consignment for his own use.

THE CARGO

Writing in the Ming-Qing transition, Gu Yanwu 顾炎武 (1613–1682) provided more details about the 1555–1556 purchase.[116] In the third month of the thirty-fourth year of Jiajing (1555), a eunuch read an edict to the Ministry of Revenue, ordering it to proceed urgently to seek out and purchase (*zuosu fangmai* 作速访买) 1,000 *jin* of aloe wood (*chenxiang*), 3,000 *jin* of purple laka wood (*zise jiangzhenxiang* 紫色降真香), and 100 *jin* of ambergris (*longxianxiang*). The ministry managed to obtain the first two in Beijing but failed to locate any ambergris. The order was then promulgated to all thirteen provinces of the empire and foreign ships in coastal areas, offering the price of 1,200 *liang* of silver per *jin* that had been fixed previously. The Grand Coordinator of Guangdong (*xunfu* 巡抚) ordered Wang Hong 王泓, a merchant from Fuliang 浮梁 County (near Jingdezhen, Jiangxi Province) to take care of this mission. Together with He Chude 何处德, an officially assigned merchant (*gangji* 纲纪), Wang inspected the goods on board foreign ships to find and purchase (*fangmai* 访买) ambergris, but they were only able to get eleven *liang* in this manner.[117] Zhu Shiwei 朱世威, a military officer of the rank of *qianhu* 千户 (lit. "one-thousand-household"), was ordered to escort a consignment of ambergris to Beijing, although this too was found to be not authentic. Guangdong was ordered to continue the purchase and Manabiedi 马那别的, a foreign prisoner, "reported and presented (*gaosong* 告送)" 1.3 *liang*, his foreign subordinates (*yishu* 夷属) in *Mididu* presented six *liang*, and Zhou Minghe 周鸣和 of *Mididu* also presented a quantity. In 1556 Zhang Luan 张鸾, another *qianhu*, escorted the 17.25 *liang* to Beijing. The emperor found this consignment to be authentic and kept it for his own use.

In the 1610s Zhang Xie directly alluded to the role of Macao in the ambergris mission.[118] Local officials and merchants went to Macao in Xiangshan County (*Xiangshan Ao* 香山澳) for the purchase of ambergris. In the Ming dynasty, Macao was under the administration of Xiangshan County and had been well known for its dependable supply of ambergris. Considering the historical context, the Chinese knew that the Portuguese would be the only people likely to possess this exotic substance. The rest of the story was the same as is recorded in other Ming sources. The eleven *liang* from Macao was not real ambergris, so Guangdong was once again ordered to find the real stuff. Manabiedi, at the time a foreign prisoner in Guangzhou, presented 1.3 *liang*, some foreign people from *Mididu* of *Midishan* presented six *liang*, and Zhou Minghe presented some other amount. All these amounted to 17.25 *liang*, and these were all sent to Beijing.

Macao continued to supply ambergris to the Inner Court after the death of Emperor Jiajing. Five *jin* in 1598, 46 *liang* in 1600, 48.51 *liang* in 1604, and 97.62 *liang* in 1605 were purchased from Guangdong. From the reign of Jiajing, foreign ships began to carry ambergris to sell in China since they had heard that the emperor was desperate for ambergris, and by then, the routine regulation of purchase was set at a fixed price of 100 *liang* in silver per *jin* of ambergris. "However, it is extremely difficult to get this" (*ran de ci shennan* 然得此甚难), commented Zhang Xie.[119] Considering the historical context, all these purchases of ambergris must have been made through the Portuguese merchants in Macao.

While most Chinese archives and sources concerning the role of Macao in the procurement of ambergris remain unclear or vague, the Portuguese documents are direct and explicit. The Portuguese in Goa, for example, understood that ambergris was greatly desired by the Chinese who used it to increase their sexual pleasure and improve health. Garcia da Orta in his *Colóquios dos simples e drogas da India* (Colloquies on the Simples and Drugs of India) published in 1563, mentioned that ambergris was not only highly appreciated by the Indians and the Moors, but also especially by the Chinese. When asked about its meaningful function in China, he stated that the Chinese understood it much as the Portuguese did, using it in accompanying women and also using it for the heart, brain, and stomach. More important, he pointed out, it was "we Portuguese" who transported ambergris to China for sale, and one *jin*, or twenty ounces, might sell for 1,500 cruzados, but because so much was shipped to China by the Portuguese, the prices continued to drop.[120] This drastic decrease in price was in line with the Chinese sources that mentioned that the price dropped from 1,200 *liang* of silver per *jin* to 100 *liang* per *jin*. This shows that by the mid-sixteenth century the Portuguese in India had known that ambergris was used in China as an aid for sexual pleasure, and thus it was greatly desired in China. This must have had something to do with the persistent demands for ambergris by Emperor Jiajing.

Manabiedi, the so-called foreign chief who was jailed in Guangzhou, was in fact Portuguese. The name Mabanbiedi was a rough translation of Mateus de Brito, a famous Portuguese merchant. Put into prison for six years, he offered 1.3 *liang* of ambergris in exchange for his freedom, and indeed this Indian Ocean commodity was utilized by the Portuguese in 1555 to save other fellows in the imperial prison, too.[121] The Jesuit Melchior Nunes Barreto used ambergris as a bargaining tool to free some Portuguese prisoners, since he must have known that the Chinese emperor had been in search of it for six years, and he went to the trouble of pointing out that according to Chinese texts, ambergris when processed with other ingredients would help seniors to achieve longevity.[122] More astonishingly, the Portuguese in the late 1550s knew that Emperor Jiajing "did eat it to sustain life, and many days were passed since they had demanded it of the Portugals."[123] The Portuguese pressed their advantage and obtained, monopolized, and presented this Indian Ocean product to the Ming state. After all, they were the first Europeans to establish bases in both the Indian Ocean and Southeast Asia and were now attempting to secure Macao as their East Asian bridgehead.

Interestingly, the Chinese knew that the Japanese (*woyi* 倭夷) in Macao used ambergris and other ingredients to make the Seed Bolus (*zhongzi wan* 种子丸). The term *zhongzi wan* not only implies its assumed function in increasing the volume and vigor of sperm and thus promoting conception, but also that it served as a metaphor of a life force that could lead to longevity. Both functions, according to Daoism, could be achieved through the Daoist manipulation of sexual intercourse. Of course, sexual pleasure was desired just as much as the procreative result. Not coincidentally, it was said that Wei Jiao 魏校 (1483–1543), a *jinshi* in 1505, presented the "secret prescription for *zhongzi* (*zhongzi mifang* 种子秘方)" to obtain special grace from Jiajing. According to Zhao Xuemin, this prescription had reputedly gone missing in China, and had once been utilized by Daoists (*fangshi* 方士) for cinnabar. The Japanese had kept it secret and refused to share it with China. It was also said that certain foreigners in Canton (*Yueyi* 粤夷) knew how to get rid of the fishy odor of ambergris.[124] All these travelers' tales demonstrated the role of the Portuguese (and Macao) in the supply and use of ambergris.

In late 1556 the Portuguese took some ambergris as a bargaining tool to Guangzhou to save another group of Portuguese prisoners. The story told by the Portuguese might have been exaggerated, but it matched the Chinese one well, even in the details. The Portuguese probably had a fair amount of ambergris, but they understood its rarity in China, so they deliberately decided to control what they declared. To exchange the freedom of the Portuguese in jail, "we carried him about eight ounces of amber (which at that time was much esteemed of them and now by carrying so much it is not so much esteemed) we not being willing to give him the amber, without his giving us both the Portugals." Eight ounces was equal to 227 grams or 0.38 *jin* (six *liang*) in the Ming dynasty. This meager amount, however, caused a big stir. The Ponchassi, or Chinese provincial official, "rose out of the chair and became red as blood, and his eyes were inflamed," and he ordered the Portuguese prisoner to be whipped. To save the countryman, the Portuguese, without any hesitation, "gave him the amber. Forthwith a chafing-dish was brought him for to prove it, and likewise the prisoner cast a little in the fire; and seeing the smoke ascend right up, he was contented, and scattering the smoke he set his nose over it and said 'Haoa,' which is to say, 'it is very good.' And he forthwith commanded to deliver us the prisoner free."[125]

Once the Ponchassi who was "desirous to have the amber" from the Portuguese had obtained it, he immediately packed it up and sent it to Beijing.

> It was wonderful to see with what speed the amber was weighed, and the pieces counted and put in a paper, and noted by a scrivener before them all, the number of the pieces and the weight that was there. And after that paper another, all glued forthwith. And after that another. And in the third, the Ponchassi set his mark with red letters, and what was contained within. And at the same instant came a little box, and the amber being put therein, it was promptly sealed up, and upon the cover a paper glued, and upon it the seal of the Ponchassi. And presently came an inferior Louthia, captain of the armada, with his soldiers, and all afar off kneeled down and there the captain received his orders on his knees, saying at every word "Quoo," which is to say "yes," inclining his head and hands to the ground. And receiving his orders, just as he had come running so he returned running with the box to take shipping for to carry the amber to the Tutão, to be sent from him to the King.[126]

All these Portuguese descriptions not only reveal how anxious the Chinese were but also match the Chinese official records well, including the fact that military officials were assigned to send ambergris to Beijing.

The official mentioned in the Portuguese sources was Wang Bai 汪柏, who played a key role in allowing the Portuguese to lease Macao. As early as 1543, the Portuguese had asked if they could "borrow" Macao to sundry their commodities. Wang rejected this proposal, but in 1556, under orders and pressure to purchase ambergris, he agreed to trade with the Portuguese. In 1557, the commonly accepted official start date of the Portuguese settlement of Macao, Wang approved their previous proposal, allowing the Portuguese to remain in Macao, under the pretext of sun-drying commodities.[127]

Both the Chinese and Portuguese sources show that it was the demand for ambergris from Emperor Jiajing himself that caused foreign ships (mainly the Portuguese) to be invited to Macao and that the Portuguese in turn manipulated the supply of ambergris to be allowed to stay and to carry out their own colonial agenda. It is clear from this that ambergris played an immediate and crucial role in the Portuguese initial interactions with the Ming state, including their settlement of Macao. No wonder some scholars conclude that China's loss of Macao was caused first by ambergris in the Ming dynasty and then by opium in the Qing.[128]

Chapter Thirteen

LAKA WOOD AND FRANKINCENSE

The land produces laka wood, (but) not in any quantity.

—MA HUAN

The eight atolls produce ambergris and frankincense (*ruxiang*).

—FEI XIN

Laka wood was known to the Chinese as *Jiangzhenxiang*, literally meaning "the aromatic that brings down the True-ones." The Chinese name shows the distinctive importance of this treasured item for religious (especially Daoist) activities, for the "True Ones" were the immortal sylphs of Daoism.[1] No wonder imperial China desired and actively sought this laka wood from overseas lands.

The Maldives was not a great supplier of this treasure. Wang Dayuan failed to mention this substance in the Maldives, probably because not much was produced there. "The land produces laka wood, (but) not in any quantity," commented Ma Huan.[2] Laka wood was a product principally of places in Southeast Asia such as the Malay Peninsula, Sumatra, Java, Borneo, and the oceanic islands, but the strongest and purest was from Srivijaya,[3] as Wang Dayuan observed. In the Malay Peninsula, Siam, Manila, Palembang, Tamiang (east coast of Sumatra), and Lambri (*Nanwuli* 喃呱哩) various kinds of laka wood were produced, and Wang Dayuan roughly classified them into three levels based on their quality. In Lambri, "laka wood is the best amongst all foreign countries," claimed Wang Dayuan.[4] Ma Huan went on to describe an almost identical situation. He noted that laka wood was produced in Champa, Palembang, and Siam, and he confirmed that Lambri (*Nanboli* 南淳里) produced the best quality laka wood, which variety was

THE CARGO

given the nickname of "lotus-flower laka wood" (*lianhuajiang* 莲花降)."[5] Chinese treasure ships visited Lambri, and its king boarded the ship and presented laka wood to the Chinese emperor. The *Quanzhou I* had carried a variety of scented woods including laka wood and frankincense, in addition to ambergris and cowrie shells.[6]

The laka wood mentioned by Ma Huan was produced locally in the Maldives. Because of its climate, the kingdom might have produced other scented woods, too, though the export volume for these would have been limited. Edrisi mentioned that "in the construction of their dwellings," the Maldivian people used "timber which comes over sea, and also scented wood."[7] Having said this, the Maldives was never a major producer or a supplier of scented woods.

FRANKINCENSE

Neither Wang Dayuan nor Ma Huan even mentioned coming across frankincense (*ruxiang*) in the Maldives, but Fei Xin claimed that the eight *liu* produced both ambergris and frankincense.[8]

Unlike laka wood and other tree resins that were principally produced in tropical and subtropical forests in Southeast Asia, frankincense was a gum resin produced by several members of the genus Boswellia growing as small trees, or rather shrubs, among the hills of the Hadhramaut and Somaliland.[9] Ding Wei 丁谓 (966–1037), a Song scholar-official and expert on the *xiang* matter, understood that it was produced in rocky mountains with scanty rainfall (*duoshi er shaoyu* 多石而少雨) in the Dashi.[10] Although this was not quite accurate, the two elements of soil and rain that Ding Wei highlighted were later confirmed by modern Western scholars.[11] Wang Dayuan mentioned frankincense in Calicut, and he was correct when he pointed out that it was indeed exported from the Arab world.[12] Ma Huan described how the barter trade at Dhofar (*Zufaer* 祖法尔) produced both frankincense and ambergris. After the Chinese treasure ships had arrived in Dhofar and the edicts had been read and the gifts granted to the local king, ministers, and people, the local king "sent chiefs everywhere to issue instructions to the people of the country; (they) all too (sent) such things as frankincense, Dragon's Blood (*xuejie* 血碣), aloes (*luhui* 芦荟), myrrh (*moyao* 没药), benzoin (*anxixiang* 安息香), liquid storax (*suheyou* 苏合香),

and *momordica cochinchinensis* (*mubiezi* 木鱉子), and came for the exchange of hemp-silk, porcelain ware, and other articles,"[13] related Ma Huan.

Ma Huan described the production of frankincense, too. "This incense is in truth the gum from a tree; this tree resembles an elm-tree, but its leaves are pointed and long; local people continually cut the tree, get the incense, and sell it."[14] While the method of frankincense production described by Ma Huan was almost exactly the same as Ye Tinggui's description a few centuries earlier on the collection of frankincense in the Dashi, Ma Huan mentioned the specific area of Dhofar where it was produced and this was later confirmed by modern scholars.[15] Ye Tinggui pointed out that frankincense was shipped to Guangzhou and Quanzhou via Palembang, a similar route that was later taken by Ma Huan's treasure ships.[16]

It was the Arab traders that brought this substance to the Middle East, Central Asia, and East Asia, in addition to the Mediterranean world. Therefore, like ambergris, frankincense arrived in China first by the overland Silk Road, but unlike ambergris, frankincense had been well known in China by the Tang period.

TAXATION OF THE *XIANG* IN THE MOON HARBOR

The quantity of the imports of various *xiang* was prodigious by the Song period. In the Yuan and Ming periods, this trade seemed to be rare in both volume and price. Zhang Xie provided a glimpse of this by providing two commodity taxation rate lists from the Moon Harbor (*Yuegang* 月港) of Zhangzhou in Fujian Province.

Zhangzhou was opened in 1567 as the only port for overseas trade, and it soon became the commercial center for the eastern part of maritime Asia. At first, eighty-eight trade permits (*yin* 引) were issued per year for ships going to various ports of Southeast Asia (but not the Indian Ocean), and this was soon increased to 110.[17] This increase not only promoted the Chinese expansion and exploration of the South China Sea, but it also connected China with the New World through the arrival of European ships such as the Manila galleons that when fully loaded with silver came either from the Indian Ocean or directly from the New World. It was during this period that China's intense involvement in Southeast Asia began, pushed by the insatiable demand for marine goods such as birds' nests, sea cucumbers, and fish fins, as well as for skins and furs. At the same time, the direct interactions between the Chinese world and the Indian Ocean world declined and vanished almost without a trace. Their indirect exchanges were thereafter made only through agents in Southeast Asia or Europe.

In Zhangzhou, taxes were imposed, including water tax (*shuixiang* 水饷), land tax (*luxiang* 陆饷), and additional tax (*jiazhengxiang* 加征饷). Water tax, essentially a ship tax, was based on the size of a ship and was paid by a ship's owners (*chuanshang* 船商). Land tax, a type of commodity tax, was based on the value of goods and was payable by shop owners (*pushang* 铺商), and additional tax was only due for ships originating from Luzon (*Lüsong* 吕宋) that did not have any other commodity than silver. In 1574, all these taxes amounted to more than 10,000 *liang* of silver, this sum increasing to over 20,000 *liang* in 1583 and 29,000 *liang* in 1594.[18]

Land tax was imposed on all commodities including various kinds of the *xiang* imported to China. In 1589, a list of tax rates was created for various commodities, and the rate scheme was revised in 1615. Table 13.1 lists the taxation rate for the *xiang*.

TABLE 13.1
Taxation rates for the *Xiang* materials in Moon Harbor, Zhangzhou (1589 and 1615)

Category of *xiang*	Rate in 1589 (silver)	Rate in 1615 (silver)
Sumu 苏木 (from Dongyang)	2 *fen*/100 jin	2.1 *fen*/100 *jin* (?)
Sumu (from Xiyang)	5 *fen*/100 jin	4.3 *fen*/100 *jin*
Tanxiang 檀香 (sandalwood, big)	5 *qian*/100 jin	4.32 *qian* /100 *jin*
Tanxiang 檀香 (small)	2.4 *qian*/100 jin	2.07 *qian* /100 *jin*
Qi'nanxiang 奇楠香	2.8 *qian* (per *jin*?)	2.42 *qian*/1 *jin*
Chenxiang 沉香	1.6 *qian*/10 *jin*	1.38 *qian* /10 *jin*
Moyao 没药 (myrrh)	3.2 *qian*/100 jin	2.76 qian /100 jin
Bingpian 冰片 (camphor, lit. Dragon's Brain)	3.2 *liang*/10 *jin* (1st class)	2.765 *liang*/10 *jin* (1st class)
	1.6 *liang*/10 *jin* (2nd class)	1.382 *liang*/10 *jin* (2nd class)
	8 *qian*/10 *jin* (3rd class)	6.91 *qian*/10 *jin* (3rd class)
Jiangzhen 降真	4 *fen*/100	3.4 *fen*/100
Xuejie 血碣 (Dragon's Blood)	4 *qian*/100 *jin*	3.46 *qian*/100 *jin*
Shuxiang 束香	2.1 *qian*/100 *jin*	1.81 *qian*/100 *jin*
Ruxiang 乳香 (frankincense)	2 *qian*/100 *jin*	1.73 *qian*/100 *jin*
Muxiang 木香 (*Rosa banksiae aiton*)	1.8 *qian*/100 *jin*	1.55 *qian*/100 *jin*
Dingxiang 丁香 (clove)	1.8 *qian*/100 *jin*	1.55 *qian*/100 *jin*
Suheyou 苏合香 (liquid storax)	1 *qian* /10 *jin*	8.6 *fen*/10 *jin*
Anxixiang 安息香 (benzoin)	1.2 *qian*/100 *jin*	1.04 *qian*/100 *jin*

Note: 1 liang = 10 qian = 100 fen = 1,000 li.

Source: Zhang Xie, *Dongxiyang Kao* 东西洋考 (An Examination of the Eastern and Western Oceans), ed. Xie Fang (Beijing: Zhonghua Shuju, 2000), 140–46.

LAKA WOOD AND FRANKINCENSE

Taking the 1589 taxation rate as an example, the first class of camphor was the most valuable, followed by *qi'nanxiang, chenxiang,* and *suheyou,* while laka wood and frankincense were among the cheapest. It cannot be assumed that ambergris continued to be much desired and thus always extremely expensive on the Chinese market. Because of the absence of Sino-Indian Ocean interactions, ambergris nearly disappeared from the Chinese world. Therefore, it is not surprising that while almost all other *xiang* (and indeed many from Southeast Asia) remained as important products on the Chinese market, ambergris was no longer included on the list of taxable items.

PART IV
Reminiscences

Chapter Fourteen

A RUINED BUDDHIST PAST

Then they broke the idols and razed the temple to the ground.
—IBN BATTUTA

The king, the chiefs, and the populace are all *huihuiren* 回回人 (Muslim).
—MA HUAN

Located in the middle of the Indian Ocean along ancient maritime trade routes from the Pacific to Africa and the Mediterranean world, early inhabitants in the Maldives were exposed to and adopted aspects of many cultures. Partially due to its small size and thus limited sources available, the Maldivian people had been great cultural synthesizers rather than innovators.[1] Their culture bore similarities to others in maritime culture from Southeast Asia all the way to the island of Madagascar. Dhivehi, the language of the Maldivian people, has been influenced by many of the languages spoken in North India, Southeast Asia, and Sri Lanka. Together with Sinhala, the two form the Insular Indo-Aryan subgroup of the Indo-European language.[2] Historically written in various scripts based on Indic and Arabic models, and contemporarily inscribed in Thanna, a unique script written from right to left, Dhivehi has demonstrated Maldivian cultural interactions and particularly adaptations from neighbors both near and far. So it was with the religious transitions in the Maldives. Slight Hindu but significant evidence of Buddhist influences has been discovered to have existed before the mid-twelfth century, when Islamic beliefs and practices began to take root.[3] Prior to Bell's efforts, Buddhism had become a distant and forgotten past in this Islamic sultanate.

When Wang Dayuan arrived in 1330, Islam was well established in the Maldives, and Buddhist beliefs had been abandoned. Unfortunately, Wang said nothing about the local religious faiths, but Ma Huan thought highly of the local people who adhered strictly to the pure teaching of Islam. And Ibn Battuta, a Muslim from Morocco with the appointment of *qāḍī* (a Muslim judge) secured in this island sultanate, went into considerable depth regarding local religious customs.

The "people of these islands used to be idolaters," Ibn Battuta noted.[4] The word "idolater" referred to Buddhists in this context, and Ibn Battuta was correct. Before its king converted to Islam in the twelfth century, the Maldives had largely been a Buddhist kingdom. Buddhism probably spread to the Maldives in the third century BCE from India and Sri Lanka. The names of some islands also reveal Buddhist influences.[5] A learned Buddhist monk mentioned that there were two famous Buddhist temples in the Maldives, and local people knew that on the Fuamulah Atoll, a southernmost islet of the Maldives, jungles covered Buddhist ruins where there was a stone image of the Buddha. In 2018, in these ruins, Michael Feener's team "unearthed a large statue base, underneath which a coral stone casket contained a devotional deposit of cowrie shells,"[6] suggesting the existence of an extensive Buddhist ritual complex.

The Buddhist complex in Fuamulah had been noticed by European travelers a few centuries earlier, though they did not understand its religious nature. In 1529 the two Parmentier brothers visited this ancient temple. "In this Island was a Temple or Mosque, a very ancient structure, composed of massive stone. The Captain desired to see the inside as well as the outside, whereupon the Chief Preset bade them open it, and entered within. The work pleased him greatly; and chiefly a woodwork screen, of ancient mouldings, the best he had ever seen, with a balustrade so neatly turned that our ship's carpenter was surprised to see the fineness of the work."[7] This temple was also seen in 1595 by the Dutch traveler Frederick De Houtman:

> The small island close to which we lay had many beautiful buildings, most in ruins, very artfully built after their fashion. They appeared to be all sorts of temples and altars, which were there in that small space, fully from ten to twelve: among them one especially of an ancient structure, all of blue stone (lazulite), and round it also mouldings, basements, capitals (pillars), and their groovings (*tandeerzel*), on the steps of the entrance breastways.[8]

A RUINED BUDDHIST PAST

It was in the ruin of this mosque that in 1922, Bell found a stone Buddha head, a glass or crystal casket and some oval-shaped beads,[9] and it was Bell who restored a solid Buddhist past to the Maldives.

DISCOVERIES OF BUDDHIST REMAINS

Bell was probably the first person to raise awareness about the presence of Buddhism in the Maldives. The Buddhist past in the Maldives was not only remote, but also obscure. Owing to the persistent state efforts to rid the country of its Buddhist influence, local people had even forgotten the existence of this religious practice that had only been rediscovered in the 1920s, thanks to Bell's work.[10] Indeed, Bell's archaeological work of the Maldives "was primarily concerned to establish without doubt that there had been a Buddhist civilisation in the Islands before the Islamic Conversion." In his short stay in 1879 Bell found "nothing conclusive," but he did notice that the first Maldivian sultan "bore the Buddhist title Darumavanta (religious or just)," and that some island names referred to "Lanka City," "Buddha's City," and so on. In addition, the Maldivian name applied to the ruins was recognizably derived from those used in Ceylon.[11] All of these findings form the evidence to conclude that Buddhism had been established as a feature in local history. Two scientific expeditions, one in 1886 by C. W. Rosset and the other in 1900 by J. Stanley Gardiner, provided further clues.

On February 2, 1922, Bell sailed for Male for his first archaeological fieldwork that would confirm his early speculation. During this stay, Bell made two expeditions to southern atolls and explored islands including Gan (or Gamuin Addu Atoll), and Fua Mulaku and Mundu (in Haddhunmathi Atoll). He visited and excavated various remains of Buddhist complexes, such as "the Dagaba with its relic-chamber, the Vihare or image house, the Pirivena or monk's residence, and even one example of the Wata-da-ge or circular relic house." On March 16, 1922, Bell found three Buddhist remains, the headdress of a Bodhisattva, a small, damaged image of a sedentary Buddha, and last and most impressively, "the face of a colossal Buddha, showing part of the forehead and skull covered with short orthodox curls."[12] Although few in number, greatly wrecked and ravaged, and sparsely located, these findings solidly confirmed the existence of Buddhist culture in the Maldives before the arrival of Islam.

In general, by the 1980s historical texts, Buddhist remains (many now no longer extant), and archaeological findings (though limited) had proven that there once existed a thriving Buddhist society in this archipelago. Buddhism reached the Maldives in the early centuries CE, soon after its adoption in Ceylon, and became the state religion. The faith achieved its heyday from the ninth to the twelfth century in these islands. It was during this Buddhist period that the people of the Maldives followed a single cultural system that was borrowed and adapted.[13] Nowadays nobody would deny that there had been a Buddhist era in Maldivian history.

In addition to Buddhist connections, Hindu influences probably came from Gujarat on the western coast of India, a traditional navigational center that connected the Mesopotamian and Indus civilizations. "Hinduism was evidently present in the Maldives before the Buddhist" era, as is demonstrated by its linguistic, religious, and astrological links and legacies. Clarence Maloney explored the *Jātakas* (stories about the previous lives of the Buddha) and the Ceylon chronicles and found that both explicitly mentioned the Maldives. At least three passages in the *Jātakas* indicated Indian contact there. The *Bharu Jātaka* recounts "a thousand islands which are yet to be seen today about the island of Nāḷikera," and the combination of "a thousand islands" and "the island of Nāḷikera" must surely refer to the Maldives. In the *Sussondī Jātaka*, Sussondī, queen-consort of King Tamba of Banaras, was carried off to a Naga island called Seruma, and Sagga was dispatched to look for her, but his ship was broken up by a monster. Clarence Maloney analyzed the context of the story and argued that this shipwreck occurred in the Maldives. In the *Suppāraka Jātaka* a blind Bodhisattva from a master mariner's family was invited by merchants to be their pilot, and together they sailed for four months into mythical seas, which, according to Maloney, would surely have included those in which the islands of the Maldives were located. Maloney thus concluded both cultural influence from Gujarat in the pre-Christian era to the Maldives and the role of the Maldives in the formation of the *Jātaka* tales.[14]

The 1959 expedition to Ariadū in Ari Atoll further revealed the elements of Hinduism in the pre-Islamic period. A carved *linga* was found, 14.5 inches (36.75 cm) long and with a circumference of 12 inches (30.5 cm), which has been the first religious artifact of Hindu origin unearthed in the Maldives. Sadly, the Ariadū *linga* was either broken up, thrown into the sea, or "misappropriated or lost, with only two photographs surviving." Hindu

A RUINED BUDDHIST PAST

elements were also discerned in the 1962 excavation at Male. Two coral "heads" were unearthed, each bearing a multifaced sculpture. With "grimacing mouths, staring eyes, and protruding, sabre-like canine teeth," the two coral heads were thought to be images of Hindu deities, probably four- or five-faced *Sivalingas* or a representation of Skanda. Of similar importance were the inscriptions written in *evāla akuru*, "the oldest known script of the Maldive Islands," on the two coral heads. While their forms and some terms indicated a Hindu influence, the content was more Buddhist in doctrine.[15] Probably Hindu culture coexisted with or preceded Buddhism in the Maldives.

The 1983 excavation led to the Hindu link between the Maldives and India, too.[16] A series of carved marble stones was found in an old mosque at Male, but marble is not a local natural source. In addition, these marble artifacts, though once utilized for a Muslim *miḥrāb* (a semicircular niche in the wall of a mosque), seemed to be Hindu in appearance. It is thought that these marble stones were crafted in northwest India, exported to the Maldives, and then reused in the decoration of the mosque.

However, archaeological findings in the Maldives related to Hindu influence have been few. Therefore, Hindu links and influences might have been fragmentary and cultural rather than systematic and religious.

THERAVADA OR TANTRIC BUDDHISM?

Bell's choice of southern and central islands for his fieldwork was no mere accident, although the tropical weather and especially the Islamic authorities based in the north for eight hundred years had nearly wiped out any evidence of pre-Islamic cultures. Since Bell's last trip in 1922, many archaeological surveys and searches have been done that have helped to clear the clouds of uncertainty over the Buddhist past of the Maldives. After World War II numerous archaeological surveys, either officially sponsored or internationally driven, were carried out. One, "The Maritime Asia Heritage Survey" led by Feener, is still ongoing at this writing. As a result, more Buddhist remains have been added to our list and have helped to revise our understanding of the Buddhist era.

Bell's findings established a definite preexistence of Buddhism in these islands, and he linked Buddhist structures with those in Sri Lanka, implying that pre-Islamic Buddhism in the Maldives spread from its eastern neighboring island and belonged to the Theravada tradition. Andrew D. W. Forbes, another famous scholar of Maldivian studies, accepted this conclusion by stating that Theravada belief was apparent in four aspects of local society: the Buddhist remains, features of the Maldivian language, aspects in local religious practice, and the reluctance of the Maldivian people to take a life, whether it be a human being or an animal. Forbes summarized the seven archaeological projects conducted from the 1950s to 1983 as doing barely more than to confirm Bell's insights.[17]

In July 1958 the expedition to Toḍḍū in Ari Atoll uncovered a statue of a robed Buddha whose mouth and cheeks "bore traces of fading color," resembling the statue of Gautama Buddha found in Sri Lanka.[18] Unfortunately, the statue of the Buddha was broken up by iconoclastic islanders on the night.[19] In October 1970, two bronze-metal statues, each a few centimeters high, were accidentally discovered during construction work at Gādū (Gaadhoo) Island, Haddhunmathi Atoll (Laamu Atoll).[20] One statue, dated to the ninth or tenth century and showing a Sri Lankan style, represented a seated Buddha whose face and robes were crudely carved, with legs crossed in the lotus position, while the other, badly worn out and showing a certain Malay-Indonesian feature, might represent an *apsarā* or female semi-divinity. *Apsarā* in Hindu mythology refers to a celestial nymph, typically the consort of a *gandharva* or heavenly musician, so the second statute rather indicated some continental influence on the islands.

Several discoveries in Suvadiva (Huvadhu) Atoll (Vādū Island in 1981 and Gamu Island in 1982 respectively) are worthy of mentioning in some detail here. A coral slab with inscriptions from Vādū Island had once been thought to resemble the Indus Valley script, and several large blocks of coral masonry from Gamu Island seem to have formed part of a temple for sun worship. If so, both finds illustrated the connection between the Indus Valley and the Maldives (indeed its southernmost part). Nevertheless, a closer reading of these artifacts ruled out this speculation. The carved coral slab was nothing but "a Buddhist pāduka (foot print), probably one of a pair, decorated with a series of *maṅgalas* (auspicious signs)."[21] In the center of the footprint (a symbol of the Buddha), decorated with lotus representations, was a "Wheel of the Law (*dharmachakra*)," and its five toes each were marked with an elephant hook or a sword. Its *maṅgala*, previously mistaken for a hieroglyphic script, consisted of a fish, a conch-shell trumpet, a vase, a *svastika* as mentioned earlier, and probably a drum, all belonging to the eight

A RUINED BUDDHIST PAST

conventional auspicious symbols in Buddhism. Not surprisingly, the large tumulus on Gamu Island was probably a major Buddhist stupa, comparable with the one excavated by Bell in 1922.

The 1996–1998 excavation of a monastery at Kaashidhoo in Kaafu Atoll proved to be crucial. It found that the building of this Buddhist architecture started in the early third century, and continued until around 600 CE, with miniature stupas and sacrificial ceremonies added in the following two centuries. In contrast with Sri Lanka, where there was only one Buddhist site that showed some similarities with this monastery, in India there were quite a few. Therefore, the local Buddhist culture in the Maldives established in the first half of the first millennium might have had an Indian origin.[22] Indeed, the 1996–1998 project began to trigger a revolutionary understanding of the sources and nature of Maldivian Buddhism, and the conventional wisdom about Ceylonese-Maldivian connections was challenged at the beginning of this century by the fresh interpretation of a few Tantric Buddhist legacies, especially inscriptions.

Jost Gippert has scrutinized the few early Buddhist inscriptions and raised some unconventional ideas. The weapon-like symbols engraved on the two statues found in Male in the 1960s suggest the context of the Vajrayana-type Buddhism, an opinion greatly differing from that of Bell. This speculation has been further supported by the inscriptions on a brick-like coral stone found in the ruined Buddhist monastery on the island of Landhoo which stone has unfortunately been broken into three pieces. Gippert has pointed out that, based on its script and the language used, this artifact presumably dates back to the sixth-eighth centuries as its content shows the influence of a northern type of Buddhism. Specifically, the Landhoo inscription is principally written in an insular Prakrit, with touches of Sanskrit-derived words inserted here and there. In terms of the text content, it was certainly a dhāraṇī spell for protecting the owner against demons, and it closely resembled the famous *Sitātapatrādhāraṇī*.[23]

By examining the inscriptions engraved on the two statutes dating to the ninth to tenth centuries that were found in Male but probably destroyed in 2012 by a group of masked bandits, Gippert has postulated the prevalence of Tantric Buddhism in the pre-Islamic Maldives. Made from coral stone, these two multifaced statues had Vajrayana Buddhist features, and more crucially, their lengthy inscriptions were written in Sanskrit, in fact, "an archaic variant of the Insular Brāhmī cursive style," and bearing greater similarity to the scripts of the early Islamic period such as those found on the copper plates rather than the Landhoo inscription. Suffice to say, the knowledge of Sanskrit possessed by the engravers was limited. More interestingly, while the deities engraved on the two statues looked quite different, the two textual inscriptions proved to be "virtually the same," a mantra "nearly identical with the version" in both the Guhyasamājatantra and the Mañjuśrīmūlakalpa, and spelled out for the invocation of Yanmāntaka.[24] Therefore, these two deity statues appear to be the Yanmāntaka, "the Kings of Wrath" in Tantric Buddhism.

In sum, the beginning of the new millennium has witnessed the challenge to Bell's Theravada hypothesis by illustrating the distinct elements of Tantric Buddhism in the Maldivian past. Its sources, agents, and spreading routes, however, remain a question to be answered by further studies.

CONVERSION TO ISLAM

While its early history remains vague, an approximate date for the transition from Buddhism to Islam has been fixed upon. In the following centuries, increasing trade between the Maldives and the Muslim world gradually led to the elite's conversion to Islam. Islam probably arrived in the ninth century.[25]

According to the Koimalā legend, the one and only local myth on the origin of the Divehi people, Prince Koimalā married the daughter of the king of Ceylon in the early twelfth century.[26] The new couple made a voyage to the Maldives, and were invited by islanders to remain there as their king and the queen. Soon, they had a son named Kalaminjā, who reigned as a Buddhist for twelve years before being converted to Islam. Supported by a traditional history called the Rūdavali, the real existence of Prince Koimalā has been confirmed by a copperplate inscription in which his name was Koimalā Kalō, who ruled for twenty-one years, and was followed by his sister's grandson, Dovemi Kalaminjā, who reigned for twelve years as a Buddhist and thirteen years as a Muslim. Koimalā Kalō, nevertheless, might represent a "generalised ancestral royal lineage" for the Maldivian people.[27] Readers may have already noticed the significance of the female lineage in the royal inheritance.

The conversion to Islam was said to have occurred in 1153, when a Muslim saint came from Morocco and converted the king. Thereafter, the

Maldives was ruled by a succession of six dynasties of ninety-three sultans for over eight hundred years.[28] Ibn Battuta shared a vivid story about how the Maldivian people suddenly completed this dramatic transition, a tale he had learned from such knowledgeable men as lawyers and school masters.

Before the conversion to Islam, an evil spirit resembling a ship full of lamps appeared from the sea once each month. The Maldivians placed a virgin girl in "an idol temple." The temple was built on the seashore and in this temple, there was a window looking out to sea so that the virgin sitting there would be visible from the sea. The following morning, the young girl was found dishonored and dead. Every month, the people drew lots to decide who would be the one to give up his daughter to appease this terrible spirit. One day, a Maghrabin Berber arrived from Morocco, and he was told about the ill fortune that had befallen his hostess.[29] He then volunteered to replace the girl that night. In the temple, he continually recited from the Koran. When the evil spirit came and heard the recitation, it "plunged into the sea and disappeared." The king was astonished, and Maghrabin Berber hence proposed to the Maldivians to "embrace the true faith." The king asked the Berber to stay for one month to see whether the evil spirit would return. At the end of that month, the king, "as well as his wives, children, and courtiers" all became Muslims. "Then they broke the idols and razed the temple to the ground .. embraced Islam, and the people of the island sent messengers to the other islands, whose inhabitants were also converted."[30] The format and plot (namely, a virgin girl presented to an evil spirit but saved by a hero) in the story are widely told in other cultures and societies, usually illustrating the magical power of a new religious faith over an old one. The Maldivian version was no exception to the rule as this local legend showed the process by which Islam replaced Buddhism in the twelfth century.

What Ibn Battuta and Bell portrayed was a sudden and rapid transition from Buddhism to Islam, whereas the real process was rather slow and gradual though still violent, as Buddhist clergy were abolished, monasteries dismantled or remodeled into mosques, images were deliberately destroyed, and Buddhist property such as land was confiscated. Some local textual documents have survived to indicate a rather long transition from Buddhism to Islam. The Isdhoo Loamaafaanu, a ring of twenty-one copper plates (13 × 2.75 inches [33.1 cm × 7 cm]), "inscribed in the old Eveyla Akuru script with a text in the Dhivehi language," for example, describes "the reallocation of lands previously held by Buddhist religious institutions on the island of Isdhoo (Laamu Atoll) to support the foundation of a mosque and the establishment of a new Islamic order."[31] Therefore, the conversion to Islam witnessed much societal and cultural disruption, from the destruction of the old belief to the establishing of the new property rights. It could not have been done in just one night. The three copper plate inscriptions from Haddhunmathi (Laamu) also serve to illustrate that the conversion continued after the king had embraced Islam. As the earliest and certainly the most complete textual sources on Islamization, they were dated almost half a century later than 1153.

By the time of Wang Dayuan and Ibn Battuta in the fourteenth century, a prosperous Muslim society was thriving in the Maldives. In this country, "the king, the chiefs, and the populace are all *huihuiren* 回回人" (Muslim). "Their customs are pure and excellent (*fengsu chunmei* 风俗淳美); they all obey the regulation of their religion." "Both their marriage and funeral rites conform exactly with the regulation of the religion." So wrote Ma Huan in the early fifteenth century, speaking highly of the local people and their culture.[32] Writing at the end of the sixteenth century, Luo Yuejiong made the mistake of claiming that "their customs are pure and excellent (*fengsu chunmei*), and they worship the Buddha (*shangfo* 尚佛)."[33] Obviously, Luo was not aware that about four centuries previously, many of the Maldivian people had followed Buddhist teachings.

Chapter Fifteen

PORT MARRIAGE

My wife is smart and pleasant (*qiaohui* 巧慧) and is able to obtain others' love (*derenaizhi* 得人爱之).

—WANG DAYUAN

I have not seen in the whole world any women whose society is more agreeable.

—IBN BATTUTA

While the Yuan-Ming texts indicate the Chinese had achieved a fair amount of information about the Maldives, in terms of the geography, climate, products, economy, trade, and social customs, their knowledge remained a mishmash of facts, misunderstandings, and mistaken beliefs, sometimes containing large gaps. Wang Dayuan and Ma Huan for example, did ignore some key issues, and prominent among these was the role of Maldivian women, especially their marriage customs.

The Maldives that Wang Dayuan and Ibn Battuta visited was an Islamic society, and thus women were relatively speaking of lower status. Nevertheless, local traditions seem to indicate the powerful role of women. According to Ibn Battuta, local marriage customs provided considerable freedom for the new couple, the husband being able to choose to go to the house of his wife, or for her to come to his.[1] Such a gender relationship was illustrated and supported by the Maldivian tradition of the queen.

According to legend, Koimala and his queen had a son called Kalaminja, who made the transition from Buddhism to Islam. It is said that he reigned as a Buddhist for twelve years and as a Muslim for thirteen before his final departure for Mecca.[2] Kalaminja's daughter married the chief minister, reigned as a nominal sultana, and initiated the tradition of a queen's role in this Islamic society. However, the queen tradition had in fact been present in the pre-Islamic period. Sulaiman explicitly wrote that these islands "are governed by a woman," and Mas'udi mentioned a queen again, indicating that during the ninth and early tenth century the island kingdom was at one time or another ruled by a queen. In the eleventh century, according to Edrisi, a queen ruled the island with her husband. "All the inhabitants of these Islands are subject to a chief, who convokes them, and protects and defends them to the best of his power. His wife administers justice, and speaks in public unveiled, after an established custom from which they never vary."[3]

It is difficult for modern readers to imagine the scene of a woman delivering a speech in public without covering her face with a veil in a medieval Islamic society, but Edrisi explained that it was a local tradition that never varied. Edrisi continued to reveal the unparalleled powers of the queen:

> The name of this queen is *Demhera*; she wears for ornaments a robe of gold tissue, and on her head a crown of the same metal, enriched with pearls and precious stones. She wears gold slippers, such as none other may use under pain of having their feet cut off. This queen, on solemn feasts and other great occasions, appears in public, along with her maids of honour, with a great array of elephants, trumpets, and flags. Her husband and the viziers follow her at a certain distance. This queen has wealth deposited in cellars, to be distributed in due course to the poor of her dominions. No distribution of alms is made but in her presence and under her eye. The inhabitants of the country suspend silk stuffs along her path, and at places which she is to pass, for she keeps up great state, as we have explained.[4]

Edrisi was here describing a kingdom ruled by a queen who held a supreme position, dominating in public ceremonies, with her husband and ministers following at a respectful distance. The queen wore gold slippers, while any other person who dared to do so would have had their feet cut off.

The queen tradition continued into the fourteenth century onward, as can be glimpsed through the two Waqf endowments. The first Waqf for a mosque was commissioned by Queen Kanba Aisha Rani Kilege, who was extraordinarily active in resisting patriarchal power by reestablishing herself as sultana three times (1347–1363, 1364–1373, and 1376–1379), a few decades later than the visit of Wang Dayuan and earlier than that of Zheng He, respectively, by means of killing her first two husbands.[5] Her reigns took place immediately after the departure of Ibn Battuta, an interesting period, and the Moroccan traveler mentioned the queen tradition quite a number of times. Ibn Battuta found that local women did not cover their hands (nor did the queen), and most of them wore an apron from their waists to the ground, with the rest of their bodies being exposed. Ibn Battuta was also surprised by the Maldivian queen. "It is a strange thing about these islands that their ruler is a woman, Khadíja," commented Ibn Battuta.[6] According to Ibn Battuta, her grandfather had passed the kingdom to her father and her father had passed it to her brother who, as a boy, had been overthrown and put to death. With only three daughters of the royal family surviving, Khadíja, the eldest, then became the queen.

The second Waqf endowment, written in 1661, identifies the endowments previously donated by Queen Kalhu Kamana Thukkamana Binth Ḥasan Ranna Bandeyri Kilegefaanu.[7] Queen Thukkamana, once a contender to the throne after the death in 1609 of her cousin, King Kalaafaan, donated two plots of land (an island and an islet), including all the trees and plants planted there.

However, by the era of Ibn Battuta, the power of the queen seemed to be in a decline, if his words are to be relied upon. "She was married to their preacher, Jamál ad-Dín, who became Wazír and the real holder of authority, but orders are issued in her name only," commented Ibn Battuta.[8] There were two more queens in the 1370s–1380s transition, and from then onward the queen tradition disappeared, indicating the dominance of patriarchy in Maldivian politics.[9] Therefore, the declining influence of the queen described by Ibn Battuta might be correct in revealing this trend.

It seems that Western travelers were aware of the existence of the queen tradition in the Maldives, but their Chinese counterparts Wang Dayuan and Ma Huan failed to utter a word about this local practice. Wang Dayuan arrived before Queen Khadíja had ascended the throne and the Zheng He voyages occurred between the two queens' reigns. It could be that they had not been informed about this custom. Or, had they perhaps heard about it but felt to be more tactful not to mention it? This omission might have been due to the heavy influence of Neo-Confucian patriarchy that regarded a queen or woman emperor as an evil omen to the empire.

"I HAD IN THAT COUNTRY FOUR LEGITIMATE WIVES, BESIDES CONCUBINES"

The Chinese visitors also paid little attention to local women. Ma Huan was the only Chinese traveler who mentioned Maldivian women, and he restricted his description to their costume alone. "Their men and women are of relatively dark skin. Men wind a white cotton cloth round the head, with a kerchief surrounding the lower part. Women wear a short garment on the upper part, and wrap the bottom with a broad cotton kerchief, with another broad cotton kerchief to pass across and cover the head and veil the face. For marriage and funeral rituals, both follow the Islamic teachings strictly."[10] To one's surprise, this is the only text in which the Chinese mentioned the local women. Although Ma's tone was highly positive, little information is provided to explore substantial differences or similarities between local women and their Chinese counterparts. By contrast, Ibn Battuta wrote expansive and detailed passages about the local women and their marriage rites, in addition to his futile efforts to change local women's "uncivilized" custom of not clothing themselves sufficiently according to Islamic custom.

While Ibn Battuta was surprised to find that local women in the Maldives "do not cover their hands, not even their queen does so," he very much enjoyed the fact that servant girls were very cheap, and he had quite a few in his house.[11] He was also very pleased with the local marriage custom in which women's dowries were of little concern. "It is easy to get married in these islands, owing to the smallness of the dowry, as well as by reasons of the agreeable society of the women. Most of them say nothing about a nuptial gift, contenting themselves with declaring their profession of the Musalmán faith, and a nuptial gift in conformity to the law is given."[12]

Ibn Battuta was equally pleased to find that local wives took great care of their men. "Among the islanders, the wife entrusts to no one the care of her husband's service; she it is who brings him his food, takes away when he has eaten, washes his hands, presents the water for his ablutions, and covers his feet when he wills to go to sleep. And it is one of their customs that the wife never eats with her husband, and he does not even know what she eats."[13] Ibn Battuta's descriptions of local women and marriage, though compromised by his own religious and patriarchal angle, were based on his own experience and observations and are reliable. Indeed, Ibn Battuta himself had four Maldivian wives during his eighteen-month stay in the Maldives.

Soon after Ibn Battuta's arrival, the Vizier Sulayman proposed a marriage between his daughter and Ibn Battuta. After a few rounds of negotiation, Ibn Battuta decided to accept the proposal. However, on the wedding day when guests all arrived for this ceremony, the vizier postponed his appearance, even after two invitations had been delivered. Soon a secret message reached Ibn Battuta, saying, "His daughter refuses to marry; and she is mistress of her own actions." This surprising episode does reflect the right of local women, at least the elite ones, to have a say in their own marriage. As a solution, the vizier proposed instead the widow whose daughter had married the vizier's own son for Ibn Battuta. He agreed and loved this lady dearly. "She was one of the best women who ever lived," commented Ibn Battuta.[14] This was Ibn Battuta's first marriage in the Maldives.

Not long after, Ibn Battuta "married another wife, daughter of a highly esteemed Vizier." And then he "married one who had been married to the Sultan Shikábuddín," and "had three houses built in the garden which the Vizier gave to me." His fourth wife was "the step-daughter of 'Abd-Allal" who lived at her own house and was the one Ibn Battuta "cherished the most." "I had in that country four legitimate wives, besides concubines," Ibn Battuta proudly boasted.[15] Obviously Ibn Battuta enjoyed a wonderful family life there.

Marriage was easy, and so was divorce. When he decided to leave the Maldives, Ibn Battuta "repudiated one of my wives. To another, who was with child, I gave a term of nine months, within which I might return; in default, she was to be mistress of her own actions. I took with me that one of my wives who had been married to the Sultan *Shihaáb uddín*, in order to restore her to her father, who dealt in the island of *Molúk*, and my first wife, whose daughter was half-sister to the Sultana."[16] At that moment, Ibn Battuta might have decided not to return to the Maldives in the future.

In the beginning, the first wife of Ibn Battuta was resolved to leave with him, despite her daughter's pleas. Therefore, Ibn Battuta's statement that local women would not leave the Maldives might not have been quite true. However, soon after their departure, she changed her mind. "My wife was in great distress and wished to return. I repudiated [divorced] her and left her there, and wrote to the Vizier, for she was the mother of his son's wife." In addition, he "repudiated also the wife to whom I have fixed the term for my return, and sent for a slave girl I was fond of."[17] In words, such a "transitionary" or "temporary" marriage was the custom of the Maldivian society.[18]

When Ibn Battuta arrived at the island of Molúk, where he stayed for seventy days, he "married two wives there." And then he departed for the Indian subcontinent. In Calicut Ibn Battuta was informed that his wife "whom he left pregnant, was delivered of a male child." This wife was highly likely the one with whom Ibn Battuta had initially fixed the term of nine months, so he returned to the Maldives to take his son, "who was now about two years old." Ibn Battuta saw his boy but eventually thought that "it would be better for him to remain among the islanders," "sent him back" and left the Maldives for Bengal.[19] Ibn Battuta's experience seems to confirm that marriage and divorce were essentially contractual.[20]

Was easy marriage (and divorce) a privilege for the likes of Ibn Battuta, a highly regarded Muslim guest in this island sultanate? It might have been so, since his wives were from noble families, and some were even the descendants of sultans. However, even common foreign men such as sailors and merchants found it equally easy to find local wives, as Ibn Battuta himself observed.

"SERVES HIM BY DAY AS HIS MAIDSERVANT AND BY NIGHT AS HIS WEDDED WIFE"

What Ibn Battuta experienced was neither a single nor an exceptional case. Indeed, he noted how local women made a living by forming contracted marriages with foreign sailors and merchants. When a commercial ship arrived, local women would sail small boats out to the foreign vessel, presenting betel nuts and coconuts and carrying foreigners to their home as if they were near and dear relations. "Any new-comer who wishes to marry is at liberty to do so. When the time comes for his departure he repudiates his wife, for the people of the Maldives do not leave their country. As for a man who does not marry, the woman of the house in which he is lodged prepares his food, serves it, and supplies him with provisions for his journey when he goes. In return she is content to receive from him a very small present."[21]

This is exactly the way in which Ibn Battuta married his four wives and divorced three of them when he departed. François Pyrard concluded that the northern parts, the commercial center, "are more frequented by foreigners, who usually marry there."[22] Bell confirmed it by highlighting more mixed blood in the north.[23] Therefore, easy marriage (and divorce) not only occurred to Ibn Battuta, but also to ordinary sailors and merchants. "When foreign ships arrive there the crews take wives, whom they repudiate on their departure; it is a kind of temporary marriage," concluded Ibn Battuta. Very pleased, Ibn Battuta exclaimed that "I have not seen in the whole world any women whose society is more agreeable."[24]

One may wonder whether Ibn Battuta was exaggerating in his account of the liberal behavior of Maldivian women. The temporary marriage that he described reveals the seemingly low status of women in a patriarchal society and yet was an essential part of a maritime culture in which women were provided with rights and freedoms that were denied to many other women such as the Chinese.[25] For example, local marriage in the Maldives did not require the wife to go and reside in her husband's house. Ibn Battuta mentioned a few times that women were their own mistresses of all their actions (though it might have been somehow exaggerated), including refusing the marriage arrangement made by their father, as had happened to Ibn Battuta himself. With the arrival of Islam, a patriarchal society had been formed in the Maldives, where the socially strong role of women was declining. This was true for many parts of Southeast Asia that accepted Islam, let alone China, which was distinguished by its Neo-Confucian emphasis on women's virginity and chastity.

One may argue that mention of his polygamous marriages merely served to illustrate that Ibn Battuta was a pious and model Muslim who stuck to the teachings of the Quran and married just four wives, neither more nor fewer. However, there had existed such a social relationship between indigenous women and itinerant traders in maritime Asia before and after the era of Ibn Battuta as vividly described by the Chinese and the earliest European adventurers.

In Patani, in the northern region of the Malay Peninsula, the Dutch naval officer Jacob Van Neck observed almost the same custom as Wang Dayuan in Champa and Ibn Battuta in the Maldives.

> When foreigners come there from other lands to do their business, men come and ask them whether they do not desire a woman; these young women and girls themselves also come and present themselves, from whom they may

choose the one most agreeable to them, provided they agree what he shall pay for certain months. Once they agree about the money (which does not amount to much for so great a convenience), she comes to his house, and serves him by day as his maidservant and by night as his wedded wife. He is then not able to consort with other women or he will be in grave trouble with his wife, while she is similarly wholly forbidden to converse with other men, but the marriage lasts as long as he keeps his residence there, in good peace and unity. When he wants to depart he gives her whatever is promised, and so they leave each other in friendship, and she may then look for another man as she wishes, in a propriety, without scandal.[26]

Temporary marriages between local women and foreign sojourners were widely practiced in port societies, including those in coastal Southeast Asia. Often misunderstood as a form of prostitution by European observers, port marriage in fact demonstrated a form of female autonomy in these societies that often shocked the Chinese literati scholars who were accustomed to the strictly brought up women in Ming-Qing China.[27] In his study of precolonial Southeast Asian women, Anthony Reid points out that "the pattern of pre-marital sexual activity and easy divorce, together with the commercial element potentially involved in the paying of bride-wealth, ensured that temporary marriage or concubinage rather than prostitution became the dominant means of coping with the vast annual influx of foreign traders to the major ports."[28] Barbara Watson Andaya critically analyzes the changing attitude adopted by European observers toward temporary marriage between Southeast Asian women and foreign merchants. She details the case of traditional Southeast Asia in which the arrangement of local wives for foreign traders was a common practice to take the outsiders into local kinfolk. The companionship and assistance provided by local wives were crucial to the reproduction of maritime trade, and therefore such a custom might not be unique to Southeast Asia.[29]

There are a few features in this form of marriage that distinguish it from prostitution or forced sexual service. First, although commercial or financial consideration constituted a crucial part in the marriage agreement, the two parties, especially the woman, made the decision "as she wishes." Without women's consent and cooperation, such a partnership could not have been forged, let alone evolved into a widespread practice for centuries.[30] Second, under this agreement both parties remained loyal to each other, which essentially refuted the accusation of prostitution or forced sexual service. In addition, although the marriage only lasted for a short period, it was by no means a one-night stand. Rather, the couple lived in "good peace and unity" until the husband had to depart for his business. Such a form of marriage, though of a short term, was agreed on by the two parties and contract-based, with the couple being equal partners, dividing labors, sharing responsibilities, enjoying benefits, and demanding mutual fidelity. The term "wedded wife" coined by Jacob Van Neck touches on the nature of this gender relationship, which shares a lot of similarities with modern marriage. Indeed, no other people mentioned port marriage more often than imperial Chinese travelers.

"FIRST THING . . . IS TO MARRY A LOCAL WOMAN"

Southeast Asia had been the major water territory for Chinese exploratory missions in the imperial period, and its socially strong women made a big impression on Chinese visitors such as Zhou Daguan and Wang Dayuan who saw women's submission as the primary principle and ideal value.

Zhou Daguan was a Yuan envoy who was dispatched by the Mongol court to Zhenla (Cambodia). He arrived at Angkor in August 1296, and remained at the court of King Indravarman III until July 1297. Zhou was extraordinarily impressed with the important role that women played there. In this country, all transactions were managed by women, "so when a Chinese merchant arrives, the first thing he does is to marry a local woman (*suoyi Tangren dao bi, bi xian na yi furen* 所以唐人到彼，必先纳一妇人), taking advantage of her because she excels at trading (*li qi neng maimai* 利其能买卖)."[31] According to this Chinese envoy, some Chinese sailors even jumped ship to stay there, since in that country it was easy to get rice, women, housing, utensils and other needs. In Zhenla, Zhou Daguan met a countryman from Wenzhou, Zhejiang, who had been there for more than three decades and who very possibly had married a local woman. Such a Champa tradition had lasted for centuries. In 1695 Dashan 大汕, a Chinese monk in the early Qing period, visited Huian 会安 (Hoi An) in central Vietnam (previously a Champa port city) and made a similar statement on port marriage between the Chinese traders and local women.[32]

Zhou Daguan was pleased to see that such a relationship brought about multiple advantages as local women were bedmates at night and business partners in the day where they provided crucial access to local society and politics. These commercial, fiscal, sexual, emotional, psychological, and political benefits of temporary marriage listed by Zhou Daguan would be shared by Ibn Battuta, who gained not only wives in each locality but also their dowries, social status, and connections.[33] Indeed, peoples in various maritime Asian societies understood the benefits of port marriage very well, as illustrated by a Palembang folktale in which a Javanese merchant simply asked himself, "Being a newcomer, how can I get close to people? I will marry one of their daughters." And an Indian merchant in a Perak chronicle was said to have one wife in India and another in Perak.[34]

Wang Dayuan made similar comments on this warm reception and arrangement in Southeast Asia such as in Champa and Timor. In Champa, Wang Dayuan joined former Chinese travelers in appreciating the loyalty of the local women to (Chinese) merchants and sailors. When a commercial ship arrived, women went out in small boats to meet it and after boarding the vessel would match themselves with a sailor. When the sailors departed, local women shed tears of farewell, and the following year when the ship returned, these women would join again with their previous sailor husbands. If some sailors were forced to remain in Champa because of some misadventure, these women maintained their loyalty and would offer clothing and food to them. When such stranded sailors finally departed, the local women would present them with many gifts. "Such was their kind affection" (*qingyi* 情义), Wang Dayuan exclaimed.[35] Wang's word "*qingyi*" shares the same tone as Ibn Battuta's comments on the Maldivian women being the most "agreeable," both travelers appreciating the local women's love and care of them. The scene observed by Wang Dayuan of the local women sailing small boats out to receive and match themselves with foreign men in big ships vividly depicts the customs of port marriage and was clearly a common sight, as would be witnessed by Ibn Battuta and other travelers, whether they were describing the Maldives, Champa, or Timor.

Wang Dayuan also visited Zhenla, where he was surprised and pleased to find that a local man was very happy (*shenxi* 甚喜) to let his wife have sex with foreign visitors (*yukeyin* 与客淫). He would show her off to people around him, saying, "my wife is smart and pleasant (*qiaohui* 巧慧) and is able to obtain others' love (*derenaizhi* 得人爱之)."[36]

Ma Huan wrote notes that combine what Zhou Daguan and Wang Dayuan had recorded and highlighted the image of strong women in Siam.

He said that all matters were managed by their wives and men, whether they be king or commoner, followed this practice, because "the mental capacity of wives certainly exceeds that of men."[37] He almost exactly repeated what Wang Dayuan had mentioned about women in Zhenla. "If a married woman is very intimate with one of our men from the Middle Kingdom, wine and food are provided, and they drink and sit and sleep together. The husband is quite calm and takes no exception to it; indeed, he says, 'my wife is beautiful and the man from the Middle Kingdom is delighted with her.'"[38] While Wang Dayuan did not specify who these foreign guests were, Ma Huan explicitly pointed out that the local women preferred Chinese men over people from other countries.

Were husbands in Zhenla really happy to let their wives have sex with foreign visitors? One should probably question Wang Dayuan on this issue. Wang's words might be correct, but it is more likely to have been a cultural misunderstanding. Local women in premodern Southeast Asian societies enjoyed a high status, the freedom to have premarital sex, and the right to voice their opinions in marriage. The "husbands" mentioned by Wang Dayuan might well have been the women's lovers. Zhou Daguan certainly provided a detailed introduction to a local custom called *zhentan* 阵毯 that did not attach any importance to virginity, and this of course shocked the Chinese traveler.

The *zhentan* was a local ritual for girls. "When they are seven to nine years old—if they are girls from wealthy homes—or only when they are eleven—if they come from the poorest families—girls have to get a Buddhist monk or a Daoist to take away their virginity, in what is called *zhentan*."[39] This ritual was also noted by Wang Dayuan, who called it *lishi* 利市, which meant "bringing fortune to her future husband's family." The ritual of the *zhentan* was crucial. Before this ritual a daughter slept with her parents, after which she was excluded from her parents' rooms, and then she "goes wherever she wants without restraint or precaution."[40] In other words, premarital sex was allowed and even encouraged in medieval Cambodia.

In addition, the local ritual for marriage in Zhenla was not as formal as the Chinese one. Although there was the ceremony of gift giving, "it is just an illicit and plain affair (*goujian congshi* 苟简从事). There are many who get married only after premarital sex (*xian jian er hou qu* 先奸而后娶). Such a local custom is regarded as neither shameful nor odd." Like Wang Dayuan, Zhou Daguan might have mistaken the lover for the husband. "When a family is bringing up a daughter, her father and mother are sure to wish her well by saying, 'May you be wanted by men, in future may you marry thousands and thousands of husbands (*jia qianbaige zhangfu* 嫁千百个丈夫).'"[41] Obviously, "husbands" here refers to lovers.

Zhou Daguan was neither the only nor the first Chinese traveler to observe premarital sex as condoned. Li Jing, a contemporary Yuan official who served in Yunnan, a southwestern Chinese frontier area, provided an account of parents who were proud of their daughter's beauty because it attracted many lovers.[42] Among many ethnic groups in Yunnan virginity was not important, and girls were free to have sex with men. In southern Yunnan along the border with Burma and Siam, if a girl died before marriage, all the men who had had relations with the girl had to hold up a banner to see her off. If the banners numbered one hundred (or more), the girl was considered to have been especially beautiful. Her parents would cry and lament: "How could we have known that our daughter who is loved by so many men would have died so young (*nü aizhe zhong, heqi yaozhe* 女爱者众, 何期夭折)?" Yunnan (especially its southern part), though landlocked and located on the tip of northern mainland Southeast Asia, was more southern Asian than Chinese before the massive arrival of Han migrants in the fifteenth century. No wonder it shared the custom of strong women with coastal Southeast Asian kingdoms such as Zhenla, Siam, and Champa, and was thus seen as culturally degenerate in the eyes of the Chinese literati.

"IF A STRANGER DESIRES TO MARRY, MARRY HE MAY"

Chinese islands, peninsulas, and port cities, just as their counterparts in the Indian Ocean or Southeast Asia, constituted integral parts of maritime Asia. Did prostitution occur in Wang Dayuan's China? Of course it did, and Wang Dayuan himself would not have denied it. Did this maritime practice of a temporary marriage exist in China? Wang Dayuan might deny this, but Ibn Battuta was not shy to confirm it.

It is well known that many foreign merchants had already lived in coastal China such as Guangzhou as early as the Tang dynasty (618–907), and some of these had married Chinese women. Their descendants continued their overseas trade, opened shops, served as local brokers, or even took imperial examinations to become officials of the Son of Heaven. Therefore,

Sino-foreign marriage was not uncommon in China's port cities. Then what about temporary marriages between foreign merchants and Chinese women? Not a single Chinese text has ever mentioned it, but Ibn Battuta succinctly described it.

The itinerant merchant Ibn Battuta probably traveled extensively in China, from coastal to inland China, and he shared his experience of being a foreign trader in China.[43] When he entered a city or town, he chose to stay in a Muslim community or at a local hostel. Whatever the case, his money would be taken into custody by the local host, who became the traveler's accounts keeper. All kinds of expenses would be deducted by the keeper from this account "with honesty and charity."[44] One expense was that of a temporary marriage between the foreign merchant and some Chinese women.

> If he desires to take a concubine, the keeper purchases a slave girl for him and lodges him in an apartment opening out of the hostelry, and purveys for them both. Slave girls fetch a low price; yet all the Chinese sell their sons and daughters, and consider it no disgrace. They are not compelled, however, to travel with those who buy them, nor on the other hand, are they hindered from going if they choose to do so. In the same way, if a stranger desires to marry, marry he may; but as for spending his money in debauchery, no, that he may not do. They say, "We will not have it noised about amongst Muslims that their people waste their substance in our country, because it is a land of riotous living and [women of] surpassing beauty."[45]

To sum up, in a Chinese port city, a male agent came to help foreign men who were looking for a wife or concubine, a similar situation to the one Jacob Van Neck encountered in Patani nearly three centuries later. While Ibn Battuta claimed such a practice in "any town in China," it is highly possible that he expanded on his own experience in Quanzhou and other coastal port cities and generalized it to have been practiced all over China. Essentially, what he described was different from neither what he experienced in the Maldives nor what the Chinese observed in maritime Asia. Although Ibn Battuta's words have remained the sole piece of evidence for the Chinese case, it is reasonable to assume that this temporary marriage arrangement also occurred in Chinese port cities.

Furthermore, like Ibn Battuta, who brought his own slave girls along on his Asian voyages, Chinese merchants, according to Ibn Battuta, took "slave girls and wives" along with them during their maritime business trips.[46] By "wives" Ibn Battuta might mean port marriage wives, like his own in the Maldives. Therefore, temporary marriages were contracted between Chinese women and foreign merchants in Chinese ports, and between Chinese merchants and foreign women in foreign lands. Such a maritime culture took root in these connected port communities, no matter whether they were under the ideologies of Neo-Confucianism, Buddhism, Islam, Hinduism, various local belief systems, or a mixture of these. The Chinese were by no means an exception.

"WOMEN WHO DO NOT KNOW SHAME"

While Ibn Battuta boasted of his sex, love, and marriage adventures in the Maldives, his contemporary but much less well-known traveler Wang Dayuan commented on port marriages, thinking highly of local women in Champa for their "kind affection," being pleased to know that Zhenla women took part in sexual partnerships with foreign guests, but remained utterly silent on the subject of port marriage in the Maldives.

Wang's sojourn in the Maldives occurred only a few years earlier than that of Ibn Battuta, and in the intervening years there were no drastic changes in this island kingdom. Neo-Confucian moral codes might have prevented Wang from writing about such an "uncivilized" social custom in which Maldivian women seemed to be licentious and cheap, an image so directly opposite to the ideal Chinese woman who prided herself on her self-restraint. It is true that accounts of foreign and exotic women often appeared in miscellaneous Chinese writings, but as the first Chinese man in the Maldives, Wang Dayuan probably deliberately chose not to mention this custom.[47]

While Wang Dayuan passed over a description of local women and marriage in the Maldives that Ibn Battuta thought so highly of, he was extremely harsh about the local women on Timor Island. Wang categorically deplored the local women there (*Gulidimen* 古里地闷), describing them as "women who do not know shame (*fu bu zhichi* 妇不知耻)." No detail or fact was provided by Wang to support this extremely negative remark, except he vaguely dismissed the local customs as obscene and indecent (*yinlan* 淫濫). However, his mention of the sexual obsession of local chiefs and foreign sailors indicates that Wang accused the local women of being cheap, lascivious, and thus shameless.[48]

It is puzzling that Wang Dayuan made such sharply opposing value judgments on the same gender relationship and maritime culture in different places, thinking highly of Cambodian women for their kind affection but denouncing those in Timor as vulgar women. Wang Dayuan was not the first Chinese traveler to see indigenous women as lascivious. In Cambodia, Zhou Daguan

> often heard people say that the local women are very lascivious, so that a day or two after giving birth they are immediately coupling with their husbands. If a husband does not meet his wife's wishes he will be abandoned right away. If the husband happens to have work to do far away, if it is only for a few nights that is all right; but if it is for more than ten nights or so the wife will say, "I am not a ghost; how could I sleep alone (*wo feishi gui ruhe dumian* 我非是鬼，如何独眠)?" Such is her eagerness of sexual desire (*yindangzhixin youqie* 淫荡之心尤切).[49]

Having said that, in many Southeast Asian societies women remained loyal and chaste even after the death of their husbands and were highly regarded for this by Chinese literati. Shocked by Zhenla women's sexual desire and activities, Zhou Daguan simultaneously highlighted their loyalty in love and marriage. "That said, I have heard that there are some who exercise self-restraint," added Zhou.[50] Wang Dayuan himself recorded a few cases, too.[51] Widows either remained unmarried, starved, or immolated themselves so as to follow their husbands to the grave.

Therefore, in general, the Chinese judged port marriages in maritime Asia harshly. Timor was a new and strong case to illustrate the Chinese accusation. This remote island had witnessed the expansion of the Chinese commercial empire by the age of Wang Dayuan and become the most distant base for Chinese sojourners in Southeast Asia. Due to the high death rate probably caused by tropical diseases categorized by the Chinese as the *zhang* 瘴, Timor was singled out by Wang who attributed these Chinese deaths to the local women's debauchery.[52]

It is generally true that accounts by Chinese sojourners about foreign women were essentially decided by these women's behaviors and attitude toward sex, but the Chinese adopted a double standard on the same social custom.[53] Local women's interactions, especially sexual relationships with Chinese men, were often thought to be affectionate, smart, and pleasant, a result of their admiration of Chinese culture personified by Chinese men and as illustrated by the proud "husbands" in Zhenla or Siam, while their intimate relationship with non-Chinese foreign men were despised as being obscene and indecent.[54] As for Chinese women's relationships with foreign merchants in Chinese port cities, the Chinese tended not to address this culturally sensitive issue. In sum, women and temporary marriage in maritime Asia were constructed to prove the superiority (and thus attraction) of Chinese masculinity individually and the magnificence of Chinese culture collectively.[55] No wonder Wang Dayuan and his fellow travelers doted on some indigenous women but despised others.

"HOW COULD YOU TOLERATE YOUR WOMEN TO BOARD AND DEAL IN SHIPS?"

It is highly possible that Wang Dayuan might have landed in Timor, and thus though his account is very brief, it might provide evidence that port marriages existed there. One edition of Fei Xin's *Xingcha Shenglan* confirms this speculation, providing crucial information on local women's relationship with sailors. "When a commercial ship arrives, women go to the ship to deal; people often get infected with illness, and of ten men, eight or nine die, due to the *zhang* vapor (*zhangqi* 瘴气) in the land and its debauchery."[56] Fei Xin's account of Timor women in their sailing boats is just like Ibn Battuta's account of this custom in the Maldives some one hundred years earlier and some ten thousand miles away, or that of Wang Dayuan's of the Champa women on the eastern side of Southeast Asia. Essentially, these accounts all referred to contracted marriages (including sexual liaisons) between local women and foreign visitors in maritime Asia.

China's Confucian tradition held the assumption of secular salvation by civilizing "barbarians." Naturally, Chinese men were sincere in providing moral indoctrination for indigenous women in Timor. In his *Xiyang Ji*, a Chinese novel completed at the end of the sixteenth century that romanticized the Zheng He voyages, Luo Maodeng helped Wang Dayuan teach the local people a Chinese lesson of correcting evil practices, thus "civilizing" the Timor people, especially its women.[57]

PORT MARRIAGE

According to this novel, when the Treasure Fleet reached a small kingdom called Jilidimen 吉里地闷, Zheng He was told that whenever barbarian ships arrived, the local women frequently boarded the ship to trade, and nine-tenths of the men who were sexually assaulted (by these women) would die. The Chinese eunuch was shocked by such vulgarity, and he had the local chief beaten with five staves. He also delivered a lecture to the chief, saying, "as a chief how could you tolerate your women to board and deal in ships (*shangchuan jiaoyi* 上船交易), and contaminate people (*dianwu ren* 玷污人)?" The chief kowtowed to the eunuch and accepted this good lesson. In this manner, Zheng He "transformed the barbarians with the Chinese way (*yongxia bianyi* 用夏变夷)."[58] Wang Dayuan's moral slur on local women in Timor was reiterated through the pen of Luo Maodeng, and the proposed solution for this malpractice, which Wang Dayuan had not deigned to offer, was carried out in Zheng He's punishment and indoctrination in the novel *Xiyang Ji*.

Despite Luo Maodeng's best literary efforts, contracted marriage for male visitors in Timor continued over the following centuries. The day after Élie Ripon, an officer of the Dutch East India Company, arrived at this island in the 1620s, the local king led servants and women aboard and provided services, and on the third day, the king came on board once again with a hundred armed soldiers and two hundred women, together with some unmarried daughters.[59] This particular scene appears to echo previous observations. Meanwhile, the presence of massive European (and Chinese) arrivals potentially presented a commercial prospect for local monarchs and elites to exploit their women for the purposes of the sex trade. Alternatively, there existed a blurred boundary between port marriages and sporadic instances of the sex trade in maritime Asia, and the large number of foreign male visitors facilitated the shift from port marriages to an organized sex trade. Because the limited availability of information, I regrettably cannot offer a conclusive response.

By connecting all these fragmentary but circumstantial accounts of port marriage, this chapter makes efforts to place women back into the story of long-distance trade in coastal cultures across the seas, thus enriching maritime history. However, there are two aspects concerning port marriage that have made it difficult to paint a fuller picture of this practice. Some challenges in fully explaining port marriage remain, and one notable omission is the absence of women's voices. The absence of a literary tradition within maritime societies has resulted in a complete dearth of written accounts by indigenous women. In premodern times the number of women who engaged in travel was very low, resulting in a lack of documents authored by women from external perspectives. Another concern pertains to the progeny resulting from port unions. There is limited mention of offspring in textual sources, but logically we can assume that port marriages served to alleviate the low rate of population growth in maritime societies (and Southeast Asia). Its biological legacy is supported by common sense and later cases in colonial Southeast Asia, for example. Furthermore, the male-female interactions in premodern maritime Asia were varied. We cannot exclude other forms of sexual relationships, such as waterborne prostitution and slave-wives.[60] Finally, can we undertake a comparative analysis of port marriage and polygamy (or polygyny), the latter being prevalent practices and institutions within Asian aristocratic circles? Probably not. In the context of polygamy it was common for wives (and concubines) to coexist within the same societal and cultural framework, albeit not always in the same building. In most instances these wives were acquainted with each other. In contrast, the port wife lived far away from the husband's primary wife, and it is more probable that they hardly knew of or interacted with each other.

Port marriage was an agreement between indigenous women and foreign men in maritime Asia, characterized by free will, contract, loyalty, and mutual benefits. In addition to its economic, commercial, and fiscal dimensions, the two parties, especially the female one, had the free will and ability to make their own decisions and remain loyal to each other during the term agreed. Although it lasted for only a short period, this temporary marriage provided a win-win situation.[61] Men were well taken care of by their wives, who not only cared for housing, clothing, food, and physical desire but also facilitated trading, access to local resources, and mediation in local affairs. Women were paid by their husbands, who provided material and economic support and contributed to the reproduction of local societies and maritime networking.

Temporary marriage in port cities sheds some fresh light on maritime activities such as navigation and trade dominated by men. It linked people from different regions in the maritime world, met the various needs of maritime sojourners (mainly sailors and merchants), crossed the boundaries of landscape, ethnicity, culture, and religion, and enabled the formation, sustainability, and population momentum of maritime Asia. In sum, it certainly represents a vivid case of the "Ocean Unbounded."[62] This social custom itself resulted from not only a combination of many indigenous cultural elements including socially strong women in Southeast Asian societies and the like, but also the mutual benefits brought about by trading. The demand and desire for interactions might have derived from human nature, both individually and collectively, which underlies the necessity of connections, no matter whether they were commercial, sexual, emotional, or psychological. Therefore, port marriage provides a rare opportunity to take a glimpse into the private lives of male sojourners who frequently and regularly spent months and years in the ocean world, a theme hardly touched on by any historical documents or anthropological studies, let alone archaeological findings. We are just left from these port marriage accounts with the faint shadows of the indigenous women who obviously had a great impact on the maritime world and its travelers, but who have since all been left out of all the maritime history accounts.

Port marriage, essentially a gender-divided and cooperative institution that fit well in maritime Asia, however, could not avoid discrimination by cultural agents who tended to emphasize women's subjection and lifelong loyalty to husbands. While port marriage illustrates the relatively powerful social status and autonomy of women, both Chinese and European travelers imposed their cultural biases and judgments on this system. Chinese sojourners such as Zhou Daguan and Wang Dayuan, followed by European ones, were unable to understand or accept the liberty and high status of indigenous women and more often than not disdainfully regarded it as a form of prostitution.[63] Many of these women, unfortunately, would be forced to become prostitutes when colonial institutions were imposed on these port societies. In Southeast Asia, for example, prostitution did not appear in major port cities until the late sixteenth century, and usually it involved slave women whose owners forced them into the trade.[64]

Tradition, nevertheless, dies out slowly. In the late Qing period many a Chinese tycoon accumulated tremendous wealth with the assistance of his port wives in Saigon, Bangkok, Malacca, Palembang, Semarang, Jakarta, and elsewhere.[65]

Chapter Sixteen

A TRUE ROMANCE

In the sea your little deity supervises, there is the *Ruanyangtan* 软洋滩 (lit. "the Soft-Ocean Shoal") of 800 *li*. Its upper water is soft, and its bottom water hard. The surface of the *ruanshui* 软水 (lit. "soft water") is unable to hold even a bird feather or a leaf of duckweed. Therefore, ships from the east, south, west, and north are not able to pass here.

—LUO MAODENG

In the sixteenth century, no advances were made on the Chinese knowledge of the Indian Ocean world. Existing information was instead circulated and recirculated through romanticizing, exoticizing, storytelling, hand-copying, and printing. The late period of the Ming dynasty was a prosperous age of commercialization, urbanization, and globalization, during which an incredible quantity of silver entered the Chinese market from Japan, but particularly from the New World. The urban culture of the time demanded sensational stories and created a large quantity of cultural consumers for this literature. As a result, many serial novels were compiled based on the oral tradition of storytelling. One by one, stories that had been largely oral and often not connected in time or space were revised, polished, and published in chaptered literary works. The *Xiyou Ji* 西游记 (The Journey to the West), based on Xuanzang's journey, and the *Fengshen Yanyi* 封神演义 (Investiture of the Gods), derived from the legendary replacement of the Shang with the Zhou Dynasty, were both completed in this period. Inspired by historical facts, these novels, with their rich mixture of seeds of truth, cultural beliefs, and mysterious or exotic hearsay, became widely circulated and retold orally among illiterate commoners who could not read the stories themselves.

Not coincidentally, in the 1590s two works were completed by two native literati in Jiangxi Province, and these two represent the last works in the

A TRUE ROMANCE

Celestial Dynasty that hark back to the Indian Ocean world. Born in Nanchang, Luo Yuejiong obtained his provincial degree in 1585 and put together the *Xianbin Lu* (A Record of All Guests) in 1591 by compiling all that was known about the barbarian regions, including those in the Indian Ocean world. Under the orthodox tone of the tributary language, the *Xianbin Lu* contributed little to Chinese knowledge of the world outside China's border. Rather, it showed in the worst light Chinese information on the Indian Ocean world that had already become erroneous, distorted, or forgotten.

The other work, the *Xiyang Ji*, was completed in the 1590s by Luo Maoden, a scholar born in Fuzhou 抚州, Jiangxi Province.[1] Fuzhou is located in eastern Jiangxi Province, neighboring Nanchang, the provincial capital, to the west and Fujian Province to the east. It is no accident that such writers as Wang Dayuan, Luo Yuejiong, and Luo Maodeng were all natives of Jiangxi Province, which had become a principal producer and supplier of porcelain for the world, especially from the Ming dynasty onward. The porcelain center of Jingdezhen was in northern Jiangxi, very close to both Nanchang and Fuzhou. Porcelainware produced in Jingdezhen was usually shipped to Hangzhou and Guangzhou, but especially to Quanzhou, en route to Southeast Asia and the Indian Ocean world. Therefore, local knowledge about the maritime world would have circulated among the literati, which explains the historical context of Jiangxi where Wang Dayuan, Luo Yuejiong, and Luo Maodeng were born.

The *Xiyang Ji*, inspired by and based on the Zheng He voyages, rather romanticized maritime Asia by merging fact and fiction. Although much less famous than the *Xiyou Ji*, the *Xiyangji* retains many facts about the Indian Ocean including the Maldives and shows that Luo Maodeng had some actual knowledge of this remote region. The novel is thought to be creatively historical, since it "makes a sedulous use of the data found in the description of these voyages," often literally copying works by Wang Dayuan, Ma Huan, Fei Xin, and others.[2]

The two Luos belonged to the same era, both being active in writing at the end of the sixteenth century. Neither Luo Yuejiong nor Luo Maodeng ventured overseas, however. While the passage concerning the Maldives in *Xianbin Lu* remained a word-for-word hand copy with just a couple of minor misunderstandings, Luo Maodeng's long novel was much more voluminous and creative. Almost every kingdom introduced in the *Xiyang Ji* could find citations from the *Yingya Shenglan* or the *Xingcha Shenglan*, as well as several other previous Chinese works.[3] For example, Jicini, a kingdom recorded in the *Xiyang Ji* that presented ambergris to Ming China, could not be found in early Ming sources. Referring to the city of Ghazni located in central Afghanistan, Jicini was the capital of the Ghaznavid Empire in the tenth century. The Zheng He voyages did not visit Jicini, and thus neither Ma Huan, Fei Xin, nor Gong Zhen mentioned this kingdom. The *Lingwai Daida* and the *Zhufan Zhi*, the two Song works, and the *Dade Nanhaizhi*, a Yuan source, however, all share an entry on Jicini, which shows that the three Song and Yuan texts served as sources for Luo Maodeng.[4] Indeed, Luo Maodeng might have been the last imperial scholar to pay attention to Jicini.

The *Xiyang Ji* provides many clues and hints to aid our understanding of the Chinese knowledge of maritime Asia. By focusing on coconuts, the Soft-Water Sea, the magnetic rock range, cowrie shells, and the Maldivian subordination to the imperial throne, the following topical discussions illustrate the influences or clues left by Wang Dayuan, Ma Huan, and the like on the *Xiyang Ji*, and help to reveal extant records or provide new information on maritime Asia and the Maldives found in texts unknown to us. Arguably, the *Xiyang Ji* symbolizes the peak of the Chinese popular fascination with the Maldives that had been accumulated, circulated, and translated among the Chinese intellectual circles over the ages.

DRAGON KING'S FOUR GIFTS

The story of the *Xiyang Ji* relates how Dīpaṃkara (*Randeng Fo* 燃灯佛, lit. the "lamp bearer Buddha") is reincarnated into a monk in Ming China and helps Zheng He to complete the journey to the eighteen kingdoms in the Western Ocean, including the Liushanguo (the Maldives). Dīpaṃkara is one of the Buddhas of the past who reached enlightenment prior to Gautama Buddha, the historical Buddha. With the colorful influence of Buddhism and to a lesser degree Daoism, the novel *Xiyang Ji* closely models itself after the *Xiyou Ji* and the *Fengshen Yanyi*, those far more popular fictitious novels completed in the Ming dynasty, but unfortunately, it did not meet with such resounding success as they had. Nonetheless, to a large degree, the *Xiyang Ji* serves better than any other imperial novel to illustrate the maritime world conceptualized and romanticized by the Chinese.

Maritime or waterborne items are immediately highlighted at the beginning of the *Xiyang Ji*. Before his reincarnation, the Master Monk

A TRUE ROMANCE

Dīpaṃkara receives four maritime-borne gifts from the four Dragon Kings (*longwang* 龙王) in charge of the four seas (East, South, West, and North): thirty-three large pearls from the East Sea, lapis lazuli (*feiliuli* 吠琉璃) from the West Sea, a Chan shoe (*chanlü* 禅履) from the North Sea, and a coconut fruit from the South Sea.[5]

All four gifts derived from the sea or were associated with water. Pearls, a highly desired exotic item for the Chinese elite for more than 1,600 years prior to this period, came from the south, with the most prized often brought in from overseas. Lapis lazuli came from the south, too, especially when Buddhism prospered in China. These two items had become standard tributary gifts for overseas kingdoms to present to the Chinese court. In the *Xiyang Ji*, pearls help to provide access to fresh water from the sea and *feiliuli* is said to be the eggshell of the Golden-Winged Bird (*jinchiniao* 金翅鸟) that loves to eat iron.[6] The so-called Golden-Winged Bird refers to Garuḍa, a giant bird in Indian mythology that was a guardian deity in both Hinduism and Buddhism. In Hindu mythology, Garuḍa, ate the *naga* (snake) as its preferred food and when this tradition spread into Chinese mythology, the *naga* was replaced with the dragon, a giant snakelike guardian creature in charge of the oceans.

The mention of the Chan shoe relates to the legendary Indian monk Bodhidharma, who introduced Chan Buddhism to China in the fifth century, and has been regarded as its first Chinese patriarch. It is said that he crossed the Yangzi River by standing on a reed, and this has become the best-known story to illustrate the magic power that Buddhism possessed. In the *Xiyang Ji*, the reed is replaced with the Chan shoe, and the Yangzi River with the North Sea, as the North Sea Dragon King claims that Bodhidharma was sitting on this shoe to bear him across the river.

The description of the coconut fruit deserves special attention here. It is described as shaggy (*maosongsong* 毛鬆鬆), with the name of *boluo xuyoujia* 波罗许由迦.[7] This Chinese name is worth discussing. The name *boluo* might be an abbreviated variation of *boluomiduo* 波罗蜜多 (*pāramitā*) or *boluomi* 波罗蜜 (*pāramī*), a Buddhist term often translated as "perfection." Meanwhile, a very popular and creative translation of *pāramitā* seems more closely related to the Chinese name. It divides *pāramitā* into *pāra* and *mita*, with *pāra* meaning "beyond," "the further bank, shore, or boundary" while *mita* meant "that which has arrived," or *ita* meant "that which goes." In this way, *pāramitā* means "that which has gone beyond," "that which goes beyond," or "transcendent," and such an understanding is also "reflected in the Tibetan translation *pha rol tu phyin pa* ("gone to the other side").[8]

Therefore, the word *boluo* might have the meaning of crossing a river to reach the other shore. If so, the three Chinese characters *xuyoujia* might be a perverted transliteration of *naukā* (small ship or boat). Hence, I would like to propose that the name *boluo xuyoujia* for the coconut in fact served as a metaphor, indicating the magical power of the coconut in its ability to float over water and thus help people complete perilous water voyages. Such an ability or means to cross water safely, which immediately reminds us with "ships without nails" constructed by coconut trunk planks and coir ropes, is further revealed in the introduction of this fruit presented by the Dragon King to Master Monk. The fruit is born from the *āmra* tree (*anluo shu* 庵罗树) in the Western Full of Joy Kingdom in the West (*Xifang Jile guo* 西方极乐国). It is round, like a ball of light, and before it was cut it represented *Taiji* 太极. When cut in half it represents the two divides (*Liangyi* 两仪), and when Pindola Bharadvaja (*Luoduoshe zunzhe* 罗堕阇尊者) descends into the sea he passes it to the Dragon King.[9] When the Master Monk asks about its use, the Dragon King explains:

> In the sea where your little deity supervises, there is the Soft-Ocean Shoal (*Ruanyangtan* 软洋滩) of 800 *li*. Its surface water is soft, and its bottom water hard. The surface soft-water (*ruanshui* 软水) is unable to hold even a bird feather or a leaf of duckweed. Therefore, ships from the east, south, west, and north are not able to pass here. If the coconut fruit is sawn into a ladle (*piao* 瓢), you will find that it is broader by ten *fen* (*shifen* 十分) than the five lakes and the four seas (*wuhusihai* 五湖四海). When a ship arrives at the Soft-Water Sea, using the ladle as a scoop, the soft water is gone, while the hard water rises up.[10]

As a result, the ship is able to sail forward. Although the use of the coconut described here is different from the Indian Ocean practice, the Chinese mythical understanding of coconuts might have been a sinicized belief mixed with or related to that of the Indian culture.

In sum, all the four special treasures presented by the four Dragon Kings are southern, exotic, water or ocean-related, and magically powerful for oceangoing navigators.

A TRUE ROMANCE

THE SOFT-WATER SEA AND THE ATTRACTING-IRON RANGE

One major feature of the Maldives recorded by early Chinese travelers, the so-called Ruoshui, had its similar counterpart in the *Xiyang ji*. When introducing the magical function of coconuts, the *Xiyang Ji* mentions the so-called Soft-Ocean Shoal, sometimes called the Soft-Water Sea (*Ruanshuiyang* 软水洋). The Soft-Ocean Shoal, 800 *li* long, is in fact a variation of the so-called Weak River (*Ruoshui*) and they share the same features.[11]

Just like the Floating-Sand-River in the *Xiyou Ji*, the Soft-Water Sea is too soft or weak to suspend even a goose feather, a piece of duckweed or dried grass, which poses an insurmountable barrier for the treasure fleet. Thus, the Master Monk pays a visit to the Dragon King of the East Sea for help. The Dragon King tells him that in the Tang dynasty Xuanzang and his three disciples faced the same problem in crossing the Soft-Water Sea, and that it was only when the Monkey King Sun managed to get the help of the Buddha (*Rulaifo* 如来佛) to withdraw the soft water and promote the hard water (*yingshui* 硬水) that they were able to proceed with their Buddhist pilgrimage to India. In the morning, the Master Monk uses his bowl (*bo* 钵) to scoop all the soft water up, the hard water rises to the surface, and the treasure fleet is able to sail forward.[12] This bowl, although not specifically described, must have been made of coconut. Luo's novel hence combines the traditional narrative of the Ruoshui and the *Xiyou Ji* and applies this fantastical treatment to the Zheng He expedition.

Immediately after their passing the Soft-Water Sea there emerges another challenge called the Attracting Iron Range (*Xitieling* 吸铁岭), which is 500 *li* long. The range is composed of magnetic rocks lying along the bottom of the sea. Anything made of iron would be magnetically attracted to these rocks, which worries all sailors, since nails, anchors, and weapons including knives, spears, swords, and other implements are all made of iron. Only with *feiliuli* attached to the head of the ship would these magnetic rocks lose their power. With the help of the Dragon King, the Master Monk is able to help the fleet cross the Attracting Iron Range.[13] This again reminds us of the magnetic rock fable mentioned by Ptolemy in the second century, Palladius in the fifth century, Zhou Qufei in the twelfth century, and Fei Xin in the fifteenth century, many of these positioning this terrible geographical feature in the Maldives.

The Chinese description of the Attracting Iron Range seems to have been more or less a copy of what had been shared more than a thousand years earlier on the other side of the globe. "The magnet-stone which attracts iron is produced; so that if any ship built with iron nails should approach these islands, it will be by the virtue of this stone be drawn thither and stayed in its course."[14] While the fable of the magnetic Maldives had disappeared from Western records, a similar legend was found in this Ming China novel. Although a solid connection between the two has not yet been established due to the lack of sources, this is more than a mere coincidence.

THE SUBORDINATION OF LIUSHAN

In its introduction to the Liushanguo (The Maldives), the *Xiyang Ji* shows itself to be a copy of early Ming works. The eight *liu* with their names, the *xiaozhailiu*, the Ruoshui, and various gifts presented to Zheng He, such as cowrie shells (and the way to collect them), dried fish, coconut wine cups (and wine making), and gold thread woven kerchiefs (their superb quality and price) are copied, nearly word for word, from the *Yingya Shenglan*, the *Xingcha Shenglan*, and the *Xiyang Fanguo Zhi*.[15] The *Xiyang Ji* also records that many precious stones are presented to Zheng He. The Maldives does not produce precious stones, but these might have been brought there from Ceylon. In addition, coconuts and coconut wine are mentioned for consumption on the Chinese voyages.

The purpose and nature of the Zheng He voyages to Southeast Asia and the Indian Ocean world have been hotly debated. Whether these were intended to be pro-colonizing, proto-colonizing, or friendly, this fleet of approximately a hundred ships and more than twenty thousand crewmen including soldiers sailing across the South China Sea to the Indian Ocean in the early fifteenth century represented the might of the Ming empire in these regions. It is no wonder that a few violent clashes broke out between the Ming forces and local rulers.

In 1407 Zheng He attacked and captured the "pirate" Chen Zuyi 陈祖义 in Palebambang and established a "Pacification Superintendency," and Zheng He's troops fought with local forces in Java. In 1411 Zheng He's troops captured the Ceylonese king and forcibly transported him to Beijing. In 1415 Zheng He seems to have been involved in a civil war in Samudera in north Sumatra, and Suganla, the reported "leader of the Samuderan bandits," was

A TRUE ROMANCE

captured and taken to Beijing. In addition, the Ming voyagers were also active as arbitrators in tensions among local polities in India, such as those between Calicut and Cochin, and between Bengal and Jaunpur. Certainly, a major theme running through the *Xiyang Ji* is how the Chinese fleet adopts force, magical or otherwise, to subdue local kingdoms. In the *Xiyang Ji*, violent clashes occur between the Chinese and nine kingdoms from mainland Southeast through Java, Sumatra, Malacca, and Ceylon to India and East Africa, many of these having been acknowledged in the Ming historical records. The subjugation of the Liushanguo, not by force but by carrot and stick, is particularly interesting.[16]

Some seven or eight days out from their departure from Ceylon, the fleet reaches the kingdom of Liushan. Eunuch Hong (*Hong Gonggong* 洪公公) and General Wu are already there when Zheng He arrives. Zheng He reports that "the letter and form of surrender" (*xiangshu xiangbiao* 降书降表), together with tributary gifts prepared by the Liushan king, have been made ready.[17] And very interestingly, the narrative states that there are two chiefs who remain unconvinced and attempt to incite the king to resist the Chinese. Informed of this, Eunuch Hong reminds Zheng He to be careful when dealing with the king.

With this knowledge of a possible counterincursion in mind, Zheng He orders that the Ceylonese king be captured and put in a cage with his shoulder blades chained with irons, and on top of the cage, a white board should be displayed that reads: "any king who dares to resist and refuse subordination will be punished in the same way as this one." He also commands that the heads of the Ceylonese soldiers killed by the Chinese should be hung up high, with a white board reading: "Any chief who dares to resist and disobey will be punished in this way."[18] On learning of this, the Liushan king is so awed that he roundly scolds the two chiefs. They then go to Zheng He's ship, presenting a letter as a form of surrender. Zheng He reads the letter, accepts the gifts, gives them the reward of Chinese gifts to be given to their king, and warns the two chiefs to behave themselves. The two chiefs are terrified, perform their kowtows, ask for forgiveness, and vow their loyalty. In this way potential violence is avoided, at least for the kingdom of Liushan.

How much does this fictional account reflect the real interactions between Zheng He and the king of the Maldives? The *Xiyang Ji* is a novel, and without any doubt the story related here appears fictional. However, some details in this account can be linked to historical texts for the purposes of a speculative discussion that might not be irrelevant. First, it is evident that the Zheng He fleet did visit the Maldives, and this is categorically stated in the *Xiyang Ji*. Second, no historical sources suggest any violence between Ming envoys and the Maldives although the *Xiyang Ji* indicates some potential tension. Concerns and tensions were natural responses to a large armed fleet, as many local kings and envoys including the Maldivian emissary to China were solicited by "invitation." Probably that is why the Maldives quickly abandoned its mission to China when the Ming suspended the Western Ocean campaign.

Finally, a look at the gifts presented from the Liushan Kingdom to the Ming court may provide some information not mentioned in the Ming sources. In the *Xiyang Ji*, the Maldivian gifts include "10,000 silver coins, twenty *shi* of cowrie shells (*haiba*), ten red *yakut* or rubies (*hongyahu* 红鸦呼) stones, ten blue *yakut* stones (*qingyahu* 青鸦呼), ten blue sapphires (*qingyelan* 青叶蓝), ten *xilani* 昔剌泥 stones, ten *kumolan* 窟没蓝 stones, ten *shi* 石 of laka wood, five *shi* of ambergris, 100 coconut wine cups, 100 embroidered silken kerchiefs, 100 gold-thread handkerchiefs, and 100 *shi* of dried bonito fish."[19] Obviously, cowrie shells, various silk or cotton kerchiefs, and dried fish were locally produced Maldivian products, laka wood and ambergris were also local commodities mentioned by Ma Huan and Fei Xin, and the silver coin was very possibly the Maldivian *larin*, while the precious stones listed most certainly originated in Ceylon or India. It is highly plausible that the Maldivian king would present cowries together with kerchiefs and dried fish to the Ming emperor, although neither Ma Huan and his fellow travelers nor contemporary archives such as the *Ming Shilu* or the *Ming Shi* mention these local items as being included in tribute gifts. It is thus fair to say that the historical value of the *Xiyang Ji* is "by no means negligible."[20] Fictitious as it is, the novel provides many Chinese transcriptions of foreign words, refers to texts known and unknown to us, and mixes facts with fiction. Its rich and diverse information has yet to be comprehensively mined for historical information on the Zheng He voyages and Chinese knowledge on maritime Asia, including the Maldives.

Chapter Seventeen

AN ECHO: THE "CHINA BIRD"

Straightway they began to dive into the water, catching great numbers of fish, and ever as they caught them putting them of their own accord into the baskets, so that before long all the three baskets were full.

—ODORICO DA PORDENONE

The king hearing of this bird wondered exceedingly how it was possible for it to have come alone from China, a distance of more than 1,200 leagues.

—FRANÇOIS PYRARD

The Maldives was "but a small country," concluded Ma Huan.[1] Despite the diminutive size of this island kingdom in the Indian Ocean, it managed to draw an unusual amount of attention from imperial China, thousands of miles away and with very different ethnic, cultural, and social systems. Chinese travelers did land in the Maldives, and Wang Dayuan was reportedly the first of these. Zheng He's fleets anchored in the Maldives, and many other Chinese travelers stayed in the Maldives, Ma Huan being the most famous sojourner. The Chinese certainly made their own contributions to the understanding of Maldivian history. Ma Huan, Fei Xin, and Gong Zhen filled the gap between Ibn Battuta in the 1330s and the Portuguese at the beginning of the sixteenth century, while Wang Dayuan preceded Ibn Battuta, and Huang Xingzeng was there at the same time as the Portuguese and other Europeans.

Ibn Battuta witnessed a commercially prosperous society in the Maldives that facilitated and was simultaneously benefited by maritime trade owing to its crucial location. Perhaps the winning qualities that made the essential nature of the Maldives so appealing throughout history were the abundance of commodities and local hospitality. It provided almost everything that indigenous and foreign people needed or desired. Ibn Battuta mentions India, Yemen, and China quite often in his accounts, indicating the significant role that the Maldives played in the broad trade network of maritime Asia. These three vast areas denoted the Indian, Arab, and Chinese worlds and spanned a vast area to the north, east, and west, with the Maldives almost at center stage. In addition, many specific areas and their merchants were mentioned, such as Coromandel, Ceylon, Bengal, Persia, various Southeast Asian polities, and so on. The Maldives in the age of Wang Dayuan, Ibn Battuta, and Ma Huan was a key constituent of maritime Asia.

It is reasonable to deduce that some private merchants or sailors from China might have traveled as far as or even farther than the Maldives, but unfortunately, after the suspension of the Zheng He fleet in 1433, the Chinese state forbade maritime activities, closed its doors, and gradually lost interest in that region altogether. Private trade was also banned, and Chinese merchants were not allowed to go overseas. Might there have been any Chinese travelers who visited the Maldives after Zheng He's era? Probably not. Today we can hardly find any influence left by imperial China on this archipelago, except for hundreds of porcelain sherds. Nonetheless, the local memory of China had once been much stronger in this island kingdom, and this was glimpsed in an anecdote shared by Francois Pyrard.

When Francois Pyrard was in the Maldives (1602–1607), a giant bird landed on an island there.

> This bird is three feet in height, the body exceedingly thick, more than a man could embrace; the plumage is all white, like a swan's; the feet are flat, as with birds that swim; the neck is half a fathom, and the beak half an ell in length; at the end of the beak above is a kind of crooked hook; the lower jaw is much larger than the upper, and has a large pocket depending on therefrom, very capacious, and of a yellowish golden colour, like parchment. The king was greatly astonished to think whence this animal could have come, and what was its nature, and inquired of all who had come from foreign parts, but none could resolve the matter. At length arrived certain strangers, who informed him that this animal was peculiar to China, being bred only there, and that the Chinese use it for catching fish, inasmuch as this animal swims in the water like other water-fowl, and for long whiles at a time. It catches fish industriously, filling the great creel or pocket which hangs beneath its beak, and is so large and capacious as to carry therein many

fish of two feet in length each. The king hearing of this bird wondered exceedingly how it was possible for it to have come alone from China, a distance of more than 1,200 leagues.[2]

The king followed the Chinese practice of having the bird's neck tied, leaving it with just enough room to breathe. This prevented the bird from swallowing a fish once it had caught one, allowing the fisherman to retrieve the fish from the bird. Francois Pyrard concluded:

> This is the artifice employed in China. I have seen it in this manner go into the sea for a long space, and return laden with fish. It used to go out to sea for a considerable time, sometimes remaining away a whole day, which leads me to believe it not impossible that it had come from China, for it loves the sea and tarries there a long time, catching fish for its food. In addition to this, I have been assured by numberless Indians of all parts that fowls of this kind are bred in China alone.[3]

In fact, centuries earlier than Pyrard, various China-related legends or tales had circulated in maritime Asia and beyond. In Quilon, Ibn Battuta was impressed by the Chinese fowl:

> The hens and cocks in China are very big indeed, bigger than geese in our country, and hens' eggs there are bigger than our goose eggs. On the other hand their geese are not at all large. We bought a hen once and set about cooking it, but it was too big for one pot, so we put it in two. Cocks over there are about the size of ostriches: often a cock will shed its feathers and [nothing but] a great red body remains. The first time I saw a Chinese cock was in the city of Kawlam. I took it for an ostrich and was amazed at it, but its owner told me that in China there were some even bigger than that, and when I got to China I saw for myself the truth of what he had told me about them.[4]

The Chinese fishing bird in the Maldives and the Chinese hens and cocks in Kawlam (Quilon) demonstrate that traditions and myths about China had emerged in the Indian Ocean world. The fishing bird witnessed by the king of the Maldives was not in fact from China, nor were the hens and cocks that Ibn Battuta had seen in Quilon. Their imagined association with China, just like various legends portrayed on Chinese silk in ancient Rome, one of which showed silk growing from a kind of tree in China, illustrates how the China factor (including Chinese products and culture) had influenced local societies that clearly had developed their own conceptualization of China.[5] No wonder "certain strangers" were able to claim that the fishing bird was bred only in China.

However, while the Chinese visited the Maldives in the fourteenth and fifteenth centuries, their cultural influence of China on the Maldives was negligible.[6] Almost nothing is visibly left of their influence except for some pieces of porcelain and some coins. For example, one bronze coin minted in 990–994 from the reign of Emperor Taizong of the Northern Song dynasty, along with some porcelain sherds, was discovered in Kaashidhoo, but it is uncertain whether or not these were directly brought there by the Chinese merchants or indirectly arrived with traders from other places.[7] It is interesting and ironic to note that while the grand imperial impact on the Maldives was impressive but not long-lasting, as illustrated by the Zheng He fleets, whereas the Maldivian impact on China proved to be rather "small," slow, and much longer lasting. This comparison draws attention to the enormous difference in size between the two, and demonstrates the contrasted roles that market and state, respectively, made in an asymmetrical relationship.

The bird thought to have come from the Celestial Dynasty was not from there at all, of course, although it is true that the method of training cormorants to catch fish seemed to be a Chinese invention.[8] Henry Yule points out that the description is "a perfectly accurate account" of the Chinese practice and that the bird was called a "fishing hawk" or "fishing duck" by the Chinese.[9] Chinese fishing hawks had certainly been a wonder that had fascinated Western observers more than two centuries earlier than Pyrard was amazed by them.

THE CHINESE HAWKS SEEN IN CHINA

When he traveled to the upper Qiantang River (*Qiantang Jiang* 钱塘江) in Zhejiang Province in about 1330, Odorico da Pordenone was amazed by a fish-catching bird called *luci* 鸬鹚. A local host invited him to see some "good fishing."

AN ECHO: THE "CHINA BIRD"

I looked and saw in some boats of his that were there certain water-fowl tied upon perches. And these he now tied with a cord round the throat that they might not be able to swallow the fish which they caught. Next he proceeded to put three great baskets into a boat, one at each end and the third in the middle, and then he let the water-fowl loose. Straightway they began to dive into the water, catching great numbers of fish, and ever as they caught them putting them of their own accord into the baskets, so that before long all the three baskets were full. And mine host then took the cord off their necks and let them dive again to catch fish for their own food. And when they had thus fed they returned to their perches and were tied up as before. And some of those fish I had for my dinner.[10]

While Henry Yule and other scholars were unable to locate the site of this scene, quite coincidentally, the place where Odorico da Pordenone saw the birds catching fish was about 12.5 miles (20 km) from the rural village where I grew up. The city in which da Pordenone lodged was Meicheng 梅城 (lit. "Plum City"), the capital of Yanzhou 严州 Prefecture, along the upper Qiantang River, also called the Jiande River (Jiande Jiang 建德江) by the Tang poet Meng Haoran 孟浩然 (689–740). That Odorico da Pordenone mistook the city of Meicheng for Belsa was reasonable, as about 18.6 (30 km) upriver there was a ferry called Baisha 白沙 (lit. "White Sands") that deeply impressed many imperial official-scholars for the turbulent rapids found there. Downriver about 12.5 miles (~20 km) away there was a bay called Luci Wan 鸬鹚湾 or 芦茨湾 (lit. "Cormorant Bay"). I never saw local fishermen using cormorants to catch fish, nor heard any senior village men talking about this scene, for the two giant dams built in the 1950s and 1960s changed the local landscape dramatically.[11] Many villages along the river were simply submerged by water, and one of them was the place where my maternal grandfather was born and grew up.

Odorico da Pordenone was the first European to observe Chinese fishing birds, and this Chinese tradition continued to fascinate the Europeans, some of whom traveled to China to witness it with their own eyes. In the early sixteenth century, when the Portuguese landed in South China, they were also immediately struck by this activity. Galeote Pereira was one of the earliest Portuguese soldiers and smugglers to seek his fortune in China. After being captured in 1549 in Fujian he was thrown into a local prison, traveled a few years across South China from Fujian through Jiangxi to

Guangxi, and probably escaped back home through Macao, providing a similar detailed description of these Chinese fishing birds.[12]

> The king hath in many rivers good store of barges full of sea-crows, that breed, are fed, and do die therein, in certain cages, allowed monthly a certain provision of rice. These barges the king bestoweth upon his greatest magistrates, giving to some two, to some three of them, as he thinketh good, to fish therewithal after this manner. At the hour appointed to fish, all the barges are brought together in a circle, where the river is shallow, and the crows, tied together under the wings, are let leap down into the water, some under, some above, worth the looking upon. Each one as he hath filled his bag, goeth to his own barge and emptieth it, which done, he returneth to fish again. Thus having taken good store of fish, they set the crows at liberty, and do suffer them to fish for their own pleasure. There were in that city, where I was, twenty barges at the least of those aforesaid crows.[13]

In fact, the Ming emperor residing in his palace in Beijing did not have his own fishing birds, nor did he grant them to his ministers. However, it might be true that local governments did have a tax for the boat people (*danjia* 疍家) who, often referred to as "sea gypsies," were placed on the bottom rung of society by the founding emperor of the Ming dynasty, out of spite, perhaps, since the boat people had supported his rival's claim to the succession. Therefore, Galeote Pereira's imagined scene of the emperor and the sea crows was not purely a fantasy. Fascinated, he "went almost every day to see them, yet could I never be thoroughly satisfied to see so strange a kind of fishing."[14]

Gaspar da Cruz (c. 1520–1570), a Portuguese Dominican friar who reached South China in late 1556, was equally amazed by this fishing bird. Although he might have seen this exotic practice himself, his description was simply a copy of Galeote Pereira's, except that he called these birds cormorants, not sea crows.[15] Bernardino de Escalante (ca. 1537–?), a Spanish soldier, left a similar account of fishing cormorants.[16] It seems that Chinese fishing birds became a sensation among Europeans, and accounts of their habits were copied and quickly circulated by the Portuguese and Spaniards so that a few decades later the French traveler Pyrard witnessed some "strangers" telling the Maldivian king all about this tradition. The source for Pyrard might have been *Historia de las cosas más notables, ritos y costumbres del gran reyno de la China* by Juan González de Mendoza (1545–1618), a Spanish bishop and scholar. Mendoza did nothing but compile accounts of several Spanish travelers in China such as Galeote Pereira and Gaspar da Cruz, but his work was the most popular of his day and was influential in spreading knowledge of Chinese things across Europe before the Jesuits' efforts in the early seventeenth century. Soon various translations of this work were completed, with both English and French versions published in 1588, three years after the original Spanish edition appeared.[17] I speculate that Pyrard had read or heard the story of the China fishing bird from this book before his departure for Asia in May 1601 and that one of those "strangers" in his recall was none other than Pyrard himself.

Fishing birds continued to be a spectacle of interest to Europeans traveling in China. On June 13, 1656, the first Dutch tributary mission (1655–1657) arrived in Jining 济宁, a port city along the Grand Canal.[18] The Dutch described the fishing birds catching fish in a pond in the same manner as in the Qiantang River or as practiced by the Maldivian king. Like Odorico da Pordenone, the Dutch bought some fish, and Johan Nieuhof (1618–1672), who came along as a member of the Dutch East India Company partly because of his artistic training, sketched a drawing of the fishing bird (figure 17.1).

FIGURE 17.1 *Louwa* (cormorant) by Johan Nieuhof. *Source*: Johan Nieuhof, *Legatio batavica ad magnum Tartariae chamum Sungteium, modernum Sinae imperatorem* . . . (Amsterdam: Jacobum Meursium, 1668), 118.

REMINISCENCES

The famous Macartney Mission, the first British embassy sent to China in 1793, also brought the image of the China bird back to Europe. William Alexander (1767–1816), a British artist and a member of the mission, created a number of paintings of Qing China, including *The Fishing Cormorant* (figure 17.2). His China pictures were frequently duplicated from engravings and thus became widely known among European audiences. As a result, the image of China's fishing bird spread throughout the West.

On October 9, 1816, Henry Ellis, part of a British mission headed by William Amherst (1773–1857), also witnessed the fishing birds along the Grand Canal:

> Just before dinner we had an opportunity of seeing the fishing birds, called *yu-ying*, fish vulture, or *yu-ye*, fish bird. Several of these birds are placed on perches in each boat, and dropped into the water from poles; the birds dive naturally for the fish, and are trained to bring them to the boat. I observed one with a stiff collar round its throat to prevent its swallowing the fish; they seem to be made to dive by striking the pole into the water; they were of the size of Muscovy ducks, and resembled the booby bird in appearance, particularly the beak.[19]

Two years after the end of the First Opium War (1839–1842), the French Catholic priest and sinologist Evariste Régis Huc (1813–1860) came

FIGURE 17.2 *The Fishing Cormorants* by William Alexander. Source: William Alexander, *Picturesque Representations of the Dress and Manners of the Chinese, illustrated in Fifty Colored Engravings, with Descriptions* (London: John Murray, 1814).

AN ECHO: THE "CHINA BIRD"

across some cormorants on a lake in the mid-Yangzi River region while traveling from Tibet to China proper. Instead of nets, local fishermen had a fair number of cormorants that were perched on the edges of their boats.

> It is a curious spectacle to see these creatures engaged in fishing, diving into the water, and always coming up with a fish in their beak. As the Chinese fear the vigorous appetite of their feathered associates, they fasten round their necks an iron ring, large enough to allow of their breathing, but too small to admit the passage of the fish they seize: to prevent their straying about in the water, and wasting the time destined for work, a cord is attached to the ring and to one claw of the cormorant, by which he is pulled up when inclined to stay too long under water. When tired, he is permitted to rest for a few minutes, but if he abuses this indulgence and forgets his business, a few strokes of a bamboo recall him to duty, and the poor diver patiently resumes his laborious occupation. In passing from one fishing ground to another, the cormorants perch side by side on the edge of the boat, and their instinct teaches them to range themselves of their own accord in nearly equal members on each side, so as not to disturb the equilibrium of the frail vessel: we saw them thus range throughout the little fleet of fishing smacks on Lake Ping-hou.
>
> The cormorant is larger than the domestic duck; it has a short neck and long beak, slightly hooked at the end. Never very elegant in appearance, it is perfectly hideous after it has passed the day in fishing. Its wet and tumbled plumage stands on end all over its meagre body, and it hunches itself up till nothing is to be seen but a frightful shapeless lump.[20]

Although he never visited China, Thomas Allom (1804–1872), an English artist, completed a series of drawings illustrating the Chinese Empire (first published in 1858), including one of cormorants[21] Never having seen the fishing birds himself but basing his drawings on sketches provided by Europeans who had traveled in China, his drawings show a peaceful and harmonious relationship between the fishermen and their cormorants, quite a contrast with the tension described by Evariste Régis Huc. The Western interest in fishing with cormorants in China continued up until the twentieth century, when photography was able to capture the real-life actions of these fishing birds.[22]

REMINISCENCES

NO CHINESE SHIPS SAILING THROUGH THE MALACCA STRAIT

Going back to the Maldives, the episode of the China bird was in fact the last echo of Chinese activity in this island country, and probably even in the entire Indian Ocean world. It shows how some knowledge about China still lingered some 170 years after the last visit of the Chinese fleet, remembered perhaps as a vast empire far, far away from the Indian Ocean. Meanwhile, by the time of Pyrard, knowledge of any Chinese influence in the Maldives had largely become diluted, and most Chinese sources concerning the Maldives simply repeated what had been previously shared.[23] In fact, virtually no Chinese ships from the mid-fifteenth century onward sailed through the Malacca Strait to reach the Indian Ocean.[24] Still, Chinese visitors including merchants and sailors probably still went to the Indian Ocean world in dribs and drabs, mainly via Southeast Asian and Indian ships. Unfortunately, little information is known to us.

The post-1567 period was widely regarded as a watershed because in this year, the Ming state partially lifted its maritime ban. Only Zhangzhou, a port near modern Amoy, was opened, permits for ships were set up with a quota, and more important, ships were allowed to sail only to the stipulated zone and only as far west as the Malacca Strait to places such as Aceh. In other words, the Ming China maritime interest focused only on Nanyang, roughly today's Southeast Asia. As a result, the Chinese began to establish an intensive commercial and diasporic network in this maritime region.

One may wonder whether during this period any Chinese vessels ventured into the Indian Ocean, at least to Keda (Kedah) on the west coast of the Malay Peninsula. Chen Lunjiong 陈伦炯, a native of Tongan 同安 County, Fujian Province, grew up in a naval family, served in the Qing army in Taiwan, Guangdong, Jiangsu, and Zhejiang, accumulated rich maritime experience including one visit to Japan, and became the general in charge of the Zhejiang provincial navy. He commented that the seas and oceans west of Johore and Malacca "had not any Chinese oceangoing ship reached, and they just stopped there" (*Zhongguo yangsou congwenjingli daocierzhi* 中国洋艘从未经历, 到此而止).[25] Considering his background and authority, it is evident that the Qing ships never sailed through the Malacca Strait.[26] Meanwhile, it is certain that many Southeast Asian and Indian vessels shipped Chinese goods from China and Southeast Asia to the Indian Ocean. Again, here is another puzzle: as early as the ninth century the Arabs sailed and traded directly between the Indian Ocean and the South China Sea (as was illustrated by the Belitung shipwreck). The Chinese followed this tradition, sailing and trading directly with ports and kingdoms in the Indian Ocean in the Song period (illustrated by the *Quanzhou I* and *Nanhai I* wrecks). Why was it that both the Arabs and the Chinese gave up these direct forms of trade? I speculate that some major regional shift occurred to disrupt the continuation of this direct trade, embodied in the rise and fall of Maldivian knowledge in China.

Even in the high Qing period of the eighteenth century, when the giant Qing Empire was more than equipped with power, wealth, and the technology to sail to the Indian Ocean, the Celestial Dynasty showed no interest in reviving this tradition. Consequently, China's knowledge of the Indian Ocean world had been stagnant since as early as the second half of the sixteenth century, which can be illustrated by the *Xianbin Lu* compiled by Luo Yuejiong in 1591, a work wholly based on secondary sources. Due to a misunderstanding or an arbitrary judgment, Luo made a few major mistakes when introducing the Maldives. First, he thought that Diegan 牒干 and Liushan were two different polities, although Ma Huan had categorically stated that Diegan was the indigenous name for Liushan. Second, while his section on Liushan was largely a summarized copy of the *Yingya Shenglan*, Luo made a huge mistake in claiming that the local people of Liushan worshiped Buddha (*shangfo* 尚佛). In addition, Luo erroneously claimed that during the Hongwu Reign (1368–1399) the king of Liushan had sent an envoy to Ming China.[27] These mistakes show that by the end of the sixteenth century the Chinese had begun to lose some of the reliable information accumulated in the previous centuries, a frequent problem caused by secondhand history. And Zhang Xie's *Dongxiyang Kao* illustrates the shift of Chinese interests from the Indian Ocean to the South China Sea by the beginning of the seventeenth century, since it does not mention anything west of the Malay Peninsula. Zhang Xie was not the only person to record this change, as can be seen from the many Chinese navigation charts produced in the Ming-Qing period that shared this trend.[28]

MAERDIWA AND THE JESUITS

The Jesuit mission to Ming-Qing China pioneered by Matteo Ricci brought the memory of those "ten thousand islands" (*wandao* 万岛) to China, and their accounts were mixed with the existing Chinese knowledge on the Maldives, gradually getting more diluted and erroneous as time went by. As a result, the two streams of information paralleled. While imperial scholars were shocked and enlightened by the brand-new knowledge and the value system behind the Jesuit works (including maps), it seems that no one at the time paid any attention to the tiny archipelago in the Indian Ocean, let alone identified it with the Chinese Liushan.

Giulio Aleni, the Italian Jesuit who visited China during the Ming-Qing transition, shared an updated version of world geography with the Chinese people. "West (of Ceylon) are some islands, with a general name of *Maerdiwa* 马儿地袜, no fewer than a few thousand in total (*buxia shuqian* 不下数千), all being inhabited. In the sea grows a kind of coco-tree, with fairly small fruits, which can cure many diseases."[29] The Chinese phrase "no fewer than a few thousand," translated from European books and written with Chinese characters by Giulio Aleni and his Chinese assistants, might have been some of the last vestiges of interactions between European and Chinese strands of knowledge on the Maldives. Its European authorship and Chinese readership literally became the final mention of these Indian Ocean islands until the era of the First Opium War.

The *Kunyu Quantu* 坤舆全图, published in 1674 by Nan Huairen, another Jesuit serving at court during the Kangxi reign (1661–1722), was an influential cartographic work made in China.[30] Nan Huairen's *Maerdewa dao* 玛儿的袜岛 (lit. "Maerdiwa Island"), although adopting a few distinctive Chinese characteristics, was obviously one and the same as the land as the one Giulio Aleni had spoken of, and this was also accurately marked as lying west of Ceylon.

The Jesuit influence had penetrated the Qing cartographical works, but their contributions also confused Chinese cartographers who had never traveled to the Indian Ocean. In the map known as *Carte de la Chine*, made in the Jiaqing reign (1796–1820) by Zhu Xiling 朱锡龄, a native of Jiaxing 嘉兴, Zhejiang Province, it was found that *Maerdiwa* 馬尔地襪 was located below and slightly to the *east* of Ceylon (*Xilanshan* 锡兰山), and that immediately below the Maerdiwa was Liushan 溜山 (map 17.1).[31] So both Maerdiwa and Liushan were erroneously placed in the Bay of Bengal, and certainly far too close to the Malay Peninsula.

Zhu Xiling claimed that his map was based on the original one made in the year of *Dingwei* 丁未 of the Qianlong reign (1787) by Huang Qianren

AN ECHO: THE "CHINA BIRD"

黄千人 (1694–1771), a native of Yuyao 余姚, Zhejiang Province. However, Huang died in 1771, seventeen years earlier than 1787, so *Dingwei* might have been mistakenly inserted by Zhu, who was probably referring to the year of *Dinghai* 丁亥 (1767).[32] It should be noted that both Jiaxing and Yuyao were situated very close to Hangzhou 杭州, the southern center of Jesuit activities during the Ming-Qing transition. Therefore, the continuing addition of Maerdiwa indicated the enduring influence of Jesuit efforts on the Chinese literati, which lasted at least for the following two centuries.

Obviously, the Chinese cartographer had learned about Maerdiwa from Giulio Aleni and Ferdinand Verbiest, but it was a pity that he did not

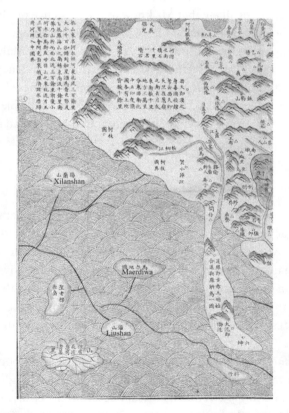

MAP 17.1 The Maldives and Liushan in Chu-Si-Ling's map of China. *Source*: "Chu-Si-Ling. Cartographe," Bibliothèque Nationale de France, département Cartes et plans, GE C-5353 (1–3 RES). The Chinese name of the map is *Daqing Wannian Yitong Tianxia Quantu* 大清万年一统天下全图 (A Comprehensive Map of All-Under-Heaven for the Ten-Thousand-Year Unification by the Grand Qing).

realize his mistake of retaining both the Jesuit Maerdiwa and the Chinese Liushan on the same map, even though they referred to the same archipelago near Ceylon, something that neither the Jesuits nor the Chinese scholars managed to figure out.

The *Jingban Tianwen Quantu* 京板天文全图 (72 cm × 119 cm), a map drawn by Ma Junliang 马俊良 and completed approximately in 1790 in the final years of the Qianlong reign (1735–1795) and three years earlier than the Macartney Mission, displays some remarkable features. On the same chart Ma drew three different maps: one a large Chinese traditional map, and over the top of the large one two hemispheric maps, one based on Chen Lunjiong's map of 1730 and the other on the map made by Matteo Ricci in 1584.[33] Because of the size of the two small maps the Maldives was not marked, although it is highly likely that Ma knew of the existence of Matteo Ricci's *wandao*. The large map is styled in the late Ming tradition, which meant leaving a tiny space for the Indian Ocean world, and the Maldives was of course missing. Ma's map seems to reveal the Chinese tendency seen at the end of the eighteenth century for both Western and Chinese knowledge of the Indian Ocean epitomized by the Maldives to be of negligible importance to the China emperor. This era of being forgotten indeed had set in by the end of the Ming.

BEING FORGOTTEN

The *Zheng He Hanghai Tu*, though printed in the 1620s, is generally regarded as a legacy of the Zheng He voyages, and thus it reveals the culmination of Chinese knowledge on maritime Asia in the early fifteenth century. The texts and maps of this era encapsulate the most comprehensive knowledge of the Indian Ocean accumulated by the Chinese, including the navigation routes and the location of the Maldives. However, some other Ming navigation guides produced in the late sixteenth century began to omit the Maldives.

The *Duhai Fangcheng* 渡海方程, a Ming navigation guidebook first compiled in 1537, was continuously revised in the following decades and probably completed in 1593. While its textual descriptions clearly detail how a ship should follow the compass to reach various ports in the Indian Ocean, its map parts are missing. This latter omission of the *Duhai Fangcheng* was made up by the *Shungfeng Xiangsong* 顺风相送, another Ming work that might have been a hand-copied manuscript of the *Duhai Fangcheng*. These two Ming maritime works provide more navigational information than the *Zheng He Hanghai Tu*, since they have retained many Indian Ocean places such as Suwendala 苏文哒喇 (Samdura), Nanwuliyang 南巫里洋 (Lamuri), Longxianyu (Ambergris Islet), Cuilanyu (the Nicobar Islands), Xilanshan (Ceylon), Xiaoju'nan 小俱南 (Kulam), Kezhigangkou 柯支港口 (Port of Cochin), Guliguo 古里国 (Calicut), and Hulumosi 忽鲁谟斯 (Ormuz), among others. Nevertheless, for reasons unknown to us, the Maldives does not appear there.[34] Was this Indian Ocean archipelago too small and thus too insignificant, or could there be another explanation for its absence on this map?

The Selden Map, a hand-colored chart made in approximately the 1620s, around the same era as Zhang Xie's *Dongxiyang Kao*, has provided a categorical illustration of such a change.[35] The map gave credit to the new extent of Fujian maritime interests and activities around the mid-Ming period and focused on just the East Sea and West Sea (roughly the eastern part of the so-called Western Ocean), exactly as Zhang Xie had done. Consequently, various navigation routes that connected China with Southeast Asia and Northeast Asia are clearly marked with textual descriptions. In contrast, the sea that was supposed to show the great Bay of Bengal and the land mass meant to represent the Indian subcontinent were much smaller than the Ryukyu Islands. In addition, Guli (Calicut) occupies half the Indian subcontinent, and the well-plied navigation routes to Adanguo 阿丹国 (Aden), Faer guo 法尔国 (Zufar), and Hulumosi (Ormuz) are only roughly sketched in. The Maldives, of course, is nowhere to be seen.

The *Zhinan Zhengfa* 指南正法 (The Correct Ways to the South), another navigational guidebook probably produced at the beginning of the eighteenth century, showed the same tendency that is seen on the Selden Map. While the major focus in the *Shunfeng Xiangsong* made in the late sixteenth century centered on the Indian Ocean with some attention paid to areas east of the Malay Peninsula and a portion on Japan, and with the Selden Map incorrectly representing the Indian Ocean and the navigational route to Ormuz, the main hub of the *Zhinan Zhengfa* was devoted to modern Southeast Asia along with the islands of Japan and Ryukyu, leaving just a brief navigational guide for Zhang Xie's Eastern Ocean and Western Ocean.[36] As the navigational guidebook used by Chinese sailors, the *Zhinan Zhengfa* entirely failed to mention anything about the regions west of the Malacca Strait, showing just how unimportant the Indian Ocean then was to China in the post-1600 Chinese maritime world.[37] By contrast, Nanyang had begun to occupy paramount attention for China, initiating China's long eighteenth-century (1683–1799) in this region.[38]

A recently discovered Chinese navigational chart in the Yale University Sterling Memorial Library is further confirmation of such a pattern.[39] Comprising 122 maps, this Qing chart provides an extraordinarily detailed guide for oceangoing ships from Nagasaki to the Malay Peninsula. Produced in the High Qing period, this chart shows how the concept of Nanyang was formed to replace the Western Ocean and Eastern Ocean.

This does not mean that no Chinese travelers ever visited the Indian Ocean in the post-1600 period. Throughout the three centuries from 1500 to 1800, a few Chinese travelers passed through the Indian Ocean.[40] They were mainly Chinese merchants, Chinese companions of European priests, or overseas Chinese living in the Dutch East Indies. These include Fan Shouyi 樊守义 (Louis Fan, 1682–1753), a Chinese priest who accompanied the Jesuit Ai Ruose 艾若瑟 (Joseph-Antoine Provana, 1662–1720) on his return to Europe in 1707, and Xie Qinggaoxie 谢清高 (1765–1821), who worked on certain European ships from 1782 onward.[41]

In his youth, Xie Qinggao, a Cantonese, had accompanied Chinese merchants on overseas trading trips, and once when rescued by a foreign ship (highly likely a European one) during a storm he traveled across Southeast Asia, the Indian Ocean, and Europe, going much further afield than Wang Dayuan had ever traveled. After fourteen years spent overseas he finally settled down in Macao and became an interpreter for Chinese traders. While in Macao, Xie went blind, but he met a certain Yang Bingnan 杨炳南 in 1820. Yang wrote down what Xie related to him into a book called *Hailu* 海录 (A Record of the Sea). This book was soon noticed by Imperial Commissioner Lin Zexu 林则徐, who was dispatched by Emperor Daoguang 道光 (r. 1820–1850) to Guangzhou in charge of the opium ban. For all information concerning European countries, technologies, and especially military posts and trade in Asia, Lin Zexu recommended this book to Emperor Daoguang.[42] Information on more than ninety countries from as far east as Timor (on which Wang Dayuan might have landed) and as far west as Holland, England, and America were included in this book. As for the Indian Ocean, while Bengal, Madras, Pondicherry, Ceylon, Cochin, Calicut, Goa, Bombay, and other places are all listed, not even a single line

AN ECHO: THE "CHINA BIRD"

was written about the Maldives. Perhaps understandably, because this Indian Ocean archipelago, once very crucial both in China's Indian Ocean activities and the maritime world in general, no longer had any trade with the Chinese at that time and had little significance to Qing China, which at that time had its hands full managing the European colonial encroachment on China's southern maritime frontiers.

In Chinese history the Maldives rose like a rocket and came down like a stick, lying deep in the seabed and covered thickly with mud. Alas, with barely a sound, the Maldives simply disappeared from the Chinese world.

NOTES

1. SMALL, REMOTE, BUT SIGNIFICANT

1. For the life of H. C. P. Bell, see Bethia N. Bell and Heather M. Bell, *H.C.P. Bell: Archaeologist of Ceylon and the Maldives* (London: Archetype Publications, 1993); Heather Bell, "H. C. P. Bell in Sri Lanka and the Maldives," *South Asian Studies* 8 (1992): 105–8.
2. H. C. P. Bell, *The Maldive Islands: Monograph on the History, Archaeology and Epigraph* (Colombo: Ceylon Government Press, 1940), 1–6.
3. Ibn Battuta, *Travels in Asia and Africa, 1325–1354*, trans. and selected by H. A. R. Gibb, with an Introduction and Notes (New York: Routledge & Kegan Paul, 2011).
4. For Ibn Battuta's stay in the Maldives, see Albert Gray and H. C. P. Bell, "Early Notices of the Maldives," in François Pyrard, *The Voyage of François Pyrard of Laval to the East Indies, the Maldives, the Moluccas and Brazil*, ed. Albert Gray and H. C. P. Bell (Cambridge: Cambridge University Press, 2011), 3:434–68.
5. For Jingdezhen and its white and blue porcelain, see Anne Gerritsen, *The City of Blue and White: Chinese Porcelain and the Early Modern World* (Cambridge: Cambridge University Press, 2020).
6. Wang Dayuan, *Daoyi Zhilue Jiaoshi* 岛夷志略校释 (Brief Record of the Island Barbarians), ed. Su Jiqing (Beijing: Zhonghua Shuju, 1981), 9. I would like to use the term "maritime Asia" in this book to emphasize seaborne societies, cultures, and networks that were based on sea and ocean trade but were simultaneously linked with land trade. Geographically speaking, maritime Asia comprised vast water regions, including the Pacific and the Indian oceans, stretching from Northeast Asia through East Asia, Southeast Asia, South Asia, and the Middle East to the east coast of Africa. Coastal areas and peoples were therefore surely part of maritime Asia by this definition.

1. SMALL, REMOTE, BUT SIGNIFICANT

7. Ma Huan, *Ming Chaoben Yingya Shenglan Jiaozhu* 明钞本瀛涯胜览校注 (An Overall Survey of the Ocean Shores: Annotation of a Ming Manuscript), ed. Wan Ming (Beijing: Haiyang Chubanshe, 2005), 1.
8. It is necessary to highlight that for the historical periods examined in this book the region known as the Maldives Islands sometimes included the Laccadive Islands (especially the southernmost Minicoy Island), due to their intimate relationship. Indeed, many historical texts did not differentiate one from the other, at least not explicitly. Although it has been politically attached to India, Minicoy has remained Maldivian, both culturally and ethnically. Andrew D. W. Forbes, "Southern Arabia and the Islamisation of the Central Indian Ocean Archipelagoes," *Archipel* 21 (1981): 56.
9. Eva-Maria Knoll, "The Maldives as an Indian Ocean Crossroads," *Oxford Research Encyclopedias: Asian History* (2018), https://oxfordre.com/asianhistory/display/10.1093/acrefore/9780190277727.001.0001/acrefore-9780190277727-e-327; R. Michael Feener, "Maldives," *The Encyclopedia of Islam Three*, ed. Kate Fleet et al. (Leiden: Brill, 2021), 89–93.
10. Xiyang was a geographical region in Chinese history. Roughly speaking, it referred to the maritime world west of the Philippines and the island of Borneo. Hence, it includes the western region of modern Southeast Asia and the entire Indian Ocean.
11. Bin Yang, *Cowrie Shells and Cowrie Money: A Global History* (New York: Routledge, 2019); "The Cowrie World," in *Oxford Research Encyclopedia of Asian History*, 2022, https://oxfordre.com/asianhistory/display/10.1093/acrefore/9780197727.001.0001/acrefore-9780190277727-e-722.
12. Bell, *The Maldive Islands*; Gray and Bell, "Early Notices." For a recent introduction to textual and archaeological work on the Maldives, see Shiura Jaufar and Anne Haour, "An Overview of Previous Historical and Archaeological Work in the Maldives," in *Archaeological Investigations of the Maldives in the Medieval Islamic Period: Ibn Battuta's Island*, ed. Anne Haour and Annalisa Christie (London: Routledge, 2022), 11–17.
13. Wang, *Daoyi Zhilue*; Xie Fang, "Zhongguo Shiji zhong zhi Maerdaifu Kao" (A Study of the Maldives in Chinese Historical Texts), *Nanya Yanjiu* (South Asia Studies) 2 (1982): 1–8.
14. John Carswell, "China and Islam in the Maldive Islands," *Transactions of the Oriental Ceramic Society 1975-77* 41 (1977): 121–98; Andrew D. W. Forbes, "Archives and Resources for Maldivian History," *South Asia: Journal of South Asian Studies* 3, no. 1 (1980): 70–82; "Dr. Andrew Forbes," https://www.britishmuseum.org/collection/term/BIOG123366.
15. Roderich Ptak, "The Maldives and Laccadive Islands (*liu-shan* 溜山) in Ming Records," *Journal of the American Oriental Society* 107, no. 4 (1987): 675–94. Ptak's paper is not only remarkably rich in sources but also touches on the key issue that this book examines, that is, the production of Chinese knowledge concerning the Maldives. Its nineteen-page-long, detailed, and insightful footnotes are no less inspiring than the text itself.
16. Yang, *Cowrie Shells and Cowrie Money*.
17. Bin Yang, "Dangzi Yinduyang Fanhang—Quanzhouwan Songdai Haichuan Hangxian Xinkao" (Sailing Home from the Indian Ocean: A New Analysis of the

Song Shipwreck Discovered in the Quanzhou Bay in 1974), *Haijiaoshi Yanjiu* (Journal of Maritime History Studies) 1 (March 2021): 18–30.
18. Sackler Gallery, Smithsonian Institution, the National Heritage Board of Singapore, and the Singapore Tourism Board, "Shipwrecked: Tang Treasures and Monsoon Winds," 2010, https://asia.si.edu/research/publications/exhibition-catalogues/shipwrecked-tang-treasures-and-monsoon-winds/.
19. Bin Yang, "'Wuding zhi Chuan': Kaogu he Wenxian zhong Zuizao Wangfan yu Xiya yu Zhongguo zhijian de Haibo" ("Ship Without Nails": Archaeological and Textual Analyses of the Earliest Ocean Vessels Sailing Directly Between China and West Asia), *Haojiaoshi Yanjiu* (Journal of Maritime History Studies) 1 (2022): 1–20.
20. Guojia Wenwuju Shuixiayichanbaohuzhongxin et al., *Nanhai I hao Chenchuan Kaogubaogao Zhiyi—1989–2004 nian Diaocha* (Archaeological Report on the *Nanhai I* Shipwreck Series I: Surveys of 1989–2004) (Beijing: Cultural Relics Press, 2017); *Nanhai I hao Chenchuan Kaogubaogao Zhier—2014–2015 nian Fajue* (Archaeological Report on the *Nanhai I* Shipwreck Series II: Excavation of 2014–2015) (Beijing: Cultural Relics Press, 2018).
21. Geoff Wade, "An Early Age of Commerce in Southeast Asia, 900–1300 CE," *Journal of Southeast Asian Studies* 40, no. 2 (2009): 221–65.
22. "The Selden Map of China," Bodleian Library, MS.Selden supra 105, https://seldenmap.bodleian.ox.ac.uk; Xiang Da, ed., *Zheng He Hanghai Tu* 郑和航海图 (The Zheng He Nautical Chart) (Beijing: Zhonghua Shuju, 2000).
23. Paul A. Cohen, *History in Three Keys: The Boxer as Event, Experience, and Myth* (New York: Columbia University Press, 1997), xv–xvi.
24. Edward H. Schafer, *The Golden Peaches of Samarkand: A Study of T'ang Exotics* (San Francisco: Hauraki Publishing, 2014).
25. Zhu Yu, *Pingzhou Ketan* 萍州可谈 (Chats in Pingzhou), ed. Li Weiguo (Shanghai: Shanghai Gujichubanshe, 1989); Derek Heng, "Shipping, Customs Procedures, and the Foreign Community: The 'Pingzhou Ketan' on Aspects of Guangzhou's Maritime Economy in the Late Eleventh Century," *Journal of Song-Yuan Studies* 38 (2008): 138.
26. Zhou Qufei, *Lingwai Daida Jiaozhu* 岭外代答校注 (Answers for Questions Concerning Out of Range), ed. Yang Wuquan (Beijing: Zhonghua Shuju, 1999). "Out of Range" refers to the Lingnan area (lit. "South of Range", including today's Guangdong and Guangxi Provinces) and beyond.
27. Zhang Xie, *Dongxiyang Kao* 东西洋考 (An Examination of the Eastern and Western Oceans), ed. Xie Fang (Beijing: Zhonghua Shuju, 2000).
28. Luo Maodeng, *Sanbao Taijian Xiyangji Tongsu Yanyi* 三宝太监西洋记通俗演义 (Romance of Eunuch Sanbao's Journey to the Western Ocean), ed. Lu Shulun and Zhu Shaohua, 2 vols. (Shanghai: Shanghai Gujichubanshe, 1982).

2. FROM ZAITUN

1. For a history of Quanzhou, especially its role in maritime trade, see Hugh R. Clark, "The Religious Culture of Southern Fujian, 750–1450: Preliminary Reflections on Contacts across a Maritime Frontier," *Asia Major* 19, nos. 1–2 (2006):

211–40; "Muslims and Hindus in the Culture and Morphology of Quanzhou from the Tenth to the Thirteenth Century," *Journal of World History* 6, no. 1 (1995): 49–74; "Quanzhou (Fujian) During the Tang-Song Interregnum, 879–978," *T'oung Pao* 68, nos. 1–3 (1982): 132–49; Angela Schottenhammer, ed., *The Emporium of the World: Maritime Quanzhou, 1000–1400* (Leiden: Brill, 2001); Billy So, *Prosperity, Region, and Institutions in Maritime China: The South Fukien Pattern, 946–1368* (Cambridge, MA: Harvard University Asia Center and Harvard University Press, 2000). Since Kuwabara Jitsuzo's work on Pu Zhougeng published in 1935, many scholars have given attention to this Muslim merchant in Quanzhou. See Sangyuan Zhizang (Kuwabara Jitsuzo), *Pu Shougeng Kao* (An Examination of Pu Shougeng), trans. and ed. Chen Yujing (Beijing: Zhonghua Shuju, 2009); John W. Chaffee, "Pu Shougeng Reconsidered: Pu, His Family, and Their Role in the Maritime Trade of Quanzhou," in *Beyond the Silk Roads: New Discourses on China's Role in East Asian Maritime History*, ed. Robert J. Antony and Angela Schottenhammer (Wiesbaden: Harrassowitz Verlag, 2017), 63–76; Hu Xiaowei, "Guanyu Quanzhou Fanshang Pu Shougeng de San'ge Wenti" (The Three Issues Concerning Pu Shougeng, the Foreign Merchant in Quanzhou), *Haijiaoshi Yanjiu* (Journal of Maritime History Studies) 1 (2015): 38–43, 63–76; Geoff Wade, "Early Muslim Expansion in South-East Asia, Eighth to Fifteenth Centuries," in *The New Cambridge History of Islam*, ed. David Morgan and Anthony Reid (Cambridge: Cambridge University Press, 2010), 3:366–408; "The Li (李) and Pu (蒲) 'Surnames' in East Asia-Middle East Maritime Silk Road Interactions during the 10th–12th Centuries," in *Aspects of the Maritime Silk Road: From the Persian Gulf to the East China Sea*, ed. Ralph Kauz (Wiesbaden: Harrassowitz, 2010), 181–93; So, *Prosperity*, 301–5; and Luo Xianglin, *Pu Shougeng Yanjiu* (A Research on Pu Shougeng) (Hong Kong: Chung-kuo Hsue-she, 1959). In his classic work, Kuwabara Jitsuzo also discussed Song China's maritime policies and the foreign merchant community in Quanzhou.

2. So, *Prosperity*, 207.
3. For the collection of stone inscriptions, see Wu Wenliang, *Quanzhou Zongjiao Shike (Zengding ben)* (Religious Stone Inscriptions in Quanzhou, Revised Version) (Beijing: Kexuechubanshe, 2005); for the literature review of this field, see Wang Liming, "Quanzhou Yindujiao Shike Yanjiu Huigu yu Sikao" (A Reflection on the Studies of Quanzhou Stone Inscriptions), *Haijiaoshi Yanjiu* (Journal of Maritime History Studies) 1 (2016): 122–36.
4. So, *Prosperity*, 27–42.
5. So, *Prosperity*, 48–49.
6. He Qiaoyuan, *Min Shu* 闽书 (A Record of Fujian) (Fuzhou: Fujian Renminchubanshe, 1994), 2:1489; So, *Prosperity*, 55.
7. Hong Mai, *Yijian Zhi* 夷坚志 (What Yijian Records), ed. He Zhuo, 4 vols. (Beijing: Zhonghua Shuju, 1981). The *Yijian Zhi* is a massive collection of miscellaneous essays on social life during the Song dynasty.
8. Hong, *Yijian Zhi*, 1:59–60.
9. Hong, *Yijian Zhi*, 1:251–52; 2:588–89.
10. Hong, *Yijian Zhi*, 3:1344–6; So, *Prosperity*, 55.
11. Xu Song, *Song Huiyao Jigao* 宋会要辑稿 (An Extracted Draft of Song Government Manuscript Compendium) (Beijing: Guoli Beiping Tushuguan, 1936), "fanyi" 7; So, *Prosperity*, 55.

2. FROM ZAITUN

12. Zhou Daguan, *Zhenla Fengtuji Jiaozhu* 真腊风土记校注 (Customs of Champa: An Annotation), ed. Xia Nai (Beijing: Zhonghua Shuju, 1981), 178.
13. For reviews of studies of this tombstone, see Johannes L. Kurz, "A Note on the Tombstone of Master Pu and the *Xishan Zazhi*," *Bijdragen tot de taal-, land- en volkenkunde* 172, no. 4 (2016): 510–37; Bin Yang, *Shangzuo Chuanjing Shi yi Wei: Rao Zongyi Xinjiapo Daxue Zhijiao Kao* (Jao Tsung-I in Singapore: Life, Research, and Chinese Scholarly Diaspora) (Hong Kong: Jao Tsung-I Petite École, Hong Kong University, Summer 2018), 117–30.
14. Kurz, "A Note," 523.
15. Chen Gaohua, "Yuandai Quanzhou Boshang (Ship Merchants in Quanzhou of the Yuan Dynasty)," in *Yuanshi Yanjiu Lungao* (On Studies of Yuan History) (Beijing: Zhonghua Shuju, 1991), 429–31; So, *Prosperity*, 116–25.
16. Ling Mengchu, *Paian Jingqi* 拍案惊奇 (Amazing Tales), ed. Zhang Peiheng and Wang Gulu (Shanghai: Shanghai Gujichubanshe, 1983), 1:1–26. The *Paian Jingqi* was a novel of many independent stories. "Wen" literally means "culture" or "being civilized," indicating that Wen Shi had a solid educational background.
17. Jiling is highly likely a translation of Keling, derived from the ancient kingdom of Kalinga in eastern India. Xuanzang once visited there, calling it *Jielinjia* 羯陵伽. In the Malay world migrants from India were called Keling, and there is a historical town of Tanjung Kling in Malacca. In modern times Keling (or Kling), however, is a derogatory term to denote a person originating from India that came to be used when the British brought over Indian laborers to work on rubber plantations.
18. For the Xiyang cloth, see Liu Yingsheng, *Hailu yu Lulu—Zhonggu Shiqi Dongxijiaoliu Yanjiu* (Maritime and Continental Routes Between East and West) (Beijing: Beijingdaxue Chubanshe, 2011), 42–45.
19. Zhao Rukuo, *Zhufan Zhi Jiaoshi* 诸蕃志校释 (A Record of Barbarians), ed. Yang Bowen (Beijing: Zhonghua Shuju, 2000), 86. The *Baolinyuan* reminds us of the "Buddhist temple" where Wang Yuanmao learned some southern foreign languages.
20. Xue Yanqiao, "Zhufanzhi 'Nanpiguo'tiao Renmin Bushi" (Supplementary Annotations to the Entry "*Nanipiguo*" in the *Zhufanzhi*), *Quannan Wenhua Yanjiu* (Studies of Southern Quanzhou Culture) 14 (September 2021): 72.
21. Zhao, *Zhufan Zhi*, 66–68. The names of the father and the son are not clear, since *Luoba* and *Zhiligan* could be one transliteration. Whatever the case, Zhao's note serves to show that maritime trade was a hereditary profession for both Chinese and non-Chinese merchants.
22. *Song Shi* 宋史 (History of the Song Dynasty) (Beijing: Zhonghua Shuju, 1977), *juan* 489, 14093.
23. Lin Zhiqi, *Zhuozhai Wenji* 拙斋文集 (Collected Works of *Zhuozhai*), in *Siku Quanshu* 四库全书 (The Complete Library of the Four Treasuries), vol. 1140 (Shanghai: Shanghai Gujichubanshe, 1987), *juan* 15; So, *Prosperity*, 53–54. In his *Zhufan Zhi*, Zhao Rukuo also abbreviated the story of Shinawei 施那帏. Zhao, *Zhufan Zhi*, 91. Billy So pointed out that Lin's essay was the source for Zhao's brief record, while Yang Bowen stated that Shinawei was a transliteration of Shilave, referring to merchants from Sirf or Shiraz, and that Sirf was known in Chinese as Silian 思莲, which Zhao Rukuo mentioned as being under the control of Dashi 大食.

2. FROM ZAITUN

"Dashi" derived from the Persian word "Tazi" or "Taziks" and referred to the Arab world in the Chinese context. So, *Prosperity*, 53; Zhao, *Zhufan Zhi*, 95n16; 97–98n36.
24. Marco Polo, *The Travels of Marco Polo (The Venetian)* (New York: Liveright, 1953), 254–55.
25. Zhu Yu, *Pingzhou Ketan* 萍州可谈 (Chats in Pingzhou), ed. Li Weiguo (Shanghai: Shanghai Gujichubanshe, 1989), 25.
26. Marco Polo, *The Travels*, 255, 268, 270.
27. Ibn Battuta, *Travels in Asia and Africa, 1325–1354*, trans. and selected by H. A. R. Gibb, with an Introduction and Notes (Abingdon [England] & New York: Routledge & Kegan Paul LTD, paperback, 2011) ,238–39. Panderani refers to today's Koyilandy.
28. Battuta, *Travels*, 259.
29. Wang Dayuan, *Daoyi Zhilue Jiaoshi* 岛夷志略校释 (Brief Record of the Island Barbarians), ed. Su Jiqing (Beijing: Zhonghua Shuju, 1981), 244.
30. Battuta, *Travels*, 287–88.
31. Battuta, *Travels*, 282–83.
32. Battuta, *Travels*, 289.

3. SAILING TO THE INDIAN OCEAN

1. Ibn Battuta, *Travels in Asia and Africa, 1325–1354*, trans. and selected by H. A. R. Gibb, with an Introduction and Notes (New York: Routledge & Kegan Paul, 2011), 235.
2. Fujian Quanzhou Haiwajiaotongshi Bowuguan, ed., *Quanzhouwan Songdai Haichuan Fajue yu Yanjiu Xiudingban* (A Report on the Excavation on the Song Boat in Quanzhou Bay; hereinafter *Songdai Haichuan*) (Beijing: Haiyang Chubanshe, revised, 2017); Bin Yang, "Dangzi Yinduyang Fanhang: Quanzhouwan Songdai Haichuan Hangxian Xinkao" (Sailing Home from the Indian Ocean: A New Analysis of the Song Shipwreck Discovered in Quanzhou Bay in 1974), *Haijiaoshi Yanjiu* (Journal of Maritime History Studies) 1 (April 2021): 12–30.
3. For the study of the *xiangyao* (aromatic medicine) trade in the Song period, see Lin Tianwei, *Songdai Xiangyao Maoyishi* (History of the Xiangyao Trade in the Song Dynasty) (Taipei: Zhongguowenhua Dauxue Chubanbu, 1986).
4. *Songdai Haichuan*, 66–67.
5. Yang, "Dangzi Yinduyang," 12–30.
6. The finding of ambergris in *Quanzhou I* has been scientifically confirmed. Jiang Jianrong, "Quanzhouwan Songdai Haichuan Chutu Bufen Xiangliao de Kexueyanjiu" (Scientific Study of Spices Excavated from the Song Boat in Quanzhou Bay), PhD diss., University of Science and Technology Beijing, 2021, 69–78.
7. *Songdai Haichuan*, 26 and 105.
8. Nanjing Yaoxueyuan, Nanjing Linchanongye Xueyuan, and Fujiansheng Yaopin Jianyansuo, "Quanzhouwan Chutu Songdai Muzao Haochuan Cangnei Jiangxiang de Xianweijianding" (A Microscopic Examination of Laka Wood in the Hold of the Wooden Song Ship Discovered in Quanzhou Bay), in *Songdai Haichuan*, 264–65; Shanghaishi Weishengyaopin Jianyansuo and Fujiansheng

3. SAILING TO THE INDIAN OCEAN

Yaopinjianyansuo, "Quanzhouwan Chutu Songdai Muzao Haochuan Cangnei Jiangxiang de Huaxuejianding" (A Chemical Examination of Laka Wood in the Hold of the Wooden Song Ship Discovered in Quanzhou Bay), in *Songdai Haichuan*, 266–71.

9. Bin Yang, *Cowrie Shells and Cowrie Money: A Global History* (New York: Routledge, 2019), 5–6, 20–39. See also chapter 10 herein.
10. *Songdai Haichuan*, 62–64 and 121–22; Li Fuxue, "Quanzhouwan Songdai Haichuan shang Beilei de Yanjiu" (A Study of the Shells in the Song Ship Discovered in Quanzhou Bay), in *Songdai Haichuan*, 238–46.
11. Li, "Quanzhouwan," 244–45; Yang, "Dangzi Yinduyang."
12. Zhou Qufei, *Lingwai Daida Jiaozhu* 岭外代答校注 (Answers for Questions Concerning Out of Range), ed. Yang Wuquan (Beijing: Zhonghua Shuju, 1999), 126; Zhao Rukuo, *Zhufan Zhi Jiaoshi* 诸蕃志校释 (A Record of Barbarians), ed. Yang Bowen (Beijing: Zhonghua Shuju, 2000), 8, 18, 34, 54, 68, 75, and 89.
13. Zhao, *Zhufan Zhi*, 8, 18, 34, 54 (*cheng* was a unit of distance); 68, 75, 89.
14. *Songdai Haichuan*, 68 and 128–29.
15. Chen Gaohua and Wu Tai, "Guanyu Quanzhouwan Chutu Haichuan de Jige Wenti" (A Few Issues of the Sea Ship Excavated in Quanzhou Bay), in *Songdai Haichuan*, 164–65; Zhuang Weiji and Zhuang Jinghui, "Quanzhouwan Songchuan Jiegou de Lishi Fenxi" (A Historical Analysis of the Structure of the Song Ship Discovered in Quanzhou Bay), in *Songdai Haichuan*, 172.
16. *Songdai Haichuan*, 75–77 and 138–39.
17. Marco Polo, *The Travels of Marco Polo (The Venetian)* (New York: Liveright, 1953), 262.
18. Marco Polo, *The Travels*, 262–63.
19. Zhu Yu, *Pingzhou Ketan* 萍州可谈 (Chats in Pingzhou), ed. Li Weiguo (Shanghai: Shanghai Gujichubanshe, 1989), 26.
20. Marco Polo, *The Travels*, 261–62.
21. Marco Polo, *The Travels*, 262.
22. Marco Polo, *The Travels*, 263.
23. Battuta, *Travels*, 235; *Songdai Haichuan*, 73–74.
24. Chen and Wu, "Guanyu Quanzhouwan," 172–73.
25. Li Qingxin, "Nansong Haiwaimaoyi zhong de Waixiaoci, Qianbi, Jinshzhipin ji Qitawenti" (Export Porcelain, Coins, Metal Items and Other Issues in the Maritime Trade of the Southern Song), *Xueshu Yuekan* 44, no. 3 (September 2012): 122.
26. Yang, "Dangzi Yinduyang," 29–30. Yang Rui argues that Quanzhou was its departure port, while some scholars believe that it departed from Guangzhou with Southeast Asia as its destination. Yang Rui, "Nanhai I Hao Nansong Chenchuan Ruoganwenti Kaobian" (Textual Research on the *Nanhai I* Shipwreck of the Southern Song Dynasty), *Bowuyuan* (Museum) 2 (2018): 27–32; Huang Chunyan and Feng Xinyi, "Nanhai I Hao Yanjiu zhong Lishiwenxian yu Kaoguziliao de Xianghubuzheng" (Historical Documents and Archaeological Data in the Research of *Nanhai I*), *Haijiaoshi Yanjiu* (Journal of Maritime History Studies) 1 (2021): 1–11.
27. Battuta, *Travels*, 235; Marco Polo, *The Travels*, 263.
28. *Songdai Haichuan*, 70 and 131.

3. SAILING TO THE INDIAN OCEAN

29. Anthony Reid, *Southeast Asia in the Age of Commerce, 1450–1680, Volume Two: Expansion and Crisis* (Chiang Mai, Thailand: Silkworms Books, 1993), 49.
30. "The Mayflower Story," https://www.mayflower400uk.org/education/the-mayflower-story/; Kate Caffrey, *The Mayflower* (Lanham, MD: Rowman & Littlefield, 2014), 52.
31. Caffrey, *The Mayflower*, 51, 69.
32. Zhu, *Pingzhou Ketan*, 26; Lin, *Songdai Xiangyao*, 124; Billy So, *Prosperity, Region, and Institutions in Maritime China: The South Fukien Pattern, 946–1368* (Cambridge, MA: Harvard University Asia Center and Harvard University Press, 2000), 208–9.
33. Battuta, *Travels*, 235–36.
34. Lin, *Songdai Xiangyao*, 124 and 127.
35. Zhu, *Pingzhou Ketan*, 26.
36. Hong Mai, *Yijian Zhi* 夷坚志 (What Yijian Records), ed. He Zhuo (Beijing: Zhonghua Shuju, 1981), 2:480.
37. Ye Daoyang, "'Nahai Yihao' Chenchuan Fanying de Songdai Haishangshenghuo Bianxi" (Maritime Life of the Song Period Reflected by *Nanhai I*), *Zhongguo Wenhua Yichan* (Chinese Cultural Heritage) 4 (2019): 101.
38. Wang Dayuan, *Daoyi Zhilue Jiaoshi* 岛夷志略校释 (Brief Record of the Island Barbarians), ed. Su Jiqing (Beijing: Zhonghua Shuju, 1981), 311.
39. He Qiaoyuan, *Min Shu* 闽书 (Fuzhou: Fujian Renminchubanshe, 1994), 2:946–47. Haicheng refers to Zhangzhou, the only port city opened to officially supervised trade from 1567 onward.
40. "Undang-undang Laut," ed. Sir Richard Winstedt and P. E. De Josselin De Jong, 51, in Sir Richard Winstedt and P. E. De Josselin De Jong, "The Maritime Laws of Malacca," *Journal of the Malayan Branch of the Royal Asiatic Society* 29, no. 3 (August 1956): 22–59; Reid, *Southeast Asia*, 125.
41. *Wakou* literally means "Japanese pirates," but many Chinese and Korean fishermen and merchants, ironically, were forced to join them after the maritime ban deprived them of their usual livelihood.
42. Battuta, *Travels*, 235–36.
43. Zhu, *Pingzhou Ketan*, 26. For a discussion on passenger-merchants, see So, *Prosperity*, 211–7.
44. Reid, *Southeast Asia*, 50–52.
45. Leonard Blussé, "Chinese Trade to Batavia During the Days of the V.O.C.," *Archipel* 18 (1979): 201; Blussé, *Strange Company: Chinese Settlers, Mestizo Women, and the Dutch in VOC Batavia* (Dordrecht: Foris Publications, 1986), xii; Chen Xiyu, *Zhongguo Fanchuan yu Haiwai Maoyi* (Chinese Junks and Overseas Trade) (Xiamen: Xiamendaxue Chubanshe, 1991), 288–89; Chen Guodong, *Dongya Haiyu Yiqiannian* (A Millennium in the Oceans of East Asia) (Ji'nan: Shandonghuabao Chubanshe, 2006), 106–11; Reid, *Southeast Asia*, 50–52; Jin Guoping, *Aomen Xue: Tanji yu Huizhi* (Studies of Macao: Exploration and Accumulation) (Guangzhou: Guangdong Renminchubanshe, 2018), 90–111.
46. Blussé, "Chinese Trade"; *Strange Company*; Chen, *Zhongguo Fanchuan*.
47. Chen, *Dongya Haiyu*, 106–11.
48. Carstair Douglas, *Chinese-English Dictionary of the Vernacular or Spoken Language of Amoy* (London: Trubner, 1873), 125.

3. SAILING TO THE INDIAN OCEAN

49. "Undang-undang Laut," 54.
50. Reid, *Southeast Asia*, 49–50.
51. Jin, *Aomen Xue*, 90–111.
52. Zhang Xie, *Dongxiyang Kao* 东西洋考 (An Examination of the Eastern and Western Oceans), ed. Xie Fang (Beijing: Zhonghua Shuju, 2000), 170–71.
53. The description of the ship crews and management in the Qing period could be referring to earlier periods. See Chen, *Zhongguo Fanchuan*, 281–84.
54. *Songdai Haichuan*, 80, 127, 143–45; Chen and Wu, "Guanyu Quanzhouwan," 161–63; Zhuang Weiji and Zhuang Jinghui, "Quanzhou Songchuan Mupai Muqian Kaoshi" (An Examination of Wooden Labels and Lots in the Song Ship Discovered in Quanzhou), in *Songdai Haichuan*, 210–16; So, *Prosperity*, 214–17.
55. Zhu, *Pingzhou Ketan*, 27. "Tang" refers to the Tang dynasty, and foreigners, especially from Southeast Asia, established a long tradition of calling China simply "Tang."
56. Wang, *Daoyi Zhilue*, 287, 285. Su Jiqing points out that there were some other Chinese terms that included the term *tu*, such as *tubu* 土布 (Chinese cloth), *tuzhu* 土珠 (Chinese pearls), and *tufen* 土粉 (Chinese powders) in Wang's book.
57. Himanshu Prabha Ray, "A 'Chinese' Pagoda at Nagapattinam on the Tamil Coast: Revisiting India's Early Maritime Networks," Occasional Publication 66 (2014), Indian International Center, 6. Noboru Karashima was one of the earliest scholars from East Asia who had studied the China Pagoda. Noboru Karashima, "Discoveries of Chinese Ceramic Sherds on the Coasts of South India," International Seminar for UNESCO Integral Study of the Silk Roads: Roads of Dialogue: "India and the Roman world Between 1st and 4th Century A.D." and "India's Cultural Relationship with East and Southeast Asia during the 4th to 13th Century A.D." (19–24 December 1990, Madras, India), 5–6.https://en.unesco.org/silkroad/sites/default/files/knowledge-bank-article/discoveries_of_chinese_ceramic_sherds_on_the_coasts_of_south_india.pdf.
58. Sir K. C. S. I. Walter Elliot, "The Edifice Formerly Known as the Chinese or Jaina Pagoda at Negapatam," *Indian Antiquary* 7 (1878): 224–27; Henry Yule, trans. and ed., *The Book of Ser Marco Polo, The Venetian Concerning the Kingdoms and Marvels of the East* (Cambridge: Cambridge University Press, 2010), 2:272–73.
59. Elliot, "The Edifice," 224.
60. Elliot, "The Edifice," 224.
61. Yule, *The Book*, 272–73.
62. Elliot, "The Edifice," 227 and 225.
63. Yule, *The Book*, 273–73.
64. Elliot, "The Edifice," 227.
65. Elliot, "The Edifice," 227.
66. Ray, "A 'Chinese' Pagoda," 3–4, 13.
67. Ray, "A 'Chinese' Pagoda," 6–7.
68. G. S. Seshadri, "New Perspectives on Nagapattinam: The Medieval Port City in the Context of Political, Religious, and Commercial Exchanges Between South India, Southeast Asia and China," in *Nagapattinam to Suvarnadwipa: Reflections on the Chola Naval Expeditions to Southeast Asia*, ed. Hermann Kulke, K. Kesavapany, and Vijay Sakhuja (Singapore: ISEAS-Yusof Ishak Institute, 2009), 121–25; Ray, "A 'Chinese' Pagoda," 13.

3. SAILING TO THE INDIAN OCEAN

69. Ray, "A 'Chinese' Pagoda," 16. All the early and medieval Tamil and Sanskrit inscriptions relating to Southeast Asia and China can be found in their original texts and English translations in N. Karashima and Y. Subbarayalu, "Ancient and Medieval Tamil and Sanskrit Inscriptions Relating to Southeast Asia and China," in *Nagapattinam to Suvarnadwipa*, 271–91.

4. WHO ONCE LANDED IN THE MALDIVES?

1. For early Chinese travelers who sailed between China and India, see Liu Yingsheng, *Hailu yu Lulu—Zhonggu Shiqi Dongxijiaoliu Yanjiu* (Maritime and Continental Routes Between East and West) (Beijing: Beijingdaxue Chubanshe, 2011), 176–226. For the Chinese conceptualization of the Indian Ocean during the Song-Yuan-Ming period, see Roderich Ptak, "Chinese Perceptions of the Sea Area from the South China Sea to the Coast of East Africa, approx. 1000–1500," in *The Indian Ocean: The Afro-Asian Mediterranean as a Cultural and Economic Area*, ed. Dietmar Rothermund and Susanne Weigelin-Schwiedrzik (Vienna: Association for History and Social Studies, ProMedia, 2004), 37–59.
2. "Daqin" was a Chinese name for the Roman Empire, especially its Near East territory. Different interpretations of "Xihai" exist that might refer to the Persian Gulf, the Black Sea, or the Mediterranean.
3. Ban Gu, *Han Shu* 汉书 (History of the Han Dynasty) (Beijing: Zhonghua Shuju, 1962), 1671; Wang Gungwu, *The Nanhai Trade: the Early History of Chinese Trade in the South China Sea* (Singapore: Times Academic Press, 1998): 1721; Yang Bin, *Renhaizhijian: Haiyang Yazhou zhong de Zhongguo yu Shijie* (Between Men and Seas: China and Its World in Maritime Asia) (Guilin: Guangxishifan Daxue Chubanshe, 2023), 22232. The *biliuli* might refer to lapis lazuli or glass, and the site of Huangzhi has remained a mystery. Ban Gu also recorded that during the reign of Yuanshi (15 CE) the Han court presented a lavish gift to the king of Huangzhi, asking for a live rhinoceros. See Ban Gu, *Han Shu*, 1671.
4. Chen Jiarong, Xie Fang, and Lu Junling, *Gudai Nanhai Diming Huishi* (Collection and Identification of Ancient Place Names in South China Sea) (Beijing: Zhonghua Shuju, 1986), 694–95. This book has been the most important reference for imperial China's maritime activities in South China Sea and the Indian Ocean.
5. Hepu was located in today's Beihai City, Guangxi Province, and Xuwen was on the southern tip of the Leizhou Peninsula, Guangdong Province, facing the island of Hainan. Both ports were situated along the Beibu Gulf (indeed a part of the Tonkin Gulf), which was flanked by northern Vietnam, mainland China, and Hainan, and thus played important roles in early maritime trade that relied on coastal navigation. Indeed, many exotic goods including glassware, precious stones, and crystal items have been unearthed from Han tombs in Hepu.
6. For an introduction to Sino-Indian navigation, see Feilang (Gabriel Ferrand), *Kunlun ji Nanhai Gudai Hangxingkao* (Le K'ouen-Louen et les anciennes navigations interocéaniques dans les Mers du Sud), trans. Feng Chengjun (Beijing: Zhonghua Shuju, 1957), 62–66; for the exchange of Buddhist and official missions

4. WHO ONCE LANDED IN THE MALDIVES?

between India and Tang China, see Wang Bangwei and Tansen Sen, eds., *India and China: Interactions Through Buddhism and Diplomacy: A Collection of Essays by Professor Prabodh Chandra Bagchi* (London: Anthem Press, 2011), 155–76; Tansen Sen, *Buddhism, Diplomacy, and Trade: The Realignment of Sino-Indian Relations, 600–1400* (Hawaii: University of Hawaii Press, 2003). For Wang Xuance's visits, see Wang and Sen, *India and China*, 158–59; Sen, *Buddhism*, 21–25 and 40–48.

7. For Tang China and the Arab world, see Zhang Guangda, *Wenben, Tuxiang yu Wenhua Jiaoliu* (Texts, Images, and Cultural Circulation) (Guilin: Guangxishifandaxue Chubanshe, 2008), 133–80; Hyunhee Park, *Mapping the Chinese and Islamic Worlds: Cross-Cultural Exchange in Pre-modern Asia* (Cambridge: Cambridge University Press, 2012).

8. Su Jiqing, "Xulun" (preface), in Wang Dayuan, *Daoyi Zhilue Jiaoshi* 岛夷志略校释 (Brief Record of the Island Barbarians), ed. Su Jiqing (Beijing: Zhonghua Shuju, 1981), 5–6; Chen, Xie, and Lu, *Nanhai*, 4089.

9. Zhang Shimin, "Yang Liangyao: The First Chinese Diplomat to the Western Ocean," *Xianyang Shifan Xueyuan Xueyuan* (Journal of Xianyang Normal College) 3 (2005): 4–8; Rong Xinjiang,"Tangchao yu Heiyi Dashi Guangxishi Xinzheng" (A New Study of the Relationship Between the Tang Dynasty and the Abbasid Caliphate), *Sichouzhilu yu Dongxi Wenhua Jiaoliu* (Silk Roads and East-West Cultural Interactions) (Beijing: Beijing University Press, 2015), 81–97; "New Evidence on the History of Sino-Arab Relations: A Study of Yang Tingyao's Embassy to the Abbasid Caliphate," in *Imperial China and Its Southern Neighbors*, ed. V. H. Mair and L. Kelly (Singapore: Institute of Southeast Asian Studies, 2015), 239–67.

10. Du Huan, *Jingxing Ji Jianzhu* 经行记笺注 (Record of Travels), ed. Zhang Yichun (Zhonghua Shuju, 2000).

11. Edward H. Schafer, *The Golden Peaches of Samarkand: A Study of T'ang Exotics* (San Francisco: Hauraki Publishing, 2014), 37. Kedah was a crucial port along the western coast of the Malay Peninsula, and many Buddhist relics have been discovered there.

12. *Song Shi* 宋史 (History of the Song Dynasty) (Beijing: Zhonghua Shuju, 1977), *juan* 489; Zhou Qufei, *Lingwai Daida Jiaozhu* 岭外代答校注 (Answers for Questions Concerning Out of Range), ed. Yang Wuquan (Beijing: Zhonghua Shuju, 1999), 91 and 99. For Song China's maritime trade, see Paul Wheatley, "Geographical Notes on Some Commodities Involved in Sung Maritime Trade," *Journal of the Malayan Branch of the Royal Asiatic Society* 32, no. 2 (1959): 3, 5–41, 43–139; Derek Heng, *Sino-Malay Trade and Diplomacy, from the Tenth Through the Fourteenth Century* (Athens: Ohio University Press, 2009).

13. Fujian Quanzhou Haiwaijiaotongshi Bowuguan, ed., *Quanzhouwan Songdai Haichuan Fajue yu Yanjiu Xiudingban* (A Report on the Excavation on the Song Boat in Quanzhou Bay; hereinafter *Songdai Haichuan*) (Beijing: Haiyang Chubanshe, revised, 2017), 24, 26–27, 51.

14. Bin Yang, "Dangzi Yinduyang Fanhang—Quanzhouwan Songdai Haichuan Hangxian Xinkao" (Sailing Home from the Indian Ocean: A New Analysis of the Song Shipwreck Discovered in Quanzhou Bay in 1974), *Haijiaoshi Yanjiu* (Journal of Maritime History Studies) 1 (2021): 18–24.

4. WHO ONCE LANDED IN THE MALDIVES?

15. For an English analysis of the official exchanges between Yuan China and India, see Tansen Sen, "The Yuan Khanate and India: Cross-Cultural Diplomacy in the Thirteen and Fourteenth Centuries," *Asia Major* 19, nos. 1–2 (2006): 299–326, at 300. For Yuan China's knowledge of the Indian Ocean, also see Park, *Mapping the Chinese*, 91–123.
16. *Yuan Shi* 元史 (History of the Yuan Dynasty) (Beijing: Zhonghua Shuju, 1974), *juan* 131, 3198–4000. Commonly known as red sanders, red sandalwood, Yerra Chandanam, or Chenchandanam, the *zitan* has been a highly valued hardwood for centuries, exclusively found in south India but much sought after by Chinese consumers.
17. Marco Polo, *The Travels of Marco Polo (The Venetian)* (New York: Liveright, 1953), 282–84.
18. Wang, *Daoyi Zhilue*, 244. Su Jiqing has provided a detailed analysis of the alms bowl. See Wang, *Daoyi Zhilue*, 246–47n3.
19. *Yuan Shi*, *juan* 210, 4669–70; Sen, "The Yuan Khanate," 302 and 303n11, 306–9.
20. Chen Gaohua, *Yuanshi Yanjiu Lungao* (On Studies of Yuan History) (Beijing: Zhonghua Shuju, 1991), 401–7; Liu Yingsheng and Ma Juan, "Mabaerguo yu Yuanchao zhi Wanglai jiqi Xiangguangwenti" (Interactions Between the Kingdom of Ma'bar and the Yuan Dynasty), *Lanzhoudaxue Xuebao* (Social Sciences) 33, no. 2 (March 2005): 20–25; Sen, "The Yuan Khanate," 313–18.
21. Chen Gaohua, "Yuandai de Hanghai Shijia Kanpu Yangshi" (The Yangs in Kanpu: a Navigation Family of the Yuan Dynasty), in *Yuanshi Yanjiu Xinlun* (New Discussions on the Studies of the Yuan History) (Shanghai: Shanghai Shehuikexueyuan Chubanshe, 2005), 238–61; Park, *Mapping the Chinese*, 112–13. Marco Polo escorted the Mongol Princess Kököchin on her journey to marry Arghun the Ilkhanate Khan, but unfortunately Arghun died before she arrived. Following Inner Asian traditions, the Mongol princess married Arghun's son, Ghazan.
22. Huang Jin, *Jinhua Huangxiansheng Wenji* 金华黄先生文集 (Collected Works of Huang Jin), *juan* 35, in *Xuxiu Siku Quanshu* (Shanghai: Shanghai Gujichubanshe, 1995), vol. 1323, 45253; Chen Gaohua, "Yuandai Hanghaishijia Kanpu Yangshi" (The Yangs–Maritime Navigators in the Yuan Dynasty), *Haiiaoshi Yanjiu* (Journal of Maritime History Studies) 1 (1995): 4–18, esp. 7–8.
23. *Yuan Shi*, *juan* 94, 2402, 2403; *juan* 205, 4566; Chen, "Yuandai Hanghaishijia," 8.
24. Huang, *Jinhua*, 453; Chen, "Yuandai Hanghaishijia," 8.
25. Guangdong Difangzhi Bianjiweiyuahui Bangongshi, ed., *Yuan Dade Nanhaizhi Canben* 元大德南海志残本 (Remains of the Nanhai Gazetteer Complied in the Dade Reign of the Yuan Dynasty) (Guangzhou: Guangdong Renminchubanshe, 1991), 44–47.
26. Park, *Mapping the Chinese*, 113.
27. Wang, *Daoyi Zhilue*, 385. There are various opinions about Wang Dayuan's biography, such as his birth year and the dates of his two overseas trips. In this respect, Su Jiqing's analysis remains the most convincing in my view. Su Jiqing, "Xulun (Preface)," in Wang, *Daoyi Zhilue*, 9–11; Xu Yongzhang, "Wang Dayuan Shengping Kaobian Santi" (Three Notes on Wang Dayuan's Life), *Hiajiaoshi Yanjiu* (Journal of Maritime History Studies) 2 (1997): 98–102; Shen Fuwei, *Sichouzhilu Zhongguo yu Feizhou Wenhua Jiaoliu Yanjiu* (The Silk Roads and the Studies of Sino-African Interactions) (Urumqi: Xinjiang Renminchubanshe, 2010): 250–59; Liu Yingsheng,

4. WHO ONCE LANDED IN THE MALDIVES?

"Wang Dayuan Liangci Chuyang Kao" (An Examination of the Two Maritime Trips of Wang Dayuan), in Liu Yingsheng, *Hailu yu Lulu*, 57–69; Xu Quansheng, *Shen Zengzhi Shidi Zhuzuo Jikao* (A Study on Shen Zengzhi's Historical and Geographical Works) (Beijing: Zhonghua Shuju, 2019), 105–42. Shen Zengzhi 沈曾植 (1850–1920), an encyclopedist, was the first Chinese to annotate the *Daoyi Zhilue*.

28. For Chinese knowledge of Ormuz see Ralph Kauz and Roderich Ptak, "Hormuz in Yuan and Ming Sources," *Bulletin de l'École Française d'Extrême-Orient* 88 (2001): 27–75. Ormuz, however, might have been introduced by the Chinese under different names.
29. Wang, *Daoyi Zhilue*, 311.
30. Chen, Xie, and Lu, *Nanhai*, 698; Wang, *Daoyi Zhilue*, 257.
31. Su, "Xulun," 1–2 and 5–6. The *Daoyi Zhilue* was attached to the Quanzhou gazette compiled by Wu Jian so that it was able to circulate. Only those Jinshi who were on the top list of palace examinations were assigned to the Hanlin Academy. For the studies of the *Daoyi Zhilue*, see Ptak, "Images of Maritime Asia in Two Yuan Texts: 'Daoyi zhilue' and 'Yiyu zhi,'" *Journal of Song-Yuan Studies* 25 (1995): 47–75; Sen, *Buddhism*, 231; Sen, "The Yuan Khanate," 312; Park, *Mapping the Chinese*, 115–18; Zhou Yunzhong, "Daoyizhilue Diming yu wang Dayuan Xingcheng Xinkao" (Toponymy in Daoyi Zhiue and a New Study of the Itinerary of Wang Dayuan), *Yuanshi ji Minzu yu Bianjiang Yanjiu Jikan* (A Collection of the History of the Yuan Dynasty and the Studies of Ethnicity and Frontier) 1 (2014): 98–131.
32. W.W. Rockhill, "Notes on the Relations and Trade of China with the Eastern Archipelago and the Coast of the Indian Ocean During the Fourteenth Century, Part II," *T'oung Pao* 16, no. 1 (1915): 61–159; "Notes on the Relations and Trade of China with the Eastern Archipelago and the Coast of the Indian Ocean During the Fourteenth Century, Part III," *T'oung Pao* 16, no. 3 (1915): 374–92, and; Roderich Ptak, "The Maldives and Laccadive Islands (*liu-shan* 溜山) in Ming Records," *Journal of the American Oriental Society* 107, no. 4 (1987): esp. 675–76.
33. Ptak, "Images of Maritime Asia," esp. 51.
34. Richard Stoneman, "Who Are the Brahmans? Indian Lore and Cynic Doctrine in Palladius' De Bragmanibus and Its Models," *Classical Quarterly* 44, no. 2 (1994): 500–10.
35. Chinese historical texts on the Maldives by Wang Dayuan, Ma Huan, and Fei Xin have all been translated into English, wholly or partially, and this book hence usually consults these English translations. Ptak, "The Maldives"; Ma Huan, *Ying-yai sheng-lan: "The Overall Survey of the Ocean's Shores," [1433]*; translated from the Chinese text edited by Feng Ch'eng-chün with introduction, notes, and appendices by J. V. G. Mills (London: Hakluyt Society, 1970); Fei Xin, *Xingcha Shenglan Jiaozhu* 星槎胜览校注 (Overall Survey of the Star Raft: An Annotation), ed. Feng Chengjun (Beijing: Huawen Chubanshe, 2019); *Hsing-ch'a-sheng-lan: The Overall Survey of the Star Raft*, trans. J. V. Mills, ed. Roderich Ptak (Wiesbaden: Harrassowitz, 1996); Gong Zhen, *Xiyang Fangguo Zhi* 西洋番国志 (Record of Foreign Kingdoms in the Western Ocean), ed. Xiang Da (Beijing: Zhonghua Shuju, 2000). As stated, the *Xiyang Fanguo Zhi* by Gong Zhen remains almost a word-for-word copy of the *Yingya Shengla*. In addition, the copy of Gong Zhen's book was not found until the 1950s and thus it was not widely circulated. This is why, unless specified, the *Xiyang Fanguo Zhi* is not discussed in this book.

4. WHO ONCE LANDED IN THE MALDIVES?

36. For an English introduction to Zheng He's seven voyages and the three Ming authors, see J. V. G. Mill, "Introduction," in Ma, *Ying-yai sheng-lan*, 1–66.
37. H. C. P. Bell, *The Maldive Islands: Monograph on the History, Archaeology and Epigraph* (Colombo: Ceylon Government Press, 1940), 1–6.
38. Bell, *The Maldive Islands*, 1.
39. Bell, *The Maldive Islands*, 1–2.
40. Bell, *The Maldive Islands*, 2, vii.
41. Bell, *The Maldive Islands*, 2.
42. Bell, *The Maldive Islands*, 3.
43. Bell, *The Maldive Islands*, 4.
44. Bell, *The Maldive Islands*, 5.
45. For the list, see Ptak, "The Maldives," 684–85.
46. Xie Fang, "Qianyan" (Preface), in Huang Xingzeng, *Chaogong Dianlu Jiaozhu* 西洋朝贡典录校注 (Record of Tributes from the Western Ocean), ed. Xie Fang (Beijing: Zhonghua Shuju, 2000), 3–6; Ptak, "The Maldives," 685–8.
47. Yu Sili, "Qianyan" (Preface), in Yan Congjian, *Shuyu Zhouzi Lu* (Comprehensive Survey and Record on Foreign Territories), ed. Yu Sili (Beijing: Zhonghua Shuju, 1993), 1–4.
48. Xiang Da, ed., *Zheng He Hanghai Tu* 郑和航海图 (The Zheng He Nautical Chart) (Beijing: Zhonghua Shuju, 2000); Ptak, "The Maldives," 689–92.
49. Luo Maodeng, *Sanbao Taijian Xiyangji Tongsu Yanyi* 三宝太监西洋记通俗演义 (Romance of Eunuch Sanbao's Journey to the Western Ocean, hereinafter the *Xiyang Ji*), ed. Lu Shulun & and Zhu Shaohua, 2 vols. (Shanghai: Shanghai Gujichubanshe, 1982). For a recent study of this novel, see Shi Ping and Roderich Ptak, eds., *Studien zum Roman Sanbao Taijian Xiyang Ji Tongsu Yanyi*, vol. 2 (Wiesbaden: Harrassowitz Verlag, 2013).
50. Xiang Da, "Lun Luo Maodeng zhu sanbao Tajian Xiyangji Tongsu Yanyi" (On Luo Maodeng's Romance of Eunuch Sanbao's Journey to the Western Ocean), in Luo, *Xiyang Ji*, 2:1291–7; Zhao Jingshen, "Saoban Taijian Xiyang Ji" (Romance of Eunuch Sanbao's Journey to the Western Ocean), in Luo, *Xiyang Ji*, 2:1298–1333; Ji Xianli, "Xinban Xu" (Preface to the New Edition), in Luo, *Xiyang Ji*, 1:1–5; Lu Shulun and Zhu Shaohua, "Qianyan" (Preface), in Luo, *Xiyang Ji*, 1:6–20; J. J. L. Duyvendak, "Desultory Notes on the His-yang chi," *T'oung Pao* 42, nos. 1–2 (1953): 1–35; Ptak, "The Maldives," 692–93.
51. Zhang Xie, *Dongxiyang Kao* 东西洋考 (An Examination of the Eastern and Western Oceans), ed. Xie Fang (Beijing: Zhonghua Shuju, 2000), 70.
52. Albert Gray and H. C. P. Bell, "Early Notices of the Maldives," in François Pyrard, *The Voyage of François Pyrard of Laval to the East Indies, the Maldives, the Moluccas and Brazil*, ed. Albert Gray and H. C. P. Bell (Cambridge: Cambridge University Press, 2011), 3:426–27.

5. THE KINGDOM OF ATOLLS

1. Clarence Maloney, *People of the Maldive Islands* (Bombay: Oriental Longman, 1980), 2.
2. Maloney, *People*, 2.

5. THE KINGDOM OF ATOLLS

3. Xuanzang and Bianji, *Datang Xiyuji Jiaozhu* 大唐西域记校注 (Great Tang Records on the Western Regions: Annotation), ed. Ji Xianlin (Beijing: Zhonghua Shuju, 1985), 8841.
4. Xuanzang and Bianji, *Datang*, 211, 213, 794.
5. Wang Dayuan, *Daoyi Zhilue Jiaoshi* 岛夷志略校释 (Brief Record of the Island Barbarians), ed. Su Jiqing (Beijing: Zhonghua Shuju, 1981), 264. For an English translation, also see Roderich Ptak, "The Maldives and Laccadive Islands (*liu-shan* 溜山) in Ming Records," *Journal of the American Oriental Society* 107, no. 4 (1987): 677–78. The last sentence, "*yi jiuyuan zhi shifa ye* 亦久远之食法也," is certainly vague, though it might refer to the cowrie money that was a traditional form of money in Bengal and Pegu.
6. H. C. P. Bell, *The Maldive Islands: Monograph on the History, Archaeology and Epigraph* (Colombo: Ceylon Government Press, 1940), 13.
7. Albert Gray and H. C. P. Bell, "Early Notices of the Maldives," in François Pyrard, *The Voyage of François Pyrard of Laval to the East Indies, the Maldives, the Moluccas and Brazil*, ed. Albert Gray and H. C. P. Bell (Cambridge: Cambridge University Press, 2011), 3:427.
8. Gray and Bell, "Early Notices," 427.
9. Gray and Bell, "Early Notices," 428.
10. Gray and Bell, "Early Notices," 429.
11. Gray and Bell, "Early Notices," 433.
12. Gray and Bell, "Early Notices," 434.
13. "The Eastern Parts of the World Described by Friar Odoric the Bohemian, of Friuli, in the Province of Saint Anthony," in Henry Yule et al., *Cathay and the Way Thither: Being a Collection of Medieval Notices of China* (London: Hakluyt Society, 1914), 1:103.
14. Gray and Bell, "Early Notices," 436.
15. Gray and Bell, "Early Notices," 469.
16. Maloney, *People*, 134.
17. Gray and Bell, "Early Notices," 477.
18. Fei Xin, *Xingcha Shenglan Jiaozhu* 星槎胜览校注 (Overall Survey of the Star Raft: An Annotation), ed. Feng Chengjun (Beijing: Huawen Chubanshe, 2019), 108; Fei Xin, *Hsing-ch'a-sheng-lan: The Overall Survey of the Star Raft*, trans. J. V. Mills, ed. Roderich Ptak (Wiesbaden: Harrassowitz, 1996), 103.
19. Cropped and edited from panel 2, in Matteo Ricci, "Kunyu wanguo quantu" (Map of the Ten Thousand Countries of the Earth), James Ford Bell Library at the University of Minnesota, https://umedia.lib.umn.edu/item/p16022coll251:8823/p16022coll251:8818.
20. Wang, *Daoyi Zhilue*, 265n1; Ptak, "The Maldives," 676 and n 4.
21. W. W. Rockhill, "Notes on the Relations and Trade of China with the Eastern Archipelago and the Coast of the Indian Ocean During the Fourteenth Century, Part II," *T'oung Pao* 16, no. 1 (1915): 67; "Notes on the Relations and Trade of China with the Eastern Archipelago and the Coast of the Indian Ocean During the Fourteenth Century, Part III," *T'oung Pao* 16, no. 3 (1915): 388–89.
22. Xie Fang, "Zhongguo Shiji zhong zhi Maerdaifu Kao" (A Study of the Maldives in Chinese Historical Texts), *Nanya Yanjiu* (South Asia Studies) 2 (1982): 3.
23. Xie, "Zhongguo Shiji," 3.

5. THE KINGDOM OF ATOLLS

24. Ptak, "The Maldives," 676n4.
25. Maloney, *People*, 41–43.
26. Maloney, *People*, 44. Here Clarence Maloney failed to realize that *liu* was first recorded or invented by Wang Dayuan rather than by Ma Huan.
27. Xie, "Zhongguo Shiji," 3.
28. Wang, *Daoyi Zhilue*, 280; Xie, "Zhongguo Shiji," 3. Dabadan, according to Su Jiqing, was located between Cannanore and Tellicherrry. Wang, *Daoyi Zhilue*, 281n1.
29. Wang, *Daoyi Zhilue*, 280.
30. Bell, *The Maldive Islands*, 13; M. Risk and R. Sluka, *Coral Reefs of the Indian Ocean* (London: Oxford University Press, 2000), 328; Mirani Litster, "Cowry Shell Money and Monsoon Trade: the Maldives in Past Globalizations," Ph.D. diss., The Australian National University, 2016, 59.
31. Bell, *The Maldive Islands*, 13.
32. Comments on my draft by Michael Feener, June 1, 2018. Currently Feener, my former colleague at the National University of Singapore and now professor of Cross-Regional Studies at the Kyoto University Center for Southeast Asian Studies, is leading a project, "The Maritime Asia Heritage Survey (MAHS)," that "works to digitally document historical and archaeological sites across the coastal and island world of Southern Asia through field survey work in the Maldives, Sri Lanka, Indonesia and Vietnam." R. Michael Feener, ed., "Maritime Asia Heritage Survey," https://maritimeasiaheritage.cseas.kyoto-u.ac.jp/.
33. Pyrard, *The Voyage of François Pyrard*, 1:106.
34. Bell, *The Maldive Islands*, 13.
35. Pyrard, *The Voyage of François Pyrard*, 1:105.
36. Pyrard, *The Voyage of François Pyrard*, 1: 105.
37. Ma Huan, *Ming Chaoben Yingya Shenglan Jiaozhu* 明钞本瀛涯胜览校注 (Overall Survey of the Ocean Shores: Annotation of a Ming Manuscript), ed. Wan Ming (Beijing: Haiyangchubanshe, 2005), 71; Ma Huan, *Ying-yai sheng-lan: The Overall Survey of the Ocean's Shores,"* [1433]; translated from the Chinese text edited by Feng Ch'eng-chün with introduction, notes, and appendices by J. V. G. Mills (London: Hakluyt Society, 1970), 147.
38. Ma, *Ying-yai sheng-lan*, 149n2; Wang, *Daoyi Zhilue*, 265n1; Chen Jiarong, Xie Farong, and Lu Junling, *Gudai Nanhai Diming Huishi* (Collection and Identification of Ancient Place Names in the South China Sea) (Beijing: Zhonghua Shuju, 1986), 8089; Ptak, "The Maldives," 678n17.
39. Guangdong Difangzhi Bianjiweiyuahui Bangongshi, ed., *Yuan Dade Nanhaizhi Canben* 元大德南海志残本 (Remains of the Nanhai Gazetteer Compiled in the Dade Reign of the Yuan Dynasty) (Guangzhou: Guangdong Renminchubanshe, 1991), 47; Wang, *Daoyi Zhilue*, 265n1; Ptak, "The Maldives," 678n17.
40. Gray and Bell, "Early Notices," 436.
41. Fei, *Xingcha Shenlan*, 107–8.
42. Ma, *Ming Chaoben*, 76, 71–73; Ma, *Ying-yai sheng-lan*, 147; Gong Zhen, *Xiyang Fanguo Zhi* 西洋番国志 (Record of Foreign Kingdoms in the Western Ocean), ed. Xiang Da (Beijing: Zhonghua Shuju, 2000), 32–3; Fei, *Xingcha Shenglan*, 107–8; Fei, *Hsing-ch'a-sheng-lan*, 102–3; Huang Xingzeng, *Xiyang Chaogong Dianlu*

5. THE KINGDOM OF ATOLLS

Jiaozhu 西洋朝贡典录校注 (Record of Tributes from the Western Ocean), ed. Xie Fang (Beijing: Zhonghua Shuju, 2000), 78.

43. Xie, "Zhongguo Shiji"; Chen, Xie and Lu, *Nanhai*; Ptak, "The Maldives;" Haijun Haiyangcehuiyanjiusuo and Dalian Haiyunxueyuan Hanghaishi Yanjiushi, eds., *Xinbian Zheng He Hanghai Tuji* (An Edited Volume of the Zheng He Nautical Chart) (Beijing: Renmin Jiaotongchubanshe, 1988).

44. It was also called Guanwu liu 官坞溜 (lit. "Official Docking Atoll") or Guanliu 官溜 (lit. "Official Atoll"), both indicating that a Ming factory was built there. George Phillips, "The Seaports of India and Ceylon: Described by Chinese Voyagers of the Fifteenth Century, Together with an Account of Chinese Navigation," *Journal of the China Branch of the Royal Asiatic Society* 20 (1885): 222. In the *Zheng He Hanghai Tu* five locations were named with the Chinese character *guan*, on which there has been a long-lasting discussion as to its meaning. If it means "official," "governmental," or even "pro-military," the issue becomes very sensitive. Do these names refer to a certain Chinese control, supervision, military station, or even "a maritime proto-colonialism," as Geoff Wade has postulated? Geoff Wade, "The Zheng He Voyages: A Reassessment," *Journal of the Malaysian Branch of the Royal Asiatic Society* 78, no. 1 (2005): 37–58. As for the Guanwu liu denoting Malé, Ptak has scrutinized all the contemporary Chinese sources produced in and after the Zheng He voyages and listed five different versions: Guanwu liu, Guanyu liu 官屿溜, Guanrui Liu 官瑞溜, Guanchang liu 官场溜, and Guangming liu 官名溜. Here again arises the question: what does the Chinese character *guan* refer to? If it simply refers to Malé as the capital of the island kingdom, then these versions simply indicate its importance. If it expresses the same meaning as other *guan* names such as *guanchang* 官场 or 官厂 in Malacca or Johore, then Malé seems to have had the same function of logistic supplies for the Ming fleets due to its navigational strategy. I lean toward the first interpretation as being relatively reasonable. Roderich Ptak, "Selected Problems Concerning the 'Zheng He Map': Questions Without Answers," *Journal of Asian History* 53, no. 2 (2019): 197–203, esp. 198. Xiang Da, ed., *Zheng He Hanghai Tu* (The Zheng He Nautical Chart) (Beijing: Zhonghua Shuju2000), 57; Ma, *Ying-yai sheng-lan*, 148n4; Xie, "Zhongguo Shiji," 4–5; Ptak, "The Maldives," 690, esp. fig. 2. For the discussion of the routes see Ptak, "The Maldives," 691–92.

45. Ma, *Ying-yai sheng-lan*, 147nn6–7; Xie, "Zhongguo Shiji," 5; Ptak, "The Maldives," 690. Philipps referred to Mulaku Atoll as Suadiva. Phillips, "The Seaports of India," 222.

46. Ma, *Ying-yai sheng-lan*, 147n8; Xie, "Zhongguo Shiji," 5; Ptak, "The Maldives," 690.

47. Phillips, "The Seaports of India," 222–23; Ma, *Ying-yai sheng-lan*, 147n9, 148nn1–3; Xie, "Zhongguo Shiji," 5, 6; Ptak, "The Maldives," 690.

48. Ma, *Ming Chaoben*, 72; Ma, *Ying-yai sheng-lan*, 151; Gong, *Xiyang Fanguo Zhi*, 32; Ptak, "The Maldives," 691.

49. Xie, "Zhongguo Shiji," 6; Ptak, "The Maldives," 690.

50. Phillips, "The Seaports of India," 222; Ptak, "Selected Problems,"193–97.

51. Recently combining modern technology and imperial texts and maps, Xu Panqing, An Junli, and Cao Shuji calculated that the length of one *geng* was equal to

5. THE KINGDOM OF ATOLLS

13.23 miles (21.3 km), which does explain most if not all historically textual records. Xu Panqing, An Junli, and Cao Shuji, "Hangxian yu Licheng: Wenchang Qizhouyang yu Xisha Qizhouyang de Diliweizhi" (Navigation Routes and Distances: The Two Qizhouyang in South Sea), *Zhongguo Lishi Dili Luncong* (Journal of Chinese Historical Geography) 37, no. 1 (January 2022): 15–28.

52. Ptak, "The Maldives," 691.
53. Ma, *Ming Chaoben*, 72; Ma, *Ying-yai sheng-lan*, 148; Fei, *Xingcha Shenglan*, 108; Fei, *Hsing-ch'a-sheng-lan*, 103; Gong, *Xiyang Fanguo Zhi*, 32; Huang, *Xiyang*, 78. It is called *Xiaoliu* 小溜 (lit. "small atolls") by Gong Zhen, and *Xiaozhai liu* 小窄溜 (lit. "small and narrow atolls") by Huang Xingzeng.
54. Ma, *Ming Chaoben*, 73; Ma, *Ying-yai sheng-lan*, 148; Fei, *Xingcha Shenglan*, 108; Fei, *Hsing-ch'a-sheng-lan*, 103.
55. Gray and Bell, "Early Notices," 434.
56. Xie, "Zhongguo Shiji," 6.
57. Bell, *The Maldive Islands*, 13.
58. The *Shanghai Jing* is an early Chinese text on mythical geography and beasts. While containing some early origins dated to the fourth century BCE, it was not completed until a few centuries later.
59. Wu Cheng'en, trans. W. J. F. Jenner, *Journal to the West* (Beijing: Foreign Language Press, 2008), 1:406.
60. Huang, *Xiyang*, 79.
61. Gray and Bell, "Early Notices," 430, 436–37, 469. A *parasang* is a historical unit of walking distance adopted in Persia.
62. Gray and Bell, "Early Notices," 482.
63. Wang, *Daoyi Zhilue*, 264; Ptak, "The Maldives," 676.
64. Maloney, *People*, 3–4, 73.
65. Ma, *Ming Chaoben*, 71; Ma, *Ying-yai sheng-lan*, 147.
66. Fei, *Xingcha Shenglan*, 107; Fei, *Hsing-ch'a-sheng-lan*, 102. The History of the Ming Dynasty repeated the idea of the three stone gates for navigation. *Ming Shi* 明史 (History of the Ming Dynasty) (Beijing: Zhonghua Shuju, 1974), *juan* 326, 8453.
67. Fei, *Hsing-ch'a-sheng-lan*, 102n105.
68. Gray and Bell, "Early Notices," 436–37.
69. Pyrard, *The Voyage of François Pyrard*, 1:99.
70. Pyrard, *The Voyage of François Pyrard*, 1:102–3.
71. Maloney, *People*, 9.
72. Pyrard, *The Voyage of François Pyrard*, 1:103.
73. Pyrard, *The Voyage of François Pyrard*, 1:103. *Caridou* might have been named after the island of Kaharidú or Karhidú, the latter derived from *karhi* (coconut), thus "Coconut Island."

6. MONSOONS AND CURRENTS

1. Ma Huan, *Ming Chaoben Yingya Shenglan Jiaozhu* 明钞本瀛涯胜览校注 (Overall Survey of the Ocean Shores: Annotation of a Ming Manuscript), ed. Wan Ming (Beijing: Haiyangchubanshe, 2005), 71, 73; Ma Huan, *Ying-yai sheng-lan*: "The

6. MONSOONS AND CURRENTS

Overall Survey of the Ocean's Shores," [1433]; translated from the Chinese text edited by Feng Ch'eng-chün with introduction, notes, and appendices by J. V. G. Mills (London: Hakluyt Society, 1970), 146–49; Fei Xin, *Xingcha Shenglan Jiaozhu* 星槎胜览校注 (Overall Survey of the Star Raft: An Annotation), ed. Feng Chengjun (Beijing: Huawen Chubanshe, 2019), 108; Fei Xin, *Hsing-ch'a-sheng-lan: The Overall Survey of the Star Raft*, trans. J. V. Mills, ed. Roderich Ptak (Wiesbaden: Harrassowitz, 1996), 103. A good wind refers to a tail wind.
2. Romero-Frias Xavier, *The Maldive Islanders: A Study of the Popular Culture of an Ancient Ocean Kingdom* (Barcelona: Nova Ethnographia Indica, 1999), 53.
3. Xavier, *The Maldive Islanders*, 65, 68.
4. H. C. P. Bell, *The Maldive Islands: Monograph on the History, Archaeology and Epigraph* (Colombo: Ceylon Government Press, 1940), 8.
5. Bell, *The Maldive Islands*, 13.
6. Wang Dayuan, *Daoyi Zhilue Jiaoshi* 岛夷志略校释 (Brief Record of the Island Barbarians), ed. Su Jiqing (Beijing: Zhonghua Shuju, 1981), 264; Roderich Ptak, "The Maldives and Laccadive Islands (liu-shan 溜山) in Ming Records," *Journal of the American Oriental Society* 107, no. 4 (1987): 677. "The Western Ocean (*Xiyang*)" here is perhaps an abbreviation of Xiyangguo 西洋国 (lit. "the kingdom of the Western Ocean"), which in the Yuan context refers to Ma'bar. One must bear in mind that the strait between India and Ceylon is too shallow for oceangoing vessels, and any ship departing from Ceylon must head toward the southern waters to reach the southwestern coast of India, which accounts for the significant role the Maldives played in navigation across the Indian Ocean.
7. Bell, *The Maldive Islands*, 8.
8. Wang, *Daoyi Zhilue*, 311, 312n1, 264 (for Dafoshan, see also 270 and 271n1); Ptak, "Images of Maritime Asia," 677.
9. Xiang Da, ed., *Zheng He Hanghai Tu* 郑和航海图 (The Zheng He Nautical Chart) (Beijing: Zhonghua Shuju, 2000), 56–68; Xie Fang, "Zhongguo Shiji zhong zhi Maerdaifu Kao" (A Study of the Maldives in Chinese Historical Texts), *Nanya Yanjiu* (South Asia Studies) 2 (1982): 4; Ptak, "The Maldives," 690.
10. Huang Xingzeng, *Xiyang Chaogong Dianlu Jiaozhu* 西洋朝贡典录校注 (Record of Tributes from the Western Ocean), ed. Xie Fang (Beijing: Zhonghua Shuju, 2000), 73–74.
11. Yijing, trans., *Genbenshuoyiqieyoubu Baiyi Jiemo* 根本说一切有部百一羯磨 (Mūlasarvāstivāda-ekaśatakarman), CBETA, https://www.cbeta.org/, juan 5, 35, http://buddhism.lib.ntu.edu.tw/BDLM/sutra/chi_pdf/sutra11/T24n1453.pdf.
12. Albert Gray and H. C. P. Bell, "Early Notices of the Maldives," in François Pyrard, *The Voyage of François Pyrard of Laval to the East Indies, the Maldives, the Moluccas and Brazil*, ed. Albert Gray and H. C. P. Bell (Cambridge: Cambridge University Press, 2011), 3:468.
13. Gray and Bell, "Early Notices," 3:469.
14. Bell, *The Maldive Islands*, 3–5, 6, 9. Pamban Island, off the southeastern coast of Tamil Nadu, is located between India and the northwestern coast of Sri Lanka.
15. Ahmed Nazim Sattar, *King Kalaafaan Manuscripts: How the Maldives Monarchy Treasured the Remembrance of a Fallen King for More Than Four Hundred Years* (Male: National Centre of Linguistic and Historical Research, 2010), 17. Sultan Ibrahim II is known as King Kalaafaan (lit. "lord").

16. Pyrard, *The Voyage of François Pyrard*, 1:314.
17. Bell, *The Maldive Islands*, 12.
18. Wang, *Daoyi Zhilue*, 264; Ptak, "Images of Maritime Asia," 677; Pyrard, *The Voyage of François Pyrard*, 1:103.
19. Ma, *Ming Chaoben*, 73; Ma, *Ying-yai sheng-lan*, 148–9.
20. Pyrard, *The Voyage of François Pyrard*, 1:101. *Oyuarou* means "river."
21. Pyrard, *The Voyage of François Pyrard*, 1:102.
22. Gray and Bell, "Early Notices," 436–37.
23. Pyrard, *The Voyage of François Pyrard*, 1:102.
24. Pyrard, *The Voyage of François Pyrard*, 1:102.
25. Bell, *The Maldive Islands*, 12. A knot is a unit of speed equal to one nautical mile per hour (1.852 km/h).
26. Pyrard, *The Voyage of François Pyrard*, 1:99–101.
27. Pyrard, *The Voyage of François Pyrard*, 1:100.

7. BETWEEN THE SON OF HEAVEN AND THE SULTAN

1. Ma Huan, *Ming Chaoben Yingya Shenglan Jiaozhu* 明钞本瀛涯胜览校注 (Overall Survey of the Ocean Shores: Annotation of a Ming Manuscript), ed. Wan Ming (Beijing: Haiyangchubanshe, 2005), 75; Ma Huan, *Ying-yai sheng-lan: "The Overall Survey of the Ocean's Shores," [1433]; translated from the Chinese text edited by Feng Ch'eng-chün with introduction, notes, and appendices by J. V. G. Mills* (London: Hakluyt Society, 1970), 151.
2. *Ming Shi*, 明史 (History of the Ming Dynasty) (Beijing: Zhonghua Shuju, 1974), *juan* 304, 7768.
3. Su Chung-jen, "Places in South-East Asia, the Middle East and Africa Visited by Cheng Ho and his Companions (A. D. 1405–1433)," in *Symposium on Historical, Archaeological and Linguistic Studies on Southern China*, ed. F. S. Drake (Hong Kong: Hong Kong University Press, 1967), 201–3, 209; Ma, *Ying-yai sheng-lan*, 12–14; Roderich Ptak, "The Maldives and Laccadive Islands (*liu-shan* 溜山) in Ming Records," *Journal of the American Oriental Society* 107, no. 4 (1987): 678–81.
4. Ptak, "The Maldives," 678–80.
5. Ptak, "The Maldives," 680–81.
6. *Ming Xuanzong Shilu* (Veritable Records of Emperor Xuanzong), *juan* 67, in *Ming Shilu* (Veritable Records of the Ming Dynasty), ed. Huang Zhangjian (Taipei: Academic Sinica, 1984), 3:2087.
7. *Ming Shi*, *juan* 326, 8453.
8. Private communications with Chen Ye, March 6, 2022.
9. "Dr Andrew Forbes," Museum number As1981,20.141, British Museum, https://www.britishmuseum.org/collection/image/1360518001; "Dr Andrew Forbes." Museum number As1981,20.140, British Museum, https://www.britishmuseum.org/collection/image/1358376001.
10. Ran Zhang, "The Glazed Pottery: Asian and Islamic Imports," in *Archaeological Investigations of the Maldives in the Medieval Islamic Period: Ibn Battuta's Island*, ed. Anne Haour and Annalisa Christie (New York: Routledge, 2022), 102. The Yuan Qinghua did not claim any fame until studies on the David Vases (a

7. BETWEEN THE SON OF HEAVEN AND THE SULTAN

pair of altar vases produced in 1351) in the British Museum and some other pieces in the Topkapı Palace in Istanbul made it well known to the world. Kinolhas is located about 95 miles (~150 km) west of Male.

11. Zhang, "Glazed Pottery," 104–5, 112–13.
12. Carswell, "China and Islam in the Maldive Islands," *Transactions of the Oriental Ceramic Society 1975–77* 41 (1977): 152–98. For some color photos of the collection, see https://maritimeasiaheritage.cseas.kyoto-u.ac.jp/country/maldives/, Maritime Asia Heritage Survey (https://maritimeasiaheritage.cseas.kyoto-u.ac.jp/); Shiura Jaufar and Anne Haour, "An Overview of Previous Historical and Archaeological Work in the Maldives," in Haour and Christie, *Archaeological Investigations*, 11–17.
13. Zhang, "Glazed Pottery," 92–113; Anne Haour, "Towards an Archaeology of the Medieval Maldives," in Haour and Christie, *Archaeological Investigations*, 156.
14. Fei Xin, *Xingcha Shenglan Jiaozhu* 星槎胜览校注 (Overall Survey of the Star Raft: An Annotation), ed. Feng Chengjun (Beijing: Huawen Chubanshe, 2019), 108; Fei Xin, *Hsing-ch'a-sheng-lan: The Overall Survey of the Star Raft*, trans. J. V. Mills, ed. Roderich Ptak (Wiesbaden: Harrassowitz, 1996), 103.
15. Fei, *Xingcha Shenglan*, 108.
16. Fei, *Xingcha Shenglan*, 8 and 11; Fei, *Hsing-ch'a-sheng-lan*, 29.
17. Ptak, "The Maldives," 678–80.
18. Fei, *Xingcha Shenglan*, 8; Fei, *Hsing-ch'a-sheng-lan*, 29; Boxihe 伯希和 (Paul Eugène Pelliot), *Zheng He Xia Xiyang Kao* (Les grands voyages maritimes chinois au début du 15ème siècle), trans. Feng Chenjun (Beijing: Zhonghua Shuju, 2003), 59.
19. Gong Zhen, "preface," in Gong Zhen, *Xiyang Fanguo Zhi* 西洋番国志 (Record of Foreign Kingdoms in the Western Ocean), ed. Xiang Da (Beijing: Zhonghua Shuju, 2000), 5.
20. Gong, *Xiyang Fanguo Zhi*, 32–33.
21. Comments by R. Michael Feener, June 1, 2018.
22. Mirani Litster, "Cowry Shell Money: The Maldives in Past Globalizations," PhD dissertation, The Australian National University, 2016, 140–43, 150–51, 155, 212.
23. Zhu Yunming, "Qianwenji Xiaxiyang" (Down to the West Ocean in A Record of What Has Been Heard), in Gong, *Xiyang Fanguo Zhi*, 55–57. J. V. Mills did a wonderful job in translating this voyage for modern readers. See Ma, *Ying-yai shenglan*, 14–19.
24. This, however, was not the largest one. Ma Huan mentioned 27,670 people and sixty-three treasure ships in the fourth voyage. Ma, *Ming Chaoben*, 5.
25. *Wuhumen* 五虎门 was also called *Wuhushan* 五虎山 (Lit. Five-Tiger Mountain). See Xiang Da, ed., *Zheng He Hanghai Tu* 郑和航海图 (The Zheng He Nautical Chart) (Beijing: Zhonghua Shuju, 2000), 26.
26. For early Ming and Calicut, see Roderich Ptak, "China and Calicut in the Early Ming Period: Envoys and Tribute Embassies," *Journal of the Royal Asiatic Society of Great Britain and Ireland* 1 (1989): 81–111; For Ormuz and Yuan-Ming China, see Ralph Kauz and Roderich Ptak, "Hormuz in Yuan and Ming sources," *Bulletin de l'École française d'Extrême-Orient* 88 (2001): 27–75.
27. Nan'ao Island was a key calling place for China's maritime activities from the Song period onward, and many stone inscriptions were left there. See Gao

7. BETWEEN THE SON OF HEAVEN AND THE SULTAN

Jianbin and Peng Liang, *Nan'ao Shike Diaocha* (A Survey of the Stone Inscriptions in Na'nao Island) (Fuzhou: Fujian Jiaoyuchubanshe, 2018).
28. Ma, *Ying-yai sheng-lan*, 18.
29. Fei, *Xingcha Shenglan*, 45; W. W. Rockhill, "Notes on the Relations and Trade of China with the Eastern Archipelago and the Coast of the Indian Ocean During the Fourteenth Century, Part III," *T'oung Pao* 16, no. 1 (1915): 375; Ma, *Ying-yai sheng-lan*, 18–9.
30. *Ming Xuanzong Shilu, juan* 67, in *Ming Shilu*, 3:2087.
31. Boxihe, *Zheng He*, 55–57. One Ming mission led by the eunuch Zhang Xuan 张璇 might have visited Bengal in the tenth year of the Yongle reign (1412). Zhang died and was buried at *Fenghuangshan* 凤凰山 (lit. "Mount Phoenix") in 1413 in *Chadigang* 察地港 (Chittagong), Bengal. See Zhou Yunzhong, "Mingchu Zhang Xuan Xia Xiyang Zu yu Mengjiala Zhengui Shiliao Jiedu" (The Precious Document on Zhang Xuan Buried in Chittagong in 1412), *Nanya Yanjiu* (Studies of South Asia), no. 2 (2010): 123–33. The Zhang Xuan mission, however, might have been a subfleet dispatched by Zheng He while the main fleet returned to China.
32. *Ming Shi, juan* 326, 8453. The *Xianbin Lu* recorded this envoy under "Diegan." Luo Yuejiong, *Xianbin Lu* 咸宾录 (A Record of All Guests), ed. Yu Sili (Beijing: Zhonghua Shuju, 1983), 103.
33. "List of Kings of the Maldives Islands Since the Conversion to Mahomedanism," in Albert Gray and Harry Charles Purvis Bell, trans. and ed., *The Voyage of François Pyrard of Laval to the East Indies, the Maldives, the Moluccas and Brazil*, vol. 3 (Cambridge: Cambridge University Press, 2010), 531–2; Ptak, "The Maldives," 681, footnote 41. The veracity of the list of Maldivian kings, however, remains a point of contention.
34. Luo, *Xianbin Lu*,101; Ptak, "The Maldives," 681.
35. Huang Xingzeng, *Xiyang Chaogong Dianlu Jiaozhu* 西洋朝贡典录校注 (Record of Tributes from the Western Ocean), ed. Xie Fang (Beijing: Zhonghua Shuju, 2000), 79. Huang might have been mistaken about the mission that occurred in 1416, the fourteenth year of the Yongle reign. A typical mission usually lasted at least more than a year, so the so-called 1416 one could be seen as having started in the fifteenth year. Also, when the text was hand-copied, the character for "ten" was missing.
36. *Ming Taizong Shilu* (Veritable Records of Ming Taizu), *juan* 134, in *Ming Shilu*, 2:1382.
37. *Ming Taizong Shilu, juan* 182, in *Ming Shilu*, 2:1463.
38. *Ming Taizong Shilu, juan* 183, in *Ming Shilu*, 2:1465.
39. Roderich Ptak, "China and Portugal at Sea: the Early Ming System and the Estado da Índia Compared," *Revista de Cultura/Review of Culture*, 13–14 (1991): 27; Tansen Sen, "The Impact of Zheng He's expeditions on Indian Ocean Interactions," *Bulletin of SOAS* 79, no. 3 (2016): 617.
40. *Ming Taizong Shilu, juan* 233, *Ming Shilu*, 2:1536.
41. Emperor Yongle moved his court from Nanjing to Beijing in 1421.
42. *Ming Taizong Shilu, juan* 263, in *Ming Shilu*, 2:1573.
43. *Ming Xuanzong Shilu, juan* 67, in *Ming Shilu*, 3:2087.
44. *Ming Xuanzong shilu, juan* 105, in *Ming Shilu*, 3:2278.

45. Chen Menglei, *Gujin Tushu Jicheng* 古今图书集成 (Complete Collection of Illustrations and Writings from the Earliest to Current Times) (n.p.: Zhonghua Shuju, 1934), *ce* 218, "bianyi dian," *juan* 106. "Yebalamo" sounds like a transliteration of Ibrahim.
46. "List of Kings of the Maldives,"532.
47. Ptak, "The Maldives," 681.
48. *Ming Shi, juan* 326, 8453.
49. *Ming Shi, juan* 326, 8453.
50. *Ming Yingzong Shilu, juan* 19, in *Ming Shilu*, 3:2455.
51. *Ming Yingzong Shilu, juan* 87, in *Ming Shilu*, 3:2797.
52. Ralph Kauz and Roderich Ptak, "Hormuz in Yuan and Ming Sources," *Bulletin de l'École française d'Extrême-Orient* 88 (2001): 54.
53. Clarence Maloney, *People of the Maldive Islands* (Bombay: Oriental Longman, 1980), 109.

8. THE TREES OF THE MALDIVES

1. Xuanzang and Bianji, *Datang Xiyuji Jiaozhu* 大唐西域记校注 (Great Tang Records on the Western Regions: Annotation), ed. Ji Xianlin (Beijing: Zhonghua Shuju, 1985), 884l.
2. Ma Huan, *Ming Chaoben Yingya Shenglan Jiaozhu* 明钞本瀛涯胜览校注 (Overall Survey of the Ocean Shores: Annotation of a Ming Manuscript), ed. Wan Ming (Beijing: Haiyangchubanshe, 2005), 74 and 75; Ma Huan, *Ying-yai sheng-lan: "The Overall Survey of the Ocean's Shores," [1433]; translated from the Chinese text edited by Feng Ch'eng-chün with introduction, notes, and appendices by J. V. G. Mills* (London: Hakluyt Society, 1970), 149 and 151.
3. Fujian Quanzhou Haiwajiaotongshi Bowuguan, ed., *Quanzhouwan Songdai Haichuan Fajue yu Yanjiu Xiudingban* (A Report on the Excavation of the Song Boat in Quanzhou Bay) (Beijing: Haiyang Chubanshe, 2017), 29.
4. Ma, *Ming Chaoben*, 68–69; Ma, *Ying-yai sheng-lan*, 143.
5. Ma, *Ming Chaoben*, 56; Ma, *Ying-yai sheng-lan*, 129.
6. Wang Dayuan, *Daoyi Zhilue Jiaoshi* 岛夷志略校释 (Brief Record of the Island Barbarians), ed. Su Jiqing (Beijing: Zhonghua Shuju, 1981), 38, 86, 93, 96, 168, 175, 187, 191, 227, 277, 282, 291, 292–93n1, 297, 321, 344.
7. Huilin, *Yiqiejingyinyi* 一切经音义 (Pronunciations and Meanings for All Buddhist Sutras) (Taipei: CBETA E-version, 2001), 581 and 1554.
8. Liu Xun, *Lingbiao Yilu* 岭表异录 (A Record of Strange Things in the South Range), ed. Lu Xun (Guangzhou: Guangzhou Renminchubanshe, 1983), *juan* 2, 20.
9. Zhou Qufei, *Lingwai Daida Dadai Jiaozhu* 岭外代答校注 (Answers for Questions Concerning Out of Range), ed. Yang Wuquan (Beijing: Zhonghua Shuju, 1999), 295; Paul Wheatley, "Geographical Notes on Some Commodities Involved in Sung Maritime Trade," *Journal of the Malayan Branch of the Royal Asiatic Society* 32, no. 2 (1959): 64.
10. Zhao Rukuo, *Zhufan Zhi Jiaoshi* 诸蕃志校释 (A Record of Barbarians), ed. Yang Bowen (Beijing: Zhonghua Shuju, 2000), 188; Wheatley, "Geographical Notes," 64.

8. THE TREES OF THE MALDIVES

11. *Song Shi* 宋史 (History of the Song Dynasty) (Beijing: Zhonghua Shuju, 1977), *juan* 489, 14,078, 14,088, 14,096, 14,091, and 14,094.
12. Zhang Xie, *Dongxiyang Kao* 东西洋考 (An Examination of the Eastern and Western Oceans), ed. Xie Fang (Beijing: Zhonghua Shuju, 2000), 142 and 145.
13. *Waqf* is an inherent religious endowment in Islam. For coconut trees as part of the Waqf, for example, see Ahmed Nazim Sattar, *King Kalaafaan Manuscripts: How the Maldives Monarchy Treasured the Remembrance of a Fallen King for More Than Four Hundred Years* (Male: National Centre of Linguistic and Historical Research, 2010), 57.
14. Clarence Maloney, *People of the Maldive Islands* (Bombay: Oriental Longman, 1980), 19, 20.
15. Albert Gray and H. C. P. Bell, "Early Notices of the Maldives," in François Pyrard, *The Voyage of François Pyrard of Laval to the East Indies, the Maldives, the Moluccas and Brazil*, ed. Albert Gray and H. C. P. Bell (Cambridge: Cambridge University Press, 2011), 429, 430, 432.
16. Gray and Bell, "Early Notices," 439.
17. Gray and Bell, "Early Notices," 439. Maldivian people boiled rather than pressed coconuts to get oil, so the oil appeared darkish. Maloney, *People*, 19.
18. Gray and Bell, "Early Notices," 439.
19. Xavier Romero-Frias, *Folk Tales of the Maldives* (Copenhagen: NIAS Press, 2012), 1–3.
20. Gray and Bell, "Early Notices," 482.
21. Gray and Bell, "Early Notices," 483.
22. Gray and Bell, "Early Notices," 483.
23. Gray and Bell, "Early Notices," 484.
24. Ai Rulue (Giulio Aleni), *Zhifang Waiji Jiaoshi* 职方外纪校释 (Chronicle of Foreign Lands), ed. Xie Fang (Beijing: Zhonghua Shuju, 2000), 58.
25. Pyrard, *The Voyage of François Pyrard*, 1:231–32.
26. Gray and Bell, "Early Notices," 484.
27. Pyrard, *The Voyage of François Pyrard*, 1:231–32n1.
28. Pyrard, *The Voyage of François Pyrard*, 1: 113.
29. González de Mendoza, *History of the great and mighty Kingdom of China and the Situation Thereof: Compiled by the Padre Juan Gonzalez de Mendoza, and now Reprinted from the early Translation of R. Parke*, ed. George T. Staunton and R. H. Major (New York: Taylor & Francis, 2010), 2:266–267.
30. Mohamed Mauroof Jameel, "Coral Stone Architecture of Maldives: A Brief Overview," *Bulletin of MIHO Museum* 18 (2018): 17–28.
31. Jameel, "Coral Stone," 22.
32. Gray and Bell, "Early Notices," 483.

9. SHIPS WITHOUT NAILS

1. Wang Dayuan, *Daoyi Zhilue Jiaoshi* 岛夷志略校释 (Brief Record of the Island Barbarians), ed. Su Jiqing (Beijing: Zhonghua Shuju, 1981), 264.
2. Wang, *Daoyi Zhilue*, 364; Ralph Kauz and Roderich Ptak, "Hormuz in Yuan and Ming Sources," *Bulletin de l'École française d'Extrême-Orient* 88 (2001): 39–40.

9. SHIPS WITHOUT NAILS

While Su Jiqing, Ptak, and others see Ganmaili as having been Ormuz/Hormuz, Shen Fuwei suspects it was Qais ben' Umaira, an island in the Persian Gulf. Shen Fuwei, "Jianlun Wang Dayuan dui Yinduyang Quyumaoyi de Kaocha—Gulifu Ganmaili, Mahesili, Manali Zaji" (On Wang Dayuan's Survey of the Indian Ocean Trading Area—Notes on Gulifu Ganmaili, Mahesili and Manali), *Zhongguoshi Yanjiu* (Studies of Chinese History) 2 (2004): 123–38. Kauz and Ptak also provide an in-depth discussion on the location of Ganmaili. Kauz and Ptak, "Hormuz," 42–45.

3. Wang, *Daoyi Zhilue*, 364, 321, 323.
4. Marco Polo, *The Travels of Marco Polo (The Venetian)* (New York: Liveright, 1953), 48–49.
5. Kauz and Ptak, "Hormuz," 40.
6. Zhou Qufei, *Lingwai Daida Jiaozhu* 岭外代答校注 (Answers for Questions Concerning Out of Range), ed. Yang Wuquan (Beijing: Zhonghua Shuju, 1999), 216–17. "Mulan" was used to refer to a Chinese tree, but here it is an abbreviation for the kingdom of Mulanpi (*Mulanpi guo* 木兰皮国), which might be a transliteration of Maghreb (*al-Maghrib*, "the west"), now known as Northwest Africa and the Arab Maghreb.
7. Zhou, *Lingwai Daida*, 217.
8. Albert Gray and H. C. P. Bell, "Early Notices of the Maldives," in François Pyrard, *The Voyage of François Pyrard of Laval to the East Indies, the Maldives, the Moluccas and Brazil*, ed. Albert Gray and H. C. P. Bell (Cambridge: Cambridge University Press, 2011), 3:430.
9. Nilakanta Sastri, ed., *Foreign Notices of South India* (Madras: University of Madras, 1939), 198, cited in Clarence Maloney, *People of the Maldive Islands* (Bombay: Oriental Longman, 1980), 154.
10. Henry Yule, *Cathay and the Way Thither: Being a Collection of Medieval Notices of China* (London: Hakluyt Society, 1914), 1:57.
11. Ma Huan, *Ming Chaoben Yingya Shenglan Jiaozhu* 明钞本瀛涯胜览校注 (Overall Survey of the Ocean Shores: Annotation of a Ming Manuscript), ed. Wan Ming (Beijing: Haiyangchubanshe, 2005), 74; Ma Huan, *Ying-yai sheng-lan: "The Overall Survey of the Ocean's Shores," [1433]; translated from the Chinese text edited by Feng Ch'eng-chün with introduction, notes, and appendices by J. V. G. Mills* (London: Hakluyt Society, 1970), 149. Bitumen for caulking or as coating for ships was in use from as early as the Sumerian period, more than four thousand years ago. Dionysius A. Agius, *Classic Ships of Islam: From Mesopotamia to the Indian Ocean* (Leiden: Brill, 2008), 137–38.
12. Huang Xingzeng, *Xiyang Chaogong Dianlu Jiaozhu* 西洋朝贡典录校注 (Record of Tributes from the Western Ocean), ed. Xie Fang (Beijing: Zhonghua Shuju, 2000), 76n6.
13. Garcia da Orta, *Colóquios dos simples e drogas da India* (Lisbon: Imprensa Nacional, 1987), folio 12; Jin Guoping, ed. and trans., *Xifang Aomen Shiliao Xiancui* (Selected Western Sources on Macao) (Guangzhou: Guangdong Renmin Chubanshe, 2005), 15. Jin Guoping, however, thinks that in this case, bitumen was mistaken for ambergris, as the latter was too expensive to be used for this purpose. Chen Xinxiong, "Ping Long Cunni 'Miren de Gongli' " (Comments on Long Cunni's 'An Attractive Tributary Gift: Ambergris'), in *Zheng He Xia Xiyang Guoji Xueshuyantaohui Lunwenji* (A Collection of Papers on the International

Conference on Zheng He's Sailing to the Western Ocean), ed. Chen Xinxiong and Chen Yunü (Taipei: Daoxiang Chubanshe, 2003), 352.

14. Michael Flecker, "Early Voyaging in the South China Sea: Implications on Territorial Claims," Nalanda-Sriwijaya Centre, Working Paper No. 19 (August 2015), 28–29. For the sewing technique, also see Ralph K. Pedersen, "Traditional Arabian Watercraft and the Ark of the Gilgamesh Epic: Interpretations and Realizations," *Proceedings of the Seminar for Arabian Studies* 34 (2004): 231–38; Agius, *Classic Ships*, 161–65.

15. George F. Hourani, *Arab Seafaring in the Indian Ocean in Ancient and Early Medieval Times*, ed. John Carswell (Princeton, NJ: Princeton University Press, 1995), 91–93, 97.

16. For an introduction to medieval Arab ships, see Hourani, *Arab Seafaring*, 87–122.

17. G. W. B. Huntingford, ed, *The Periplus of the Erythraean Sea, by an Unknown Author: With Some Extracts from Agatharkhides "on the Erythraean Sea"* (London: Hakluyt Society, 2010), 29; Tom Vosmer, "Sewn Boats in Oman and the Indian Ocean," *International Journal of Nautical Archaeology* 48, no. 2 (2019): 302.

18. Himanshu Prabha Ray, "Seafaring and Maritime Contacts: An Agenda for Historical Analysis," *Journal of the Economic and Social History of the Orient* 39, no. 4 (1996): 422–31; Eric Staples and Lucy Blue, "Archaeological, Historical, and Ethnographic Approaches to the Study of Sewn Boats: Past, Present, and Future," *International Journal of Nautical Archaeology* 48, no. 2 (2019): 269–85.

19. For their differences, see Pierre-Yves Manguin, "Sewn Boats of Southeast Asia: The Stitched-Plank and Lashed-Lug Tradition," *International Journal of Nautical Archaeology* 48, no. 2 (2019): 412.

20. Manguin, "Sewn Boats," 412. For similarities and differences between Maldivian ships and Southeast Asian one, see Pierre-Yves Manguin, "Les techniques de construction navale aux Maldives originaires d'Asie du Sud-Est," *Techniques & Culture* 35–36 (2001): 21–47; Pierre-Yves Manguin, "The Maldives Connection: Pre-Modern Malay World Shipping Across the Indian Ocean," in *Civilisations des mondes insulaires*, ed. Radimilahy and N. Rajaonarimanana (Paris: Éditions Karthala, 2011), 261–84; Manguin, "Sewn Boats," 413.

21. Agius, *Classic Ships*, 166–67; Geoff Wade, "Southeast Asia in the 15th Century," in *Southeast Asia in the Fifteenth Century: The China Factor*, ed. Geoff Wade and Sun Laichen (Singapore: NUS Press, 2010), 19–21; Pierre-Yves Manguin, "New Ships for New Networks: Trends in Shipbuilding in the South China Sea in the 15th and 16th Centuries," in *Southeast Asia in the Fifteenth Century: The China Factor*, ed. Geoff Wade and Sun Laichen (Singapore: NUS Press, 2010), 333–58.

22. Ibn Battuta, *Travels in Asia and Africa, 1325–1354*, trans. and selected by H. A. R. Gibb, with an Introduction and Notes (New York: Routledge & Kegan Paul, 2011), 114, 243.

23. Stevenson Edward Luther, trans. and ed., *Geography of Claudius Ptolemy, based upon Greek and Latin Manuscripts and Important Late Fifteenth and Early Sixteenth Century Printed Editions, including Reproductions of the Maps from the Ebner Manuscript, ca. 1460. With an Introduction by Professor Joseph Fischer, S.J.* (New York: New York Public Library, 1932), 157.

9. SHIPS WITHOUT NAILS

24. Gedaisi (George Coedès), ed., *Xila Lading Zuojia Yuandong Guwenxian Jilu* 希腊拉丁作家远东古文献辑录 (Selected Works by Ancient Greek and Latin Writers on the Far East), trans. Geng Sheng (Beijing: Zhonghua Shuju, 1987), 43–44.
25. Gray and Bell, "Early Notices," 428.
26. Li Fang, *Taiping Yulan* 太平御览 (Readings of the Taiping Era) (Beijing: Zhonghua Shujua, 1960), vol. 4, *juan* 988, 4372.
27. Rao Zongyi (Jao Tsung-I), "Taiqing Jinyeshendan Jing (juan xia) yu Nanhai Dili" ("T'ai-ch'ing chin-I shen-tan ching" and Southern Ocean Geography), *Zhongguo Wenhuayanjiusuo Xuebao* (Journal of Chinese Studies) 3, no. 1 (1970): 43.
28. Gray and Bell, "Early Notices," 430.
29. Gray and Bell, "Early Notices," 479; also see Mansel Longworth Dames, *The Book of Duarte Barbosa: An Account of the Countries Bordering on the Indian Ocean and Their Inhabitants* (New Delhi: Asian Educational Services, 1989), 2:107–8.
30. Gray and Bell, "Early Notices," 482.
31. Battuta, *Travels*, 243.
32. Pyrard, *The Voyage of François Pyrard*, 3:379.
33. Pyrard, *The Voyage of François Pyrard*, 3:385.
34. Flecker, "Early Voyaging," 34–35. The term "dhow" refers to a number of traditional sailing vessels in the Indian Ocean.
35. Michael Flecker, "A Ninth-Century Arab or Indian Shipwreck in Indonesia: The First Archaeological Evidence of Direct Trade with China," in *Shipwrecked: Tang Treasures and Monsoon Winds*, ed. Regina Krahl, John Guy, J. Keith Wilson, and Julian Raby (Washington, DC: Smithsonian Institution Press, 2010), 101.
36. Michael Flecker, Pauline Burger, Armelle Charrié-Duhaut, Jacques Connan, and Pierre Albrecht, "The 9th-Century-AD Belitung Wreck, Indonesia: Analysis of a Resin Lump," *International Journal of Nautical Archaeology* 37 (2008): 384.
37. John Guy, "The Phanom Surin Shipwreck, a Pahlavi Inscription, and Their Significance for the History of Early Lower Central Thailand," *Journal of the Siam Society* 105 (2017): 179–96, esp. 180.
38. Flecker, "Early Voyaging," 34; Jacques Connan, Seth Priestman, et al., "Geochemical Analysis of Bitumen from West Asian Torpedo Jars from the c. 8th Century Phanom-Surin Shipwreck in Thailand," *Journal of Archaeological Science* 117 (May 2020): 111; Qian Jiang, "Taiguowan Fujin Chushui de Bosibo" (The Persian Sewn-Plank Ship Excavated off the Coast of the Gulf of Thailand), *Guojia Hanghai* (National Maritime Research) 27, no. 2 (2021): 133–60.
39. Flecker, "A Ninth-Century Arab or Indian"; Tom Vosmer, "Sewn Boats," 307–8.
40. Luca Belfioretti and Tom Vosmer, "Al-Balīd Ship Timbers: Preliminary Overview and Comparisons," *Proceedings of the Seminar for Arabian Studies* 40 (2010): 111–18.
41. Huilin, *Yiqiejingyinyi* 一切经音义 (Pronunciations and Meanings for All Buddhist Sutras) (Taipei: CBETA E-version, 2001), 1014, 1467, 1554, 581.
42. For foreign ships sailing to Tang China, see Edward H. Schafer, *The Golden Peaches of Samarkand: A Study of T'ang Exotics* (San Francisco: Hauraki Publishing, 2014), 36–37. Both *kunlun* and *Bosi* here refers to some peoples in Southeast Asia or South Asia.
43. Yuankai, *Tang Daheshang Dongzheng Zhuan* 唐大和上东征传 (The Record of the Eastern Journey by the Tang Master Monk) (Beijing: Zhonghua Shuju, 1979),

9. SHIPS WITHOUT NAILS

74; also see Feilang (Gabriel Ferrand), *Kunlun ji Nanhai Gudai Hangxingkao* 昆仑及南海古代航行考 (Le K'ouen-Louen et les anciennes navigations interocéaniques dans les Mers du Sud), trans. Feng Chengjun (Beijing: Zhonghua Shuju, 1957), 8.
44. Ji Han, *Nanfang Caomu Zhuang* 南方草木状 (An Introduction to the Plants in the South), ed. Yang Weiqun, in *Lidai Lingnan Biji Bazhong* (The Eight Historical Records on the South Range) (Guangzhou: Guangdong Renminchubanshe, 2011), 1:8, 17.
45. Liu Xun, *Lingbiao Yilu* 岭表异录 (A Record of Strange Things in the South Range), ed. Lu Xun (Guangzhou: Guangzhou Renminchubanshe, 1983), 19; Flecker, "Early Voyaging," 26.
46. Zhou, *Lingwai Daida*, 218.
47. Zhou, *Lingwai Daida*, 218.
48. Wang, *Daoyi Zhilue*, 199 and 200–201n1.
49. González de Juan Mendoza, *History of the great and mighty Kingdom of China and the Situation Thereof: Compiled by the Padre Juan Gonzalez de Mendoza, and now Reprinted from the early Translation of R. Parke*, ed. George T. Staunton and R. H. Major (New York: Taylor & Francis, 2010), 266.
50. Mendoza, *History*, 266–67.
51. Qu Dajuan, *Guangdong Xinyu* 广东新语 (New Notes of Canton), ed. Li Mo, in *Qu Dajuan Quanji* (Comprehensive Works of Qu Dajun), ed. Ou Chu and Wang Guichen (Beijing: Renminwenxue Chubanshe, 1998), vol. 4, *juan* 18, 436.
52. Yin Guangren and Zhang Rulin, *Aomen Jilue* 澳门记略 (A Sketch of Macao), ed. Zhao Chunchen (Guangzhou: Guangdong Gaodengjiaoyuchubanshe, 1988), 67. *Mesua ferrea*, also known as Ceylon ironwood, was named for the heaviness and hardness of its timber and was widely native to humid, tropical regions of South Asia and Southeast Asia. Heavy, hard, and strong, this timber has been frequently used in ship construction in maritime Asia.
53. Xie Qinggao, *Hailu Jiaoshi* 海录校释 (Annotations to A Record of the Seas), ed. An Jing (Beijing: Shangwu Yinshuguan, 2002), 11. Xie also described the making of coconut wine in Siam in great detail (11).
54. Yin and Zhang, *Aomen Jilue*, 67.
55. Gray and Bell, "Early Notices," 482.

10. COWRIE SHELLS

1. Susmita Basu Majumdar and Sharmistha Chatterjee, "Cowries in Eastern India: Understanding Their Role as Ritual Objects and Money," *Journal of Bengal Art* 19 (2014): 44.
2. Wang Dayuan, *Daoyi Zhilue Jiaoshi* 岛夷志略校释 (Brief Record of the Island Barbarians), ed. Su Jiqing (Beijing: Zhonghua Shuju, 1981), 264; Roderich Ptak, "The Maldives and Laccadive Islands (*liu-shan* 溜山) in Ming Records," *Journal of the American Oriental Society* 107, no. 4 (1987): 677–78.
3. Bin Yang, *Cowrie Shells and Cowrie Money: A Global History* (New York: Routledge, 2019).

10. COWRIE SHELLS

4. Jan Hogendorn and Marion Johnson, *The Shell Money of the Slave Trade* (Cambridge: Cambridge University Press, 1986), 6–7.
5. For the global trajectory of cowrie shells from the Maldives, see Hogendorn and Johnson, *The Shell Money*; Yang, *Cowrie Shells and Cowrie Money*.
6. Wang, *Daoyi Zhilue*, 264, 330, 339, 337.
7. Faxian, *Faxian Zhuan Jiaozhu* 法显传校注 (Annotations to the Biography of Faxian), ed. Zhang Xun (Beijing: Zhonghua Shuju, 2008), 1–2, 46; James Legge, *A Record of Buddhistic Kingdoms: Being an Account by the Chinese Monk Fa-Hien of His Travels in India and Ceylon (A.D. 399–414) in Search of the Buddhist Books of Discipline* (Oxford: Clarendon Press, 1886), 43 and 43n2.
8. Xuanzang and Bianji, *Datang Xiyuji Jiaozhu* 大唐西域记校注 (Great Tang Records on the Western Regions: Annotation), ed. Ji Xianlin (Beijing: Zhonghua Shuju, 1985), 217.
9. Yijing, *Nanhai Jigui Neifa Zhuan* 南海寄归内法传 (A Record of Buddhist Practices Sent Home from the Southern Sea), ed. Wang Bangwei (Beijing: Zhonghua Shuju, 2009), 46, 167n22, 219.
10. Huilin, *Yiqiejingyinyi* 一切经音义 (Pronunciations and Meanings for All Buddhist Sutras) (Taipei: CBETA E-version, 2001).
11. Wang, *Daoyi Zhilue*, 114.
12. Wang, *Daoyi Zhilue*, 115, 155, 126, 376.
13. Marco Polo, *The Travels of Marco Polo (The Venetian)* (New York: Liveright, 1953), 194.
14. Citing from Hogendorn and Johnson, *The Shell Money*, 15.
15. Marco Polo, *The Travels*, 195, 198, 273.
16. Ma Huan, *Ming Chaoben Yingya Shenglan Jiaozhu* 明钞本瀛涯胜览校注 (Overall Survey of the Ocean Shores: Annotation of a Ming Manuscript), ed. Wan Ming (Beijing: Haiyangchubanshe, 2005), 36, 74; Ma Huan, *Ying-yai sheng-lan: "The Overall Survey of the Ocean's Shores," [1433]; translated from the Chinese text edited by Feng Ch'eng-chün with introduction, notes, and appendices by J. V. G. Mills* (London: Hakluyt Society, 1970), 107, 161, 150. The statement that "they do not use gold, silver, or copper coins" seems to be an error. Another version says that gold, silver, and copper coins were optionally used. Ma, *Ying-yai sheng-lan*, 107.
17. Gong Zhen, *Xiyang Fanguo Zhi* 西洋番国志 (Record of Foreign Kingdoms in the Western Ocean), ed. Xiang Da (Beijing: Zhonghua Shuju, 2000, 14, 38).
18. Huang Xingzeng, *Xiyang Chaogong Dianlu Jiaozhu* 西洋朝贡典录校注 (Record of Tributes from the Western Ocean), ed. Xie Fang (Beijing: Zhonghua Shuju, 2000), 69, 87, 76.
19. Yan Congjian, *Shuyu Zhouzi Lu* 殊域周咨录 (Comprehensive Survey and Record of Foreign Territories), ed. Yu Sili (Beijing: Zhonghua Shuju, 1993), 285 and 388. One *guan* was equal to one *liang*.
20. Zhang Xie, *Dongxiyang Kao* 东西洋考 (An Examination of the Eastern and Western Oceans), ed. Xie Fang (Beijing: Zhonghua Shuju, 2000), 40.
21. Albert Gray and H. C. P. Bell, "Early Notices of the Maldives," in François Pyrard, *The Voyage of François Pyrard of Laval to the East Indies, the Maldives, the Moluccas and Brazil*, ed. Albert Gray and H. C. P. Bell (Cambridge: Cambridge University Press, 2011), 3:428–29.

10. COWRIE SHELLS

22. H. C. P. Bell, *The Maldive Islands: Monograph on the History, Archaeology and Epigraph* (Colombo: Ceylon Government Press, 1940), 17.
23. Gray and Bell, "Early Notices," 430–32.
24. Egil Mikkelsen, "Archaeological Excavations of a Monastery at Kaasidhoo: Cowrie Shells and Their Buddhist Context in the Maldives," National Centre for Linguistic and Historical Research, Male' Republic of Maldives, 2000, 8, 13, 18. Some scholars also conducted an archaeological project in the Maldives searching for cowrie shells. Shiura Jaufar, "Second Season of Excavation in the Maldives for the 'Cowrie Shells: An Early Global Commodity' Project, 2017," *ACCU Nara International Correspondent* 18 (2017): 27–30; Shiura Jaufar, "Cowrie—an Early Global Commodity: An Archaeological Research on the Islamic Period of the Maldive Islands," ACCU Nara International Correspondent 17 (2017): 30–1; Anne Haour, Annalisa Christie, Shiura Jaufar, and David Vigoureux, "Back to Ibn Battuta's Island—Excavations in the Maldives, 2017," *Nyame Akuma* 88 (December 2017): 33–40; Anne Haour, Annalisa Christie, and Shiura Jaufar, "Tracking the Cowrie Shell: Excavations in the Maldives, 2016," *Nyame Akuma* 85 (June 2016): 69–82; Anne Haour and Annalisa Christie, eds., *Archaeological Investigations of the Maldives in the Medieval Islamic Period: Ibn Battuta's Island* (London: Routledge, 2021). Kaashidhoo, where a seventh-eighth century Buddhist monastery was found, is about 53 miles (86 km) north of Male.
25. MAHS-MDV-COL-003-O-0014; MAHS-MDV-COL-003-O-0084, MAHS-MDV-COL-003-O-0069, all at https://maritimeasiaheritage.cseas.kyoto-u.ac.jp/manuscript-viewer/waqf-endowment.
26. Gray and Bell, "Early Notices," 444.
27. Gray and Bell, "Early Notices," 444, 453, 457. Here one should bear in mind that cowrie shells were not counted in decimals.
28. Gray and Bell, "Early Notices," 473.
29. Gray and Bell, "Early Notices," 485.
30. For the previous summary, see Peng Ke and Zhu Yanshi, "New Research on the Origin of Cowries in Ancient China," *Sino-Platonic Papers* 68 (1995), www.sinoplatonic.org/complete/spp068_cowries_china.pdf; Bin Yang, "The Rise and Fall of Cowry Shells: The Asian Story," *Journal of World History* 22, no. 1 (March 2011): 1–26; Bin Yang, "Cowry Shells in Eastern Eurasia," in *The Silk Road: Long-Distance Trade, Culture, and Society: Interwoven History*, ed. Namba Mariko Walter and James P. Ito-Adler (Cambridge, MA: Cambridge Institutes Press, 2014), 1–32; Yang, *Cowrie Shells and Cowrie Money*, 124–596.
31. *Quanzhouwan Songdai Haichuan Fajue yu Yanjiu Xiudingban* (A Report on the Excavation of the Song Boat in Quanzhou Bay), ed. Fujian Quanzhou Haiwajiaotongshi Bowuguan (Beijing: Haiyang Chubanshe, 2017), 30 and 62.
32. Fang Linggui, trans. and ed., *Tongzhi Tiaoge Jiaozhu* 通制条格校注 (Regulation of the [Book of the] Comprehensive Rules [of the Great Yuan]) (Beijing: Zhonghua Shuju, 2001), 552; Fang Hui, "Cong Jingshi Wenqi Kan Yuan Ming ji Qingchu Yunnan Shiyong beibi de Qingkuang" (The Use of Cowrie Money in Yunnan of the Yuan-Ming-Early Qing Period: Based on Texts and Inscriptions in Bronze and Stone Items), in *Beibi Yanjiu* (Studies of Cowrie Money), ed. Yang Shouchuan (Kunming: Yunnan University Press, 1997), 149–51; Hans Ulrich Vogel, *Marco Polo Was in China: New Evidence From Currencies, Salts and Revenues* (Leiden: Brill, 2013), 250; Yang, *Cowrie Shells and Cowrie Money*, 105–7.

11. DRIED FISH, GRAINS, AND HANDKERCHIEFS

33. Guangdong Difangzhi Bianjiweiyuahui Bangongshi, ed., *Yuan Dade Nanhaizhi Canben* 元大德南海志残本 (Remains of the Nanhai Gazetteer Compiled in the Dade Reign of the Yuan Dynasty) (Guangzhou: Guangdong Renminchubanshe, 1991), 45.
34. Namio Egami, "Migration of Cowrie-Shell Culture East Asia," *Acta Asiatica* 26 (1974): 20; Li Yung-Ti, "On the Function of Cowries in Shang and Western Zhou China," *Journal of East Asian Archaeology* 5 (2006): 17, 13.
35. Yang, "Rise and Fall"; Yang, "Cowry Shells"; Yang, *Cowrie Shells and Cowrie Money*.
36. Huang Xiquan, "Chu Tongbei Beiwen Shiyi Xintan" (A New Exploration of the Chu Bronze Cowrie Inscriptions), in Huang Xiquan, *Xianqin Huobi Yanjiu* (A Study of the Pre-Qin Currencies) (Beijing: Zhonghua Shuju, 2001), 225.
37. "The He Zun," http://www.bjqtm.com/dzzp/qtq/2021-02-24/430.html, Baoji Bronze Ware Museum. "Zun" was a vaselike vessel.
38. For cowrie money in Yunnan, see Vogel, *Marco Polo*; Hans Ulrich Vogel, "Cowrie Trade and Its Role in the Economy of Yunnan: From the Ninth to the Mid-Seventeenth Century (Part I)," *Journal of the Economic and Social History of the Orient* 36, no. 3 (1993): 211–52; Hans Ulrich Vogel, "Cowrie Trade and Its Role in the Economy of Yunnan: From the Ninth to the Mid-Seventeenth Century (Part II)," *Journal of the Economic and Social History of the Orient* 36, no. 4 (1993): 309–53; Egami, "Migration."
39. Fang, "Cong Jingshu," 149–51; Vogel, *Marco Polo*, 250.
40. *Ming Yingzong Shilu* (Veritable Records of Emperor Yingzong), *juan* 68, in *Ming Shilu* (Veritable Records of the Ming Dynasty), ed. Huang Zhangjian (Taipei: Academic Sinica, 1984), 3:2684.
41. Shunzō Sakamaki, "Ryukyu and Southeast Asia," *Journal of Asian Studies* 23, no. 3 (1964): 383–89.
42. Anthony Reid, "An 'Age of Commerce' in Southeast Asian History," *Modern Asian Studies* 24, no. 1 (1990): 6.
43. Huang, *Xiyang*, 53; Yan, *Shuyu Zhouzi Lu*, 166. In terms of name and order, their lists of tributary goods are identical and thus are highly reliable.
44. The Ryukyu Kingdom continued to send students to the imperial university in Beijing and adopted the Chinese writing system.
45. *Lidai Baoan* 历代宝案 (Precious Documents of Successive Generations) (Taipei: Taiwan University Library, 1972), vol. 1, *juan* 12, 401.
46. *Lidai Baoan*, *juan* 161, 534–36.
47. *Lidai Baoan*, *juan* 188–89 and 196.
48. Zhang, *Dongxiyang*, 142–43, 145.
49. *Ming Yingzong Shilu*, *juan* 15, in *Ming Shilu*, 3:2427–28; *Ming Yingzong Shilu*, *juan* 27, in *Ming Shilu*, 3:2493. The court records cited earlier can also be seen in *Mingshi*. *Ming Shi* 明史 (History of the Ming Dynasty) (Beijing: Zhonghua Shuju, 1974), *juan* 323, 8384.

11. DRIED FISH, GRAINS, AND HANDKERCHIEFS

1. Ma Huan, *Ming Chaoben Yingya Shenglan Jiaozhu* 明钞本瀛涯胜览校注 (Overall Survey of the Ocean Shores: Annotation of a Ming Manuscript), ed. Wan Ming

11. DRIED FISH, GRAINS, AND HANDKERCHIEFS

(Beijing: Haiyangchubanshe, 2005), 73–74; Ma Huan, *Ying-yai sheng-lan: "The Overall Survey of the Ocean's Shores," [1433]; translated from the Chinese text edited by Feng Ch'eng-chün with introduction, notes, and appendices by J. V. G. Mills* (London: Hakluyt Society, 1970), 148–49.

2. François Pyrard, *The Voyage of François Pyrard of Laval to the East Indies, the Maldives, the Moluccas and Brazil*, ed. Albert Gray and H. C. P. Bell (Cambridge: Cambridge University Press, 2011), 1:100.
3. Clarence Maloney, *People of the Maldive Islands* (Bombay: Oriental Longman, 1980), 18–19.
4. Albert Gray and H. C. P. Bell, "Early Notices of the Maldives," in Pyrard, *The Voyage of François Pyrard*, 3:437–39.
5. Ma, *Ming Chaoben*, 74; Ma, *Ying-yai sheng-lan*, 150; Boxihe 伯希和 (Paul Eugène Pelliot), *Zheng He Xia Xiyang Kao* (Les grands voyages maritimes chinois au début du 15ème siècle), trans. Feng Chenjun (Beijing: Zhonghua Shuju, 2003), 128–29. *Majiaoyu* is a popular dish in local Portuguese restaurants in Macao, where I once resided. It is thought that the Portuguese brought this tradition from South Asia to its first East Asian colonial port, although the dried fish in Macao is currently salted. Very interestingly, the Chinese term *majiaoyu*, invented by Ma Huan some six hundred years ago, has remained in use.
6. Gong Zhen, *Xiyang Fanguo Zhi* 西洋番国志 (Record of Foreign Kingdoms in the Western Ocean), ed. Xiang Da (Beijing: Zhonghua Shuju, 2000), 33.
7. Fei Xin, *Xingcha Shenglan Jiaozhu* 星槎胜览校注 (Overall Survey of the Star Raft: An Annotation), ed. Feng Chengjun (Beijing: Huawen Chubanshe, 2019), 108.
8. Ma, *Ming Chaoben*, 75n2.
9. Boxihe, *Zheng He*, 129.
10. Pyrard, *The Voyage of François Pyrard*, 3:485; Gray and Bell, "Early Notices," 3:472–73.
11. Gray & Bell, "Early Notices," 240.
12. Pyrard, *The Voyage of François Pyrard*, 1:189–90.
13. Maloney, *People*, 17.
14. Ma, *Ying-yai sheng-lan*, 150n7; Pyrard, *The Voyage of François Pyrard*, 1:190–91.
15. Pyrard, *The Voyage of François Pyrard*, 1:191–92.
16. Maloney, *People*, 18.
17. Pyrard, *The Voyage of François Pyrard*, 3: 351.
18. Pyrard, *The Voyage of François Pyrard*, 3: 352.
19. Ma, *Ming Chaoben*, 75; Ma, *Ying-yai sheng-lan*, 151.
20. Fei, *Xingcha Shenglan*, 108; Fei Xin, *Hsing-ch'a-sheng-lan: The Overall Survey of the Star Raft*, trans. J. V. Mills, ed. Roderich Ptak (Wiesbaden: Harrassowitz, 1996), 103.
21. Pyrard, *The Voyage of François Pyrard*, 1:112.
22. H. C. P. Bell, *The Maldive Islands: Monograph on the History, Archaeology and Epigraph* (Colombo: Ceylon Government Press, 1940), 13.
23. Gray and Bell, "Early Notices," 453–54.
24. Gray and Bell, "Early Notices," 439.
25. Pyrard, *The Voyage of François Pyrard*, 1:113.
26. Pyrard, *The Voyage of François Pyrard*, 1:113.
27. Pyrard, *The Voyage of François Pyrard*, 1:112.

11. DRIED FISH, GRAINS, AND HANDKERCHIEFS

28. Maloney, *People*, 21.
29. Pyrard, *The Voyage of François Pyrard*, 1:111.
30. Maloney, *People*, 23.
31. Pyrard, *The Voyage of François Pyrard*, 1:111–12.
32. Maloney, *People*, 26.
33. Gray and Bell, "Early Notices," 485.
34. Pyrard, *The Voyage of François Pyrard*, 1:116.
35. Gray and Bell, "Early Notices," 454, 456.
36. Gray and Bell, "Early Notices," 443.
37. Maloney, *People*, 26.
38. Pyrard, *The Voyage of François Pyrard*, 1:111.
39. Wang Dayuan, *Daoyi Zhilue Jiaoshi* 岛夷志略校释 (Brief Record of the Island Barbarians), ed. Su Jiqing (Beijing: Zhonghua Shuju, 1981), 110–13, 267–68, 274–76, 280; Ibn Battuta, *Travels in Asia and Africa, 1325–1354*, trans. and selected by H. A. R. Gibb, with an Introduction and Notes (New York: Routledge & Kegan Paul, 2011), 242–43.
40. Xiali was probably Alwave (near Cochin) on the Malabar Coast, and Jinta was most likely Tirukalikunram on the Coromandel Coast. Wang, *Daoyi Zhilue*, 267–68, 274–76.
41. W. W. Rockhill, "Notes on the Relations and Trade of China with the Eastern Archipelago and the Coast of the Indian Ocean During the Fourteenth Century, Part II," *T'oung Pao* 16, no. 1 (1915): Part II," 109n2.
42. Ma, *Ming Chaoben*, 74; W. W. Rockhill, "Notes on the Relations and Trade of China with the Eastern Archipelago and the Coast of the Indian Ocean During the Fourteenth Century, Part III," *T'oung Pao* 16, no. 3 (1915): 390.
43. Wang, *Daoyi Zhilue*, 280; Xie Fang, "Zhongguo Shiji zhong zhi Maerdaifu Kao" (A Study of the Maldives in Chinese Historical Texts), *Nanya Yanjiu* (South Asia Studies) 2 (1982): 2. Dabadan, according to Su Jiqing, refers to Dharmapatanam, located between Cannanore and Tellicherrry. Wang, *Daoyi Zhilue*, 281n1.
44. Wang, *Daoyi Zhilue*, 110–13. Rockhill asserts that Luowei was located on the southern Malay Peninsula, while he agrees that the *liu* cloth was from the Maldives. Rockhill, "Notes Part II," 109n2. It is possible that Wang might have been mistaken.
45. Ma, *Ming Chaoben*, 74–75; Ma, *Ying-yai sheng-lan*, 150; Rockhill, "Notes Part III," 390.
46. Gong, *Xiyang Fanguo Zhi*, 33; Luo Yuejiong, *Xianbin Lu* 咸宾录 (A Record of All Guests), ed. Yu Sili (Beijing: Zhonghua Shuju, 1983), 101.
47. Yan Congjian, *Shuyu Zhouzi Lu* 殊域周咨录 (Comprehensive Survey and Record of Foreign Territories), ed. Yu Sili (Beijing: Zhonghua Shuju, 1993), 285, 308.
48. Ma, *Ming Chaoben*, 97; Ma, *Ying-yai sheng-lan*, 171.
49. Zheng Linzhi, *Gaoli Shi* (History of Goryeo) (Taipei: Wenshizhe Press, 1972), vol. 1, *juan* 33, 514; Chen Gaohua, "Yindu, Mabaer Wangzi Bohaoli Laihua Xinkao" (A New Study of the Indian Prince Bohali Visiting China), in *Yuanshi Yanjiu Lungao* (On Studies of Yuan History) (Beijing: Zhonghua Shuju, 1991), 401–7; Liu Yingsheng, "Cong Buali Shendao Beiming Kan Nanyindu yu Yuanchao ji Bosiwan de Jiaotong" (The Gateway Tablet Inscription of Buali and the Communications Among the Yuan Dynasty, Southern India, and the Persian Gulf), *Lishi Dili*

11. DRIED FISH, GRAINS, AND HANDKERCHIEFS

(Historical Geography) (Shanghai: Shanghai Renminchubanshe, 1990), 7:90–95; Ma Juan, "Mabaer Guo yu Yuanchao zhi Laiwang jiqi Xiangguan Wenti" (The Interactions Between Kingdom Ma'bar and the Yuan Dynasty and Some Related Issues), *Lanzhou Dauxue Xuebao* (Journal of Lanzhou University, Social Science) 33, no. 2 (March 2005): 20–25. "Bohali" might be a transliteration of Abu Ali.
50. Gray and Bell, "Early Notices," 430, 432.
51. Gray and Bell, "Early Notices," 473.
52. Gray and Bell, "Early Notices," 478, 485; Mansel Longworth Dames, *The Book of Duarte Barbosa: An Account of the Countries Bordering on the Indian Ocean and Their Inhabitants* (New Delhi: Asian Educational Services, 1989), 2:106.

12. DRAGON'S SPITTLE

1. Albert Gray and H. C. P. Bell, "Early Notices of the Maldives," in François Pyrard, *The Voyage of François Pyrard of Laval to the East Indies, the Maldives, the Moluccas and Brazil*, ed. Albert Gray and H. C. P. Bell (Cambridge: Cambridge University Press, 2011), 3:440. Makdashau was on the Zanzibar coast; Ibn Battuta made one visit there.
2. Ma Huan, *Ming Chaoben Yingya Shenglan Jiaozhu* 明钞本瀛涯胜览校注 (Overall Survey of the Ocean Shores: Annotation of a Ming Manuscript), ed. Wan Ming (Beijing: Haiyangchubanshe, 2005), 75; Ma Huan, *Ying-yai sheng-lan: "The Overall Survey of the Ocean's Shores," [1433]; translated from the Chinese text edited by Feng Ch'eng-chün with introduction, notes, and appendices by J. V. G. Mills* (London: Hakluyt Society, 1970), 149–50.
3. Gong Zhen, *Xiyang Fanguo Zhi* 西洋番国志 (Record of Foreign Kingdoms in the Western Ocean), ed. Xiang Da (Beijing: Zhonghua Shuju, 2000), 33.
4. Xavier Romero-Frias, *The Maldive Islanders—A Study of the Popular Culture of an Ancient Ocean Kingdom* (Barcelona: Nova Ethnographia Indica, 1999), 158.
5. Gray and Bell, "Early Notices," 428–29. For medieval records of ambergris in the Indian Ocean, see Kentaro Yamada, "A Short History of Ambergris by the Arabs and Chinese in the Indian Ocean (I)," *Report of the Institute of World Economics* 8 (1955): 1–26.
6. Feilang (Gabriel Ferrand), *Kunlun ji Nanhai Gudai Hangxingkao* 昆仑及南海古代航行考 (Le K'ouen-Louen et les anciennes navigations interocéaniques dans les Mers du Sud), trans. Feng Chengjun (Beijing: Zhonghua Shuju, 1957), 1:161.
7. Mansel Longworth Dames, *The Book of Duarte Barbosa: An Account of the Countries Bordering on the Indian Ocean and Their Inhabitants* (New Delhi: Asian Educational Services, 1989), 2:106.
8. Dames, *The Book of Duarte Barbosa*, 2:106–7; Roderich Ptak, "The Maldives and Laccadive Islands (*liu-shan* 溜山) in Ming Records," *Journal of the American Oriental Society* 107, no. 4 (1987): 687n78.
9. Pyrard, *The Voyage of François Pyrard*, 3:359, 2:229. The term *gomen* means cow dung, and ambergris does indeed look like that at first sight, though the term *meccuare* means something like "very sweet smelling" (see 2: 229n1).
10. Xavier Romero-Frias, *Folk Tales of the Maldives* (Copenhagen: NIAS Press, 2012), 287–88. Shipwrecks and their belongings were seen as the property of local chiefs,

12. DRAGON'S SPITTLE

a widespread custom in maritime Asia, such as Gaolangfu 高郎阜 (Colombo) in Sri Lanka, as recorded by Wang Dayuan. Wang Dayuan, *Daoyi Zhilue Jiaoshi* 岛夷志略校释 (Brief Record of the Island Barbarians), ed. Su Jiqing (Beijing: Zhonghua Shuju, 1981), 270.

11. Pyrard, *The Voyage of François Pyrard*, 1:229-30.
12. Ernest J. Parry, *Parry's Cyclopedia of Perfumery; A Handbook on The Raw Materials Used by The Perfumer, Their Origin, Properties, Characters and Analysis; And on Other Subjects of Theoretical and Scientific Interest to The User of Perfume Materials, and to Those Who Have to Examine and Value Such Materials* (London: J. & A. Churchill, 1925), 36-7; Yamada, "A Short History I," 18-25; T. M. Srinivasan, "Ambergris in Perfumery in the Past and Present Indian Context and the Western World," *Indian Journal of History of Sciences* 50, no. 2 (2015): 313-14.
13. Garcia da Orta, *Coloquios dos simples e drogas da India* (Lisbon: Imprensa Nacional, 1891), 46. For the English translation, see Garcia da Orta, *Colloquies on the Simples and Drugs of India*, trans. Clements Markham (London: H. Sotheran and Co., 1913), 21.
14. Ai Rulue (Giulio Aleni), *Zhifang Waiji Jiaoshi* 职方外纪校释 (Chronicle of Foreign Lands), ed. Xie Fang (Beijing: Zhonghua Shuju, 2000), 108; Kentaro Yamada, "A Short History of Ambergris by the Arabs and Chinese in the Indian Ocean (II)," *Report of the Institute of World Economics* 11 (1956): 2-32. Regarded as the "Confucius from the West" (Xilai Kongzi 西来孔子) by Chinese literati, Giulio Aleni through his book introduced Western knowledge about the world to China.
15. Ai Rulue, *Zhifang Waiji*, 154; Yamada, "A Short History II," 20
16. Karl H. Dannenfeldt, "Ambergris: The Search for Its Origin," *Isis* 73, no. 3 (1982): 382.
17. P. K. Gode, "History of Ambergris in India Between About A.D. 700 and 1900," *Chymia* 2 (1949): 51-56; Srinivasan, "Ambergris in Perfumery," 306-23. Albert Gray also provides a relatively comprehensive literature review of ambergris. See Pyrard, *The Voyage of François Pyrard*, 1:229-30n1; H. Elliot and J. Dowson, *The History of India, as Told by Its Own Historians: The Muhammadan Period* (London: Cambridge University Press, 2013), 1:1-11; Suleiman, *Ancient Accounts of Indian and China by Two Mohammedan Travelers Who Went to Those Parts in the 9th Century*, trans. Eusebius Rennaudot (London: 1733), 1:10. Quite a few iron items were found in *Nanhai I*, the Southern Song ship sailing for Southeast Asia or the Indian Ocean.
18. S. M. H. Nainar, *Arab Geographers Knowledge of South Indian up to the 14th Century A.D.* (Madras: University of Madras, 1942): 187-90; Srinivasan, "Ambergris in Perfumery," 309.
19. Gray and Bell, "Early Notices," 432.
20. Marco Polo, *The Travels of Marco Polo (The Venetian)* (New York: Liveright, 1953), 310.
21. Polo, *The Travels*, 310.
22. Dames, *The Book of Duarte Barbosa*, 1:63.
23. Polo, *The Travels*, 315-16.
24. J. Tavernier and V. Ball, *Travels in India* (n.p., 1889), 2:138.
25. Long Cunni, "Miren de Gongli: Longxianxiang" (An Attractive Tributary Gift: Ambergris), in *Zheng He Xia Xiyang Guoji Xueshuyantaohui Lunwenji* (A

Collection of Papers from the International Conference on Zheng He's Sailing to the Western Ocean), ed. Chen Xinxiong and Chen Yunü (Taipei: Daoxiang Chubanshe, 2003), 52–4.
26. Yamada, "A Short History I," 25.
27. John Crawfurd, *A Descriptive Dictionary of the Indian Islands and Adjacent Countries* (Cambridge: Cambridge University Press, 2012), 11; Yamada, "A Short History I," 3.
28. Gode, "History of Ambergris," 51; Yamada, "A Short History I," 4,5; Ma, *Ming Chaoben*, 77.
29. Yamada, "A Short History I," 6.
30. Paul Wheatley, "Geographical Notes on Some Commodities Involved in Sung Maritime Trade," *Journal of the Malayan Branch of the Royal Asiatic Society* 32, no. 2 (1959): 45–139; Edward H. Schafer, *The Golden Peaches of Samarkand: A Study of T'ang Exotics* (San Francisco: Hauraki Publishing, 2014), 201–24; Yamada, "A Short History I," 7–8.
31. Liu Yu, *Xishi Ji* 西使记 (The Ambassador to the West), in *Congshu Jicheng Chubian* (Comprehensive Collection of Rare Book Series, I), ed. Wang Yunwu (Shanghai: Shangwuchubanshe, 1936), 4; Yamada, "A Short History I," 11.
32. E. Bretschneider, *Medieval Researches from Eastern Asiatic Sources: Fragments Towards the Knowledge of the Geography and History of Central and Western Asia from the 13th to the 17th Century* (London: K. Paul, Trench, Trübner & Co., 1910), 1:152n409; Friedrich Hirth and W. W. Rockhill, trans. & eds., *Chau Ju-kua: His Work on the Chinese and Arab Trade in the Twelfth and Thirteenth Centuries, Rntitled Chu-fan-chï* (St. Petersburg: Imperial Academy of Sciences, 1911), 237, note; Yamada, "A Short History I," 12.
33. Fei Xin, *Xingcha Shenglan Jiaozhu* 星槎胜览校注 (Overall Survey of the Star Raft: An Annotation), ed. Feng Chengjun (Beijing: Huawen Chubanshe, 2019), 27–58; Yamada, "A Short History I," 12.
34. Yamada, "A Short History I," 6.
35. Steven John Rowland, Paul Andrew Sutton, and Timothy D. J. Knowles, "The Age of Ambergris," *Natural Product Research* 33, no. 21 (2019): 3135.
36. Schafer, *The Golden Peaches*, 223, 225.
37. Bai Juyi, "You Wuzhensi Shi" (A Poem on the Visit to the Wushen Monastery), *Baishi Changqi Ji* 白氏长庆集 (Collections of Bai Juyi's Poems) (Shanghai: Shanghai Gujichubanshe, 1994), *juan* 6, 67; Yamada, "A Short History I," 7.
38. Schafer, *The Golden Peaches*, 224.
39. Li Fang, *Taiping Guangji* 太平广记 (Extensive Records of the Taiping Era) (Beijing: Zhonghua Shuju, 1961), vol. 5, *juan* 237, 1827.
40. Yamada, "A Short History I," 7.
41. Su Shi, *Su Shi Shiji* 苏轼诗集 (A Collection of Poems by Su Shi) (Beijing: Zhonghua Shuju, 1992), 7:2316–17; Yamada, "A Short History II," 3.
42. Quoted in Yamada, "A Short History II," 3.
43. Duan Chengshi, *Youyang Zazu* 酉阳杂组 (Miscellaneous Writings in Youyang), ed. Xu Yimin and Xu Heng (Beijing: Zhonghua Shuju, 2018), 1:112; Schafer, *The Golden Peaches*, 224. For Chinese records of ambergris, see Yamada, "A Short History II."

12. DRAGON'S SPITTLE

44. *Xin Tangshu* 新唐书 (New History of the Tang Dynasty) (Beijing: Zhonghua Shuju, 1975), *juan* 221, 6262.
45. Schafer, *The Golden Peaches*, 222.
46. Chen Jing, *Chenshi Xinagpu* 陈氏香谱 (The Chen's Catalog of Incenses), in *Xiangpu Waisiizhong* (Guide of the Xiang and Four Others), ed. Tian Yuan (Shanghai: Shanghai Shudian), 2018, 72–73; Yamada, "A Short History II," 5. *Wulingzhi*, the dried dung of the complex-toothed flying squirrel, was a traditional Chinese medicine. *Baiyaojian* was another traditional Chinese medicine, a fermented mixture of Chinese gall and tea.
47. Ma, *Ming Chaoben*, 100–102; *Ying-yai sheng-lan*, 174–72n7, 176.
48. Zhou Qufei, *Lingwai Daida Jiaozhu* 岭外代答校注 (Answers for Questions Concerning Out of Range), ed. Yang Wuquan (Beijing: Zhonghua Shuju, 1999), 266; Yamada, "A Short History II," 5. The *Lingwai Daida* contains one category of the *xiang* 香, whereas *longxian* is placed under another of the "treasured goods" (*baohuo* 宝货).
49. Zhao Rukuo, *Zhufan Zhi Jiaoshi* 诸蕃志校释 (A Record of Barbarians), ed. Yang Bowen (Beijing: Zhonghua Shuju, 2000), 212, 105; Yamada, "A Short History II," 8–9.
50. Zhang Shinan, *Huanyou Jiwen* 宦游纪闻 (A Record of What's Heard on Official Travel), ed. Zhang Maopeng (Beijing: Zhonghua Shuju, 1981), 61–62; Yamada, "A Short History II," 3–6.
51. Wang, *Daoyi Zhilue*, 43–44; Yamada, "A Short History II," 10–11. *Qielanmu*, also called *qinan* 奇楠, refers to the best type of aloe wood; *meihua nao* refers to the so-called *Longnaoxiang* (camphor), since its white color looks just like that of the plum flower, and the *chensu* wood was another type of aloe wood.
52. *The Book of the Thousand and One Nights, Rendered into English from the Literal and Complete French Translation of Dr. J. C. Mardrus by Powys Mathers* (London: Routledge & Kegan Paul, 1986), 2:219–23.
53. *The Book of the Thousand and One Nights*, 220.
54. *The Book of the Thousand and One Nights*, 223.
55. Garcia de Orta, *Coloquios dos*, 49; *Colloquies on the Simples*, 24; Yamada, "A Short History II," 17–18.
56. Jan Huygen van Linschoten, William Phillip, Pieter Anton Tiele, and Arthur Coke Barnell, *The Voyage of John Huyghen Van Linschoten to the East Indies: From the Old English Translation of 1598* (London: Hakluyt Society, 1885), 2:93; Yamada, "A Short History II," 18.
57. Fei, *Xingcha Shenglan*, 43; Xiang Da,ed, *Zheng He Hanghai Tu* (The Zheng He Nautical Chart) (Beijing: Zhonghua Shuju, 2000), 55.
58. Fei, *Xingcha Shenglan*, 43; Fei Xin, *Hsing-ch'a-sheng-lan: The Overall Survey of the Star Raft*, trans. J. V. Mills, ed. Roderich Ptak (Wiesbaden: Harrassowitz, 1996), 60–61; Yamada, "A Short History II," 11. In the same passage, the Chinese term *dumuzhou* meaning a canoe is given, and it might be one of the earliest uses of this term, if not of Fei's own coining.
59. Fei, *Xingcha Shenglan*, 44 and 46; Yamada, "A Short History II," 12–13; Wang, *Daoyi Zhilue*, 44–45n1.
60. Wang, *Daoyi Zhilue*, 44–45n1.

12. DRAGON'S SPITTLE

61. Yamada, "A Short History II," 14–19.
62. Dames, *The Book of Duarte Barbosa*, 2:181.
63. Huang Xingzeng, *Xiyang Chaogong Dianlu Jiaozhu* 西洋朝贡典录校注 (Record of Tributes from the Western Ocean), ed. Xie Fang (Beijing: Zhonghua Shuju, 2000), 77.
64. Ptak, "The Maldives," 687n77.
65. Huang, *Xiyang*, 77; Ptak, "The Maldives," 687, 687n77. Pelliot argues that Huang's book certainly contains some passages originally written by Ma Huan, but which were gradually missed out in the process of hand copying and printing. Boxihe (Paul Eugène Pelliot), *Zheng He Xia Xiyang Kao* (Les grands voyages maritimes chinois au début du 15ème siècle), trans. Feng Chenjun (Beijing: Zhonghua Shuju, 2003), 128–29. *Dou* is a Chinese container and a volume unit that roughly speaking is equivalent to more than a dozen pounds, *liang* was a Chinese weight unit, equaling one sixteenth of a *jin*, about one ounce (31 g).
66. Yan Congjian, *Shuyu Zhouzi Lu* 殊域周咨录 (Comprehensive Survey and Record of Foreign Territories), ed. Yu Sili (Beijing: Zhonghua Shuju, 1993), 311.
67. Schafer, *The Golden Peaches*, 201–2.
68. Hong Chu, *Xiangpu* 香谱 (Guide of the Xiang), in Hong Chu et al., *Xiangpu Waisizhong* (Guide of the Xiang and Four Others), ed. Tian Yuan (Shanghai: Shanghai Shudian, 2018), 6–39.
69. Chen, *Chenshi Xinagpu*, 53–227.
70. Chen, *Chenshi Xinagpu*, 80 and 168; Yang Zhishui, "Longxian Zhenpin yu Longxian Xiangpin (Authentic Ambergris and Catalogues of Ambergris Incenses)," *Gushiwen Mingwu Xinzheng* (New Explorations of Names and Objects in Ancient Poems and Essays) (Beijing: Gugong Chubanshe, 2013), 1:120–21.
71. Chen, *Chenshi Xiangpu*, 117–26; Luo Meng, "Luetan Gudai Minggui Xianyao—Longxian de Chuanru" (A Sketchy Discussion on the Spread of Ambergris, an Ancient Precious Perfume-Medicine), *Haijiaoshi Yanjiu* (Journal of Maritime History Studies) 2 (1986): 101; Yang, "Longxian Zhenpin," 120, 122–25.
72. Xu Song, *Song Huiyao Jigao* 宋会要辑稿 (An Extracted Draft of the Song Government Manuscript Compendium), "fanyi 7" (Beijing: Guoli Beiping Tushuguan, 1936), 32; Yamada, "A Short History II," 4.
73. *Song Shi* 宋史 (History of the Song Dynasty) (Beijing: Zhonghua Shuju, 1977), juan 119, 2814.
74. Zhao Yanwei, *Yunlu Manchao* 云麓漫钞 (Loose Notes of the Cloud-Covered Foothill), ed. Fu Genqing (Beijing: Zhonghua Shuju, 1996), 88. In 1025 the Chola kingdom, based in South India, launched a maritime expedition against Srivijaya, a commercial center in Sumatra, and thus exerted a heavy influence on the latter. See Hermann Kulke, K. Kesavapany, and Vijay Sakhuja, eds. *Nagapattinam to Suvarnadwipa: Reflections on Chola Naval Expeditions to Southeast Asia* (Singapore: Institute of Southeast Asian, 2009).
75. Fujian Quanzhou Haiwajiaotongshi Bowuguan, *Quanzhouwan Songdai Haichuan Fajue yu Yanjiu Xiudingban* (A Report on the Excavation of the Song Boat in Quanzhou Bay), 26–31.
76. Xu, *Song Huiyao*, "zhiguan 44," 15, 21.
77. Cai Tao, *Tieweishan Congtan* 铁围山丛谈 (Miscellaneous Notes in Mount Iron) (Beijing: Zhonghuashuju, 1983), juan 2, 47; Yamada, "A Short History II," 2.

12. DRAGON'S SPITTLE

78. Ye Shaoweng, *Sichao Wenjian Lu* 四朝闻见录 (Record of Four Reigns), ed. Shang Cheng (Shanghai: Shanghai Gujichubanshe, 2012), *juan* 2, 60; Yang, "Longxian Zhenpin," 119.
79. Cai, *Tieweishan*, 97. One *min* is 1,000 coins, optimally equal to one silver tael.
80. Schafer, *The Golden Peaches*, 209.
81. Zhou Mi, *Wulin Jiushi* 武林旧事 (Old Stories of Hangzhou) (Hangzhou: Zhejiang Renmin Chubanshe, 1984), 125.
82. Yang, "Longxian Zhenpin," 119. Here the price was extraordinarily high, and I suspect that the character *wan* (ten thousand) was inserted by mistake.
83. *Yuan Shi* 元史 (History of the Yuan Dynasty) (Beijing: Zhonghua Shuju, 1976), *juan* 76, 1881.
84. *Ming Taizong Shilu* (Veritable Records of Emperor Taizu), *juan* 237, 1541, in *Ming Shilu* (Veritable Records of the Ming Dynasty), ed. Huang Zhangjian (Taipei: Institute of History and Philology, Academic Sinica, 1984); *Ming Shi* 明史 (History of the Ming Dynasty) (Beijing: Zhonghua Shuju, 1974), *juan* 325, 8244; *juan* 326, 8441, 8449, and 8451. For their locations, see Ma, *Ying-yai sheng-lan*, "Introduction," 20.
85. Luo Maodeng, *Sanbao Taijian Xiyangji Tongsu Yanyi* 三宝太监西洋记通俗演义 (Romance of Eunuch Sanbao's Journey to the Western Ocean), ed. Lu Shulun and Zhu Shaohua (Shanghai: Shanghai Gujichubanshe, 1982)2:1274–5, 1279, 1280–81; Long, "Miren de Gongli," 51. Jicini refers to Ghazni, located in central Afghanistan. Zhou, *Lingwai Daida*, 100, 104–5n23; Zhao, *Zhufan Zhi*, 90 and 112.
86. Shen Defu, *Wangli Yehuo Bian* 万历野获编 (Miscellaneous Notes of Wanli), ed. Li Xin (Beijing: Wenhuayishu Chubanshe, 1998), 576.
87. *Ming Shi*, *juan* 307, 7895; *juan* 17, 231; *juan* 307, 7896.
88. Luo, "Luetan Gudai," 101.
89. Li Shizhen, *Bencao Gangmu* 本草纲目 (Compendium of Materia Medica), ed. Chen Guiting (Beijing: Zhongyiguji Chubanshe, 1994), 1001.
90. Zhao Xuemin, *Bencao Gangmu Shiyi* 本草纲目拾遗 (Supplement to Compendium of Materia Medica) (Beijing: Renmin Weisheng Chubanshe, 1983), 416; Luo, "Luetan Gudai," 101.
91. Zhao, *Bencao*, 416.
92. *Ming Shi*, *juan* 307, 7896, 7902; Shen, *Wanli*, 582–83.
93. Shen, *Wanli*, 583.
94. *Ming Shizong Shilu* (Veritable Records of Emperor Shizong), *juan* 375, *Ming Shilu*, 9:9141.
95. *Ming Shizong Shilu*, *juan* 413, *Ming Shilu*, 10:9277. For Jiajing's efforts to procurement of ambergris, see Jin Guoping and Wu Zhiliang, *Zaoqi Aomen Shilun* (On the Early History of Macao) (Guangzhou: Guangdong Renminchubanshe, 2007), 44–53, 117–38; *Dongxi Wangyang* (Em busca de história[s] de Macau apagada[s] pelo tempo) (Macao: Aomen Chengrenjiaoyuxueyuan, 2002), 77–154; *Jinghai Piaomiao* (Historia[s] de Macau: Ficção e realidade) (Macao: Aomen Chengrenjiaoyuxueyuan, 2001), 38–59.
96. *Ming Shizong Shilu*, *juan* 422, *Ming Shilu*, 10:9313.
97. Shen, *Wanli*, 787.
98. *Ming Shizong Shilu*, *juan* 441 in *Ming Shilu* 10:9369; *juan* 449, in *Ming Shilu*, 10:9390.

99. *Ming Shizong Shilu, juan* 454, in *Ming Shilu*, 10:9403.
100. *Ming Shizong Shilu, juan* 487, in *Ming Shilu*, 10:9508.
101. *Ming Shizong Shili, juan* 512, in *Ming Shilu*, 10:9583.
102. Yan, *Shuyu Zhouzi Lu*, 311.
103. *Ming Shizong Shilu, juan* 512, in *Ming Shilu*, 10:9583; *Ming Shizong Shilu, juan* 520, in *Ming Shilu*, 10:9609, 9611, 9619; *Ming Shizong Shilu, juan* 543, in *Ming Shilu*, 10:9675.
104. *Ming Shizong Shilu, juan* 543, in *Ming Shilu*, 10:9675.
105. *Ming Shi, juan* 194, 5151; *juan* 202, 5329; *juan* 307, 7902; *Ming Shizong Shilu, juan* 544, in *Ming Shilu*, "Jiaokanji," 16:16,401.
106. *Ming Muzong Shilu* (Veritable Records of Emperor Muzong), *juan* 1, in *Ming Shilu*, 10:9763–64.
107. Zhang Xie, *Dongxiyang Kao* 东西洋考 (An Examination of the Eastern and Western Oceans), ed. Xie Fang (Beijing: Zhonghua Shuju, 2000),141–46.
108. *Ming Shenzong Shilu* (Veritable Records of Emperor Shenzong), *juan* 295, in *Ming Shilu*, 12:11,577; *juan* 323, in *Ming Shilu*, 12:11,738; *juan* 339, in *Ming Shilu*, 12:11,775; juan 499, in *Ming Shilu*, 13:12,566.
109. *Qingshi Gao* 清史稿 (Draft History of the Qing Dynasty) (Beijing: Zhonghua Shuju, 1977), *juan* 528, 14,690; juan 528, 14,694 and 14,696.
110. Wan Xiufeng, "Gongting Cangxiang III: Longxianxiang" (Incenses Stored in the Inner Court III: Ambergris), *Zijincheng* (The Forbidden City) 2 (2013): 128–35.
111. *Ming Shi, juan* 82, 1993–94.
112. *Ming Huidian* 明会典 (The Law Code of the Ming Dynasty) (Beijing: Zhonghua Shuju, 1989), 1118; *Ming Shi, juan* 82, 1994.
113. For ambergris and the Portuguese occupation of Macau, see Liang Jiabin, *Mingshigao Folangjizhuan Koazheng* (An Empirical Study of Chapter *Folangji* in *Draft History of the Ming Dynasty*), in *Mingdai Guoji Guanzi* (International Relationships in the Ming Period), ed. Bao Zunpeng (Taipei: Xuesheng Shuju, 1968), 7–60; Dai Yixuan, *Mingshi Folangjizhuan Jianzheng* (Annotations on Chapter Folangji in *History of the Ming Dynasty*) (Beijing: Zhongguo Shehuikexuechubanshe, 1984); Chen Yuying, "Mingdai Gongbo Yanjiu" (A Study of the Tributary Ships in the Ming Dynasty), in *Mingshi Yanjiu Luncong* (Papers on the Studies of the Ming History), ed. Wu Zhihe (Taipei: Dalichubanshe, 1984): 343–98; Jin and Wu, *Jinghai Piaomiao, Dongxi Wangyang* and *Zaoqi Aomen*.
114. *Ming Shizong Shilu, juan* 441, in *Ming Shilu*, 10:9369.
115. Gu Yanwu, *Tianxia Junguo Libing Shu* 天下郡国利病书 (The Advantages and Disadvantages of the Provinces and Prefectures of the Empire), in *Gu Yanwu Quanji* (Comprehensive Works of Gu Yanwu) (Shanghai: Shanghai Gujichubanshe, 2012), 17:3443; Jin and Wu, *Zaoqi Aomen*, 46–47. "Midishan" might refer to Aceh, because the *Guangdong Tongzhi* (Provincial Gazetteer of Guangdong) from which Zhang Xie cited this, put it under "Yaqi" 哑齐. Zhang, *Dongxiyang*, 248; Jin and Wu, *Zaoqi Aomen*, 46n5.
116. Gu, *Tianxia Junguo*, 3827.
117. *Gangji* refers to those merchants who were assigned by the Guangdong government to deal with foreign trade and foreign merchants, indeed a precedent of the Hong merchants in the Canton System before the Opium War (1839–1842).
118. Zhang, *Dongxiyang*, 248: Jin and Wu, *Zaoqi Aomen*, 48.

13. LAKA WOOD AND FRANKINCENSE

119. Zhang, *Dongxiyang*, 248.
120. Garcia da Orta, *Coloquios*, 51–52; *Colloquies on the Simples*, 26–27; Jin and Wu, *Zaoqi Aomen*, 48.
121. Jin and Wu, *Zaoqi Aomen*, 46, 48; Jin and Wu, *Jinghai Piaomiao*, 43.
122. Jin and Wu, *Zaoqi Aomen*, 49; Rebecca Catz, *Cartas de Fernão Mendes Pinto e outros documentos* (Lisbon: Editorial Presença/Biblioteca Nacional, 1983), 71.
123. Charles R. Boxer, *South China in the Sixteenth Century: Being the Narratives of Galeote Pereira, Fr. Gaspar da Cruz, O.P., Fr. Martin de Rada, O.E.S.A. (1550–1575)* (Bangkok: Orchid Press, 2004), 169.
124. Zhao, *Benchao*, 416, 958.
125. Boxer, *South China*, 168–70; Jin and Wu, *Zaoqi Aomen*, 49–51. Here the "him" refers to the Chinese official and "amber" refers to ambergris. In his translation, He Gaoji unfortunately mistook ambergris for amber (*hupo* 琥珀). He Gaoji, trans., *Shiliu Shiji Zhongguo Nanbu Xinji* (South China in the Sixteenth Century) (Beijing: Zhonghua Shuju, 1990), 115–17.
126. Boxer, *South China*, 170.
127. Liang, *Mingshigao*, 37–39.
128. Jin and Wu, *Zaoqi Aomen*, 123–28; Liang, *Mingshigao*, 39.

13. LAKA WOOD AND FRANKINCENSE

1. Edward H. Schafer, *The Golden Peaches of Samarkand: A Study of T'ang Exotics* (San Francisco: Hauraki Publishing, 2014), 212.
2. Ma Huan, *Ming Chaoben Yingya Shenglan Jiaozhu* 明钞本瀛涯胜览校注 (Overall Survey of the Ocean Shores: Annotation of a Ming Manuscript), ed. Wan Ming (Beijing: Haiyangchubanshe, 2005), 74; Ma Huan, *Ying-yai sheng-lan: "The Overall Survey of the Ocean's Shores," [1433]; translated from the Chinese text edited by Feng Ch'eng-chün with introduction, notes, and appendices by J. V. G. Mills* (London: Hakluyt Society, 1970), 149; Gong Zhen, *Xiyang Fanguo Zhi* 西洋番国志 (Record of Foreign Kingdoms in the Western Ocean), ed. Xiang Da (Beijing: Zhonghua Shuju, 2000), 33.
3. Paul Wheatley, "Geographical Notes on Some Commodities Involved in Sung Maritime Trade," *Journal of the Malayan Branch of the Royal Asiatic Society* 32, no. 2 (1959): 118–19.
4. Wang Dayuan, *Daoyi Zhilue Jiaoshi* 岛夷志略校释 (Brief Record of the Island Barbarians), ed. Su Jiqing (Beijing: Zhonghua Shuju, 1981), 79, 89, 99, 120, 141, 237, 261.
5. Ma, *Ming Chaoben*, 10, 29, 35, 50, 51; Ma, *Ying-yai sheng-lan* 81, 100, 106, 107, 113, 124. The *chenxiang* has remained a much sought-after luxurious commodity in China and Southeast Asia.
6. Fujian Quanzhou Haiwajiaotongshi Bowuguan, ed., *Quanzhouwan Songdai Haichuan Fajue yu Yanjiu Xiudingban* (A Report on the Excavation of the Song Boat in Quanzhou Bay) (Beijing: Haiyang Chubanshe, 2017), 26–31.
7. Albert Gray and H. C. P. Bell, "Early Notices of the Maldives," in François Pyrard, *The Voyage of François Pyrard of Laval to the East Indies, the Maldives, the Moluccas and Brazil*, ed. Albert Gray and H. C. P. Bell (Cambridge: Cambridge University Press, 2011), 3:432.

13. LAKA WOOD AND FRANKINCENSE

8. Fei Xin, *Xingcha Shenglan Jiaozhu* 星槎胜览校注 (Overall Survey of the Star Raft: An Annotation), ed. Feng Chengjun (Beijing: Huawen Chubanshe, 2019), 108; Fei Xin, *Hsing-ch'a-sheng-lan: The Overall Survey of the Star Raft*, trans. J. V. Mills, ed. Roderich Ptak (Wiesbaden: Harrassowitz, 1996), 103.
9. Vían Beek, "Frankincense and Myrrh in Ancient South Arabia," *Journal of American Oriental Society* 78, no. 3 (1958): 141–44.
10. Ding Wei, *Tianxiang Zhuan* 天香传 (Biography of the Celestial Xiang), in Hong Chu et al., *XiangpuWaisizhong* (Guide of the Xiang [and Four Others]), ed. Tian Yuan (Shanghai: Shanghai Shudian, 2018), 5.
11. Beek, "Frankincense and Myrrh," 142–43.
12. Wang, *Daoyi Zhilue*, 325.
13. Ma, *Ming Chaoben*, 77; Ma, *Ying-yai sheng-lan*, 152–53.
14. Ma, *Ming Chaoben*, 76; Ma, *Ying-yai sheng-lan*, 152.
15. Chen Jing, *Chenshi Xiangpu* 陈氏香谱 (The Chen Guide to the Xiang), in *Xiangpu Waisizhong*, 63; Beek, "Frankincense and Myrrh," 142.
16. Chen, *Chenshi Xiangpu*, 63.
17. Zhang Xie, *Dongxiyang Kao* 东西洋考 (An Examination of the Eastern and Western Oceans), ed. Xie Fang (Beijing: Zhonghua Shuju, 2000), 132.
18. Zhang, *Dongxiyang*, 132, 133.

14. A RUINED BUDDHIST PAST

1. Hassan Ahmed Maniku, "Conversion of Maldives to Islam," *Journal of the Royal Asiatic Society Sri Lanka Branch* 31 (1986–87): 74.
2. R. Michael Feener, "Maldives," *The Encyclopedia of Islam Three*, ed. Kate Fleet et al. (Leiden: Brill, 2021), 89.
3. Evidence supporting the practice of Hinduism in the Maldives primarily comes from linguistic studies, and the only archaeological findings are two *lingas*. Andrew D. W. Forbes, "The Pre-Islamic Archaeology of the Maldive Islands," *Bulletin de l'École française d'Extrême-Orient* 76 (1987): 285–86.
4. Albert Gray and H. C. P. Bell, "Early Notices of the Maldives," in François Pyrard, *The Voyage of François Pyrard of Laval to the East Indies, the Maldives, the Moluccas and Brazil*, ed. Albert Gray and H. C. P. Bell (Cambridge: Cambridge University Press, 2011), 3:446.
5. Pyrard, *The Voyage of François Pyrard*, 1:123–24n2.
6. Email from R. Michael Feener, June 1, 2018.
7. Clarence Maloney, *People of the Maldive Islands* (Bombay: Oriental Longman, 1980), 85–86.
8. Maloney, *People*, 84–85.
9. Maloney, *People*, 86.
10. For the ruined Buddhist past in the Maldives, see Andrew D. W. Forbes, "The Mosque in the Maldive Islands: A Preliminary Historical Survey," *Archipel* 26 (1983): 43–74; Jost Gippert, "A Glimpse into the Buddhist Past of the Maldives. II. Two Sanskrit Inscriptions," *Wiener Zeitschrift für die Kunde Südasiens* 55 (2014): 111–44.

14. A RUINED BUDDHIST PAST

11. H. C. P. Bell, *The Maldive Islands: Monograph on the History, Archaeology and Epigraph* (Colombo: Ceylon Government Press, 1940), 1 and 4; Bethia N. Bell and Heather M. Bell, *H. C. P. Bell: Archaeologist of Ceylon and the Maldives* (London: Archetype Publications, 1993), 233.
12. Bell and Bell, *H. C. P. Bell*, 224, 234. For Buddhist findings in this expedition, see also Bell, *The Maldive Islands*.
13. Maloney, *People*, 75, 83.
14. Maloney, *People*, 30–47; quotes at 51 and 38–39.
15. Forbes, "Pre-Islamic Archaeology," 286. The relationship between the *linga* and Buddhist stupas found on the island is still unknown, and so is the fate of the two photographs, as far as I can tell.
16. Forbes, "Pre-Islamic Archaeology," 288.
17. Andrew D. W. Forbes, "Southern Arabia and the Islamicisation of the Central Indian Ocean Archipelagoes," *Archipel* 21 (1981): 59; Forbes, "Pre-Islamic Archaeology," 283–88.
18. Forbes, "The Pre-Islamic Archaeology," 284. Toḍḍū is 36 miles (58 km) west of Male. Very interestingly, a coral relic casket (probably a miniature stupa) discovered in this expedition contained one coin identified as a Roman Republican *denarius* of Caius Vibius Pansa, minted in Rome around 90 BCE. This Roman coin, however, thereafter went missing. Andrew D. W. Forbes, "A Roman Republican Denarius of c. 90 B.C., from the Maldive Islands, Indian Ocean," *Archipel* 28 (1984): 53–60; Forbes, "Pre-Islamic Archaeology," 284.
19. Forbes, "A Roman Republican Denarius," 56.
20. Forbes, "Pre-Islamic Archaeology," 286–87. Haddhunmathi Atoll forms the southern limit of Central Maldives, and Gaadhoo is 162 miles (260 km) south of Male.
21. Forbes, "Pre-Islamic Archaeology," 287. Suvadiva Atoll, the southernmost atoll in the Maldives, is about 250 miles (400 km) south of Male.
22. Mikkelsen, "Archaeological Excavations," 21–22. The monastery was partially used as a cemetery from the tenth to the late twelfth century.
23. Jost Gippert, "A Glimpse into the Buddhist Past of the Maldives. I. An Early Prakrit Inscription," *Wiener Zeitschrift für die Kunde Südasiens* 48 (2004): 81–109; "A Glimpse II," 111–44; "Sanskrit as a Medium of Maldivian Buddhism," in *Indische Kultur im Kontext: Rituale, Texte und Ideen aus Indien und der Welt—Festschrift für Klaus Mylius*, ed. Lars Gohler (Wiesbaden: Harrassowitz 2005), 213–20, 487–88. The stone is 22 × 7.5 × 8.3 inches (56 × 19 × 21 cm) in size.
24. Gippert, "A Glimpse II," 113–14, 133–34; Gippert, "Sanskrit as a Medium," 218.
25. Bell, *The Maldive Islands*, 13; Feener, "Maldives," 89.
26. Bell, *The Maldive Islands*, 16; Maloney, *People*, 29–31. The Koimalā legend has many versions, and the following is based on Maloney's record.
27. Maloney, *People*, 29–31.
28. Clarence Maloney, "The Maldives: New Stresses in an Old Nation," *Asian Survey* 16, no. 7 (July 1976): 655; Maloney, *People*, 98–100; Feener, "Maldives," 92.
29. The year 1147–48 has been suggested rather than 1153, and the saint was certainly thought to have come from Ceylon instead of Maghreb (Morocco). Hassan Ahmed Maniku, "Conversion of Maldives to Islam," *Journal of the Royal Asiatic*

14. A RUINED BUDDHIST PAST

Society Sri Lanka Branch 31 (1986–87): 72–81; Jost Gippert, "Early New Persian as a Medium of Spreading Islam," in *Persian Origins: Early Judaeo-Persian and the Emergence of New Persian*, ed. Ludwig Paul (Wiesbaden: Harrassowitz, 2003), 31–47.
30. Gray & Bell, "Early Notices," 446–8.
31. MAHS-MDV-COL-001-O-0024, https://maritimeasiaheritage.cseas.kyoto-u.ac.jp/manuscript-viewer/waqf-endowment.
32. Ma Huan, *Ming Chaoben Yingya Shenglan Jiaozhu* 明钞本瀛涯胜览校注 (Overall Survey of the Ocean Shores: Annotation of a Ming Manuscript), ed. Wan Ming (Beijing: Haiyangchubanshe, 2005), 74; Ma Huan, *Ying-yai sheng-lan: "The Overall Survey of the Ocean's Shores,"* [1433]; translated from the Chinese text edited by Feng Ch'eng-chün with introduction, notes, and appendices by J. V. G. Mills (London: Hakluyt Society, 1970), 149.
33. Luo Yuejiong, *Xianbin Lu* 咸宾录 (A Record of All Guests), ed. Yu Sili (Beijing: Zhonghua Shuju, 1983), 101.

15. PORT MARRIAGE

1. Albert Gray and H. C. P. Bell, "Early Notices of the Maldives," in François Pyrard, *The Voyage of François Pyrard of Laval to the East Indies, the Maldives, the Moluccas and Brazil*, ed. Albert Gray and H. C. P. Bell (Cambridge: Cambridge University Press, 2011), 3:441.
2. H. C. P. Bell, *The Maldive Islands: Monograph on the History, Archaeology and Epigraph* (Colombo: Ceylon Government Press, 1940), 16.
3. Gray and Bell, "Early Notices," 429, 430–32; Bell, *The Maldive Islands*, 17.
4. Gray and Bell, "Early Notices," 431–32.
5. MAHS-MDV-COL-003-O-0004 (https://maritimeasiaheritage.cseas.kyoto-u.ac.jp/manuscript-viewer/miscellaneous/); MAHS-MDV-COL-003-O-0009 (https://maritimeasiaheritage.cseas.kyoto-u.ac.jp/manuscript-viewer/waqf-endowment/; "Timeline of Maldives History," 3, in R. Michael Feener, ed., Maritime Asia Heritage Survey, https://maritimeasiaheritage.cseas.kyoto-u.ac.jp/wp-content/uploads/2021/03/Maldives-Timeline-MHS.pdf.
6. Ibn Battuta, *Travels in Asia and Africa, 1325–1354*, trans. and selected by H. A. R. Gibb, with an Introduction and Notes (New York: Routledge & Kegan Paul, 2011), 244.
7. Ahmed Nazim Sattar, *King Kalaafaan Manuscripts: How the Maldives Monarchy Treasured the Remembrance of a Fallen King for More Than Four Hundred Years* (Male: National Centre of Linguistic and Historical Research, 2010), 36, 56–58.
8. Ibn Battuta, *Travels*, 244–45.
9. "List of Kings of the Maldive Islands," in Pyrard, *The Voyage of the Francois Pyrard*, 3: 528–43.
10. Ma Huan, *Ming Chaoben Yingya Shenglan Jiaozhu* 明钞本瀛涯胜览校注 (Overall Survey of the Ocean Shores: Annotation of a Ming Manuscript), ed. Wan Ming (Beijing: Haiyangchubanshe, 2005), 74; Ma Huan, *Ying-yai sheng-lan: "The Overall Survey of the Ocean's Shores,"* [1433]; translated from the Chinese text edited by

15. PORT MARRIAGE

Feng Ch'eng-chün with introduction, notes, and appendices by J. V. G. Mills (London: Hakluyt Society, 1970), 149.
11. Ibn Battuta, *Travels*, 243.
12. Gray and Bell, "Early Notices," 445–46. For the discussion of Ibn Battuta's love, sex life, marriage, and divorce throughout his journey in Europe, Africa, and Asia, see Marina A. Tolmacheva, "Concubines on the Road: Ibn Battuta's Slave Women," in *Concubines and Courtesans: Women and Slavery in Islamic History*, ed. Matthew S. Gordon and Kathryn A. Hain (New York: Oxford University Press, 2017), 163–89; Ross E. Dunn, *The Adventures of Ibn Battuta: A Muslim Traveler of the Fourteenth Century, with a New Preface* (Berkeley: University of California Press, 2012), 191–98; Rachel Singer, "Love, Sex, and Marriage in Ibn Battuta's Travels," (2019) MAD-RUSH Undergraduate Research Conference, 1, https://commons.lib.jmu.edu/madrush/2019/love/1. While Tolmacheva illustrates that Ibn Battuta was a serial enslaver of women and master of numerous concubines in his travel across various Islamic societies, this approach unfortunately dilutes the difference between maritime and overland boundaries and ignores Ibn Battuta's love of his wives, concubines and even slave women.
13. Gray and Bell, "Early Notices," 446.
14. Gray and Bell, "Early Notices," 458, 455, 459; Ibn Battuta, *Travels*, 249–50.
15. Gray and Bell, "Early Notices," 439.
16. Gray and Bell, "Early Notices," 463. Molúk was an island, probably in the northern part of the Maldives, and it only took three days from there to reach Malabar.
17. Gray and Bell, "Early Notices," 460, 442, 464; Ibn Battuta, *Travels*, 253.
18. Dunn, *The Adventures of Ibn Battuta*, 197; Barbara D. Metcalf, "Ibn Battuta as a Qadi in the Maldives," in *Islam in South Asia in Practice*, ed. Barbara D. Metcalf (Princeton, NJ: Princeton University Press, 2010), 272.
19. Gray and Bell, "Early Notices," 465–67; Ibn Battuta, *Travels*, 253, 266.
20. G. H. Bousquet, "Ibn Baṭṭūṭa et les institutions musulmanes," *Studia Islamica* 24 (1966): 95; Singer, "Love, Sex, and Marriage in Ibn Battuta's Travels," 6–7.
21. Gray and Bell, "Early Notices," 442.
22. Pyrard, *The Voyage of François Pyrard*, 1:105.
23. Bell, *The Maldive Islands*, 13.
24. Battuta, *Travels*, 244; see also Gray and Bell, "Early Notices," 446.
25. This, however, should not be overinterpreted; women, especially poor women, still constituted the second sex in the Maldives. For example, the vizier, Ibn Battuta's future father-in-law, presented "a young female slave from Coromandel" to Ibn Battuta the day after his arrival. Gray and Bell, "Early Notices," 441 and 455.
26. Jacob Van Neck, "Journaal van Jacob van Neck," in *De vierde schipvaart der Nederlanders naar Oost-Indie onder Jacob Wilkens en Jacob van Neck (1599–1604)*, ed. H. A. van Foreest and A. de Booy (S-Gravenhage: Martinus Nijhoff, 1980 [1604]), 1:225; Anthony Reid, *Southeast Asia in the Age of Commerce 1450–1680*, vol. 1, *The Lands Below the Winds* (New Haven, CT: Yale University Press, 1988), 155.
27. Barbara Watson Andaya, "From Temporary Wife to Prostitute: Sexuality and Economic Change in Early Modern Southeast Asia," *Journal of Women's History* 9, no. 4 (1998): 11–12, 21–24. It is necessary to point out that the commercialization of

sexual trade in Southeast Asia muse be placed in the context of urbanization brought about by the large flow of European merchants. Barbara Watson Andaya, "Historical Perspectives on Prostitution in Early Modern Southeast Asia," *Antropologi Indonesia* 66 (2001): 59, 63–68; Anthony Reid, "Female Roles in Pre-colonial Southeast Asia," *Modern Asian Studies* 22, no. 3 (1988): 633–34.
28. Reid, *The Lands Below the Winds*, 155–56; Reid, "Female Roles," 632.
29. Andaya, "From Temporary Wife to Prostitute," 11–34, esp. 12–13 and 29n5; Barbara Watson Andaya, *To Live as Brothers: Southeast Sumatra in the Seventeenth and Eighteenth Centuries* (Honolulu: University of Hawaii Press, 1993), 40–41.
30. Andaya, "From Temporary Wife to Prostitute," 13.
31. Zhou Daguan, *Zhenla Fengtuji* 真腊风土记 (Customs of Cambodia), ed. Xia Nai (Beijing: Zhonghua Shuju, 1981), 146.
32. Zhou, *Zhenla*, 178, 180; Reid, *The Lands Below the Winds*, 155; Reid, "Female Roles," 634–35; Zhao Daguan, *A Record of Cambodia: The Land and Its People*, trans. Peter Harris (Chiang Mai, Thailand: Silkworm Books, 2011), 94; Dashan, *Haiwai Jishi* 海外纪事 (An Overseas Record), ed. Yu Sili (Beijing: Zhonghua Shuju, 2000), 80. Hoi An (lit. "Peaceful Meeting"), or Fai-Fo or Faifoo in European languages, was a prosperous trading port where the Chinese, Japanese, and later Europeans sojourned during their trade in Southeast Asia from the sixteenth to the eighteenth centuries. Dashan claimed that "all the (Chinese) visiting here must marry a local woman to smooth commercial transactions" (*Fan kecizhe, bi qu yifu, yibian jiaoyi* 凡客此者，必娶一妇，以便交易). See also Andaya, "From Temporary Wife to Prostitute," 20.
33. Remke Kruk, "Ibn Baṭṭūṭa: Travel, Family Life, and Chronology: How Seriously Do We Take a Father?" *Al-Qantara* 16, no. 2 (1995): 377; Singer, "Love, Sex, and Marriage," 6–7.
34. Andaya, *To Live as Brothers*, 40.
35. Wang Dayuan, *Daoyi Zhilue Jiaoshi* 岛夷志略校释 (Brief Record of the Island Barbarians), ed. Su Jiqing (Beijing: Zhonghua Shuju, 1981), 55, 69, 209. For Chinese records of Timor see Roderich Ptak, "Some References to Timor in Old Chinese Records," *Ming Studies* 1 (1983): 37–48; Roderich Ptak, "Images of Maritime Asia in Two Yuan Texts: 'Daoyi zhilue' and 'Yiyu zhi,'" *Journal of Song-Yuan Studies* 25 (1995): 68.
36. Wang, *Daoyi Zhilue*, 69.
37. Ma, *Ying-yai sheng-lan*, 104; Ma, *Ming Chaoben*, 32.
38. Ma, *Ying-yai sheng-lan*, 104; Ma, *Ming Chaoben*, 32–33.
39. Zhou, *Zhenla*, 106; Zhou, *A Record of Cambodia*, 62.
40. Wang, *Daoyi Zhilue*, 69, 107. Ma Huan mentioned the ritual of *lishi* in Siam. Ma, *Ming Chaoben*, 33; Ma, *Ying-yai sheng-lan*, 104.
41. Zhou, *Zhenla*, 106–7; Zhou, *A Record of Cambodia*, 62–63.
42. Li Jing, *Yunnan Zhilue* 云南志略 (Sketchy Record of Yunnan), in *Yunnan Shiliao Congkan* (Historical Sources of Yunnan), ed. Fang Guoyu (Kunming: Yunnandaxue Chubanshe, 1998), 3:121; Bin Yang, *Between Winds and Clouds: The Making of Yunnan (Second Century BCE to Twentieth Century CE)* (New York: Columbia University Press, 2009), 142–43.
43. Whether Ibn Battuta reached China is still a matter of discussion, but his descriptions must have been based on either what he had heard and read or what he had

15. PORT MARRIAGE

experienced, or probably both. Therefore, it would be incautious to wholly discount his information about China.

44. Battuta, *Travels*, 286–87.
45. Battuta, *Travels*, 286.
46. Battuta, *Travels*, 235, 240.
47. For an analysis of foreign women in the *Daoyi Zhilue*, see Ptak, "Images of Maritime Asia," 66–69.
48. Wang, *Daoyi Zhilue*, 209; Ptak, "Images of Maritime Asia," 67.
49. Zhou, *Zhenla*, 105; Zhou, *A Record of Cambodia*, 65.
50. Zhou, *Zhenla*, 105; Zhou, *A Record of Cambodia*, 65.
51. Wang, *Daoyi Zhilue*, 33, 86; Ptak, "Images of Maritime Asia," 67.
52. For the Chinese disease concept of the Zhang, see Bin Yang, "The Zhang on Southern Chinese Frontiers: Disease-Construction, Environmental Changes, and Imperial Colonization," *Bulletin of the History of Medicine* 84, no. 2 (Summer 2010): 163–92.
53. Ptak, "Images of Maritime Asia," 67.
54. Wang, *Daoyi Zhilue*, 69: Ma, *Ming Chaoben*, 32–3.
55. Reid, *The Lands Below the Winds*, 156–58; Reid, "Female Roles," 629–45.
56. Fei Xin, *Xingcha Shenglan Jiaozhu* 星槎胜览校注 (Overall Survey of the Star Raft: An Annotation), ed. Feng Chengjun (Beijing: Huawen Chubanshe, 2019), 80.
57. Luo Maodeng, *Xiyang Ji Sanbao Taijian Xiyangji Tongsu Yanyi* 三宝太监西洋记通俗演义 (Romance of Eunuch Sanbao's Journey to the Western Ocean), ed. Lu Shulun and Zhu Shaohua (Shanghai: Shanghai Gujichubanshe, 1982), 2:583; Ptak, "Images of Maritime Asia," 67–68.
58. Luo, *Xiyang Ji*, 2:583. The Chinese character *ji* 吉 is similar to that for *gu* 古. *Jili* is the transliteration of *giri*, which means reef or island. Therefore, highly likely, Gulidimen 古里地闷 was a mistake for Jilidimen 吉里地闷, that is, Timor.
59. Aili Libang (Elie Ripon), *Haishang Maoxian Huiyiliu—Yiwei Yongbing de Rizhi (1617–1627)* (Voyages et aventures du Capitaine Ripon aux Grandes Indes), trans. Lai Huiyun (Hangzhou: Zhejiang University Press, 2015), 197.
60. For slave-wives purchased by Chinese sojourners in certain Southeast Asian ports, see Andaya, "From Temporary Wife to Prostitute," 20–21.
61. This chapter does not attempt to deny that women in maritime Asia were also assaulted, kidnapped, and raped during this violent period, nor does it intend to exclude any other form of sexual relationship in maritime Asia, including maritime prostitution. To ensure a regular and continuing trade, however, the port marriage was primarily based on mutual trust and cooperation.
62. Barbara Watson Andaya, "Oceans Unbounded: Transversing Asia Across 'Area Studies,'" *Journal of Asian Studies* 65, no. 4 (2006): 669–90.
63. Andaya, "From Temporary Wife to Prostitute."
64. Reid, "Female Roles," 633.
65. The phenomenon of transnational polygyny, known as the *Liangtou jia* 两头家 (literally meaning "a family of both ends"), refers to the practice among Chinese migrants in Southeast Asia of maintaining a primary wife in their home villages while entering a marital relationship with a Southeast Asian woman in their working community. One could posit that the advent of modern modes of transportation played a pivotal role in overcoming the obstacles provided by the

nature, hence facilitating many port wives' lifelong partnerships. Jiemin Bao, *Marital Acts: Gender, Sexuality, and Identity Among the Chinese Thai Diaspora* (Honolulu: Hawaii University Press, 2005); Huifen Shen, *China's Left-Behind Wives: Families of Migrants from Fujian to Southeast Asia, 1930s–1950s* (Singapore: NUS Press, 2012).

16. A TRUE ROMANCE

1. Luo completed a preface to his *Xiyang Ji* in 1597.
2. J. J. L. Duyvendak, "Desultory Notes on the His-yang chi," *T'oung Pao* 42, nos. 1–2 (1953): 4.
3. Xiang Da, "Lun Luo Maodeng zhu sanbao Tajian Xiyangji Tongsu Yanyi" (On Luo Maodeng's Romance of Eunuch Sanbao's Journey to the Western Ocean), in Luo Maodeng, *Sanbao Taijian Xiyangji Tongsu Yanyi* 三宝太监西洋记通俗演义 (Romance of Eunuch Sanbao's Journey to the Western Ocean, hereinafter *Xiyang Ji*), ed. Lu Shulun and Zhu Shaohua (Shanghai: Shanghai Gujichubanshe, 1982), 2:, 1291–97; Zhao Jingshen, "Saoban Taijian Xiyang Ji" (Romance of Eunuch Sanbao's Journey to the Western Ocean), in Luo, *Xiyang Ji*, 2:1298–333; Duyvendak, "Desultory Notes"; Roderich Ptak, *Cheng Hos Abenteuer im Drama und Roman der Ming-Zeit* (Stuttgart: Franz Steiner Verlag Wiesbaden GMBH XXX, 1986), 238–40. Robert Finlay once compared *The Lusiads*, a Portuguese epic poem written by Luís Vaz de Camões (c. 1524/45–1580) praising Da Gama's discovery of a sea route to India to the *Xiyang Ji*, and he points out that the two works, though "fanciful and incredible," structured "the story of a historical event as a quest" and "grounded their fictional narrations in historical reality." Robert Finlay, "Portuguese and Chinese Maritime Imperialism: Camoes' *Lusiads* and Luo Maodeng's Voyage of the San Bao Eunuch," *Comparative Studies in Society and History* 34, no. 2 (April 1992): 232.
4. Zhou Qufei, *Lingwai Daida Jiaozhu* 岭外代答校注 (Answers for Questions Concerning Out of Range), ed. Yang Wuquan (Beijing: Zhonghua Shuju, 1999), 100, 104–5n23; Zhao Rukuo, *Zhufan Zhi Jiaoshi* 诸蕃志校释 (A Record of Barbarians), ed. Yang Bowen (Beijing: Zhonghua Shuju, 2000), 90 and 112; Guangdong Difangzhi Bianjiweiyuahui Bangongshi, ed., *Yuan Dade Nanhaizhi Canben* 元大德南海志残本 (Remains of the Nanhai Gazetteer Compiled in the Dade Reign of the Yuan Dynasty) (Guangzhou: Guangdong Renminchubanshe, 1991), 47.
5. Luo, *Xiyang Ji*, 1:15–17. "Feiliuli" might be the transcription of *veḷuriya* (Pali) or *vaiḍūrya* (Sanskrit). Because of its blue-green color, it is also called "blue *liuli*" (*biliuli* 碧琉璃) in Chinese.
6. Luo, *Xiyang Ji*, 1:15–6.
7. Luo, *Xiyang Ji*, 1:15.
8. Donald S. Lopez Jr., *The Heart Sutra Explained: Indian and Tibetan Commentaries* (Albany: SUNY Press, 1988), 21–22.
9. Luo, *Xiyang Ji*, 1:15–16. The *āmra* tree is native to India and was often mentioned in Chinese Buddhist sutras as early as the Tang period. Instead of the *āmra* tree, the *māra* tree (*moluo shu* 摩罗树), is given. *Moluo* is the Chinese transliteration of

16. A TRUE ROMANCE

māra, which simply meant a demon, and is associated with death, rebirth, and desire, all these being barriers to obtaining enlightenment. The characters of *mo* 摩 and *an* 庵 are very similar, and hence could easily be mistaken for one another. Considering the context, the author tends to believe that *moluo* was the intended meaning. *Jile* is the Chinese translation of Sukhāvatī (the Western Paradise), which refers to the pure western land of Amitābha in Mahayana Buddhism. Here the metaphor of a fruit grown from a tree of barriers that could help to reach the land of joy indeed confirms the author's suspicion that coconut fruit is seen as the magic vehicle to cross the Soft-Water Sea. *Taiji* is a Chinese cosmological term for the "Supreme Ultimate" from which *Yin* and *Yang* originate; *Liangyi* refers to two primary forces, namely *Yin* and *Yang*. Pindola Bharadvaja (Piṇḍola Bhāradvāja) is a popular Arhat in Buddhism.

10. Luo, *Xiyang Ji*, 1:16. *Fen* is a Chinese unit of length. Very interestingly, in a Maldivian folktale a young man recited a spell and broke the three coconuts to clear a storm that prevented his navigation. Xavier Romero-Frias, *The Maldive Islanders—A Study of the Popular Culture of an Ancient Ocean Kingdom* (Barcelona: Nova Ethnographia Indica, 1999), 112.
11. Luo, *Xiyang Ji*, 1:16, 269–70, 275–76.
12. Luo, *Xiyang Ji*, 1:275–78.
13. Luo, *Xiyang Ji*, 1:279–80.
14. Albert Gray and H. C. P. Bell, "Early Notices of the Maldives," in François Pyrard, *The Voyage of François Pyrard of Laval to the East Indies, the Maldives, the Moluccas and Brazil*, ed. Albert Gray and H. C. P. Bell (Cambridge: Cambridge University Press, 2011), 3:428.
15. Luo, *Xiyang Ji*, 2:774–5.
16. Geoff Wade, "The Zheng He Voyages: A Reassessment," *Journal of the Malaysian Branch of the Royal Asiatic Society* 78, no. 1 (2005): 47–50; Tansen Sen, "The Impact of Zheng He's Expeditions on Indian Ocean Interactions," *Bulletin of SOAS* 79, no. 3 (2016): 613–16, 620; Tansen Sen, "The Formation of Chinese Maritime Networks to Southern Asia, 1200–1450," *Journal of the Economic and Social History of the Orient* 49, no. 4 (2006): 443–45, 438; Luo, *Xiyang Ji*, 2:774–6.
17. Eunuch Hong Bao 洪保 served under Zheng He and visited Champa, Java, Malacca, Sumatra, Ceylon, Cochin, Calicut, Ormuz, and Aden and was mentioned in two imperial edicts kept by Gong Zhen. Thus, Hong Gonggong might refer to Hong Bao. Gong Zhen, *Xiyang Fanguo Zhi* 西洋番国志 (Record of Foreign Kingdoms in the Western Ocean), ed. Xiang Da (Beijing: Zhonghua Shuju, 2000), 15–16; Roderich Ptak, "The Maldives and Laccadive Islands (*liu-shan* 溜山) in Ming Records," *Journal of the American Oriental Society* 107, no. 4 (1987): 692n110.
18. Luo, *Xiyang Ji*, 2:774.
19. Luo, *Xiyang Ji*, 2:1277. English translation from Ptak, "The Maldives," 692–93. For the word *yagu* or *yahu* see also George Phillips, "The Seaports of India and Ceylon: Described by Chinese Voyagers of the Fifteenth Century, Together with an Account of Chinese Navigation," *Journal of the China Branch of the Royal Asiatic Society* 20 (1885): 213. One *shi* was about 100 *jin* in the Ming period (approximately 130 pounds in weight). Four hundred cowrie shells from the

16. A TRUE ROMANCE

Maldives weighed one pound, so twenty *shi* amounts to more than a million shells.
20. Duyvendak, "Desultory Notes," 6.

17. AN ECHO: THE "CHINA BIRD"

1. Ma Huan, *Ming Chaoben Yingya Shenglan Jiaozhu* 明钞本瀛涯胜览校注 (Overall Survey of the Ocean Shores: Annotation of a Ming Manuscript), ed. Wan Ming (Beijing: Haiyangchubanshe, 2005), 75.
2. François Pyrard, *The Voyage of François Pyrard of Laval to the East Indies, the Maldives, the Moluccas and Brazil*, ed. Albert Gray and H. C. P. Bell (Cambridge: Cambridge University Press, 2011), 3:353–54. A league is a unit of length commonly used in Europe and Latin America, originally referring to the distance a person could walk in an hour.
3. Pyrard, *The Voyage of François Pyrard*, 3:354.
4. Ibn Battuta, *Travels in Asia and Africa, 1325–1354*, trans. and selected by H. A. R. Gibb, with an Introduction and Notes (New York: Routledge & Kegan Paul, 2011), 283.
5. Certainly, Ibn Battuta himself still thought that "the silk-worm attaches itself to fruits and feeds on them without requiring much care." Battuta, *Travels*, 284. In fact, raising silkworms is highly labor-intensive, as I learned myself through much hardship and suffering as a teenager and not surprisingly quickly became very tired of it.
6. Clarence Maloney, *People of the Maldive Islands* (Bombay: Oriental Longman, 1980), 111.
7. Egil Mikkelsen, "Archaeological Excavations of a Monastery at Kaasidhoo: Cowrie Shells and Their Buddhist Context in the Maldives," National Centre for Linguistic and Historical Research, Male, Republic of Maldives, 2000, 19–21.
8. Albert Gray was reminded that this bird might be a great white pelican, which was common in Afro-Eurasia. Pyrard, *The Voyage of François Pyrard*, 3:354n1.
9. Henry Yule, *Cathay and the Way Thither: Being a Collection of Medieval Notices of China* (London: Hakluyt Society, 2010), 1:111n2.
10. Yule, *Cathay and the Way Thither*, 112.
11. For early studies of cormorants in China as well as Western accounts of the cormorant there, see E. W. Gudger, "Fishing with the Cormorant in China," *The American Naturalist* 60, no. 666 (January–February 1926): 5–41; C. B. Laufer, "The Domestication of the Cormorant in China and Japan," Field Museum of Natural History Anthropology Series 3, 1931, 205–62.
12. Charles R. Boxer, *South China in the Sixteenth Century: Being the Narratives of Galeote Pereira, Fr. Gaspar da Cruz, O.P., Fr. Martin de Rada, O.E.S.A. (1550–1575)* (Bangkok: Orchid Press, 2004), 42–43.
13. Boxer, *South China*, 42–43.
14. Boxer, *South China*, 43.
15. Boxer, *South China*, 136.
16. Bernardino de Escalante, *An Account of the Empire of China*, trans. John Frampton (Bad Mergentheim, Germany: Ascanio-Verlag, 2008), 73–74.

17. AN ECHO: THE "CHINA BIRD"

17. He Gaoji, "Xulun" (Preface), in Menduosa (Juan González de Mendoza), *Zhonghua Dadiguo Shi* (The History of the Great and Mighty Kingdom of China and the Situation Thereof), trans. He Gaoji (Beijing: Zhonghua Shuju, 1998), 52.
18. Bao Leshi (Leonard Blussé) and Zhuang Guotu, *Heshi Chufang Zhongguo Ji Yanjiu* (A Study of an Embassy from the East India Company of the United Provinces) (Xiamen: Xiamendaxue Chubanshe, 1989), 74; Gudger, "Fishing with the Cormorant," 13–14.
19. Ellis Henry, *Journal of the Proceedings of the Late Embassy to China* (London: Elibron Classics, 2006), 278.
20. Evariste Régis Huc, *A Journey Through the Chinese Empire* (New York: Harper, 1855), 2:100–101.
21. Thomas Allom and G. N. Wright, *The Chinese Empire Illustrated: being a series of views from original sketches, displaying the scenery, architecture, social habits etc. of that ancient and exclusive nation* (London Printing and Publishing Company, 1858), 1:20; see also Liu Jia and Ma Jing, trans, *Qingdiguo Tuji: Gudai Zhongguo de Fengjing, Jianzhu yu Shehuishenghuo* (Illustrations of the Qing Empire: Displaying the Scenery, Architecture, and Social Habits in Ancient China) (Tianjin: Tianjin Jiaoyuchubanshe, 2011), 169.
22. Gudger, "Fishing with the Cormorant."
23. Roderich Ptak, "Images of Maritime Asia in Two Yuan Texts: 'Daoyi zhilue' and 'Yiyu zhi,'" *Journal of Song-Yuan Studies* 25 (1995): 75.
24. Xie Fang, "Qianyan" (Foreword), in Ai Rulue (Giulio Aleni), *Zhifang Waiji Jiaoshi* 职方外纪校释 (Chronicle of Foreign Lands), ed. Xie Fang (Beijing: Zhonghua Shuju, 2000), 2.
25. Chen Lunjiong, *Haiguo Wenjianlu Jiaozhu* 海国闻见录校注 (What Is Heard and Seen on the Maritime Countries: An Annotation), ed. Li Changfu and Chen Daiguan (Zhengzhou: Zhongzhou Gujichubanshe, 1984), 54.
26. Jin Feng, "Qingchuan Buguo Maliujia Yuanyou Kaoxi" (An Examination on Why Qing Ships Did Not Sail Through the Malacca Strait), *Haijiaoshi Yanjiu* (Journal of Maritime History Studies) 2 (2018): 1–16.
27. Luo Yuejiong, *Xianbin Lu* 咸宾录 (A Record of All Guests), ed. Yu Sili (Beijing: Zhonghua Shuju, 1983), 101, 103–4; Ma, *Ming Chaoben*, 71. As discussed, *Deigan* is supposed to be *Diew*.
28. Qian Jiang and Chen Jiarong, "Niujin Cang 'Mingdai Dongxiyang Hanghaitu' Jiemeihua—Yelu Cang 'Qingdai Dongnanyang Hanghaitu' Tuijie" (An Introduction to a Qing Navigation Chart in Yale University: A Sister Work of the Ming Navigation Chart in Oxford University), *Haijiaoshi Yanjiu* (Journal of Maritime History Studies) 2 (2013): 15.
29. Ai Rulue, *Zhifang Waiji*, 58.
30. "Kun yu quan tu / Nan huai ren," https://gallica.bnf.fr/ark:/12148/btv1b7200283b#.
31. Here 馬尔地襪, the four traditional Chinese characters of Maerdiwa, are kept as they were marked on the map.
32. Vera Dorofeeva-Lichtmann realized this mistake and concluded that Huang's map was made in 1767, the year of Dinghai. Vera Dorofeeva-Lichtmann, "Zhongguo Ditu" 中国地图 (Chinese Maps), China National Library, https://heritage.bnf.fr/france-chine/zh-hans/cartes-de-chine-article-chinois. The Year of Dinghai certainly appears on another Qing Map made by Zhu Xiling, *Daqing*

17. AN ECHO: THE "CHINA BIRD"

Wannian Yitong Dili Quantu 大清万年一统地理全图 (A Comprehensive Map of Geography for the Ten-Thousand-Year Unification by the Grand Qing). Huang Qianren was a grandson of Huang Zonqxi 黃宗羲 (1610–1695) and one of the great minds of the Ming-Qing transition. His map had its earlier sources from works completed by his grandfather.

33. "Jing ban tian wen quan tu / Ma jun liang," Bibliothèque Nationale de France, département Cartes et plans, GE AA-1656 (RES), https://gallica.bnf.fr/ark: /12148/btv1b72001830#.
34. *Duhai Fangcheng*, literally means "Directions and Distances for Crossing Seas," and *Shungfeng Xiangsong*, literally means "Escort by Tail Winds." Xiang Da, ed., *Liangzhong Haidao Zhenjing* 两种海道针经 (The Two Compass Guidebooks of Navigation Routes) (Beijing: Zhonghua Shuju, 2000); Chen Jiarong and Zhu Jianqiu, eds., *Duhai Fangfeng Jizhu* (Routes for Crossing Seas: A Compilation and Annotation) (Shanghai: Zhongxi Shuju, 2013), esp. 307–35.
35. Qian Jiang, "Yifu Xinjin Faxian de Mingchao Zhongye Caihui Hanghaitu" (A Recently Discovered Mid-Ming Colorful Navigation Chart), *Haojiaoshi Yanjiu* (Journal of Maritime History Studies) 1 (2011): 4.
36. Xiang Da, "Liangzhong Haidao Zhenjing Xuyan" (Preface to the Two Compass Guidebooks of Navigation Routes), in *Liangzhong*, 3–4 and 110–95.
37. "The Selden Map of China," Bodleian Library, MS.Selden supra 105, https:// seldenmap.bodleian.ox.ac.uk/. As for Faerguo for Zufar, the first character of *zu* is probably missing. See Robert Batchelor, "The Selden Map Rediscovered: A Chinese Map of East Asian Shipping Routes, c.1619," *Imago Mundi* 65, no. 1 (2013): 37–63.
38. For Qing China as a maritime empire, see Ronald C. Po, *The Blue Frontier: Maritime Vision and Power in the Qing Empire* (Cambridge University Press, 2018).
39. Qian and Chen, "Niujin," 1–101.
40. Chen Guodong, *Dongya Haiyu Yiqiannian* (A Millennium in the Oceans of East Asia) (Ji'nan: Shandonghuabao Chubanshe, 2006), 159–87.
41. Xie Fang, "Qianyan" (Preface), in Ai Rulue, *Zhifang Waiji*, 4. Joseph-Antoine Provana and Fan Shouyi were dispatched by the Kangxi Emperor to the Vatican to represent him in the Chinese rites controversy.
42. An Jing, "Xulun (Preface)," in Xie Qinggao, *Hailu Jiaoshi* 海录校释 (Annotations to a Record of the Seas), ed. An Jing (Beijing: Shangwu Yinshuguan, 2002), 7–8.

BIBLIOGRAPHY

Agius, Dionysius A. *Classic Ships of Islam: From Mesopotamia to the Indian Ocean.* Leiden: Brill, 2008.
Ai, Rulue (Giulio Aleni). *Zhifang Waiji Jiaoshi* (Chronicle of Foreign Lands). Ed. Xie Fang. Beijing: Zhonghua Shuju, 2000.
Alexander, William. *Picturesque Representations of the Dress and Manners of the Chinese, Illustrated in Fifty Colored Engravings, with Descriptions.* London, Printed for John Murray, Albemarle-Street, by W. Bulmer and Co. Cleveland-Row, 1814.
Allom, Thomas, and G. N. Wright. *The Chinese Empire Illustrated: Being a series of views from original sketches, displaying the scenery, architecture, social habits, &c., of that ancient and exclusive nation.* London: London Printing and Publishing Company, 1858.
Andaya, Barbara Watson. "From Temporary Wife to Prostitute: Sexuality and Economic Change in Early Modern Southeast Asia." *Journal of Women's History* 9, no. 4 (1998): 11–34.
———. "Historical Perspectives on Prostitution in Early Modern Southeast Asia." *Antropologi Indonesia* 66 (2001): 58–71.
———. "Oceans Unbounded: Transversing Asia Across 'Area Studies.'" *Journal of Asian Studies* 65, no. 4 (2006): 669–90.
———. *To Live as Brothers: Southeast Sumatra in the Seventeenth and Eighteenth Centuries.* Honolulu: University of Hawaii Press, 1993.
Bai, Juyi. *Baishi Changqi Ji* (Collections of Bai Juyi's Poems). Shanghai: Shanghai Gujichubanshe, 1994.
Ban, Gu. *Han Shu* (History of the Han Dynasty). Beijing: Zhonghua Shuju, 1962.
Bao, Jiemin. *Marital Acts: Gender, Sexuality, and Identity Among the Chinese Thai Diaspora.* Honolulu: Hawaii University Press, 2005.

BIBLIOGRAPHY

Bao, Leshi (Leonard Blussé), and Zhuang Guotu. *Heshi Chufang Zhongguo Ji Yanjiu* (A Study of an Embassy from the East India Company of the United Provinces). Xiamen: Xiamendaxue Chubanshe, 1989.

Batchelor, Robert. "The Selden Map Rediscovered: A Chinese Map of East Asian Shipping Routes, c.1619." *Imago Mundi* 65, no. 1 (2013): 37–63.

Battuta, Ibn. *Travels in Asia and Africa, 1325–1354, trans. and selected by H. A. R. Gibb, with an Introduction and Notes.* New York: Routledge & Kegan Paul, 2011.

Beek, Vían. "Frankincense and Myrrh in Ancient South Arabia." *Journal of American Oriental Society* 78, no. 3 (1958): 141–44.

Belfioretti, Luca, and Tom Vosmer. "Al-Balīd Ship Timbers: Preliminary Overview and Comparisons." *Proceedings of the Seminar for Arabian Studies* 40 (2010): 111–18.

Bell, Bethia N., and Heather M. Bell. *H. C. P. Bell: Archaeologist of Ceylon and the Maldives.* London: Archetype Publications, 1993.

Bell, H. C. P. *The Maldive Islands: Monograph on the History, Archaeology and Epigraph.* Colombo: Ceylon Government Press, 1940.

Bell, Heather. "H. C. P. Bell in Sri Lanka and the Maldives." *South Asian Studies* 8 (1992): 105–8.

Blussé, Leonard. "Chinese Trade to Batavia During the Days of the V.O.C." *Archipel* 18 (1979): 195–214.

———. *Strange Company: Chinese Settlers, Mestizo Women, and the Dutch in VOC Batavia.* Dordrecht: Foris Publications, 1986.

The Book of the Thousand and One Nights, Rendered into English from the Literal and Complete French Translation of Dr. J. C. Mardrus by Powys Mathers. London: Routledge & Kegan Paul, 1986.

Bousquet, G. H. "Ibn Baṭṭūṭa et les institutions musulmanes." *Studia Islamica* 24 (1966): 81–106.

Boxer, Charles R. *South China in the Sixteenth Century: Being the Narratives of Galeote Pereira, Fr. Gaspar da Cruz, O.P., Fr. Martin de Rada, O.E.S.A. (1550–1575).* Bangkok: Orchid Press, 2004.

Boxihe (Paul Eugène Pelliot). *Zheng He Xia Xiyang Kao* (Les grands voyages maritimes chinois au début du 15ème siècle). Trans. Feng Chenjun. Beijing: Zhonghua Shuju, 2003.

Bretschneider, E. *Medieval Researches from Eastern Asiatic Sources: Fragments Towards the Knowledge of the Geography and History of Central and Western Asia from the 13th to the 17th Century.* 2 vols. London: K. Paul, Trench, Trübner & Co., 1910.

Caffrey, Kate. *The Mayflower.* Lanham, MD: Rowman & Littlefield, 2014.

Cai, Tao. *Tieweishan Congtan* (Miscellaneous Notes in Mount Iron). Beijing: Zhonghua Shuju, 1983.

Carswell, John. "China and Islam in the Maldive Islands." *Transactions of the Oriental Ceramic Society 1975–77* 41 (1977): 121–98.

Catz, Rebecca. *Cartas de Fernão Mendes Pinto e outros documentos.* Lisbon: Editorial Presença/Biblioteca Nacional, 1983.

Chaffee, John W. "Pu Shougeng Reconsidered: Pu, His Family, and Their Role in the Maritime Trade of Quanzhou." In *Beyond the Silk Roads: New Discourses on China's Role in East Asian Maritime History,* ed. Robert J. Antony and Angela Schottenhammer, 63–76. Wiesbaden: Harrassowitz Verlag, 2017.

BIBLIOGRAPHY

Chen, Gaohua. "Yuandai Hanghaishijia Kanpu Yangshi" (The Yangs: Maritime Navigators in the Yuan Dynasty). *Haiiaoshi Yanjiu* (Journal of Maritime History Studies) 1 (1995): 4–18.

———. *Yuanshi Yanjiu Lungao* (On Studies of Yuan History). Beijing: Zhonghua Shuju, 1991.

———. *Yuanshi Yanjiu Xinlun* (New Discussions on Studies of Yuan History). Shanghai: Shanghai Shehuikexueyuan Chubanshe, 2005.

Chen, Gaohua, and Wu Tai. "Guanyu Quanzhouwan Chutu Haichuan de Jige Wenti" (A Few Issues of the Sea Ship Excavated in Quanzhou Bay). In *Quanzhouwan Songdai Haichuan Fajue yu Yanjiu Xiudingban* (A Report on the Excavation of the Song Boat in Quanzhou Bay), ed. Fujian Quanzhou Haiwajiaotongshi Bowuguan, 160–65. Beijing: Haiyang Chubanshe, 2017.

Chen, Guodong. *Dongya Haiyu Yiqiannian* (A Millennium in the Oceans of East Asia). Ji'nan: Shandonghuabao Chubanshe, 2006.

Chen, Jiarong, and Zhu Jianqiu, eds. *Duhai Fangfeng Jizhu* (Routes for Crossing Seas: A Compilation and Annotation). Shanghai: Zhongxi Shuju, 2013.

Chen, Jiarong, Xie Fang, and Lu Junling. *Gudai Nanhai Diming Huishi* (Collection and Identification of Ancient Place Names in the South China Sea). Beijing: Zhonghua Shuju, 1986.

Chen, Jing. *Chenshi Xinagpu* (The Chen Guide to the Xiang). In Hong Chu et al., *Xiangpu Waisizhong* (Guide of the Xiang and Four Others), ed. Tian Yuan, 53–227. Shanghai: Shanghai Shudian, 2018.

Chen, Lunjiong. *Haiguo Wenjianlu Jiaozhu* (What Is Heard and Seen on the Maritime Countries: An Annotation). Ed. Li Changfu and Chen Daiguan. Zhengzhou: Zhongzhou Gujichubanshe, 1984.

Chen, Menglei. *Gujin Tushu Jicheng* (Complete Collection of Illustrations and Writings from the Earliest to Current Times). n.p.: Zhonghua Shuju, 1934.

Chen, Xinxiong. "Ping Long Cunni 'Miren de Gongli'" (Comments on Long Cunni's "An Attractive Tributary Gift: Ambergris"). In *Zheng He Xia Xiyang Guoji Xueshuyantaohui Lunwenji* (A Collection of Papers from the International Conference on Zheng He's Sailing to the Western Ocean), ed. Chen Xinxiong, and Chen Yunü, 351–53.Taipei: Daoxiang Chubanshe, 2003.

Chen, Xiyu. *Zhongguo Fanchuan yu Haiwai Maoyi* (Chinese Junks and Overseas Trade). Xiamen: Xiamendaxue Chubanshe, 1991.

Chen, Yuying. "Mingdai Gongbo Yanjiu" (A Study of the Tributary Ships in the Ming Dynasty). In *Mingshi Yanjiu Luncong* (Papers on the Studies of the Ming History), ed. Wu Zhihe, 343–98. Taipei: Dalichubanshe, 1984.

"Chu-Si-Ling. Cartographe." Bibliothèque Nationale de France. https://gallica.bnf.fr/ark:/12148/btv1b7200281h/f5.item.

Clark, Hugh R. "Muslims and Hindus in the Culture and Morphology of Quanzhou from the Tenth to the Thirteenth Century." *Journal of World History* 6, no. 1 (1995): 49–74.

———. "Quanzhou (Fujian) During the Tang-Song Interregnum, 879–978." *T'oung Pao* 68, nos. 1–3 (1982): 132–49.

———. "The Religious Culture of Southern Fujian, 750–1450: Preliminary Reflections on Contacts Across a Maritime Frontier." *Asia Major* 19, nos. 1–2 (2006): 211–40.

Cohen, Paul A. *History in Three Keys: The Boxer as Event, Experience, and Myth*. New York: Columbia University Press, 1997.

Connan, Jacques, Seth Priestman, et al. "Geochemical Analysis of Bitumen from West Asian Torpedo Jars from the c. 8th Century Phanom-Surin Shipwreck in Thailand." *Journal of Archaeological Science* 117 (May 2020): 1–18.

Crawfurd, John. *A Descriptive Dictionary of the Indian Islands and Adjacent Countries*. Cambridge: Cambridge University Press, 2012.

Dai, Yixuan. *Mingshi Folangjizhuan Jianzheng* (Annotations on Chapter Folangji in History of the Ming Dynasty). Beijing: Zhongguo Shehuikexue Chubanshe, 1984.

Dames, Mansel Longworth. *The Book of Duarte Barbosa: An Account of the Countries Bordering on the Indian Ocean and Their Inhabitants*. New Delhi: Asian Educational Services, 1989.

Dannenfeldt, Karl H. "Ambergris: The Search for Its Origin." *Isis* 73, no. 3 (1982): 382–97.

Dashan. *Haiwai Jishi* (An Overseas Record). Ed. Yu Sili. Beijing: Zhonghua Shuju, 2000.

Ding, Wei. *Tianxiang Zhuan* (Biography of the Celestial Xiang). In Hong Chu et al., *Xiangpu Waisizhong* (Guide of the Xiang and Four Others), ed. Tian Yuan, 1–5. Shanghai: Shanghai Shudian, 2018.

Dorofeeva-Lichtmann, Vera. "Zhongguo Ditu" (Chinese Maps). China National Library, https://heritage.bnf.fr/france-chine/zh-hans/cartes-de-chine-article-chinois.

Douglas, Carstair. *Chinese-English Dictionary of the Vernacular or Spoken Language of Amoy*. London: Trubner, 1873.

"Dr. Andrew Forbes." https://www.britishmuseum.org/collection/term/BIOG123366.

Du, Huan. *Jingxing Ji Jianzhu* (Record of Travels). Ed. Zhang Yichun. Zhonghua Shuju, 2000.

Duan, Chengshi. *Youyang Zazu* (Miscellaneous Writings in Youyang). Ed. Xu Yimin and Xu Heng. Beijing: Zhonghua Shuju, 2018.

Dunn, Ross E. *The Adventures of Ibn Battuta: A Muslim Traveler of the Fourteenth Century, with a New Preface*. Berkeley: University of California Press, 2012.

Duyvendak, J. J. L. "Desultory Notes on the His-yang chi." *T'oung Pao* 42, nos. 1–2 (1953): 1–35.

Egami, Namio. "Migration of Cowrie-Shell Culture East Asia." *Acta Asiatica* 26 (1974): 1–52.

Elliot, H., and J. Dowson. *The History of India, as Told by Its Own Historians: The Muhammadan Period*. Vol. 1. London: Cambridge University Press, 2013.

Elliot, Walter. "The Edifice Formerly Known as the Chinese or Jaina Pagoda at Negapatam." *Indian Antiquary* 7 (1878): 224–27.

Escalante, Bernardino de. *An Account of the Empire of China*. Bad Mergentheim, Germany: Ascanio-Verlag, 2008.

Fang, Hui. "Cong Jingshi Wenqi kan Yuan Ming ji Qingchu Yunnan Shiyong Beibi de Qingkuang" (The Use of Cowrie Money in Yunnan of the Yuan-Ming-Early Qing Period: Based on Texts and Inscriptions in Bronze and Stone Items). In *Beibi Yanjiu* (Studies of Cowrie Money), ed. Yang Shouchuan, 127–57. Kunming: Yunnan University Press, 1997,

BIBLIOGRAPHY

Fang, Linggui, trans. *Tongzhi Tiaoge Jiaozhu* (Regulation of the [Book of the] Comprehensive Rules [of the Great Yuan]). Beijing: Zhonghua Shuju, 2001.
Faxian. *Faxian Zhuan Jiaozhu* (Annotations to Biography of Faxian). Ed. Zhang Xun. Beijing: Zhonghua Shuju, 2008.
Feener, R. Michael. "Maldives." *The Encyclopedia of Islam Three*. Ed. Kate Fleet et al., 89–93. Leiden: Brill, 2021.
———, ed. *Maritime Asia Heritage Survey*. https://maritimeasiaheritage.cseas.kyoto-u.ac.jp/.
Fei, Xin. *Hsing-ch'a-sheng-lan: The Overall Survey of the Star Raft*. Trans. J. V. Mills. Ed. Roderich Ptak. Wiesbaden: Harrassowitz, 1996.
———. *Xingcha Shenglan Jiaozhu* (Overall Survey of the Star Raft: An Annotation). Ed. Feng Chengjun. Beijing: Huawen Chubanshe, 2019.
Feilang (Gabriel Ferrand). *Kunlun ji Nanhai Gudai Hangxingkao* (Le K'ouen-Louen et les anciennes navigations interocéaniques dans les Mers du Sud). Trans. Feng Chengjun. Beijing: Zhonghua Shuju, 1957.
Flecker, Michael. "Early Voyaging in the South China Sea: Implications on Territorial Claims." Nalanda-Sriwijaya Centre, Working Paper 19 (August 2015).
———. "A Ninth-Century Arab or Indian Shipwreck in Indonesia: The First Archaeological Evidence of Direct Trade with China." In *Shipwrecked: Tang Treasures and Monsoon Winds*, ed. Regina Krahl, John Guy, J. Keith Wilson, and Julian Raby, 101–19. Washington, DC: Smithsonian Institution Press, 2010.
Flecker, Michael, Pauline Burger, Armelle Charrié-Duhaut, Jacques Connan, and Pierre Albrecht. "The 9th-Century-AD Belitung Wreck, Indonesia: Analysis of a Resin Lump." *International Journal of Nautical Archaeology* 37 (2008): 383–86.
Forbes, Andrew D. W. "Archives and Resources for Maldivian History." *South Asia: Journal of South Asian Studies* 3, no. 1 (1980): 70–82.
———. "The Mosque in the Maldive Islands: A Preliminary Historical Survey." *Archipel* 26 (1983): 43–74.
———. "The Pre-Islamic Archaeology of the Maldive Islands." *Bulletin de l'École française d'Extrême-Orient* 76 (1987): 281–88.
———. "A Roman Republican Denarius of c. 90 B.C., from the Maldive Islands, Indian Ocean." *Archipel* 28 (1984): 53–60.
———. "Southern Arabia and the Islamicisation of the Central Indian Ocean Archipelagoes." *Archipel* 21 (1981): 55–92.
Gao, Jianbin, and Peng Liang. *Nan'ao Shike Diaocha* (A Survey of the Stone Inscriptions in Nan'ao Island). Fuzhou: Fujian Jiaoyuchubanshe, 2018.
Gedaisi (George Coedès), ed. *Xila Lading Zuojia Yuandong Guwenxian Jilu* (Selected Works by Ancient Greek and Latin Writers on the Far East). Trans. Geng Sheng. Beijing: Zhonghua Shuju, 1987.
Gerritsen, Anne. *The City of Blue and White: Chinese Porcelain and the Early Modern World*. Cambridge: Cambridge University Press, 2020.
Gippert, Jost. "Early New Persian as a Medium of Spreading Islam." In *Persian Origins: Early Judaeo-Persian and the Emergence of New Persian*, ed. Ludwig Paul, 31–47. Wiesbaden: Harrossowitz, 2003.
———. "A Glimpse Into the Buddhist Past of the Maldives. I. An Early Prakrit Inscription." *Wiener Zeitschrift für die Kunde Südasiens* 48 (2004): 81–109.

BIBLIOGRAPHY

———. "A Glimpse Into the Buddhist Past of the Maldives. II. Two Sanskrit Inscriptions." *Wiener Zeitschrift für die Kunde Südasiens* 55 (2014): 111–44.

———. "Sanskrit as a Medium of Maldivian Buddhism." In *Indische Kultur im Kontext: Rituale, Texte und Ideen aus Indien und der Welt. Festschrift für Klaus Mylius*, ed. Lars Gohler, 213–20, 487–88. Wiesbaden: Harrassowitz, 2005.

Gode, P. K. "History of Ambergris in India Between About A.D. 700 and 1900." *Chymia* 2 (1949): 51–56.

Gong, Zhen. *Xiyang Fanguo Zhi* (Record of Foreign Kingdoms in the Western Ocean). Ed. Xiang Da. Beijing: Zhonghua Shuju, 2000.

Gray, Albert, and H. C. P. Bell. "Early Notices of the Maldives." In François Pyrard, *The Voyage of François Pyrard of Laval to the East Indies, the Maldives, the Moluccas and Brazil*, ed. Albert Gray and H. C. P. Bell, 3:434–68. Cambridge: Cambridge University Press, 2011.

Gu, Yanwu. *Gu Yanwu Quanji* (Comprehensive Works of Gu Yanwu). Shanghai: Shanghai Gujichubanshe, 2012.

Guangdong Difangzhi Bianjiweiyuahui Bangongshi, ed. *Yuan Dade Nanhaizhi Canben* (Remains of the Nanhai Gazetteer Compiled in the Dade Reign of the Yuan Dynasty). Guangzhou: Guangdong Renminchubanshe, 1991.

Gudger, E. W. "Fishing with the Cormorant in China." *The American Naturalist* 60, no. 666 (January–February 1926): 5–41.

Guojia Wenwuju Shuixiayichanbaohuzhongxin et al. *Nanhai I hao Chenchuan Kaogubaogao Zhiyi—1989–2004 nian Diaocha* (Archaeological Report on the Nanhai I Shipwreck Series I: Surveys of 1989–2004), 2 vols. Beijing: Cultural Relics Press, 2017.

———. *Nanhai I hao Chenchuan Kaogubaogao Zhier—2014–2015 nian Fajue* (Archaeological Report on the Nanhai I Shipwreck Series II: Excavation of 2014–2015). 2 vols. Beijing: Cultural Relics Press, 2018.

Guy, John. "The Phanom Surin Shipwreck, a Pahlavi Inscription, and Their Significance for the History of Early Lower Central Thailand." *Journal of the Siam Society* 105 (2017): 179–96.

Haijun Haiyangcehuiyanjiusuo and Dalian Haiyunxueyuan Hanghaishi Yanjiushi, eds. *Xinbian Zheng He Hanghai Tuji* (An Edited Volume of the Zheng He Nautical Chart). Beijing: Renmin Jiaotongchubanshe, 1988.

Haour, Anne, and Annalisa Christie, eds. *Archaeological Investigations of the Maldives in the Medieval Islamic Period: Ibn Battuta's Island*. London: Routledge, 2022.

Haour, Anne, Annalisa Christie, and Shiura Jaufar. "Tracking the Cowrie Shell: Excavations in the Maldives, 2016." *Nyame Akuma* 85 (June 2016): 69–82.

Haour, Anne, Annalisa Christie, Shiura Jaufar, and David Vigoureux. "Back to Ibn Battuta's Island—Excavations in the Maldives, 2017." *Nyame Akuma* 88 (December 2017): 33–40.

He, Qiaoyuan. *Min Shu* (A Record of Fujian). Fuzhou: Fujian Renminchubanshe, 1994.

Heng, Derek. "Shipping, Customs Procedures, and the Foreign Community: The Pingzhou ketan' on Aspects of Guangzhou's Maritime Economy in the Late Eleventh Century." *Journal of Song-Yuan Studies*, no. 38 (2008):1–38.

———. *Sino-Malay Trade and Diplomacy, from the Tenth Through the Fourteenth Century*. Athens: Ohio University Press, 2009.

BIBLIOGRAPHY

Henry, Ellis. *Journal of the Proceedings of the Late Embassy to China.* London: Elibron Classics, 2006.
"The *Hezun.*" Baoji Bronze Ware Museum, Baoji, China. http://www.bjqtm.com/dzzp/qtq/2021-02-24/430.html.
Hirth, Friedrich, and W.W. Rockhill, trans. & eds. *Chau Ju-kua: His Work on the Chinese and Arab Trade in the Twelfth and Thirteenth Centuries, Entitled Chu-fan-chï.* St. Petersburg: Imperial Academy of Sciences, 1911.
Hogendorn, Jan, and Marion Johnson. *The Shell Money of the Slave Trade.* Cambridge: Cambridge University Press, 1986.
Hong, Chu, et al. *Xiangpu Waisizhong* (Guide of the Xiang and Four Others). Ed. Tian Yuan. Shanghai: Shanghai Shudian, 2018.
Hong, Mai. *Yijian Zhi* (What Yijian Records). Ed. He Zhuo. 4 vols. Beijing: Zhonghua Shuju, 1981.
Hourani, George F. *Arab Seafaring in the Indian Ocean in Ancient and Early Medieval Times.* Ed. John Carswell. Princeton, NJ: Princeton University Press, 1995.
Hu, Xiaowei. "Guanyu Quanzhou Fanshang Pu Shougeng de San'ge Wenti" (The Three Issues Concerning Pu Shougeng, the Foreign Merchant in Quanzhou). *Haijiaoshi Yanjiu* (Journal of Maritime History Studies) 1 (2015): 38–43.
Huang, Chunyan, and Feng Xinyi. "Nanhai I Hao Yanjiu zhong Lishiwenxian yu Kaoguziliao de Xianghubuzheng" (Historical Documents and Archaeological Data in the Research on the Nanhai I). *Haijiaoshi Yanjiu* (Journal of Maritime History Studies) 1 (2021): 1–11.
Huang, Jin. *Jinhua Huangxiansheng Wenji* (Collected Works of Huang Jin). In *Xuxiu Siku Quanshu,* vol. 1323, 91–544. Shanghai: Shanghai Gujichubanshe, 1995.
Huang, Xingzeng. *Xiyang Chaogong Dianlu Jiaozhu* (Record of Tributes from the Western Ocean). Ed. Xie Fang. Beijing: Zhonghua Shuju, 2000.
Huang, Xiquan. *Xianqin Huobi Yanjiu* (A Study of the Pre-Qin Currencies). Beijing: Zhonghua Shuju, 2001.
Huc, Evariste Régis. *A Journey Through the Chinese Empire.* New York: Harper, 1855.
Huilin. *Yiqiejingyinyi* (Pronunciations and Meanings for All Buddhist Sutras). Taipei: CBETA E-version, 2001.
Huntingford, G. W. B., ed. *The Periplus of* Guangzhou *the Erythraean Sea, by an Unknown Author: With Some Extracts from Agatharkhides "On the Erythraean Sea."* London: Hakluyt Society, 2010.
Jameel, Mohamed Mauroof. "Coral Stone Architecture of Maldives: A Brief Overview." *Bulletin of MIHO Museum* 18 (2018): 17–28.
Jaufar, Shiura. "Cowrie—an Early Global Commodity: An Archaeological Research on the Islamic Period of the Maldive Islands." *ACCU Nara International Correspondent* 17 (2017): 30–31.
———. "Second Season of Excavation in the Maldives for the 'Cowrie Shells: An Early Global Commodity' Project, 2017." *ACCU Nara International Correspondent* 18 (2017): 27–30.
Jaufar, Shiura, and Anne Haour. "An Overview of Previous Historical and Archaeological Work in the Maldives." In *Archaeological Investigations of the Maldives in the Medieval Islamic Period: Ibn Battuta's Island,* ed. Anne Haour and Annalisa Christie, 11–17. London: Routledge, 2022.

Ji, Han. *Nanfang Caomu Zhuang* (An Introduction to the Plants in the South). Ed. Yang Weiqun. In *Lidai Lingnan Biji Bazhong* (The Eight Historical Records on the South Range), vol. 1. Guangzhou: Guangdong Renminchubanshe, 2011.

Ji, Xianlin. "Xinban Xu" (Preface to the New Edition). In Luo Maodeng, *Sanbao Taijian Xiyangji Tongsu Yanyi* (Romance of Eunuch Sanbao's Journey to the Western Ocean), ed. Lu Shulun and Zhu Shaohua, 1:1–5. Shanghai: Shanghai Gujichubanshe, 1982.

Jiang, Jianrong. "Quanzhouwan Songdai Haichuan Chutu Bufen Xiangliao de Kexueyanjiu" (Scientific Study of Spices Excavated from the Song Boat in Quanzhou Bay). PhD dissertation, University of Science and Technology Beijing, 2021.

Jin, Feng. "Qingchuan Buguo Maliujia Yuanyou Kaoxi" (An Examination on Why Qing Ships Did Not Sail Through the Malacca Strait). *Haijiaoshi Yanjiu* (Journal of Maritime History Studies) 2 (2018): 1–16.

Jin, Guoping. *Aomen Xue: Tanji yu Huizhi* (The Studies of Macao: Exploration and Accumulation). Guangzhou: Guangdong Renminchubanshe, 2018.

———, ed. and trans. *Xifang Aomen Shiliao Xiancui* (Selected Western Sources on Macao). Guangzhou: Guangdong Renmin Chubanshe, 2005.

Jin, Guoping, and Wu Zhiliang. *Dongxi Wangyang* (Em busca de história[s] de Macau apagada[s] pelo tempo). Macao: Aomen Chengrenjiaoyuxueyuan, 2002.

———. *Jinghai Piaomiao* (Historia[s] de Macau: Ficção e realidade). Macao: Aomen Chengrenjiaoyuxueyuan, 2001.

———. *Zaoqi Aomen Shilun* (On the Early History of Macao). Guangzhou: Guangdong Renminchubanshe, 2007.

"Jing ban tian wen quan tu/Ma jun liang." Bibliothèque Nationale de France, département Cartes et plans, GE AA-1656 (RES). https://gallica.bnf.fr/ark:/12148/btv1b72001830#.

Karashima, N., and Y. Subbarayalu. "Ancient and Medieval Tamil and Sanskrit Inscriptions Relating to Southeast Asia and China." In Kulke, Kesavapany, and Sakhuja, *Nagapattinam to Suvarnadwipa*, 271–91.

Karashima, Noboru. "Discoveries of Chinese Ceramic Sherds on the Coasts of South India." International Seminar for UNESCO Integral Study of the Silk Roads: Roads of Dialogue, 19–24, Madras, December 1990. https://en.unesco.org/silkroad/sites/default/files/knowledge-bank-article/discoveries_of_chinese_ceramic_sherds_on_the_coasts_of_south_india.pdf.

Kauz, Ralph, and Roderich Ptak. "Hormuz in Yuan and Ming Sources." *Bulletin de l'École française d'Extrême-Orient* 88 (2001): 27–75.

Knoll, Eva-Maria. "The Maldives as an Indian Ocean Crossroads." *Oxford Research Encyclopedias: Asian History*. 2018. https://oxfordre.com/asianhistory/display/10.1093/acrefore/9780190277727.001.0001/acrefore-9780190277727-e-327.

Kruk, Remke. "Ibn Baṭṭūṭa: Travel, Family Life, and Chronology—How Seriously Do We Take a Father?" *Al-Qantara* 16, no. 2 (1995): 369–84.

Kulke, Hermann, K. Kesavapany, and Vijay Sakhuja, eds. *Nagapattinam to Suvarnadwipa: Reflections on Chola Naval Expeditions to Southeast Asia*. Singapore: ISEAS-Yusof Ishak Institute, 2009.

"Kun yu quan tu/Nan huai ren." https://gallica.bnf.fr/ark:/12148/btv1b7200283b#.

Kurz, Johannes L. "A Note on the Tombstone of Master Pu and the Xishan Zazhi." *Bijdragen tot de taal-, land- en volkenkunde* 172, no. 4 (2016): 510–37.

BIBLIOGRAPHY

Laufer, C. B. "The Domestication of the Cormorant in China and Japan." Field Museum of Natural History Anthropology Series 3 (1931): 205–62.
Legge, James. *A Record of Buddhistic Kingdoms: Being an Account by the Chinese Monk Fa-Hien of His travels in India and Ceylon (A.D. 399–414) in Search of the Buddhist Books of Discipline.* Oxford: Clarendon Press, 1886.
Li, Fang. *Taiping Guangji* (Extensive Records of the Taiping Era). Beijing: Zhonghua Shuju, 1961.
———. *Taiping Yulan* (Readings of the Taiping Era). Beijing: Zhonghua Shuju, 1960.
Li, Fuxue. "Quanzhouwan Songdai Haichuan shang Beilei de Yanjiu" (A Study of the Shells in the Song Ship Discovered in Quanzhou Bay). In Fujian Quanzhou Haiwajiaotongshi Bowuguan, *Quanzhouwan Songdai Haichuan Fajue yu Yanjiu Xiudingben* (A Report on the Excavation of the Song Boat in Quanzhou Bay), 238–46.
Li, Jing. *Yunnan Zhilue* (Sketchy Record of Yunnan). In *Yunnan Shiliao Congkan* (Historical Sources of Yunnan), ed. Fang Guoyu, 3:120–32. Kunming: Yunnandaxue Chubanshe, 1998.
Li, Qingxin. "Nansong Haiwaimaoyi zhong de Waixiaoci, Qianbi, Jinshzhipin ji Qitawenti" (Export Porcelain, Coins, Metal Items and Other Issues in the Maritime Trade of the Southern Song). *Xueshu Yuekan* 44, no. 3 (September 2012): 121–31.
Li, Shizhen. *Bencao Gangmu* (Compendium of Materia Medica). Ed. Chen Guiting. Beijing: Zhongyiguji Chubanshe, 1994.
Li, Yung-Ti. "On the Function of Cowries in Shang and Western Zhou China." *Journal of East Asian Archaeology* 5 (2006): 1–26.
Liang, Jiabin. *Mingshigao Folangjizhuan Koazheng* (An Empirical Study of the Chapter Folangji in Draft History of the Ming Dynasty). In *Mingdai Guoji Guanzi* (International Relationships in the Ming Period), ed. Bao Zunpeng, 7–60. Taipei: Xuesheng Shuju, 1968.
Libang, Aili (Elie Ripon). *Haishang Maoxian Huiyiliu—Yiwei Yongbing de Rizhi (1617–1627)* (Voyages et aventures du Capitaine Ripon aux Grandes Indes). Trans. Lai Huiyun. Hangzhou: Zhejiang University Press, 2015.
Lidai Baoan (Precious Documents of Successive Generations). Taipei: Taiwan University Library, 1972.
Lin, Tianwei. *Songdai Xiangyao Maoyishi* (History of the Xiangyao Trade in the Song Dynasty). Taipei: Zhongguowenhua Dauxue Chubanbu, 1986.
Lin, Zhiqi. *Zhuozhai Wenji* (Collected Works of Zhuozhai). In *Siku Quanshu* (The Complete Library of the Four Treasuries), vol. 1140. Shanghai: Shanghai Gujichubanshe, 1987.
Ling, Mengchu. *Paian Jingqi* (Amazing Tales). Ed. Zhang Peiheng and Wang Gulu. 2 vols. Shanghai: Shanghai Gujichubanshe, 1983.
Linschoten, Jan Huygen van, William Phillip, Pieter Anton Tiele, and Arthur Coke Barnell. *The Voyage of John Huyghen Van Linschoten to the East Indies: From the Old English Translation of 1598.* 2 vols. London: Hakluyt Society, 1885.
Litster, Mirani. "Cowry Shell Money and Monsoon Trade: The Maldives in Past Globalizations." PhD dissertation, The Australian National University, 2016.
Liu, Jia, and Ma Jing, trans. *Qingdiguo Tuji: Gudai Zhongguo de Fengjing, Jianzhu yu Shehuishenghuo* (Illustrations of the Qing Empire: Displaying the Scenery,

Architecture, and Social Habits in Ancient China). Tianjin: Tianjin Jiaoyuchubanshe, 2011.

Liu, Xun. *Lingbiao Yilu* (A Record of Strange Things in the South Range). Ed. Lu Xun. Guangzhou: Guangzhou Renminchubanshe, 1983.

Liu, Yingsheng. "Cong Buali Shendao Beiming Kan Nanyindu yu Yuanchao ji Bosiwan de Jiaotong" (The Gateway Tablet Inscription of Buali and the Communications Among the Yuan Dynasty, Southern India, and the Persian Gulf). *Lishi Dili* (Historical Geography) 7 (1990): 90–95.

———. *Hailu yu Lulu—Zhonggu Shiqi Dongxijiaoliu Yanjiu* (Maritime and Continental Routes Between East and West). Beijing: Beijingdaxue Chubanshe, 2011.

Liu, Yu. *Xishi Ji* (The Ambassador to the West). In *Congshu Jicheng Chubian* (Comprehensive Collection of Rare Book Series, I). Ed. Wang Yunwu. Shanghai: Shangwuchubanshe, 1936.

Long, Cunni. "Miren de Gongli: Longxianxiang" (An Attractive Tributary Gift: Ambergris). In *Zheng He Xia Xiyang Guoji Xueshuyantaohui Lunwenji* (Collected Papers from the International Workshop on the Zhenghe Voyages to the Western Ocean), ed. Chen Xinxiong and Chen Yunü, 41–60. Taipei: Daoxiang Chubanshe, 2003.

Lu, Shulun, and Zhu Shaohua. "Qianyan" (Preface). In Luo Maodeng, *Sanbao Taijian Xiyangji Tongsu Yanyi* (Romance of Eunuch Sanbao's Journey to the Western Ocean), ed. Lu Shulun and Zhu Shaohua, 1:6–20. Shanghai: Shanghai Gujichubanshe, 1982.

Luo, Maodeng. *Sanbao Taijian Xiyangji Tongsu Yanyi* (Romance of Eunuch Sanbao's Journey to the Western Ocean). Ed. Lu Shulun and Zhu Shaohua. 2 vols. Shanghai: Shanghai Gujichubanshe, 1982.

Luo, Meng. "Luetan Gudai Minggui Xianyao—Longxian de Chuanru" (A Sketchy Discussion on the Spread of Ambergris, an Ancient Precious Perfume-Medicine). *Haijiaoshi Yanjiu* (Journal of Maritime History Studies) 2 (1986): 95–103.

Luo, Xianglin. *Pu Shougeng Yanjiu* (A Research on Pu Shougeng). Hong Kong: Chungkuo Hsue-she, 1959.

Luo, Yuejiong. *Xianbin Lu* (A Record of All Guests). Ed. Yu Sili. Beijing: Zhonghua Shuju, 1983.

Luther, Stevenson Edward, trans. and ed. *Geography of Claudius Ptolemy, Based Upon Greek and Latin Manuscripts and Important Late Fifteenth and Early Sixteenth Century Printed Editions, Including Reproductions of the Maps from the Ebner Manuscript, ca. 1460*. New York: New York Public Library, 1932.

Ma, Huan. *Ming Chaoben Yingya Shenglan Jiaozhu* (Overall Survey of the Ocean Shores: Annotation of a Ming Manuscript). Ed. Wan Ming. Beijing: Haiyangchubanshe, 2005.

———. *Ying-yai sheng-lan: "The Overall Survey of the Ocean's Shores," [1433]; translated from the Chinese text edited by Feng Ch'eng-chün with introduction, notes, and appendices by J. V. G. Mills*. London: Hakluyt Society, 1970.

Ma, Juan. "Mabaer Guo yu Yuanchao zhi Laiwang jiqi Xiangguan Wenti" (The Interactions Between Kingdom Ma'bar and the Yuan Dynasty and Some Related Issues). *Lanzhoudaxue Xuebao* (Social Sciences) 33, no. 2 (March 2005): 20–25.

Majumdar, Susmita Basu, and Sharmistha Chatterjee. "Cowries in Eastern India: Understanding Their Role as Ritual Objects and Money." *Journal of Bengal Art* 19 (2014): 39–56.

BIBLIOGRAPHY

Maloney, Clarence. "The Maldives: New Stresses in an Old Nation." *Asian Survey* 16, no. 7 (July 1976): 654–71.
———. *People of the Maldive Islands*. Bombay: Oriental Longman, 1980.
Manguin, Pierre-Yves. "Les techniques de construction navale aux Maldives originaires d'Asie du Sud-Est." *Techniques & Culture* 35–36 (2001): 21–47.
———. "The Maldives Connection: Pre-modern Malay World Shipping Across the Indian Ocean." In *Civilisations des mondes insulaires*, ed. Chantal Radimilahy and N. Rajaonarimanana, 261–84. Paris: Éditions Karthala, 2011.
———. "New Ships for New Networks: Trends in Shipbuilding in the South China Sea in the 15th and 16th Centuries." In *Southeast Asia in the Fifteenth Century: The China Factor*, ed. Geoff Wade and Sun Laichen, 333–58. Singapore: NUS Press, 2010.
———. "Sewn Boats of Southeast Asia: The Stitched-Plank and Lashed-Lug Tradition." *International Journal of Nautical Archaeology* 48, no. 2 (2019): 400–15.
Maniku, Hassan Ahmed. "Conversion of Maldives to Islam." *Journal of the Royal Asiatic Society Sri Lanka Branch* 31 (1986–87): 72–81.
"The Mayflower Story." https://www.mayflower400uk.org/education/the-mayflower-story/.
Mendoza, Juan González de. *History of the great and mighty Kingdom of China and the Situation Thereof: Compiled by the Padre Juan Gonzalez de Mendoza, and now Reprinted from the early Translation of R. Parke*. Vol. 2. Ed. George T. Staunton and R. H. Major. New York: Taylor & Francis, 2010.
Menduosa (González de Mendoza). *Zhonghua Dadiguo Shi* (The History of the Great and Mighty Kingdom of China and the Situation Thereof). Trans. He Gaoji. Beijing: Zhonghua Shuju, 1998.
Metcalf, Barbara D. "Ibn Battuta as a Qadi in the Maldives." In *Islam in South Asia in Practice*, ed. Barbara D. Metcalf, 271–78. Princeton, NJ: Princeton University Press, 2010.
Mikkelsen, Egil. "Archaeological Excavations of a Monastery at Kaasidhoo: Cowrie Shells and Their Buddhist Context in the Maldives." National Centre for Linguistic and Historical Research, Male, Republic of Maldives, 2000.
Ming Huidian (The Law Code of the Ming Dynasty). Beijing: Zhonghua Shuju, 1989.
Ming Shi (History of the Ming Dynasty). Beijing: Zhonghua Shuju, 1974.
Ming Shilu (Veritable Records of the Ming Dynasty). Ed. Huang Zhangjian. Taipei: Academic Sinica, 1984.
Nainar, S. M. H. *The Knowledge of India Possessed by Arab Geographers down to the 14th Century A.D., with Special Reference to Southern India*. Madras: University of Madras, 1942.
Nanjing Yaoxueyuan, Nanjing Linchanongye Xueyuan, and Fujiansheng Yaopin Jianyansuo. "Quanzhouwan Chutu Songdai Muzao Haochuan Cangnei Jiangxiang de Xianweijianding" (A Microscopic Examination of Laka Wood in the Hold of the Wooden Song Ship Discovered in the Quanzhou Bay). In Fujian Quanzhou Haiwajiaotongshi Bowuguan, *Quanzhouwan Songdai Haichuan Fajue yu Yanjiu Xiudingban* (A Report on the Excavation of the Song Boat in Quanzhou Bay), 264–65.
National Institute of Korean History. "Veritable Records of the Ming/Veritable Records of the Qing." http://sillok.history.go.kr/mc/main.do.
Nieuhof, Johan. *Legatio batavica ad magnum Tartariae chamum Sungteium, modernum Sinae imperatorem; Historiarum narratione, quæ legatis in provinciis*

Quantung, Kiangsi, Nanking, Xantung, Peking, & aula imperatoriâ ab anno 1655 A.D. annum 1657 obtigerunt.... Amsterdam: Jacobum Meursium, 1668.
Orta, Garcia da. *Colloquies on the Simples and Drugs of India.* Trans. Clements Markham. London: H. Sotheran and Co., 1913.
———. *Colóquios dos simples e drogas da India.* 1891. Lisbon: Imprensa Nacional, 1987.
Park, Hyunhee. *Mapping the Chinese and Islamic Worlds: Cross-Cultural Exchange in Pre-modern Asia.* Cambridge: Cambridge University Press, 2012.
Parry, Ernest J. *Parry's Cyclopedia of Perfumery: A Handbook on The Raw Materials Used by The Perfumer, Their Origin, Properties, Characters and Analysis.* London: J. & A. Churchill, 1925.
Pedersen, Ralph K. "Traditional Arabian Watercraft and the Ark of the Gilgamesh Epic: Interpretations and Realizations." *Proceedings of the Seminar for Arabian Studies* 34 (2004): 231–38.
Peng, Ke, and Zhu Yanshi. "New Research on the Origin of Cowries in Ancient China." *Sino-Platonic Papers* 68 (1995). www.sino platonic.org/complete/spp068_ cowries_ china.pdf.
Phillips, George. "The Seaports of India and Ceylon: Described by Chinese Voyagers of the Fifteenth Century, Together with an Account of Chinese Navigation." *Journal of the China Branch of the Royal Asiatic Society* 20 (1885): 209–26.
Po, Ronald C. *The Blue Frontier: Maritime Vision and Power in the Qing Empire.* Cambridge University Press, 2018.
Polo, Marco. *The Travels of Marco Polo (The Venetian).* New York: Liveright, 1953.
Ptak, Roderich. *Cheng Hos Abenteuer im Drama und Roman der Ming-Zeit: Hsia hsi-yang, eine Übersetzung und Untersuchung; Hsi-yang chi, ein Deutungsversuch.* Stuttgart: Franz Steiner Verlag Wiesbaden GMBH, 1986.
———. "China and Calicut in the Early Ming Period: Envoys and Tribute Embassies." *Journal of the Royal Asiatic Society of Great Britain and Ireland* 1 (1989): 81–111.
———. "China and Portugal at Sea: The Early Ming System and the Estado da Índia Compared." *Revista de Cultura/Review of Culture* 13–14 (1991): 21–38.
———. *China, the Portuguese, and the Nanyang.* Burlington, VT: Ashgate & Variorum, 2004.
———. "Chinese Perceptions of the Sea Area from the South China Sea to the Coast of East Africa, Approx. 1000–1500." In *The Indian Ocean: The Afro-Asian Mediterranean as a Cultural and Economic Area*, ed. Dietmar Rothermund and Susanne Weigelin-Schwiedrzik, 37–59. Vienna: Association for History and Social Studies, 2004.
———. "Images of Maritime Asia in Two Yuan Texts: 'Daoyi zhilue' and 'Yiyu zhi.'" *Journal of Song-Yuan Studies* 25 (1995): 47–75.
———. "The Maldives and Laccadive Islands (*liu-shan* 溜山) in Ming Records." *Journal of the American Oriental Society* 107, no. 4 (1987): 675–94.
———. "Some References to Timor in Old Chinese Records." *Ming Studies* 1 (1983): 37–48.
Pyrard, François. *The Voyage of François Pyrard of Laval to the East Indies, the Maldives, the Moluccas and Brazil.* Ed. Albert Gray and H. C. P. Bell. 3 vols. Cambridge: Cambridge University Press, 2011.
Qian, Jiang. "Taiguowan Fujin Chushui de Bosibo" (The Persian Sewn-Plank Ship Excavated off the Coast of the Gulf of Thailand). *Guojia Hanghai* (National Maritime Research) 27, no. 2 (2021): 133–60.

BIBLIOGRAPHY

———. "Yifu Xinjin Faxian de Mingchao Zhongye Caihui Hanghaitu" (A Recently Discovered Mid-Ming Colorful Navigation Chart). *Haojiaoshi Yanjiu* (Journal of Maritime History Studies) 1 (2011): 1–7, 141.
Qian, Jiang, and Chen Jiarong. "Niujin Cang 'Mingdai Dongxiyang Hanghaitu' Jiemeihua—Yelu Cang 'Qingdai Dongnanyang Hanghaitu' Tuijie' " (An Introduction to a Qing Navigation Chart in Yale University: A Sister Work of the Ming Navigation Chart in Oxford University). *Haijiaoshi Yanjiu* (Journal of Maritime History Studies) 2 (2013): 1–101.
Qingshi Gao (Draft History of the Qing Dynasty). Beijing: Zhonghua Shuju, 1977.
Qu, Dajuan. *Guangdong Xinyu* (New Notes of Canton). Ed. Li Mo. In *Qu Dajuan Quanji* (Comprehensive Works of Qu Dajun), vol. 4, ed. Ou Chu and Wang Guichen. Beijing: Renminwenxue Chubanshe, 1998.
Rao, Zongyi (Jao Tsung-I). "Taiqing Jinyeshendan Jing (juan xia) yu Nanhai Dili" (The "T'ai-ch'ing chin-I shen-tan ching" and Southern Ocean Geography). *Zhongguo Wenhuayanjiusuo Xuebao* (Journal of Chinese Studies) 3, no. 1 (1970): 31–76.
Ray, Himanshu Prabha. "A 'Chinese' Pagoda at Nagapattinam on the Tamil Coast: Revisiting India's Early Maritime Networks." Occasional Publication 66 (2014), Indian International Center.
———. "Seafaring and Maritime Contacts: An Agenda for Historical Analysis." *Journal of the Economic and Social History of the Orient* 39, no. 4 (1996): 422–31.
Reid, Anthony. "An 'Age of Commerce' in Southeast Asian History." *Modern Asian Studies* 24, no. 1 (Feb. 1990): 1–30.
———. *Southeast Asia in the Age of Commerce 1450–1680*, vol. 1, *The Lands Below the Winds*. New Haven, CT: Yale University Press, 1988.
———. *Southeast Asia in the Age of Commerce, 1450–1680*, vol. 2, *Expansion and Crisis*. Chiang Mai, Thailand: Silkworms Books, 1993.
Ricci, Matteo. "Kunyu wanguo quantu" (Map of the Ten Thousand Countries of the Earth). James Ford Bell Library at the University of Minnesota. https://umedia.lib.umn.edu/item/p16022coll251:8823/p16022coll251:8818.
Risk, M., and R. Sluka. *Coral Reefs of the Indian Ocean*. London: Oxford University Press, 2000.
Rockhill, W. W. "Notes on the Relations and Trade of China with the Eastern Archipelago and the Coast of the Indian Ocean During the Fourteenth Century, Part II." *T'oung Pao* 16, no. 1 (1915): 61–159.
———. "Notes on the Relations and Trade of China with the Eastern Archipelago and the Coast of the Indian Ocean During the Fourteenth Century, Part III." *T'oung Pao* 16, no. 3 (1915): 374–92.
Romero-Frias, Xavier. *Folk Tales of the Maldives*. Copenhagen: NIAS Press, 2012.
———. *The Maldive Islanders—A Study of the Popular Culture of an Ancient Ocean Kingdom*. Barcelona: Nova Ethnographia Indica, 1999.
Rong, Xinjiang. "New Evidence on the History of Sino-Arabic Relations: A Study of Yang Liangyao's Embassy to the Abbasid Caliphate." In *Imperial China and Its Southern Neighbors*, ed. V. H. Mair and L. Kelly, 239–67. Singapore: Institute of Southeast Asian Studies, 2015.
———. "Tangchao yu Heiyi Dashi Guangxishi Xinzheng" (A New Study of the Relationship Between the Tang Dynasty and the Abbasid Caliphate). In *Sichouzhilu yu*

Dongxi Wenhua Jiaoliu (Silk Roads and East-West Cultural Interactions), 81–97. Beijing: Beijing University Press, 2015.
Rowland, Steven John, Paul Andrew Sutton, and Timothy D. J. Knowles. "The Age of Ambergris." *Natural Product Research* 33, no. 21 (2019): 3134–42.
Sackler Gallery, Smithsonian Institution, the National Heritage Board of Singapore, and the Singapore Tourism Board. "Shipwrecked: Tang Treasures and Monsoon Winds." 2010. https://asia.si.edu/research/publications/exhibition-catalogues/shipwrecked-tang-treasures-and-monsoon-winds/.
Sakamaki, Shunzō. "Ryukyu and Southeast Asia." *Journal of Asian Studies* 23, no. 3 (1964): 383–89.
Sangyuan Zhizang (Kuwabara Jitsuzo). *Pu Shougeng Kao* (An Examination of Pu Shougeng). Trans. and ed. Chen Yujing. Beijing: Zhonghua Shuju, 2009.
Sastri, Nilakanta, ed. *Foreign Notices of South India*. Madras: University of Madras, 1939.
Sattar, Ahmed Nazim. *King Kalaafaan Manuscripts: How the Maldives Monarchy Treasured the Remembrance of a Fallen King for More Than Four Hundred Years*. Male: National Centre of Linguistic and Historical Research, 2010.
Schafer, Edward H. *The Golden Peaches of Samarkand: A Study of T'ang Exotics*. San Francisco: Hauraki Publishing, 2014.
Schottenhammer, Angela, ed. *The Emporium of the World: Maritime Quanzhou, 1000–1400*. Leiden: Brill, 2001.
"The Selden Map of China." Bodleian Library, MS.Selden supra 105, https://seldenmap.bodleian.ox.ac.uk/.
Sen, Tansen. *Buddhism, Diplomacy, and Trade: The Realignment of Sino-Indian Relations, 600–1400*. Honolulu: University of Hawaii Press, 2003.
———. "The Impact of Zheng He's Expeditions on Indian Ocean Interactions." *Bulletin of SOAS* 79, no. 3 (2016): 609–36.
———. "The Yuan Khanate and India: Cross-Cultural Diplomacy in the Thirteen and Fourteenth Centuries." *Asia Major* 19, nos. 1–2 (2006): 299–326.
Seshadri, G. S. "New Perspectives on Nagapattinam: The Medieval Port City in the Context of Political, Religious, and Commercial Exchanges Between South India, Southeast Asia and China." In Kulke, Kesavapany, and Sakhuja, *Nagapattinam to Suvarnadwipa: Reflections on the Chola Naval Expeditions to Southeast Asia*, 102–34.
Shanghaishi Weishengyaopin Jianyansuo and Fujiansheng Yaopinjianyansuo. "Quanzhouwan Chutu Songdai Muzao Haochuan Cangnei Jiangxiang de Huaxuejianding" (A Chemical Examination of Laka Wood in the Hold of the Wooden Song Ship Discovered in the Quanzhou Bay). In Fujian Quanzhou Haiwajiaotongshi Bowuguan, *Quanzhouwan Songdai Haichuan Fajue yu Yanjiu Xiudingban* (A Report on the Excavation of the Song Boat in Quanzhou Bay), 266–71.
Shen, Defu. *Wangli Yehuo Bian* (Miscellaneous Notes of Wanli). Ed. Li Xin. Beijing: Wenhuayishu Chubanshe, 1998.
Shen, Fuwei. "Jianlun Wang Dayuan dui Yinduyang Quyumaoyi de Kaocha—Gulifu Ganmaili, Mahesili, Manali Zaji" (On Wang Dayuan's Survey of the Indian Ocean Trading Area—Notes on Gulifu Ganmaili, Mahesili and Manali). *Zhongguoshi Yanjiu* (Studies of Chinese History) 2 (2004): 123–38.
———. *Sichouzhilu Zhongguo yu Feizhou Wenhua Jiaoliu Yanjiu* (The Silk Roads and Studies of Sino-African Interactions). Urumqi: Xinjiang Renminchubanshe, 2010.

BIBLIOGRAPHY

Shen, Huifen. *China's Left-Behind Wives: Families of Migrants from Fujian to Southeast Asia, 1930s–1950s.* Singapore: NUS Press, 2012.

Shi, Ping, and Roderich Ptak, eds. *Studien zum Roman Sanbao Taijian Xiyang Ji Tongsu Yanyi*, vol. 2. Wiesbaden: Harrassowitz, 2013.

Singer, Rachel. "Love, Sex, and Marriage in Ibn Battuta's Travels." MAD-RUSH Undergraduate Research Conference, 2019. https://commons.lib.jmu.edu/madrush/2019/love/1.

So, Billy. *Prosperity, Region, and Institutions in Maritime China: The South Fukien Pattern, 946–1368.* Cambridge, MA: Harvard University Asia Center and Harvard University Press, 2000.

Song Shi (History of the Song Dynasty). Beijing: Zhonghua Shuju, 1977.

Srinivasan, T. M. "Ambergris in Perfumery in the Past and Present Indian Context and the Western World." *Indian Journal of History of Sciences* 50, no. 2 (2015): 306–23.

Staples, Eric, and Lucy Blue. "Archaeological, Historical, and Ethnographic Approaches to the Study of Sewn Boats: Past, Present, and Future." *International Journal of Nautical Archaeology* 48, no. 2 (2019): 269–85.

Stoneman, Richard. "Who Are the Brahmans? Indian Lore and Cynic Doctrine in Palladius' De Bragmanibus and Its Models." *Classical Quarterly* 44, no. 2 (1994): 500–10.

Su, Chung-jen. "Places in South-East Asia, the Middle East and Africa Visited by Cheng Ho and His Companions (A. D. 1405–1433)." In *Symposium on Historical, Archaeological and Linguistic Studies on Southern China*, ed. F. S. Drake, 198. Hong Kong: Hong Kong University Press, 1967.

Su, Shi. *Su Shi Shiji* (A Collection of Poems by Su Shi). 8 vols. Beijing: Zhonghua Shuju, 1992.

Suleiman. *Ancient Accounts of Indian and China by Two Mohammedan Travelers Who Went to Those Parts in the 9th Century.* Trans. Eusebius Rennaudot. London: n.p., 1733.

Tavernier, J., and V. Ball. *Travels in India*, vol. 2. n.p., 1889.

Thomson, John. *Through China with a Camera.* Westminster: A. Constable & Co., 1898.

Tolmacheva, Marina A. "Concubines on the Road: Ibn Battuta's Slave Women." In *Concubines and Courtesans: Women and Slavery in Islamic History*, ed. Matthew S. Gordon and Kathryn A. Hain, 163–89. New York: Oxford University Press, 2017.

Van Neck, Jacob. "Journaal van Jacob van Neck." In *De vierde schipvaart der Nederlanders naar Oost-Indie onder Jacob Wilkens en Jacob van Neck (1599–1604)*, vol. 1, ed. H. A. van Foreest and A. de Booy. 1604. S-Gravenhage: Martinus Nijhoff, 1980.

Vogel, Hans Ulrich. "Cowrie Trade and Its Role in the Economy of Yunnan: From the Ninth to the Mid-Seventeenth Century (Part I)." *Journal of the Economic and Social History of the Orient* 36, no. 3 (1993): 211–52.

———. "Cowrie Trade and Its Role in the Economy of Yunnan: From the Ninth to the Mid-Seventeenth Century (Part II)." *Journal of the Economic and Social History of the Orient* 36, no. 4 (1993): 309–53.

———. *Marco Polo Was in China: New Evidence from Currencies, Salts and Revenues.* Leiden: Brill, 2013.

Vosmer, Tom. "Sewn Boats in Oman and the Indian Ocean." *International Journal of Nautical Archaeology* 48, no. 2 (2019): 302–13.

BIBLIOGRAPHY

Wade, Geoff. "An Early Age of Commerce in Southeast Asia, 900–1300 CE." *Journal of Southeast Asian Studies* 40, no. 2 (2009): 221–65.

———. "Early Muslim Expansion in South-East Asia, Eighth to Fifteenth Centuries." In *The New Cambridge History of Islam*, ed. David Morgan and Anthony Reid, 3:366–408. Cambridge: Cambridge University Press, 2010.

———. "The Li (李) and Pu (蒲) 'Surnames' in East Asia-Middle East Maritime Silk Road Interactions During the 10th–12th Centuries." In *Aspects of the Maritime Silk Road: From the Persian Gulf to the East China Sea*, ed. Ralph Kauz, 181–93. Wiesbaden: Harrassowitz, 2010.

———. "Southeast Asia in the 15th Century." In *Southeast Asia in the Fifteenth Century: The China Factor*, ed. Geoff Wade and Sun Laichen, 1–43. Singapore: NUS Press, 2010.

———. "The Zheng He Voyages: A Reassessment." *Journal of the Malaysian Branch of the Royal Asiatic Society* 78, no. 1 (2005): 37–58.

Wan, Xiufeng. "Gongting Cangxiang III: Longxianxiang" (Incenses Stored in the Inner Court III: Ambergris). *Zijincheng* (The Forbidden City) 2 (2013): 128–35.

Wang, Bangwei, and Tansen Sen, eds. *India and China: Interactions Through Buddhism and Diplomacy: A Collection of Essays by Professor Prabodh Chandra Bagchi*. London: Anthem Press, 2011.

Wang, Dayuan. *Daoyi Zhilue Jiaoshi* (Brief Record of the Island Barbarians). Ed. Su Jiqing. Beijing: Zhonghua Shuju, 1981.

Wang, Gungwu. *The Nanhai Trade: The Early History of Chinese Trade in the South China Sea*. Singapore: Times Academic Press, 1998.

Wang, Liming. "Quanzhou Yindujiao Shike Yanjiu Huigu yu Sikao" (A Reflection on the Studies of Quanzhou Stone Inscriptions). *Haijiaoshi Yanjiu* (Journal of Maritime History Studies) 1 (2016): 122–36.

Wheatley, Paul. "Geographical Notes on Some Commodities Involved in Sung Maritime Trade." *Journal of the Malayan Branch of the Royal Asiatic Society* 32, no. 2 (1959): 3, 5–41, and 43–139.

Winstedt, Sir Richard, and P. E. De Josselin De Jong. "The Maritime Laws of Malacca." *Journal of the Malayan Branch of the Royal Asiatic Society* 29, no. 3 (August 1956): 22–59.

Wu, Cheng'en. *Journal to the West*. Trans. J. F. Jenner. Beijing: Foreign Language Press, 2008.

Wu, Wenliang. *Quanzhou Zongjiao Shike (Zengding ben)* (Religious Stone Inscriptions in Quanzhou, Revised Version). Beijing: Kexuechubanshe, 2005.

Xiang, Da, ed. *Liangzhong Haidao Zhenjing* (Two Navigation Documents). Beijing: Zhonghua Shuju, 2000.

———. "Lun Luo Maodeng zhu sanbao Tajian Xiyangji Tongsu Yanyi" (On Luo Maodeng's Romance of Eunuch Sanbao's Journey to the Western Ocean. In Luo Maodeng, *Sanbao Taijian Xiyangji Tongsu Yanyi* (Romance of Eunuch Sanbao's Journey to the Western Ocean), ed. Lu Shulun and Zhu Shaohua, 2:1291–97. Shanghai: Shanghai Gujichubanshe, 1982.

———, ed. *Zheng He Hanghai Tu* (The Zheng He Nautical Chart). Beijing: Zhonghua Shuju, 2000.

Xie, Fang. "Zhongguo Shiji zhong zhi Maerdaifu Kao" (A Study of the Maldives in Chinese Historical Texts). *Nanya Yanjiu* (South Asia Studies) 2 (1982): 1–8.

BIBLIOGRAPHY

Xie, Qinggao. *Hailu Jiaoshi* (Annotations to a Record of the Seas). Ed. An Jing. Beijing: Shangwu Yinshuguan, 2002.
Xin Tangshu (New History of the Tang Dynasty). Beijing: Zhonghua Shuju, 1975.
Xu, Panqing, An Junli, and Cao Shuji. "Hangxian yu Licheng: Wenchang Qizhouyang yu Xisha Qizhouyang de Diliweizhi" (Navigation Routes and Distances: The Two Qizhouyang in the South Sea). *Zhongguo Lishi Dili Luncong* (Journal of Chinese Historical Geography) 37, no. 1 (January 2022): 15–28.
Xu, Quansheng. *Shen Zengzhi Shidi Zhuzuo Jikao* (A Study on Shen Zengzhi's Historical and Geographical Works). Beijing: Zhonghua Shuju, 2019.
Xu, Song. *Song Huiyao Jigao* (An Extracted Draft of the Song Government Manuscript Compendium). Beijing: Guoli Beiping Tushuguan, 1936.
Xu, Yongzhang. "Wang Dayuan Shengping Kaobian Santi" (Three Notes on Wang Dayuan's Life). *Hiajiaoshi Yanjiu* (Journal of Maritime History Studies) 2 (1997): 98–102.
Xuanzang and Bianji. *Datang Xiyuji Jiaozhu* (Great Tang Records on the Western Regions: Annotation). Ed. Ji Xianlin. Beijing: Zhonghua Shuju, 1985.
Xue, Yanqiao. "Zhufanzhi 'Nanpiguo'tiao Renmin Bushi" (Supplementary Annotations to the Entry of "*Nanipiguo*" in the *Zhufanzhi*). *Quannan Wenhua Yanjiu* (Studies of Southern Quanzhou Culture) 14 (September 2021): 71–77.
Yamada, Kentaro. "A Short History of Ambergris by the Arabs and Chinese in the Indian Ocean (I)." *Report of the Institute of World Economics* 8 (1955): 1–26.
———. "A Short History of Ambergris by the Arabs and Chinese in the Indian Ocean (II)." *Report of the Institute of World Economics* 11 (1956): 2–32.
Yan, Congjian. *Shuyu Zhouzi Lu* (Comprehensive Survey and Record of Foreign Territories). Ed. Yu Sili. Beijing: Zhonghua Shuju, 1993.
Yang, Bin. *Cowrie Shells and Cowrie Money: A Global History*. New York: Routledge, 2019.
———. "The Cowrie World." In *Oxford Research Encyclopedia of Asian History*. 2022. https://oxfordre.com/asianhistory/display/10.1093/acrefore/9780190277727.001.0001/acrefore-9780190277727-e-722.
———. "Cowry Shells in Eastern Eurasia." In *The Silk Road: Long-Distance Trade, Culture, and Society: Interwoven History*, ed. Namba Mariko Walter and James P. Ito-Adler, 1–32. Cambridge, MA: Cambridge Institutes Press, 2014.
———. "Dangzi Yinduyang Fanhang—Quanzhouwan Songdai Haichuan Hangxian Xinkao" (Sailing Home from the Indian Ocean: A New Analysis of the Song Shipwreck Discovered in Quanzhou Bay in 1974). *Haijiaoshi Yanjiu* (Journal of Maritime History Studies) 1 (2021): 18–30.
———. *Renhaizhijian: Haiyang Yazhou zhong de Zhongguo yu Shijie* (Between Men and Seas: China and Its World in Maritime Asia). Guilin: Guangxishifan Daxue Chubanshe, 2023.
———. "The Rise and Fall of Cowry Shells: The Asian Story." *Journal of World History* 22, no. 1 (March 2011): 1–26.
———. *Shangzuo Chuanjing Shi yi Wei: Rao Zongyi Xinjiapo Daxue Zhijiao Kao* (Jao Tsung-I in Singapore: Life, Research, and Chinese Scholarly Diaspora). Hong Kong: Jao Tsung-I Petite Ecole, Hong Kong University, 2018.
———. "'Wuding zhi Chuan': Kaogu he Wenxian zhong Zuizao Wangfan yu Xiya yu Zhongguo zhijian de Haibo" ("Ship Without Nails": Archaeological and Textual

Analyses of the Earliest Ocean Vessels Sailing Directly Between China and West Asia). *Haojiaoshi Yanjiu* (Journal of Maritime History Studies) 1 (2022): 1–20.

——. "The Zhang on Southern Chinese Frontiers: Disease-Construction, Environmental Changes, and Imperial Colonization." *Bulletin of the History of Medicine* 84, no. 2 (Summer 2010): 163–92.

Yang, Huanxin. "Maerdaifu Chutu de Zhongguo Ciqi—Jiantan Zhongma Haishang Jiaotong" (Chinese Porcelains Unearthed in the Maldives—Notes on the Maritime Communication Between China and the Maldives). *Jiandezhen Ciqi* (Porcelains of Jingdezhen) 59–60 (1993): 81–86.

Yang, Rui. "Nanhai I Hao Nansong Chenchuan Ruoganwenti Kaobian" (Textual Research on the "Nanhai I" Shipwreck of the Southern Song Dynasty). *Bowuyuan* (Museum) 2 (2018): 27–32.

Yang, Zhishui. *Gushiwen Mingwu Xinzheng* (New Explorations of Names and Objects in Ancient Poems and Essays). Beijing: Gugong Chubanshe, 2013.

Ye, Daoyang. "'Nahai Yihao' Chenchuan Fanying de Songdai Haishangshenghuo Bianxi" (Maritime Life of the Song Period Reflected by the Nanhai I). *Zhongguo Wenhua Yichan* (Chinese Cultural Heritage) 4 (2019): 99–104.

Ye, Shaoweng. *Sichao Wenjian Lu* (A Record of Four Reigns). Ed. Shang Cheng. Shanghai: Shanghai Gujichubanshe, 2012.

Yijing. *Nanhai Jigui Neifa Zhuan* (A Record of Buddhist Practices Sent Home from the Southern Sea). Ed. Wang Bangwei. Beijing: Zhonghua Shuju, 2009.

——, trans. *Genbenshuoyiqieyoubu Baiyi Jiemo* (Mūlasarvāstivāda-ekaśatakarman). http://buddhism.lib.ntu.edu.tw/BDLM/sutra/chi_pdf/sutra11/T24n1453.pdf.

Yin, Guangren, and Zhang Rulin. *Aomen Jilue* (A Sketch of Macao). Ed. Zhao Chunchen. Guangzhou: Guangdong Gaodengjiaoyuchubanshe, 1988.

Yuan Shi (History of the Yuan Dynasty). Beijing: Zhonghua Shuju, 1976.

Yuankai. *Tang Daheshang Dongzheng Zhuan* (The Record of the Eastern Journey by the Tang Master Monk). Beijing: Zhonghua Shuju, 1979.

Yule, Henry, trans. and ed. *The Book of Ser Marco Polo, The Venetian Concerning the Kingdoms and Marvels of the East*. Cambridge: Cambridge University Press, 2010.

——, ed. *Cathay and the Way Thither: Being a Collection of Medieval Notices of China*, vol. 1. London: Hakluyt Society, 1914.

Zhang, Guangda. *Wenben, Tuxiang yu Wenhua Jiaoliu* (Texts, Images, and Cultural Circulation). Guilin: Guangxishifandaxue Chubanshe, 2008.

Zhang, Ran. "The Glazed Pottery: Asian and Islamic Imports." In *Archaeological Investigations of the Maldives in the Medieval Islamic Period: Ibn Battuta's Island*, ed. Anne Haour and Annalisa Christie, 92–113. London: Routledge, 2022.

Zhang, Shimin. "Yang Liangyao: The First Chinese Diplomat to the Western Ocean." *Xianyang Shifan Xueyuan* (Journal of Xianyang Normal College) 3 (2005): 4–8.

Zhang, Shinan. *Huanyou Jiwen* (A Record of What's Heard on Official Travel). Ed. Zhang Maopeng. Beijing: Zhonghua Shuju, 1981.

Zhang, Xie. *Dongxiyang Kao* (An Examination of the Eastern and Western Oceans). Ed. Xie Fang. Beijing: Zhonghua Shuju, 2000.

Zhao, Jingshen. "Saoban Taijian Xiyang Ji" (Romance of Eunuch Sanbao's Journey to the Western Ocean). In Luo Maodeng, *Sanbao Taijian Xiyangji Tongsu Yanyi* (Romance of Eunuch Sanbao's Journey to the Western Ocean), ed. Lu Shulun and Zhu Shaohua, 2:1298–333. Shanghai: Shanghai Gujichubanshe, 1982.

BIBLIOGRAPHY

Zhao, Rukuo. *Zhufan Zhi Jiaoshi* (A Record of Barbarians). Ed. Yang Bowen. Beijing: Zhonghua Shuju, 2000.

Zhao, Xuemin. *Bencao Gangmu Shiyi* (Supplement to Compendium of Materia Medica). Beijing: Renmin Weisheng Chubanshe, 1983.

Zhao, Yanwei. *Yunlu Manchao* (Loose Notes of the Cloud-covered Foothill). Ed. Fu Genqing. Beijing: Zhonghua Shuju, 1996.

Zheng, Linzhi. *Gaoli Shi* (History of Goryeo). Taipei: Wenshizhe Press, 1972.

Zhou, Daguan. *A Record of Cambodia: The Land and Its People*. Trans. Peter Harris. Chiang Mai, Thailand: Silkworm Books, 2011.

———. *Zhenla Fengtuji Jiaozhu* (Customs of Cambodia: An Annotation). Ed. Xia Nai. Beijing: Zhonghua Shuju, 1981.

Zhou, Mi. *Wulin Jiushi* (Old Stories of Hangzhou). Hangzhou: Zhejiang Renmin Chubanshe, 1984.

Zhou, Qufei. *Lingwai Dadai Jiaozhu* (Answers for Questions Concerning Out of Range). Ed. Yang Wuquan. Beijing: Zhonghua Shuju, 1999.

Zhou, Yunzhong. "Daoyizhilue Diming yu wang Dayuan Xingcheng Xinkao" (Toponymy in *Daoyi Zhiue* and a New Study of the Itinerary of Wang Dayuan). *Yuanshi ji Minzu yu Bianjiang Yanjiu Jikan* (A Collection of the History of the Yuan Dynasty and the Studies of Ethnicity and Frontier) 1 (2014): 98–131.

———. "Mingchu Zhang Xuan Xia Xiyang Zu yu Mengjiala Zhengui Shiliao Jiedu" (The Precious Document on Zhang Xuan Buried in Chittagong in 1412). *Nanya Yanjiu* (Studies of South Asia) 2 (2010): 123–33.

Zhu, Yu. *Pingzhou Ketan* (Chats in Pingzhou). Ed. Li Weiguo. Shanghai: Shanghai Gujichubanshe, 1989.

Zhu, Yunming. "Qianwenji Xiaxiyang" (Down to the West Ocean in Record of What Has Been Heard). In Gong Zhen, *Xiyang Fanguo Zhi* (A Record of Foreign Kingdoms in the Western Ocean), ed. Xiang Da, 55–57. Beijing: Zhonghua Shuju, 2000.

Zhuang, Weiji, and Zhuang Jinghui. "Quanzhou Songchuan Mupai Muqian Kaoshi" (An Examination of Wooden Labels and Lots in the Song Ship Discovered in Quanzhou). In Fujian Quanzhou Haiwajiaotongshi Bowuguan, *Quanzhouwan Songdai Haichuan Fajue yu Yanjiu Xiudingban* (A Report on the Excavation of the Song Boat in Quanzhou Bay), 210–16.

———. "Quanzhouwan Songchuan Jiegou de Lishi Fenxi" (A Historical Analysis of the Structure of the Song Ship Discovered in the Quanzhou Bay). In Fujian Quanzhou Haiwajiaotongshi Bowuguan, *Quanzhouwan Songdai Haichuan Fajue yu Yanjiu Xiudingban* (A Report on the Excavation of the Song Boat in Quanzhou Bay), 166–73.

INDEX

Abder-Razzak, 66
Addu Atoll, 68, 81
Aden, 95, 277; Ming relation to, 113–15
Ai, Ruose, 278
Alberuni, 64, 132, 154
alchemy, 203–6
Aleni, Giulio (Ai Rulue), 126, 274, 275, 276; on ambergris, 182–83
Alexander, William, 269
Ali, Fawzia, 105
Allom, Thomas, 271
"All under Heaven," 6, 7–8
aloe wood, 212, 317n51
ambergris, 11, 15, 55, 60, 103, 127, 180–81, 215, 221, 305n13, 314n9; in alchemy, 203–4; Arabs and, 186–87; bitumen relation to, 133; from Bobali, 189–90; Brito and, 213–14; Fei on, 217; G. He on, 321n125; Huizong and, 201–2; for incenses, 190–92; from Indian Ocean, 32, 182, 184–85; Jiajing and, 9, 205–8, 212, 214, 216; from Longxian Yu, 193–94, 195–96, 197–98; Macao relation to, 211, 212–13; Maritime Ban relation to, 209–10; as medicine, 9, 199, 204–5; on Quanzhou I, 31, 56, 158, 191, 201, 286n6; Seed Bolus relation to, 214; in *The Seven Voyages of Sinbad the Sailor*, 194–95; sperm whales relation to, 183, 188; as tributary gifts, 200–201, 202–3, 210
Amherst, William, 269
Amitābha, 328n9
āmra tree, 328n9
Andaya, Barbara Watson, 242
Androth Island, 85, 87
Anduli Liu. *See* Androth Island
Angkor, 243
anhua (secret decorations), 106
animals, 175–76
ant-nose bronze coins, 160
aphrodisiacs, 208–9
apsarā, 230
Arabs, 272–73; ambergris and, 186–87
Archaeological Survey, of Ceylon, 66
Arghun, 292n21; Kököchin relation to, 57
Ariadū, in Ari Atoll, 228
Ari Atoll: Ariadū in, 228; Toḍḍū in, 230
Ariq Böke, 57
aromatic materials, 180, 186; on Quanzhou I, 31–32. *See also* ambergris
atollon, 100–101

INDEX

Attracting Iron Range, 259–60
auspicious signs (*maṅgalas*), 230–31

Bai Juyi, 62, 189
Baiyaojian, 190, 198, 317n46
al-Balīd, 142
Baolinyuan, 23
Barbosa, Duarte, 66, 77; on ambergris, 181, 185; on handkerchiefs, 178; on stitched ships, 137–38
Barreto, Melchior Nunes, 214
Barros, Joao de, 64, 66, 91, 178–79; on animals, 175; on coconuts, 125–26; on coir ropes, 128, 138; on cowrie shells, 155–56; on dried fish, 169–70; on stitched ships, 147
Battle of Talas, 55
Bay of Bengal, 54, 97, 110, 135, 136, 148, 163, 183, 198, 274, 277; ambergris from, 185
Beibu Gulf, 290n5
Beiliu, 74, 78, 79–80, 83, 176
Belitung shipwreck, 11–12, 35, 71, 140, 142–43, 273; bitumen on, 141
Bell, Harry Charles Purvis, 3–4, 66, 68–69, 81–82; Buddhism relation to, 227, 229–30; on cowrie shells, 154; Gray and, 10; Maldive Islands and, 74–75, 98–99; "The Maldive Islands" of, 67; on *Mary*, 97–98; on monsoon winds, 95–96; shipwreck of, 91; on soil, 173; on tidal currents, 101
Bencheng, 19
Bengal, 6, 74, 94, 97, 111, 148, 150–55, 166, 172, 178, 202, 240, 261, 264, 278, 152–53; cowrie shells in, 149
Berber, Maghrabin, 233
Bharadvaja, Pindola, 258
Bharu Jātakas, 78, 228
biliuli, 53, 290n3
bin Šāṣh, Ibrāhīm, 181
Bipaluo, 192
bitumen, 134, 182, 305n11, 305n13; ambergris relation to, 133, 181; on Belitung shipwreck, 141; on *fanbo*, 147; in horse ships, 133
Blussé, Leonard, 42
boat people, 268

Bobali, 189–90, 200
Bodhidharma, 257
Bohali, 177–78
boluo xuyoujia, 257–58
Borneo, 21, 123, 146, 217
Bretschneider, E., 187
British Museum, 10, 105, 106
Brito, Mateus de, 213–14. *See also* Manabiedi
bronze coins, 109; ant-nose, 160
bronze cowries, 157, 160; in Warring States period, 161
bronze mirror, 23, 140, 141
Buddha's alms bowl, 58–59
Buddhism, 27, 54, 88–89, 225, 233–34; Amitābha in, 328n9; Bell relation to, 227, 229–30; Chan, 257; China Pagoda and, 46, 48; cowrie shells relation to, 154; on Fuamulah Atoll, 81; Ibn Battuta relation to, 226; in Maldive Islands, 67–68, 69, 228; *maṅgalas* in, 230–31; stupas of, 323n15; Tantric, 231–32; Theravada, 4, 229–30; *zhentan* in, 245
Buddhist sutras, 90, 143; *āmra* tree in, 328n9
Buddhist temples, at Fuamulah Atoll, 226–27
Burnell (Dr.), 46

Cai Jing, 201
Cai Tao, 201
Calicut, 24, 27, 33, 66, 87, 122, 130, 133, 155, 177, 202, 218, 261, 277, 278; Ibn Battuta in, 30, 37, 240; Ming relation to, 110–15
Cambodia, 20, 33, 40, 245; D. Zhou in, 243, 249
camphor: 20, 186, 188, 192, 202; on Quanzhou I, 34; taxes on, 26, 220–24
canoe (*dumuzhou*), 196, 317n58
Canton, 28–29
Canton Bay, 146
Canton System, 43; Hong merchants in, 320n117
Carswell, John, 10; porcelain and, 106
Carte de la Chine, 274–75
Celestial Dynasty, 43, 254–55, 266
cemetery, in Quanzhou, 24–25

INDEX

Cengtan, 200
Central Plain, 13, 157
Central Secretariat, of Yuan Dynasty, 158, 163
Ceylon, 4, 55, 323n29; Archaeological Survey of, 66; coconuts in, 122; Maldive Islands relation to, 75; precious stones in, 76; Quanzhou relation to, 27; in *The Seven Voyages of Sinbad the Sailor*, 195; tidal currents near, 96; D. Wang in, 61, 111; Yiheimishi in, 58
Ceylon ironwood (*Mesua ferrea*), 308n52
Chagatai Khanate, 57
Chagos Islands, 72, 85, 95
Champa, 20, 26, 33, 40, 58, 110, 112, 113, 123, 146, 217; local women in, 241–44, 246, 248, 250
Chan Buddhism, 257
Chang Ning, 210
Chao Phraya River basin, 153
Chen Baosheng, 21–22
Chen Dazhen, 60
Cheng (King), 161
Cheng Ho, 104
Chen Guodong, 42
Chen Jing, 199–200
Chen Lunjiong, 272, 276
chensu wood, 193, 317n51
chenxiang, 31, 177, 186, 212, 220, 221, 321n5
Chen Xiyu, 42
Chen Ye, 105
Chen Zuyi, 260
chickens, 172–74, 176
children, on Chinese ships, 40–41
China. *See specific topics*
"China Bird," 15, 269, 272
China Pagoda, at Nagapattinam, 47, 21, 45–46, 48–49, 289n57
Chinese cabins, 42
Chinese rites controversy, 332n41
Chinese ships, 34; children on, 40–41; crews on, 38, 39; Ibn Battuta on, 30, 37, 38, 39–40. *See also* shipbuilding technology
Chola, 6, 33, 123, 318n74

Christopher (Lieutenant), 3, 91
Chunyao (meiyao), 203
cinnabar, 19, 214; gold cinnabar, 203–5; red cinnabar, 209
Cishishan (Mount Magnetic Rock), 145
Cobolly masse, 170–71
Cochin, 6, 87, 95, 97, 133, 203, 261, 277, 278; Ming relation to, 112–15
coconuts, 56, 72–73, 75, 103, 108, 111, 121–25, 127–28, 172, 240; as *boluo xuyoujia*, 257–58; coir ropes relation to, 129, 138–39; as medicine, 126
Cohen, Paul, 13
coins, 20, 22, 31, 46, 48, 140, 150, 151, 153, 192, 196, 198, 202, 262, 266, 309n16; bronze, 109, 160; *denarius*, 323n18; *min*, 319n79; on *Nanhai I*, 37
coir ropes, 121, 123, 128, 131, 133, 135; coconuts relation to, 129, 138–39; Ji on, 144; on *Kunlun bo*, 143; for navigation, 63, 147; on Phanom Surin shipwreck, 142. *See also* coconuts
Colóquios dos simples e drogas da India (Orta), 213
communication portals, 99–100
compass, 35, 43, 86, 102, 197, 276
Compendium of Materia Medica (Li), 204
complex-toothed flying squirrel dung, 317n46
Comus, HMS, 67, 68
concubines, 125, 239, 247, 252; Ibn of Battuta, 5, 325n12
contracted marriage, 15, 240, 250
copper coins, 152, 192, 198, 207, 309n16; on *Quanzhou I*, 31
coral reef islands, 72, 83, 90; gateways in, 91–93
coral stones, 128
cormorants, 266, 267, 268, 270; Huc on, 271. *See also* fishing birds
Coronelli Isole di Divandurou, 85
Cosmos, 75
cotton, 23, 145, 168, 170, 176, 178, 179, 238, 262
counting, of cowrie shells, 310n27
cow dung (*gomen*), 314n9

cowrie shells, 8, 11, 15, 26, 71, 108, 310n24, 329n19; counting of, 310n27; at Fuamulah Atoll, 226; *Hezun* relation to, 162; imitation, 160, *160*, 161, 167; in Ming Dynasty, 163, 164–65, 166; as money, 148–59, 162–63, 167; on *Quanzhou I*, 31, 32, 158; taxes on, 166–67
crews: on Chinese ships, 38, 39, 243; navigation relation to, 43
Cruz, Gaspar da, 268, 269
Cudamanivihara, 48
Cudrania tricuspidata, 145

Dabadan, 81; southern clothing and southern silk in, 176–77
Dade Nanhaizhi, 158–59; Jicini in, 256; Longya Men in, 188
dagaba mound, 68
Dali, 8, 151, 153, 162
Danmolidi, kingdom of, 97
Daoguang (Emperor), 278
Daoism, 18, 199, 201, 205, 211; Jiajing and, 203–4; sexual pleasure relation to, 214; "True Ones" of, 217
Daoyi Zhilue (Wang, D.), 5, 61, 63, 293n31; *Beiliu* in, 78; J. Su and, 10; Z. Zhang and, 62
Daqin (Roman Empire), 290n2; Gan in, 53
Dashan, 243
Dashi, 30, 33, 55, 56, 132, 144; ambergris from, 190–92, 200–201; frankincense from, 218, 219
David Vases, 300n10
Da Wudie, 150
Daxi Hongtong (Daxi Tong), 55
De Bragmanibus (Palladius), 64–65, 136
Demhera (Queen), 236
denarius coins, 323n18
De Silva, W. L., 68
Dharmapatanam, 176–77
Dhivehi language, 225; on Isdhoo Loamaafaanu, 233–34
Dhofar, Oman, 142, 203; frankincense from, 218, 219
Dian Kingdom, in Yunnan, 162–63

Dickens, Charles, 41
Didi, H. Haji Ismail, 68
Diegan, 82, 273
ad-Dín, Jamál, 237
Ding Wei, 218
Dīpaṃkara, 256–57
Divehi ruh (Maldivian palm), 125. *See also* coconuts
Division, of *Xingren*, 70
divorce, 239–42
Dongxiyang Kao (Zheng, X.), 14, 71, 273, 277
dou, 318n65
Dragon Kings, 257–59
"dragon's spittle" (*longxian*). See ambergris
dried fish, 15, 63, 74, 84, 108, 168–70, 176, 178, 260, 262
dried madder, 145
Duan Chengshi, 189–90, 200; on Bipaluo, 192
Duhai Fangcheng, 276–77
Du Huan, 55
dumuzhou (canoe), 196, 317n58
dung: complex-toothed flying squirrel, 317n46; cow, 314n9

East Africa, 5, 32, 63, 70, 85, 87, 95, 134, 189–90, 261
Eastern Ocean, the, 277, 278
Edrisi, 64, 124, 154, 178, 218; on ambergris, 184; on queens, 236
Elliot, Walter, 45–46
Ellis, Henry, 269–70
envoys, 6, 53, 55, 56, 105, 110–11, 167, 200, 208, 211, 262; of Kublai Khan, 57–59; of Liushan, 112–16, 273; H. Ma relation to, 107; of Taizu, 70; Western Ocean, 7; of Yisufu, 112; to Yongle, 113–14; H. Zheng and, 104, 115
erronea errones, 156
Escalante, Bernardino de, 268
evāla akuru, 229

Fadiffolu Atoll, 97
Fai-Fo, 326n32

INDEX

fanbo, 147
Fangbai, 150
Fan Shouyi, 332n41
Faxian, 54, 75; on cowrie shells, 150; on maritime Silk Road, 64
Feener, R. Michael, 81, 108–9, 296n32; at Fuamulah Atoll, 226; "The Maritime Asia Heritage Survey" of, 229
Fei Xin, 64, 65, 77, 78, 83, 85, 87, 169, 172, 187, 250, 255–56; on frankincense, 217, 218; on gateways, 91, 93; on Longxian Yu, 196; magnetic rocks and, 259; Maldive Islands and, 104, 107–8, 263; on treasure fleet, 111; on *xiaozhai zhi liu*, 88
Fengshen Yanyi, 254; *Xiyang Ji* relation to, 256
Finlay, Robert, 328n3
fishing, 168, 170–72
fishing birds, 263, 264–69
The Fishing Cormorant, 269, 270
Five-Tiger Gate, 109
Flecker, Michael, 133–34
Floating-Sand-River, 89–90, 259
Fodiffolu Atoll, 84
Fonadhoo Island, 96
food, 172–75. *See also* coconuts; fishing
Forbes, Andrew D. W., 10, 230; porcelain of, 105
Forbidden City Museum, 210
frankincense, 19, 31, 56, 107, 158, 186, 200; Fei on, 217, 218; taxes on, 26, 221; trade for, 218–19
fresh water, 75, 122, 172, 257
fruits, 73, 123, 124, 126, 172–76, 274
Fuamulah Atoll, 81; Buddhist temple at, 226–27
Fua Mulaku, 74, 95, 227
Fujian Province, 18. *See also* Quanzhou
Funadhoo Mosque, 154–55
Fuzhou (抚州), 255
Fuzhou (福州), 18, 19, 40, 109

Gaadhoo, 230, 323n20
Gādū Island, Haddhunmathi Atoll, 230
Gamuin Addu Atoll, 227
Gamu Island, 230–31

gandharva, 230
gangji, 212, 320n117
gangshou, 20, 39, 42, 43; in Malay Maritime Code, 42
Gan Island, 68
gan labels, 44
Ganlantang, 144
Gan Ying, 53, 227
Gao Yao, 207–8
Gaozong (Emperor), 201
Gardiner, Stanley, 227
Garuḍa, 257
gateways, in coral reef islands, 91–93
Gelishengxialaxilibajiaola, 114
geng, 297n51
Genghis Khan, 57
Geography (Ptolemy), 135–36
Ghazan, 292n21; envoys of, 59
Ghazni, 256
ghost-face coin, 160
Gippert, Jost, 231
Giridīpa, 80
Goa, 9, 145, 185, 195, 213, 278
gold coins, 98, 196, 198, 309n16
Golden Horde Khanate, 57
Golden Peaches of Samarkand, The (Schafer), 13
gomen (cow dung), 182, 314n9
Gong Zhen, 64, 65, 77, 104, 108, 293n35; on ambergris, 181; on cowrie shells, 152; on dried fish, 169; on gateways, 93; on handkerchiefs, 177; Maldive Islands and, 263
González de Mendoza, Juan, 268–69
Gordon, Arthur, 66
Gray, Albert, 10, 69
Guanbenchuan, 59–60
Guangdong, 37, 110, 144–45, 272, 283n26; ambergris and, 205, 206, 208, 211, 212, 213; *gangji* in, 320n117
Guangdong Tongzhi, 114, 320n115
Guangxi Province, 144–45, 283n26
Guangzhou, 11, 14, 17, 26, 33, 45, 55, 123, 142, 143, 144, 192, 201, 209, 219, 246, 255, 278, 287n26; ambergris in, 192, 208, 211–14; incenses in, 200
Guangzong (Emperor), 209

Guanwu liu, 297n44
Guanyu Liu. *See* Male Island
Guhyasamājatantra, 232
Gujarat, 11, 61, 123, 228
Gujin Tushu Jicheng, 114
Gu Kexue, 205
Gulidimen, 248, 327n58
Gulin, 33, 56
Guo Xizong, 24
Gu Yanwu, 212

Haddhunmathi Atoll, 68, 85, 97, 227, 234, 323n20; Gādū Island, 230
haiba dao, 165–66
Hailu (Xie, Q.), 278
handkerchiefs, 15, 74, 168, 176–78, 262
Han Dynasty, 53, 75
Hanlin Academy, 293n31
Hat Island, 197
Havaru-bassavá Duvahu, 95–96
Hayton (Prince), 64, 65, 76, 78, 88–89
Heavenly Mandate, 161
He Chude, 212
Heiyi Dashi, 55
Hepu, 53, 290n5
He Qiaoyuan, 41
hexiang (mixed incense), 191, 194, 200
Hezun, 161, 162
Hinduism, 225, 228, 322n3; *apsarā* in, 230; Garuḍa and, 257; at Male Island, 229
Hirth, Friedrich, 187
Historia de las cosas más notables, ritos y costumbres del gran reyno de la China (de Mendoza), 268–69
History in Three Keys (Cohen), 13
homosexual relationships, 41
Hong Bao, 111
Hong Chu, 199–200
Hong Gonggong, 261
Hong Mai, 19–20
Hong merchants, 320n117
hongqian, 205
horses, 60, 113, 130, 175; of Ormuz, 116
horse ships, 129–31, 133, 145
De Houtman, Frederick, 226
Huairen, Nan, 274

Hualuo, 123
Huang Qianren, 274–75, 331n32
Huang Xingzeng, 66, 69–70, 87, 90, 112, 152, 302n35; on ambergris, 198; on coir ropes, 133; *haiba dao* and, 165–66; Maldive Islands and, 97, 263
Huangzhi, 53, 290n3
Huc, Evariste Régis, 270, 271
Huian, 243
Huilin, 123, 143; on cowrie shells, 151
Huizong, 201–2
Huvadhu Atoll, 95, 230
Hu Zongxian, 70

Ibn Battuta, 4, 238–39, 326n43; on animals, 175–76; on aromatic materials, 180; on Chinese cabins, 42; on Chinese ships, 30, 37, 38, 39–40; on coconuts, 121, 124–25; on coir ropes, 129, 135, 138; concubines of, 5, 325n12; on cowrie shells, 150, 155; on dried fish, 168–69; on food, 172–73; on *gangshou*, 41–42; on gateways, 92; on idols, 225; Islam relation to, 226, 233; Maldive Islands and, 53, 72, 76–77, 90, 97, 235, 263–64; marriage of, 239–40, 241, 244; on Quanzhou, 17, 27–29; on queens, 237; in Quilon, 265–66; on silkworms, 330n5; on slave girls, 248; on temporary marriage, 247; women relation to, 325n12, 325n25
Ibrahim II (Sultan), 98
idols, 88, 225, 233
Ilkhanate, 57, 59
incenses, 60, 190–92, 193, 199–200, 202, 205, 211
India: *āmra* tree in, 328n9; cowrie shells in, 149, 150; Maldive Islands relation to, 229; Roman Catholic missions in, 65; silk from, 178; D. Wang in, 49; *zitan* from, 292n16
Indian Ocean, 282n10; ambergris from, 32, 182, 184–85; China relation to, 6, 10, 13, 74, 210, 220, 272–73, 278–79; Kublai Khan relation to, 57; marine biology in, 32–33; Mulan ships in, 131–32; *Quanzhou I* and, 32–33, 56, 56, 57;

INDEX

stitched ships in, 137–38; treasure fleet in, 103, 114; *Xianbin Lu* relation to, 255
Indicopleustes, Cosmas, 65
Indo-European language, Insular Indo-Aryan subgroup of, 225
Indravarman III (King), 243
Indus Valley, 230
iron nails: on Chinese ships, 34; and horse ships, 129–35; magnetic rocks relation to, 136–37
Isdhoo Loamaafaanu, 233–34
Islam, 89, 225–26, 233–34; *miḥrāb* and, 229; Muhammadan Conversion to, 68; patriarchy relation to, 241; queens relation to, 236; trade relation to, 232; *woyi*, in, 304n13
ivory, 19; taxes on, 26

Jalal-ud-din, 'Umar Vira, 68–69
Japan, 26, 165, 166, 254, 272, 277
Japanese pirates (*wakou*), 70, 288n41; *woyj*, 214
Jātakas, 228
Java, 21, 26, 32, 33, 58, 123, 146, 165, 217; Ming relation to, 110–13
Jesuits, 10, 12, 48, 77, 182–83, 273–76
Jiabannian Liu, 85–85. *See also* Kalpeni Island
Jiajia Liu, 84, 85
Jiajing (Emperor), 209; ambergris and, 9, 205–8, 212, 214, 216; Daoism and, 203–4; in *Ming Shi*, 210–11
Jiang Gongwang, 18–19
Jiangxi Province, 5, 19, 205, 212, 254; porcelain of, 255
Jiangzhenxiang. *See* laka wood
Jianweiluo, 166
Jianzhen, 144
Jicini, 202, 256
Ji Han, 144
ji labels, 44
Jilidimen, 251, 327n58
Jiling, 22, 285n17
Jindan, 203
Jin Dynasty, 13
Jingban Tianwen Quantu, 276

Jingdezhen, 5, 28–29, 37, 212, 255
Jin Guoping, 43
Jingxing Ji (Du), 55
Jin River, 18
jinshi, 19, 24, 70, 190, 199, 201, 214
Jinta, 176
John, of Montecorvino, 64, 65, 132
Jordanus (Friar), 64, 65, 76
jun labels, 44

Kaafu Atoll, 154, 231
Kaashidhoo, 154, 231, 266, 310n24
Kalaminjā, Dovemi, 232, 235
Kalō, Koimalā, 232
Kalpeni Island, 85
Kangxi (Emperor), 210, 332n41
Kayarohanaswami temple, 48
kegang, 43
keji, 43
Kelai Island, 85
Keling, 285n17
kewei (passenger space), 42
Khadíja (Queen), 237
Khadijah, Rehendi, 68–69
Kilege, Kanba Aisha Rani, 236–37
Kilegefaanu, Kalhu Kamana Thukkamana Binth Ḥasan Ranna Bandeyri, 237
Kinolhas, 300n10; porcelain at, 105–6
kiwi, 42–43
Koimalā (Prince), 235, 323n26
Kököchin, 57, 292n21
Kollam, 6, 57, 59, 63, 97, 130
Koryo, 18
Kublai Khan, 7, 58–59; Bohali and, 177; Indian Ocean relation to, 57
Kunlun bo, 143–44
Kunyu Quantu (Huairen), 274
Kuruhinna Tharaagadu Ceramic Assemblage, 109

Laccadive Islands, 134; Maldive Islands relation to, 282n8
laka wood, 31, 32, 211; lotus-flower, 217–18; purple, 212; on *Quanzhou I*, 31–32; taxes on, 221
Lakshadweep Islands, 72

Lambri, 33, 112–13, 185, 195–96, 207, 217–18
Landhoo Island, 231–32
land tax, 220
Lanli, 33
lapis lazuli, 257
Liang Cai, 207–8
Lidai Baoan, 166
Li Jing, 246
lingas, 322n3, 323n15; at Ariadū, 228
Ling Mengchu, 22–23, 285n16
Lingnan area, 283n26
Lingwai Daida (Zhou, Q.), 14, 33, 56, 60, 61, 256; coconuts in, 123
Linschoten, Jan Huygen van, 195
Lin Zexu, 278
Lin Zhiqi, 24–25
Li Shizhen, 204
liu, 77, 78, 79, 83, 84; *xiaozhai zhi*, 88–89; F. Xie on, 80, 81; in *Zheng He Hanghai Tu* (Mao), 88
liu cloth, 176–78
Liuqiu, 165
Liushan (King), 261–62; envoys of, 114–15, 273
Liushanguo, 72, 80, 82, 83, 152, 256, 260, 261
Liu Xun, 123, 144, 146
Lizong (Emperor), 21
local chiefs, 249; shipwrecks and, 314n10
Lohu, 152
Longnaoxiang, 186, 317n51
Longqing (Emperor), 208, 209
longxian ("dragon's spittle"). *See* ambergris
longxianxiang, 180, 187, 200, 201, 210, 212
Longxian Yu, 188, 193–94, 195, 198; in *Zheng He Hanghai Tu*, 196, 197, 197
Longya Men, 188
Longya Shan, 188
Luchuan, 164
Luci Wan, 267
luoba, 166
Luoba, 23–24
Luohu, 151
Luohuna, 23
Luo Maodeng: *Sanbao Taijian Xiyangji Tongsu Yanyi* of, 15; *Xiyang Ji* of, 70, 202, 250–51, 254, 255–57, 259–62

Luowei, 177
Luo Yuejiong, 234; on handkerchiefs, 177; *Xianbin Lu* of, 112, 255, 273
Lusiads, The (Vaz de Camões), 328n3
Luzon, 165, 220

Mabaoha, 22, 23
Ma'bar, 58, 63, 96, 100, 123, 175, 177, 299n6; Kollam relation to, 59
Macao, 9, 216, 278, 312n5; ambergris relation to, 211, 212–13; Qianlong relation to, 146–47
Macartney Mission, 269
Maerdiwa, 274, 275, 276
Maghreb, 305n6, 323n29
magnetic rocks, 135–37, 145; in Attracting Iron Range, 259–60
MAHS. *See* Maritime Asia Heritage Survey
Ma Huan, 74, 77, 84–85, 312n5, 318n65; on ambergris, 180–81, 191; on coconuts, 121, 122; on coir ropes, 133; on cowrie shells, 152; on Diegan, 273; on dried fish, 169; envoys relation to, 107; on food, 173; on frankincense, 218–19; on gateways, 91, 93; on handkerchiefs, 168; on Islam, 234; on laka wood, 217; on *liu* cloth, 176, 177; *Liushanguo* and, 82, 83; Maldive Islands and, 80–81, 104, 195–96, 263; monsoon winds and, 94; on Muslims, 225, 226; on Ormuz, 116; Ruoshui and, 90; on tidal currents, 99; on vegetables, 172; on women, 238, 244–45; on *xiaozhai zhi liu*, 88; *Xiyang Ji* relation to, 255–56; *Yingya Shenglan* of, 65, 255, 260, 273
majiaoyu, 169, 312n5
Ma Junliang, 276
Malabar, 27, 55, 98, 133, 138, 139, 186, 325n16
Malacca, 9, 165, 198, 253, 261; Ming relation to, 110–14; Tanjung Kling in, 285n17
Malacca Strait, 55, 110, 111, 167, 188, 272, 278
maladvipa, 72
Malay Maritime Code, 42–43

INDEX

Malay Peninsula, 48, 54, 55, 71, 97, 137, 146, 151, 188, 217, 241, 272–74, 277, 278
Maldive Islands, 7, 78, 84. *See also* specific topics
Maldives and Liushan in Chu-Si- Ling's map of China, 275
Maldivian language, 3–4, 93, 225; Theravada Buddhism and, 230
Maldivian palm (*Divehi ruh*), 125. *See also* coconuts
Maldivian people, 101–2; ambergris relation to, 181–82; fishing and, 171
Male Island, 67–68, 85, 93, 97, 104; *Beiliu* relation to, 79; Buddhism at, 231; Hinduism at, 229
Male Old Friday Mosque, 128
Maliqi Liu. *See* Minicoy Island
Maloney, Clarence, 69, 80, 323n26; *Jātakas* and, 228; on Male Island, 93; on shipwrecks, 91
Manabiedi, 211, 212–13
maṅgalas (auspicious signs), 230–31
Maniolae Islands, 136
Mañjuśrīmūlakalpa, 232
Mantuolang, 61
Mao Yuanyi, 69, 70
maps: *Carte de la Chine*, 274–75; *Jingban Tianwen Quantu*, 276; Maldives and Liushan in Chu-Si- Ling's map of China, 275; Qing, 331n32; Ricci, 77, 79; *Selden Map of China*, 12, 14, 277; in *Zheng He Hanghai Tu*, 196, 197
māra tree, 328n9
Marco Polo, 5, 76, 292n21; on ambergris, 184; on Chinese ships, 38; on coir ropes, 138; on cowrie shells, 151–52; on horse ships, 130–31, 133; Kököchin relation to, 57; on Kublai Khan, 58; on Quanzhou, 17, 25–26, 29; on shipbuilding technology, 30, 34, 35–36; on Silk Road, 65
marine biology, in Indian Ocean, 32–33
Maritime Ban, 9, 16, 208, 272; ambergris relation to, 209–10
Maritime Customs Office (Shibosi), 18, 39, 44, 201

Maritime Customs Superintendent (Shiboshi), 17, 18, 24
maritime Silk Road, 6, 54–55; ambergris on, 191; Faxian on, 64
marriage, 15, 82, 235, 251, 327n61; of Ibn Battuta, 239–40, 241, 244; nuptial gift and, 238; temporary, 242–44, 246–48, 250, 252–53; in Zhenla, 245; in Zhu-Chen Village, 61–62
Mary, 97–98
Al Mas'udi, 65, 76, 78, 90, 154; on ambergris, 183–84; on coconuts, 124; on queens, 236
Mathurā transactions, 150
Mayflower, 38, 40
medicine, 31, 58, 60, 89, 317n46; ambergris as, 9, 190, 199, 204–5; coconuts as, 126
Meicheng, 267
meihua nao, 193, 317n51
Meng Haoran, 267
Mesua ferrea (Ceylon ironwood), 147, 308n52
Mididu, 211, 212–13
Midishan, 211, 212–13, 320n115
miḥrāb, 229
Miladu Madulu Atoll, 85
millet, 174
Mills, J. V. G., 85, 103
min, 19–20, 319n79
Ming Dynasty, 7, 69, 216; ambergris in, 202, 215; boat people in, 268; commercialization in, 254; cowrie shells in, 163, 164, 164–65, 166; handkerchiefs and, 177; Macao relation to, 212; Maritime Ban and, 9, 16; Ormuz relation to, 116
Ming-Qing transition, 212
Ming Shi, 69, 115, 203, 262; Jiajing in, 210–11; Yisufu in, 112; Zheng He in, 103, 111
Ming Shilu, 69, 105, 111, 114–15, 262; Maldive Islands in, 112; Ormuz in, 116
Minicoy Island, 85, 282n8
Ministry of Revenue, 205–7, 211–12
Ministry of Ritual, 113–14
Min River, 109

INDEX

mixed incense (*hexiang*), 191, 200
Modeliya, Yebala, 114
Mohwa tree, 46, 48
Molúk, 325n16; Ibn Battuta at, 240
Monetaria annulus, 57, 149, 156, 158
Monetaria moneta, 57, 149, 156, 158
money, 8; cowrie shells as, 148–59, 162–63, 167
money-shell coin, 160
monsoon winds, 95–97; treasure fleet and, 94, 112
Montecorvino, John of, 65, 132
Moon Harbor, 219, 220
Mount Fudou, 109
Mount Kunlun, 89
Mount Magnetic Rock (*Cishishan*), 145
Mozambique, 185
Muhammadan Conversion, 68
Mulaku Atoll, 85
Mulanpi, 305n6
Mulan ships, 131–32
musk oil, 180
Muslim, 225–26, 233, 247

Nagapattinam, China Pagoda at, 47, 21, 45–46, 48–49, 289n57
Nakhoda (ship owner), 43
Nāḷikera, 228
Naluojiluo, 73, 121
Nan'ao Island, 110, 301n27
Nanchang, 5, 255
Nanfan Xianglu (Ye), 199
Nanhai I, 11–12, 14, 315n17; children on, 40; *Quanzhou I* compared to, 37–38
Nanhai Zhi (Chen, D.), 60, 82, 159, 188, 256
nanliu bu, 81, 82
Nanpi, 24, 33, 56, 63, 123
Nanyang, 16, 272, 278
Nanzhao, 8, 153, 162
Nanzhou Yiwuzhi, 137
navigation, 276–77, 299n6; coastal, 290n5; coir ropes for, 63, 147; crews relation to, 43; fishing relation to, 171; of Maldivian people, 102; monsoon winds relation to, 94, 95, 97; of *xiaozhai zhi liu*, 89; in *Zheng He Hanghai Tu*, 86–87

Neo-Confucianism, 237, 241, 248
Nicobar Islands, 37, 55, 94, 111, 195–98; ambergris from, 183, 185, 198
Nieuhof, Johan, 269
Noboru Karashima, China Pagoda and, 289n57
Northern Song Dynasty, 187, 201, 266
nuptial gift, 238

oakum: on Chinese ships, 34; in horse ships, 133
Oliver Twist (Dickens), 41
olive tree bark, 144
One-and-a-half Degree Channel, 81
One-Belt-One-Road Initiative, 4
Ormuz, 59, 61, 103, 177, 187, 277; Ming relation to, 110–16; Tūrānshāh of, 116
Orta, Garcia da, 182, 195; *Colóquios dos simples e drogas da India* of, 213
oyuarou, 99. See also tidal currents

Pacification Superintendency, 260
Paian Jingqi (Ling), 22–23, 285n16
Palladius, 64–65, 75, 259; on magnetic rock, 136–37, 145
pāramitā, 257–58
parasang, 90, 298n61
partition (*petak*), 43
Patani, 165, 241–42, 247
patriarchy, 237; Islam relation to, 241
Pax Mongolica, 57
pearls, 19, 20, 22, 23, 53, 75, 63, 88, 150, 189, 195, 208, 211, 236, 257; taxes on, 26; as tributary gifts, 200, 201
Pegu, 66, 74, 77, 97, 148, 150, 151, 172
Pelliot, Paul Eugène, 63, 111, 169, 196
Pereira, Galeote, 267–68, 269
Periplus of the Erythraean Sea, The, 10, 71, 134
Persia, 57, 66
petak (partition), 43
Phanom Surin shipwreck, 142
Phillips, George, 85
Pingzhou Ketan (Zhu), 14
pirates, 40, 54, 98; Japanese, 70, 288n41
polygamy, 252
polygyny, 252, 327n65

INDEX

Ponchassi, 215
porcelain, 71, 105, 107, 109; *anhua* on, 106; on Belitung shipwreck, 140; of Jiangxi Province, 255; of Nanchang, 5; of Quanzhou, 28
Pordenone, Odorico da, 57, 64, 65, 76, 263; on fishing birds, 266–67; on stitched ships, 132
port marriage, 242–53, 327n61
Powell (Lieutenant), 3
Prakrit, 231
precious stones, 27, 53, 55, 75, 88, 194, 195, 211, 236, 260, 262; in Ceylon, 76
premarital sex, 245–46
Proserpine, HMS, 96
prostitution, 242–43, 246, 327n61; in slave trade, 253
Provana, Joseph-Antoine, 278, 332n41
Providence Atoll, 95
Ptak, Roderich, 10–11, 63, 85, 86, 104, 282n15; on *Beiliu*, 80; on Fei, 108; on Guanwu liu, 297n44; on Zheng He, 115
Ptolemy, Claudius, 135–36, 259
purple laka wood, 212
Pu Shougeng, 17, 19, 21
Pu Xiaxin, 25
Pyrard, François, 3, 4, 66, 82, 168; on ambergris, 182; on coconuts, 126, 127; on coir ropes, 138–39; on dried fish, 170; on fishing, 170–72; on fishing birds, 263, 264–65, 269; on food, 174–75; on fruits, 173, 176; on gateways, 92, 93; on Ibrahim II, 98; on marriage, 240–41; on *oyuarou*, 99; on tidal currents, 100–101

Qiandao reign, of Southern Song Dynasty, 37
Qianlong (Emperor), 146–47
Qianwenji (Zhu Yunming), 109
Qilai Liu. *See* Kelai Island
Qing Empire, 273
qiushi, 205
Quanbo, 33
Quanzhou, 4, 19, 287n26; Baolinyuan in, 23; cemetery in, 24–25; Ceylon relation to, 27; envoys in, 59; Ibn Battuta on, 17, 27–29; Marco Polo on, 17, 25–26, 29; Shiboshi of, 17, 18, 24; Y. Wang in, 20; Ye in, 190–91
Quanzhou I, 11–12, 20–21, 30, 34, 218; ambergris on, 191, 201, 286n6; coconuts on, 122; cowrie shells on, 31, 32, 158; Indian Ocean and, 32–33, 56, 56, 57; *Nanhai I* compared to, 37–38; shipbuilding technology of, 34, 35; wooden labels on, 44
Qu Dajun, 146
queens, 235–37
Quilon, 27, 33, 66, 76, 87, 265–66

Rajaraja I, 48
Rajendra I, 48
Rao Zongyi, 137
rattan ships, 145
Ray, Himanshu Prabha, 48
Reid, Anthony, 42; on temporary marriage, 242
Renbuzhi Liu, 84, 85, 87
"Report on a Visit to Male, January 20 to February 21, 1920" (Bell), 67
Ricci, Matteo, 12, 77, 78, 273–74, 276
Ricci Map, 77, 79
rice, 74, 88, 107, 126, 148–51, 155, 173–74, 178–79
Ripon, Élie, 251
Rockhill, W. W., 63, 176, 187, 196; on *Beiliu*, 79
Roman Catholic missions, 65
Roman Empire (*Daqin*), 290n2; *denarius* of, 323n18
rosewater, 172, 180, 193, 201; ambergris and, 191
Rosset, C. W., 227
Royal Asiatic Society, 3
Rūdavali, 232
Rukh (Shah), 66
Ruoshui, 89–90, 261; in *Xiyang Ji*, 259
Ryukyu kingdom, 165–66, 167, 277

Sagga, 228
Sanbao Taijian Xiyangji Tongsu Yanyi (Luo, M.), 15

sandalwood oil, 180
Sanfoqi, 19, 33, 123, 200, 201
Sanskrit, 48, 72, 73, 80, 82, 143, 195, 231–32
Santo Stefano, Hieronimo di, 64, 66, 77, 90–91; on monsoon winds, 94, 97
sappanwood, taxes on, 26
Sarandib. *See* Ceylon
sarīradhātu, 58
Schafer, Edward H., 13, 55
Schouten, Wouter, 45
secret decorations (*anhua*), 106
Seed Bolus (*zhongzi wan*), 214
Selden Map of China, 12, 14, 277
Semudera, Ming relation to, 110–15
Sengjialuo. See Ceylon
Seruma, 228
Seven Voyages of Sinbad the Sailor, The, 194–95
sex, 249–50; premarital, 245–46
sex trade, 251
sexual pleasure: ambergris for, 208, 213; Daoism relation to, 214
Shaivism, 48
Sha Liu. *See* Mulaku Atoll
Shams-ud-din, Muhammad, III, 67
Shanghai Jing, 89, 90, 298n58
Shao Yuanjie, 205
Shenzong (Emperor), 208–9
Shiboshi (Maritime Customs Superintendent), 17, 26, 190; Guo as, 24
Shibosi, 18, 163, 201, 209
Shi Nawei, 24–25
shipbuilding technology, 30, 33–34, 135; watertight compartments, 35–36. *See also* horse ships; stitched ships
ship owner (*Nakhoda*), 43
shipwrecks, 30, 91, 195, 228; Belitung, 11–12, 71, 140, 141–43; local chiefs and, 314n10; *Nanhai I*, 37–38. *See also* Quanzhou I
Shiva temple, 48–49
Shungfeng Xiangsong, 276–77
Shuyu Zhouzilu (Yan, C.), 69, 70
Siam, 146, 147, 152, 153, 165, 166, 210, 217; handkerchiefs, 177; women in, 244, 246, 250

Sichuan, 145, 192
silk, 179; of Dabadan, 81; from India, 178; of Quanzhou, 28; southern, 177
Silk Road: Marco Polo on, 65; maritime, 6, 54–55, 64, 191
silkworms, 330n5
Silong Liu, 84–86. *See also* Haddhunmathi Atoll
silver, 22, 37, 108, 122, 124, 140, 150, 254, 262
silver coins, 150, 309n16; in Pegu, 151
Sima Qian, 8, 157
Sinhala, 225
Sino-foreign marriage, 246–47
Sīnu Kara, 117
Sitātapatrādhāranī, 231
Sivalingas, 229
Skanda, 229
slave girls, 39, 42, 247, 248
slave trade, 156; prostitution in, 253
So, Billy, 17
Sodré, Vicente, 155
Soft-Ocean Shoal, 254, 258, 259
Soft-Water Sea, 256, 258, 259
soil, 28, 35, 75, 183, 192; of the Maldives, 172
Song Shi, 24; coconuts in, 123
South China Sea, 32, 110, 135, 137, 140, 142, 143, 145–47, 260, 273; cowrie shells relation to, 157–58; Zhangzhou relation to, 219
southern silk, 81, 177
Southern Song Dynasty, 15; Lizong of, 21; Qiandao reign of, 37; Quanzhou relation to, 18; in Yangzi Delta, 13
sperm whales, 183, 185, 188
Sri Lanka, 94, 97, 104, 136, 168, 171, 225, 226, 229–31
Srivijaya, 19, 24, 33, 48, 123, 217, 318n74
SS *Sea Gull*, 67
stitched ships, 11, 129–30, 132–35, 139–40, 145–46; *fanbo* as, 147; in Indian Ocean, 137–38; Phanom Surin shipwreck, 142
stupas, 231, 323n18; of Buddhism, 323n15

INDEX

Su Chung-jen, 103
Su Dongpo, 62, 189
Su Jiqing, 10, 79, 82–83, 197
Sukhāvatī (Western Paradise), 328n9
Sulaiman, 64, 65, 66, 78, 124; on ambergris, 181, 183; on cowrie shells, 153–54; on queens, 236
Sulayman (Vizier), 239
Sumatra, 48, 55, 66, 77, 86, 94, 97, 111, 112, 139, 146, 165, 170, 186, 188, 196, 200, 202, 217, 260, 261
Sunda Strait, 85, 86
Sun Tianfu, 21–22
Supreme Ultimate (*Taiji*), 328n9
Sussondī Jātakas, 228
Suvadiva Atoll, 81, 230–31

Taicang, 110, 112
Taiping Yulan, 137
Taizong (Emperor), 266
Taizu (Emperor), 70, 163, 164, 165, 209; Ryukyu kingdom relation to, 165
al-Tajir, Sulaiman, 65
Tamba (King), 228
Tamil inscriptions, 48–49
Tang Dynasty, 140, 143, 151, 189, 190, 246, 259, 289n55
Tanjung Kling, in Malacca, 285n17
Tantric Buddhism, 231–32
Tao Zhongwen, 205
Tauarcarré, 126–27. See also coconuts
Tavernier, Jean-Baptiste, 185
taxes: on camphor, 26, 221; on cowrie shells, 166–67; at Moon Harbor, 219, 220; in Zhangzhou, 220
"ten thousand islands" (*wandao*), 77, 79, 273, 276
Thailand, 153, 163
Thakurufan, Mohamed, 98
Thanna, 225
Theravada Buddhism, 4, 229–30
Thousand and One Nights, The, 137, 194
tianbai, 106. See also porcelain
Tibet-Nepal Road, 54
tidal currents, 53, 74, 99–101; near Ceylon, 96

Tiladummati Atoll, 85, 97
Timor, 61, 244, 248–49, 278; marriage in, 250–51
Toḍḍū, in Ari Atoll, 230
Toluid Civil War, 57
Tongchang (Princess), 189
Toyohachi, Fujita, 79
trade, 263–64; for frankincense, 218–19; Islam relation to, 232; for rice, 173–74; sex, 251; slave, 156, 253; women relation to, 243–44; in Zhangzhou, 209
Tranquebar, 96
treasure fleet, 10, 109, 196, 202; Fei and, 77; in Indian Ocean, 103, 114; in Java, 111; at Jilidimen, 251; Maldive Islands and, 104–5, 107; monsoon winds and, 94, 112; in Ormuz, 110; at Soft-Water Sea, 259; *xiaozhai zhi liu* and, 87, 88. See also Zheng He
trees, 173. See also coconuts
tributary gifts, 163, 261; ambergris as, 200–201, 202–3, 210; cowrie shells as, 164, 165; pearls as, 257; from Ryukyu kingdom, 166
"True Ones," 186, 217
tubers, 174–75
tuolong, 22
Tūrānshāh (Sultan), 116
turtle shells, 19, 22; taxes on, 26
Tuta, 45

Vādū Island, 230
Vajrayana, 231
Van Neck, Jacob, 241–42, 243; in Patani, 247
Vaz de Camões, Luís, 328n3
vegetables, 172; on Chinese ships, 40
Verbiest, Ferdinand, 12, 275, 276

Wade, Geoff, 12
waiyang yibo, 146–47
wakou (Japanese pirates), 42, 70, 209, 288n41
wandao ("ten thousand islands"), 77, 79, 273, 276
Wang Bai, 216

INDEX

Wang Dayuan, 60–61, 72; on ambergris, 180, 193–94; *Beiliu* and, 78, 79, 80, 83; on Buddha's alms bowl, 58–59; on Buddhism, 27; in Ceylon, 61, 111; in Champa, 244; on China Pagoda, 45; on coconuts, 123; on coral reef islands, 91; on cowrie shells, 148, 150, 151; on crews, 39; on Dabadan, 81; on dried fish, 168; on frankincense, 218; on handkerchiefs, 176–77; on horse ships, 131; in India, 49; on laka wood, 217; Maldive Islands and, 4–6, 10, 63, 73–77, 195, 225–26, 235, 263; on monsoon winds, 94, 96; on rattan ships, 145; on stitched ships, 129–30; on tidal currents, 53, 99; Wen Shi compared to, 23; on women, 243, 245, 248–49, 251, 253; *Xiyang Ji* relation to, 255–56; Z. Zhang and, 62
Wang Gao, 208
Wang Hong, 212
Wang Huai, 206
Wang Jian, 206
Wang Jinghong, 114
Wang Xuance, 54
Wang Yuanmao, 20, 39, 41
Wang Zhi, 42
Waqf, 124, 154, 173, 236–37; in Islam, 304n13
Waqf endowment, 173; queens in, 236–37
Warring States period, 161
water tax, 220
watertight compartments, 35–36
Weh Island, 94, 195
Wei Jiao, 214
Wen Shi, 22–23, 39, 285n16
Western Full of Joy Kingdom, 258
Western Ocean, the, 7, 14, 53, 59, 65, 71, 74, 96, 110, 164, 220, 256, 262, 277, 278
Western Paradise (Sukhāvatī), 328n9
whales, 184; sperm, 183, 185, 188
wheat, 172, 174
women, 238–39, 246, 253; in Fai-Fo, 326n32; Ibn Battuta relation to, 325n12, 325n25; prostitution and, 327n61; on Timor Island, 248–49, 250;

trade relation to, 243–44; in *Xiyang Ji*, 250–51; in Zhenla, 244–45
wooden labels, on *Quanzhou I*, 44
Wu Da, 20
Wu Jian, 62
Wudi (Emperor), 53
Wulingzhi, 190, 198, 317n46
Wuxun, 200

Xiali, 176
Xianbin Lu (Luo, Y.), 112, 255, 273
Xiangpu, 199
Xiangshan County, 212
xiangyao, 31, 201
Xiaozhailiu, 168, 260
xiaozhai zhi liu, 87, 88–89
Xie Fang, 10, 81; on *Beiliu*, 79–80
Xie Qinggao, 278
Xingcha Shenglan (Fei), 65, 104, 108, 250; dried fish in, 169; Longxian Yu in, 196; *Xiyang Ji* relation to, 255, 260
Xingren, Division of, 70
Xinjiang, 53
Xin Tangshu, 190
Xiyang bu, 23
Xiyang Chaogong Dianlu (Huang, X.), 69–70
Xiyang Fanguo Zhi (Gong), 65, 108, 293n35; *Xiyang Ji* relation to, 260
Xiyang Ji (Luo, M.), 70, 202, 255–57, 261–62, 328n3; Attracting Iron Range in, 259–60; women in, 250–51
Xiyou Ji, 89–90, 254; Floating-Sand-River in, 259; *Xiyang Ji* relation to, 256
Xuande (Emperor), 105, 114
Xuanzang, 54, 65, 73, 285n17; Soft-Water Sea and, 259; in *Xiyou Ji*, 89–90
Xuwen, 53, 290n5

Yamada, xvi, 187, 189, 197
Yan Congjian, 69, 70, 165–66; on ambergris, 207; on cowrie shells, 153; on Longxian Yu, 198
Yang Bingnan, 278
Yang Liangyao, 55
Yang Shu, 57, 59–60
Yang Tingbi, 57, 59

INDEX

Yangzi River, 110, 112, 140, 145, 158, 160, 257, 271
Yangzi Delta, 34, 201; Southern Song Dynasty in, 13
Yanmāntaka, 232
Yan Song, 205
Yaqubi, 183
Ye Tinggui, 190–91, 199; on frankincense, 219
Yiheimishi, 57–58, 59
Yijian Zhi (Hong, M.), 19–20
Yijing, 45, 54, 97; on cowrie shells, 150–51
Yin Guangren, 146–47
Yingwuluo, 166
Yingya Shenglan (Ma, H.), 65, 70, 108, 169, 273; *Xiyang Ji* relation to, 255, 260
Yingzong (Emperor), 115; cowrie shells and, 167
Yiqie Jingyinyi (Huilin), 143
Yisufu, 103, 112
Yizong (Emperor), 189
Yongchang, 152
Yongle (Emperor), 7–8, 106, 302n35; envoys to, 113–14
Yongle Dadian, 207
Yuan Dynasty, 40, 57; Central Secretariat of, 158, 163; cowrie shells during, 163
Yuan Qinghua, 105, 300n10. *See also* porcelain
Yuan Shi, 202
Yule, Henry, 45–46, 266, 267
Yunnan, 152, 158, 246; Dian Kingdom in, 162–63
Yusub (King), 112

Zaitun. *See* Quanzhou
Zhancheng, 20, 33, 40, 123
Zhang Chengyun, 22
zhanghai. *See* South China Sea
Zhang Rulin, 146–47
Zhang Shinan, 192–93
Zhang Xie, 14, 71, 213, 273, 277, 320n115; on cowrie shells, 153; on crews, 43; on Macao, 212; on Moon Harbor, 219
Zhangzhou, 166–67, 272; Moon Harbor of, 219, 220; taxes in, 220; trade in, 209
Zhang Zhu, 62
Zhao Rukuo, 26, 56, 61, 192, 285n23; on coconuts, 123; *Quanbo* and, 33; as Shiboshi, 24
Zhao Xuemin, 204–5; on *zhongzi mifang*, 214
Zhao Yanwei, 201
Zhaozong (Emperor), 144
Zhejiang, 167, 243
Zheng Chenggong, 42
Zheng He, 4, 6, 110, 112; ambergris and, 9; *Daoyi Zhilue* relation to, 5; envoys and, 104, 115; H. Ma and, 65; Maldive Islands and, 107, 263; in *Ming Shi*, 103, 111; porcelain and, 105–6; *Sanbao Taijian Xiyangji Tongsu Yanyi* and, 15; in *Xiyang Ji*, 70, 250–51, 255, 256, 260–62; Xuande relation to, 114; Yongle relation to, 8, 113
Zheng He Hanghai Tu (Mao), 12, 70, 79, 97, 276–77, 297n44; Haddhunmathi Atoll on, 85; *liu* in, 88; Longxian Yu in, 196, 197, *197*; navigation in, 86–87
Zheng Zhilong, 42
Zhenla, 20, 33, 40, 115, 243; women in, 244–45
Zhenlu, 151
zhentan, 245
Zhezong (Emperor), 201
Zhiligan, 23–24
Zhinan Zhengfa, 277–78
Zhiyongyuan, 60
Zhongguo, 161, 162
Zhongtong chao, 151
zhongzi mifang, 214
zhongzi wan (Seed Bolus), 214
Zhou Daguan, 20; in Cambodia, 249; on women, 243–44, 245–46, 253
Zhou Dynasty, 254
Zhou Minghe, 213
Zhou Qufei, 14, 26, 56, 61, 123; on ambergris, 191–92; on Dashi, 30; magnetic rocks and, 259; on Mulan ships, 131–32; *Quanbo* and, 33; on rattan ships, 145

Zhu-Chen Village, 61–62
zhufan, 45
Zhufan Zhi (Zhao), 24, 33, 56, 61, 285n23; Jicini in, 256
Zhunian, 33, 123
Zhu Shiwei, 212
zhutang, 45
Zhu Xiling, 274–75, 331n32
Zhu Yu, 14; on pirates, 40; on taxes, 26
Zhu Yunming, 109, 110–11
Zhu Zicai, 189
zitan, 58; from India, 292n16